The Final Elegy:
The Consolation of the Classics in Old Age

The Final Elegy:

The Consolation of the Classics in Old Age

Richard Oliver Brooks

To order additional copies of this book, contact:
Xlibris
844-714-8691
www.Xlibris.com
Orders@Xlibris.com
844078

CONTENTS

CONCLUSION

PREFACE

"Go, little book… but kiss the steps where
pass though ages spacious Vergil and Ovid,
Homer, Lucan, and Statius" - Chaucer

In this book, I am talking to three audiences. The first audience is composed of those who share with me the delights and burdens of age or who anticipate experiencing them in the near future. Although the entire book is addressed to the elderly reader, Part IV of this book, in which I discuss each of the seven losses which old age encounters may be of special interest to them. This discussion seeks to illustrate the thesis that the classic works can provide an understanding of specific losses in old age, offer expressions of the mourning that results from these losses, help us to detach ourselves from these losses and find some consolations. The "classic works" are that collection of great works, great books, works of fine art, and great practical accomplishments or their accounts.

Another audience of this work are those who are seriously interested in liberal education. Since I suggest that the classics can be helpful in understanding old age, I recognize that the reader must gain access to these works. This access requires a liberal education which teaches the classics and the skills for interpreting them. Contemporary proponents of liberal education view the reading or beholding of these classics as a vehicle to cultivate basic general capabilities for effective citizenship and to prepare the youth for a more specialized education to follow. To those proponents of liberal education, I suggest a third purpose: to provide the means for a continuing consolation for the losses of age. We old persons may view the classics in a unique way – through the lens of old age after having experienced an almost complete life. We bring a unique vantage point along with the experience of old age losses and the consequent emotions to an appreciation of the classic works. In so doing, we can test the classic against the reality of our own lives to make sense of both.

To make sense of our lives, we look for permanent truths in the classics. This search for permanent truths contrasts with the quest of many modern proponents of liberal arts who are content to appeal to the classics as simply part of a valuable tradition of thought, "cultural knowledge," or as the raw material for cultivating the arts of reading, discussing and listening to be used in the future lives of their students. We elderly look to the classics for something more. We seek the truth among the variety of competing truths to be found in these works. For us, facing old age and death, liberal education is more important; it is the pursuit of final and permanent truths.

The third audience for this book is not the elderly nor to those interested in the liberal arts, but to everyone who must anticipate or cope with fundamental losses during the span of their lives. At some stage of our lives, most of us encounter some of these losses, such as significant health problems, involuntary unemployment, unwelcome dependency, loss of hope, or the death of a loved one. These losses are not unique to the elderly, although they are more certain to occur in the later stages of life. The final chapter in the book seeks to draw some general conclusions about losses and consolation at any stage of life testing the general conclusions set forth in the earlier chapters with the author's personal experience. In sum *this book supplies an understanding of old age, a rethinking of liberal education, and a consolation for losses in life for the old and others.*

When I reflected upon the three audiences I had "chosen," I came to realize that I, myself, was an upstanding member of all three audiences! I was old and beginning to encounter old age losses. I had undertaken to write this book in old age because I was looking for an excuse – a project – which would enable me to do what I wanted to do anyway – read and appreciate the classic works I had been introduced to in my early liberal education and I have continued to think about their implication for old age and its losses. This realization led to the conclusion that, like Montaigne's *Essays*, I was writing this book for me – an audience of one. Therefore, I preface each chapter with a brief relevant autobiographical account pertaining to the subject discussed in the chapter, while setting forth more general, dare I say, universal, observations in the body of the chapter itself. Whether the audience of this book reaches beyond myself as an audience depends upon how much my thoughts and feelings successfully mirror those of the three audiences I have identified and whether I communicate effectively to myself and them.

INTRODUCTION

The Final Elegy: The Consolations of the Classics in Old Age

An aged man is but a paltry thing
A tattered coat upon a stick, unless
Soul clap its hands and sing, and louder sing
For every tatter in its mortal dress
Nor is there singing school but studying
Monuments of its own magnificence
And therefore I have sailed the sea and come
To the holy city of Byzantium – Yeats

This book is a report on my "sailing the sea" to the holy city of old age, to study the "monuments of un-aging intellect". For the past t6 years, beginning at age 72 when I retired, I have undertaken an old age experiment in which I sought to embrace old age and its losses by consulting the classics, hoping to find within them a detachment and consolation I believed would be necessary in this period of life. Unlike those who glorify old age as "the best is yet to be" nor those who believe with Matthew Arnold that "in last stage of all…we are frozen up within", I hypothesize that old age would be a time of losses and emotions which follow close upon these losses, but which, with reflective meditation, I could find avenues of solace.

There are several premises to my old age venture. I assume that old age is a distinct stage of life dominated by loss and the emotions of sadness, regret, nostalgia and alienation; that these losses may be understood through the components of the literary form of elegy, (loss, sadness, detachment, consolation;) these elegiac components are explored through meditative reflection, which enables detachment and consolation from old age loss and emotion; that such reflection is assisted by a consultation with the classics, especially when these losses are placed within the old age vision of one's completed life.

In this Introduction, to guide the reader, I shall explain briefly these premises, although they will receive more extended treatment in the chapters of the book. After this introductory explanation, I shall set forth the order of the book and acknowledge those who have helped me in this venture.

The Premises

- Old Age - a Distinct Stage of Life

Old age is a period of our lives in which we encounter serious losses and the prospect of death. On the other hand, if we are fortunate, we are granted a period of leisure when we can reflect upon these losses in the context of our entire life and its meaning. The old age losses are obvious. Physical losses may include the thinning of bones and joint diseases, the advent of heart disease, arthritis, and hypertension, increased dental problems, digestive disorders, tremors, impaired eyesight, changes in gait, thinner hair, diminished hearing, hardening arteries, less efficient immunity, diminished lung capacity, impairment of mobility, decreased sexual desire, less elastic skin, sleep problems, deadened taste buds, incontinence, and weakening vocal cords. Not all elderly persons suffer all old age maladies, and when these arrive, they may arrive at different stages of old age. Some of these health issues may not be serious enough to impede our everyday functioning. A variety of mental problems also may arrive including reduced cognitive abilities, depression, anxiety and fear. Many of these marks of old age appear inevitable for many, and they are often irreversible, cumulative over time, and, given proximity to our deaths, they may be tinged with a certain finality.

With the arrival of these unwelcome guests to our house of old age, society has conspired to erect the fence of an oft-required retirement age which excludes older people from the fields of paid work, but, at least in the developed world, rewards them with a meagre retirement income and health insurance, if not much respect. Such exclusion from work means that many elderly persons have reduced income and some are thrown into poverty. Others often rest in alienated affluence. The unwelcome guests of physical and mental decline may bring with them a painful financial and physical dependency either upon the state, the non-profit sector, or upon families and friends.

There are also often more subtle harms in old age. Old people may lose their memory of the past and, if serious, such a loss can erode a sense of identity. Since future time is limited for the elderly, a loss of ambition and initiative may ensue. Why make long term plans and organize one's life in pursuit of them? At the same time, it is not surprising that the elderly often abandon optimism for themselves and others, instead embracing caution and love of routine; they adopt a conservative way of life and outlook seeking to avoid risks which might be treated as adventures when they were young. Finally, there is the heightened anticipation of their own death and they cannot avoid the frequent encounter of the deaths of friends and loved ones. In this book, I have treated these marks of old age as seven losses: loss of biological capacities, loss of paid employment; loss of the past, loss of an extended future, loss of autonomy and initiative, loss of faith in personal and societal progress, and loss of life itself. In Chapters XIII- XIX, I report my reflective meditations on each of these losses.

Few will debate the reality of old age as a stage of loss, but they will suggest that there are blessings in old age as well, and some old age losses may be prevented or minimized. In addition, some will claim that there no "stage" of old age, but rather a continuum of "aging". To be sure, the boundaries of a stage of old age are fuzzy, but losses which accumulate in the sixth or seventh decade of life also begin to establish the stage of old age. The importance of viewing old age as a stage of life is that it can be conveniently understood as part of the development through an entire lifespan and both linked and contrasted with earlier stages of that lifespan. Old age is perhaps best regarded as that stage of life in which the losses of aging become evident and for most, soon eventuate in death,

- The Elegy of Old Age

Based upon my own old age experience and the classics I have read, I have chosen to view old age as an elegy. It may seem odd to rely upon a poetic form by which to understand this stage of life, but, once one understands the nature of elegy, its' suitability becomes evident. Relying upon an appeal to a poetic form gives unity to the old age experience. Elegy was originally a form of poetry about the death of a loved one. The poem conveyed sadness, but also yielded a message or at least a sense of consolation. As a work of art, it embodied a certain aesthetic detachment, both for the writer and the reader. Modern critics have expanded the poetic form of elegy to include losses aside from death, evoking other emotions, finding the elegiac form in prose as well as poetry. Such an expansion of elegy permits the extension and applicability of elegy to the losses of old age and to a wider range of emotions including anger, melancholy, alienation, regret, and nostalgia. The modern expanded view of elegy permits one to look at prose and even fine art works as well as poetry as vehicles by which one might achieve a sense of detachment from the old age losses found within these works. Finally, the expansion of the scope of elegy permits consideration of kinds of consolation different from those suited to the death of a loved one; as we shall see below, such consolations are found in elegies applicable to old age.

- Meditative reflection in old age

Three classic works inform my approach to meditative reflection. First is Petrarch's *The Solitary Life* which discusses his own approach to his periodic solitary meditation and he reports on the lives of other, more ancient, solitaries. Second is Montaigne's *Essays,* written in his Tower library, after he retreated from an active public life. Specific essays focus on old age losses and all the essays are exercises in meditative reflection. The third classic work is Thoreau's *Walden,* in which he tries his own short experiment with solitude and reflects upon nature, the classics and other subjects. Each of these authors give accounts of their engagement in "classical leisure", a leisure in which the reflective activity is undertaken for its own sake.

The activity of meditative reflection in old age focuses upon the elements in elegy – loss, emotion, detachment, and consolation – as those elements apply to old age. I envisage a meditation which is *reflective* - a looking back upon the past losses, interpreting the present losses, and anticipating the future losses and the completion of life encountered in old age. The reflection also seeks to identify, define and accept the emotions resulting from such loss, abstracting from the immediacy of these losses and emotions, and aiming at consolation. Consolation requires a deliberation among the "avenues of solace": available for consolation. Such meditative reflection differs from the kinds of currently popular version of Buddhist meditation in America, since the reflections which focus upon the four elements of elegiac old age are dependent, in part, upon intellectual processes of abstraction from experience, consultation with the classics, and employing the ideas they generate. Such reflection is different from reflection described by John Dewey, since meditative reflection is not aimed at action aimed at resolving problems.

- Consultation with the Classics

I propose a consultation with the classics to assist in the process of meditative reflection. Such classics will help to identify and describe the nature of the losses encountered in old age as well as evoking and defining those emotions experienced in old age. The classics will enable one to abstract from the immediate experience of old age and understand that experience through the light of more universal ideas. The classics will also suggest avenues of consolation.

By "classics", I mean as Matthew Arnold stated: "The best that has been thought and said" and, in addition, the best products of the fine arts and historical accounts of great deeds. I am aware of the recent attacks on the various canons of "great works" and I shall respond to those criticisms in Chapter IX) where I outline the method of meditative reflection. The ultimate test of the value of these works lies in whether they can facilitate the meditative reflection I recommend. The ultimate proof of the effectiveness of them is to be found in the reports of my reflections on each of the specific old age losses in Chapters 13-19 will demonstrate the value of the classics to an understanding of old age.

It is my contention that such classics yield universal ideas. Such ideas derived from the classics not only assist in the understanding of old age loss, but also offer a 'resting place" for the consolation of that loss. Ideas such as *work and leisure* help one to understand the nature of retirement., Notions of *biological functioning, equilibrium* and *the cycles of nature* help us in facing biological decline. The concepts of *wealth* and *poverty* are easily abstracted from discussions of the economic situation of the elderly, The loss of the past and the foreclosure of the future introduces the importance of *time* in understanding old age. *Autonomy, self-reliance, initiative* and *self-determination* are invoked in the discussions of dependency. The ideas of *history* and *progress* are immediately important to an understanding the old age rejection of the Enlightenment ideal of progress. Even *death* is more fully understood in light of the notions of *consciousness* and *being.*

- Liberal Education

Some will suggest that only a minority of the population has access to the classics. The majority, it is said, alleged lack the ability to read or appreciate the classics, let alone probe the ideas they generate. This is a valid criticism and I freely admit that meditative reflection on old age with the help of the classics is not available to everyone. Nevertheless, there are many elderly persons who have benefitted from a liberal education, many more citizens who approaching old age with a liberal education and, of course, thousands presently enrolled in liberal arts colleges. This liberal education should equip them to gain access to the classics. In this book, (Chapters X-XII), I have described the kind of liberal education ideally suited to equip one to engage in reflective meditation in old age and, by implication argue for the expansion of liberal education in the future.

- Finding Truth About One's Old Age and Entire Life

There are three kinds of truths. First, truths may be "correspondence truths" in which the conclusions reached in meditative reflection correspond to an independent reality discoverable in other ways. The general truths about old age which I have uncovered will be tested by my more specific personal experience of old age. Second, the truths of the conclusions reached may also be "coherence truths", that is, they may be consistent with the other realities not only of one's old age. I shall explore the coherence of the truths I have uncovered in reflection with the other truths of my life. Finally, the truths uncovered by reflection may be "pragmatic truths", that is, ones which, in the words of William James, turn out to "work" when believed. I shall explore whether the pragmatic truths revealed in reflection, when acted upon as part of my way of life, have led to a satisfactory old age way of life.

The conclusions of meditative reflection lead, not only to consolations for each of the losses, and for old age generally. Meditative reflection may lead to consolations derived from discovery of truths about one's entire life as revealed in that reflection. In short, the conclusions of meditative reflection lead, not only to consolations for each of the losses in old age, but also consolation derived from a discovery of the truths about one's entire life. In the final chapter, I shall report upon the these truths and consolations which I have found (or not found) in my own decade of old age meditative reflection.

The Organization of the Book

Based upon the premises outlined above, this book is divided into six parts. Part I discusses in general the components of elegy – loss, emotion, detachment, and consolation. In Part II, since some do not adopt the view that old age is elegiac, I review these "enemies of elegy"- proponents who advocate life extension, religious belief, search for pleasure, and continued "busyness" as the proper answer to coping with old age. I discuss the ways in which each of these approaches is both correct and mistaken. Since I base the method and success of meditative reflection upon consulting the classics, in Part III, I set forth a description and defense of the classics, how a liberal education can prepare one for access to the classics; and how the method of meditative reflection can "make use" of the classics. In Part IV, I offer my own reflections on each of the seven losses of old age. In the Conclusion, I summarize the conclusions of these reflections and I "test" their general truths against my own decade long old age experience. In each of the chapters, I have introduced the more abstract discussion with a brief autobiographical account which pertains to the subject of the chapter.. I have added two appendices: Appendix A. A List of Selected Classics on Old Age; Appendix B: A List of Selected Recent Works on Old Age. These may be helpful for the reader who wished to dig more deeply into the classics and their contributions to understanding and coping with old age.

ACKNOWLEDGEMENTS

Several friends, Carl Yirka,, a fellow lover of books, James Murphy, Professor and scholar of classics, Stephen Dycus, and Tom Seessel reviewed chapters of the book and supplied comments. Genie and the late Jeff Shields reviewed two different versions of the Introduction. I have presented two different summaries of the work, one to Genie Shield's "salon" and one to the Dartmouth Psychoanalysis Study Group. Both groups had many observations and criticisms, many of which I have tried to address in later versions. I have also benefitted from written comments on an earlier summary of the book from Melissa Zeiger, a Dartmouth professor and scholar of elegy, and Dr. Sarah Ackerman, a practicing psychoanalyst. I have sent selected materials out to my son and daughter who have not been sparing in their criticisms. Detailed editing was carried out by my friend, Laura Gillen, (who, at the same time, takes a completely different view of her own old age and retirement!). Eric Levy, a professional editor, edited an earlier manuscript and supplied excellent critical comments to the entire text.

My deepest personal debt is to my late loving and patient wife, Mollie, who supported my venture and reviewed many of the chapters of this book, voicing her disagreement to my general view of a loss-laden old age. Although my deepest philosophical debt is to the ancient Greek philosopher, Aristotle, and the modern British philosopher, Alfred North Whitehead, three contemporary philosophers have inspired me:

Mortimer Adler and his much maligned but magnificent *Syntopicon,* John Kekes and his myriad of thoughtful works, especially, *Moral Wisdom and Good Lives* and Walter Watson and his remarkable *The Architectonics of Meaning, Foundations of a New Pluralism.*

CHAPTER I

The Reluctant Acceptance of Old-Age Loss

. . . but as we advance in the journey of life, we drop
some of the things that have pleased us . . .

—Samuel Johnson

When I have seen Time's fell hand defaced
The rich-proud cost of outworn buried age….

__ Willian Shakespeare

*Old age Loss! Indeed! I used to run marathons, and now I helplessly watch
as students from the nearby college run by. I am old, fat and my knees
hurt. I have lost my "mojo!" Although retired, I visit the school where I
once taught, hoping to offer wise advice to younger faculty members only to
be ignored. Now, I turn to reflecting upon my past, hoping in some weird
way to lengthen my life backward. Unfortunately, I cannot quite remember
much of the past, including any past accomplishments or failures of my life.
Did they really happen? Where did my future and its possibilities disappear?
Into the mists of old age? Did this old age "loss of possibilities" suck away my
ambitions and grand plans? Even my personal plans for self-improvement
now seem ridiculous. With old age, a new dependency quietly arrives.
Now, given our infirmities, in the last few years, my wife and I clung to the
present and each other—both in body and soul. We had a host of old age
maladies-some merely inconvenient, others threatening to become serious.*

We regarded each other with a reciprocal compassion. (Compassion is the old-age virtue to be cultivated and practiced; my wife has lots of it while I didn't have enough.) We slowly became bystanders of life. We watched the news, like fans in the bleachers—able to cheer or boo—but unable to really affect the game before us, since we were out of date and out of energy. Then, my wife died – the ultimate loss in old age, both for her and me. Our losses have not been only individual losses.. In our lifetime, there have been wars, economic depressions, the Holocaust and other mass killings, famine, epidemic diseases, and other disasters, and we were unable to do anything about them. I see nothing in history or our present politics which will prevent these catastrophes from repeating. How can I hold onto belief in the inevitable progress of mankind? As for death, the "ultimate loss," although I have been deeply saddened by my wife's death, I view with equanimity the proximity of my own. Is this denial? I have discovered the losses of old age.

Introduction: The Losses of Old Age

In the literature of old age, there is a well-known poem by Matthew Arnold:

Growing Old

> What is it to grow old?
> Is it to lose the glory of the form,
> The lustre of the eye?
> Is it for beauty to forego her wreathe
> —Yes, but not this alone

Arnold proceeds, stanza by stanza, to itemize physical decay and lack of strength, the absence of sunset glow, the failure of any prophetic visions, the slow suffering of a weary pain, the loss of emotion, and then:

> It is—last stage of all—
> When we are frozen up within, and quite
> The phantom of ourselves

Unlike Arnold, I am not quite as pessimistic; I propose to view such losses as part of an elegy of old age, constituting old age wounds to be soothed by the poultices of detachment and the bandages of consolation. But Arnold and I agree that old age is a time of losses—permanent, inherent, inevitable, irreversible, cumulative, and final. They are permanent, not to be ultimately defeated by modern science or other remedies. They are an inherent part of the human condition. They are predictable and inevitable. At least for the present, they are not reversible. Unlike losses at other times of our lives, old age losses accumulate and often grow more serious, finally leading to death.

These old age losses come in different packages. The most important loss rests upon a slow or precipitous biological decline, whether physical or mental. Many of the other old-age losses result from this decline. The reality of such decline leads society to expect or mandate the aged to retire from work. Or in anticipation of society's demands we elders are persuaded that we should "voluntarily" retire (The question: "Are you still working?" was often asked of me well before retirement!). As old age advances, the past is eclipsed—the real past of the history in which we lived our lives recedes as time marches on, but also our memory of that past fades as well. We try to remember, often without success, the people and places which surrounded our past lives as well as the events of our own personal pasts. The eclipse of our memory of the past is documented by scientific findings of the frequent loss of episodic historical memory among the elderly population. Often ignored is the fact that as others in our own age cohort die, we lose those who have memories of our shared past. There is the fading of a collective memory of which we are a part.

The eclipse of the past is an especially important loss in old age, especially when we elders become aware that as we age, our future is steadily shrinking. With that shrinkage, the hopes and ambitions, which were dependent upon an extended future as well as the energy it brings with it —the winds in our sails—are reduced or abandoned. One way we can lengthen our lives is to retrieve the past.

Biological decline, loss of the past and shrinkage of the future are not the only losses in old age. Our biological decline leads inevitably to a growing dependency upon others, and that dependency poses a real or imagined threat to our autonomy and "agency"—our ability to deliberate, decide, and initiate our own actions for ourselves and others. We must increasingly look to others to help us with daily living. In old age, we also may become "politically dependent". Most of us do not assume responsibility for the problems of our community, except perhaps to make a donation to our favorite charity or political party or write the occasional diatribe to the local newspaper. Many of us, i.e., the elderly poor, are "economically crippled" in old age as we suffer a drastic reduction in income.

The weakening of our commitment to the community may have a deeper origin. Having witnessed catastrophes, evils, and brave ideals frustrated in the course of our lives, many of us abandon hope for any progress, whether in self-improvement or in the historical advance of our local or national community. Such hope may be further diminished by the awareness of our biological decline, which leads, from time to time, to an old-age anticipation of dying and death. At the very least, we reach the sobering realization that our lives are ending and soon we shall cease to exist.

Perhaps biological decline and the imminent prospect of death are the most objective and ruthless facts of old age. Old age biological decline means the loss of teeth, hair, muscle strength, and reproductive powers, accompanied by joint pain, wrinkles, and a plethora of diseases. Underlying these most obvious markers are cell senescence, limited cell reproduction, decline in hormones, and the aging of the brain and nervous system. (It is ironic that modern biologists and medical researchers, in their efforts to extend lives, also manage to document the many signs of biological decline!) Since such biological changes dictate eventually the retirement from work, an overwhelming number of people are "retired" from their occupation by their seventies, despite the fact that a majority of these retirees may wish to work after their retirement. Statistics also document that despite pension plans and social security in the affluent Western nations, the retirement from work requires many to face significant economic adjustments since retirement income is significantly less than work income. Retirement also often carry with it a subtle loss of status, a depressing loss of stimulation often offered by the workplace, the fading of a sense of mastery and competence as work skills are abandoned, and a frequent lapse of friendships which were forged in the workplace.

Other kinds of losses occur in old age and can be documented. One such loss is the inability of many of us elderly to keep up with the future; an example is our difficulty in coping with modernization and its technological changes. The eminent social philosopher, Norberto Bobbio, in *Old Age and Other Essays,* claims that it is a person's failure to cope with new technology which best marks the arrival of his old age. The fact that we elderly are slower to adopt new technologies and integrate them into our lives serves to alienate us from a younger population in love with new gadgets.

Beyond a failure to embrace the future, most elderly persons are aware that our future is limited. (Ironically, despite old age awareness of our shrinking future, many of us do not even contemplate the importance of that loss, as indicated by the fact that 70 percent of Americans die without wills, (the one legal instrument for extending one's life beyond death)! However, it is this shrinking of the future which makes many of us elderly less willing to undertake long-term projects. Of course, undertaking such projects may also be discouraged by the reality of growing old-age dependency. Physical dependency is evidenced by a visit to any hospital (such visits become more frequent as we grow older); in the hospital corridors, one can see a myriad of old people needing assistance of all sorts.

The presence of the ultimate loss, death, lurks in old age consciousness and deliver the message of its proximity in many ways. We furtively read the obituaries noting the ages at death along with the diseases which preceded it.. If older than us, the reading gives us hope. If younger than us, along with sympathy, we harbor a secret sense of triumph that we outlived persons younger than ourselves, as if some sick contest were at hand.

The brutal facts of old age are not ignored by the classics. Like Arnold's poem, other classic works have not shrunk from giving brutal descriptions of the losses of old age. Euripides, the ancient Greek playwright, described his characters' old age as sorrowful, heavy, accursed, difficult, bitter, hateful, and even murderous. His elderly players hobble on- and offstage with help from younger characters. The walking staff is standard property for these ancient elders, much as canes and wheelchairs are for us. Euripides paints the aged with colors like the gray of hair and the white and blue of skin and vein, describes our stooped postures, and notes our wrinkled skin along with our gnarled and spotted hands. The old man in *Electra* states, "How steep is the climb to this house here for wrinkled old feet like mine to make. But for your friends you have to drag yourself along with doubled-over back and tottering knees."

The ancient playwrights are not alone in their description of us elderly. As we shall see in the following chapters, medieval and modern authors rival the ancients in their brutally honest descriptions of the aged. Honoré de Balzac offers a depressingly objective account of old age in *Old Goriot*, in which one of several elderly occupants of the pension is old Poiret, described as follows:

> M. Poiret was a sort of automaton. He might be seen any day sailing like a gray shadow along the walks of the Jardin des Plantes, on his head a shabby cap, a cane with an old yellow ivory handle with the tips of his thin fingers. The outspread skirts of his threadbare overcoat failed to conceal his meager figure; his breeches hung loosely on shrunken limbs; the thin, blue-stockinged legs trembled like those of a drunken man.

Balzac provides descriptions not only of the dreary old denizens of the Maison Vauquer rooming house, but also of its' drab surroundings in which the elderly lead their lives. In one part of Balzac's account, "the paneled walls of that apartment were once painted some color, now a matter of conjecture, but the surface is encrusted with accumulated layers of grimy deposit, which cover it with curious patterns." Such a description of the room may reflect the appearance of the elderly who lived there as well as the dreariness and hopelessness of their lives.

In the preoccupation with our individual losses in old age, we may easily ignore the social dimensions of these losses, including the frequent loss of loved ones. In old age, there may be a loss of community. Our old-age losses may be accompanied by a state of poverty, an experience which many elderly experience. The lack of resources of many elderly compounds their loss of mobility, energy, and ambition, which can interrupt or destroy the social relationships the they might have enjoyed in younger years. And whether rich or poor, the fading of a collective memory of our past, often in the form of the death of our contemporaries, may weaken or eliminate the already frayed bonds with the community.

The losses of the aging individual are also losses to society. In aging, society may lose active citizens, employable adults, and the other contributions which aging individuals might make. Retirement often represents a social loss of talents; when society retires an individual, it sacrifices possible future productive contributions which might have been made by the retiree. These "opportunity costs" are added to the real social costs of aging. The physical and mental declines of old age call upon society to attempt to prevent or mitigate the consequences of the decline by launching medical and support services, often at great cost to society. Massive economic resources are also expended simply to support retirees. But retirement and physical decline are not the only source of expense that society bears. Old-age economic and physical dependency also places a heavy burden on others. Less obvious, the elderly's loss of hope and ambition, and our abandonment of commitment to societal progress, leads to the withdrawal of many talented individuals, who, in their earlier lives, had been agents for societal change and improvement. Society is the poorer as a result of such a loss.

Few notice the immense collective cost which growing old places upon society. This heavy cost is eased by the societal assumption that new generations will take the place of the old. The necessity of generational change is recognized, and with that recognition, the loss of the oldest generation is accepted as well, (often with enthusiasm!) But in that substitution of the young generation for the old, there is a collective loss of knowledge that the elderly possess. The kind of knowledge lost may include a kind of historical wisdom of the aged—a knowledge admittedly less respected in modern society, but nevertheless valuable, if not valued.

The periodic turnover of the old age cohort and the losses which individuals and societies experience in our contemporary world should be viewed in the context of a broader history of western civilization. For example, the "normal" systematic disappearance of entire generations over time takes place in the context of other historical losses of the twentieth century. In the last century, we oldsters have witnessed the brutal consequences of the continuation of the industrial revolution, two world wars, the Holocaust, mass genocidal crimes, epidemics, forced migrations, modern tortures, and natural catastrophes.. These historical events contribute to and compound the specific individual and social losses encountered by old persons, their families, and communities living today.

The Remains of the Day

I have described a bleak picture of our old age losses. As I shall suggest in later chapters, there is some relief from such losses in elegiac detachment and consolation. But as we shall see, such detachment and consolation rests upon the "remains of the day". What are "the remains of the day"? Given the losses of old age, and our recognition of them, "these remains of the day" are what is left after the losses of old age are encountered. *These losses are the variety of goods found in the rubble left by the losses.* Biological decline carries with it a tranquility which accompanies the decline of wayward passions which accompanies such decline. Retirement with its loss of opportunity for economically productive work, may result in a welcome escape from burdens of such work and an opportunity to pursue a valuable leisure. The loss of our past may not be tragic since it allows us to ignore the painful past we have lived through, escaping to live in the present. Such a loss of the past may enable us to freely reach back to imaginatively recreate a better past! Similarly, given the foreshortening of our future, we may welcome old-age freedom from demanding ambitions for that future, (whether these ambitions are for self-improvement or for making contributions to others). Lacking a future, we may discover ways of establishing legacies we can leave to others—legacies which extend beyond our admittedly limited lives. Most of us cannot deny our growing dependency, but the dependency of ourselves and our loved ones may strengthen ties of compassion and love with others. In the process of giving or receiving help, we may also discover a dignity which does not depend upon self-sufficiency. For many of us, the abandonment of historical progress, with its customary pursuits of individual perfection and community self-improvement, is difficult to swallow. However, giving up active efforts to promote an illusory political progress may allow us to reach a new appreciation of the past and the present and a more realistic understanding of history. Anticipation of death and dying itself may result in accepting the limits of our own being and may lead to the realization that our life is complete.

Thus, the remains of the day, after old age loss may be old-age serenity, contentment in leisure, recreating the past, discovery of new legacies, deepening of dignity and compassion in our relationships, contemplative understanding of history, and acceptance of the completion of our life. These "remains of the day" are *the goods of old age left over after the losses of old age take place.* As we shall see below, the classics will help us better understand and value these "remains of the day" through detachment and consolation. But whether such left over goods outweigh old age losses remains to be seen. I shall return to a discussion of the "remains of the day" in Chapter III.

The Nature of Old Age Loss: A Philosophical Digression

Old-age and its losses are fundamental changes which take place during the time of our lives. These changes can be understood in various ways—as simple facts to be found in everyday experience and carefully documented by gerontology research as well as the classics. One particularly excellent philosophical assessment of scientific research is Joseph Esposito's *The Obsolete Self.* Esposito explores the losses of old age and the various theories of the causes of aging. He draws upon the biological, psychological, social and political studies of the aged in an effort to promote the humane understanding of old age loss. Rather than repeat his fine work, (which I urge the reader to find and read), I wish to focus upon three principal ideas which lie at the heart of old age loss: change, time, and the goods, (including "the self") A brief review of some selected philosophical classics impart a heightened awareness of the nature of change, time and the goods lost in old age leading to a better understanding of the transience of life.

1. *Change*

Part of the experience of old age is change – change which took place in the past leading to experience of loss in the present old age- change in the present as each old age loss is experienced and change anticipated in the future including, of course, the change from life to death. How are we to understand the nature of change which constitutes an important part of our old age experience?

The history of thought – novels and poems, philosophies and theologies, and science – not only describes change but seeks to grapple with determining the nature of change itself. To help us understand the reality of our transience, we can turn to classics that offer a rich portrait and analysis of change. Philosophical inquiry into the nature of change has dominated the thoughts of philosophers and writers from Heraclites, Democritus, and Lucretius, to Michel de Montaigne, Sigmund Freud, Charles Darwin, and Karl Marx, to moderns such as William James, Henri-Louis Bergson, John Dewey, and Alfred North Whitehead.

These and other works may be usefully classified in terms of the different ways in which the reality of change is understood. Thus, Montaigne, in his essays, sees change as simply an existential reality which we all must face. Thus, in old age, at the end of his *Essays*, he captures the phenomenon of changes in himself in eating, sleeping and all the mundane activities of life. Following Montaigne, we would understand our old age losses by our immediate existential experience of them. Freud, like Montaigne, in his marvelous little essay "Transience," written during the First World War, accepts total transience and yet preserves his belief in the emotional value of the present experiences of truth and beauty, even if they are to be destroyed. In Freud's words,

> A time may indeed come when the pictures and statues which we admire today will crumble to dust, or a race of men may follow us who no longer understand the works of our poets and thinkers or a geological epoch may even arrive when all animate life upon the earth ceases: but since the value of all this beauty and perfection is determined only by its significance for our own emotional lives, it has no need to survive us and is therefore independent of absolute duration.

The ancient Epicurean philosopher and poet, Lucretius, like the modern physicist, sees change as reflections of the deeper workings of an underlying atomic substructure, Following Lucretius, we can regard our old age and death with a detached view since it is simply the blind workings of the flux of atoms in the universe.

. On the other hand, Plato views change not as an underlying material reality, but unreality—a mere "becoming" which is radically distinct from the reality of the changeless ideas he claims to discover. This allows Plato to regard his old age and death with equanimity, since it is simply unreal when compared to the eternity of ideas. In a related notion, modern Christian religious belief, following Augustine, and the end of his *Confessions,* finds the time of changes in this life best understood when contrasted with the eternity of the next life to be found in religious faith.

Perhaps the most unique and difficult effort to understand change is formulated by Whitehead, who sees the universe as constituting a comprehensive process of change. The elements which are part of this change he calls "occasions" to highlight their transience. We momentarily grasp these occasions when they are infiltrated by "ideas", (not unlike Platonic ideas) which, in Whitehead's words "ingress" into the actual "occasions", thus constituting our experience of actual entities undergoing change. Thus, for Whitehead, unlike Plato, change is part of an essential reality of beings, including, of course aging humans. As occasions, our reality as humans is merely the ingression of the universal idea of humanity, (an idea, eternal in itself), "ingressing" into us to make us for the moment, "actual" human beings. Despite the difficulty of understanding Whitehead's philosophy, it suggests that our change to and within old age are essential parts of who we are!

One ancient thinker, Aristotle, identifies four kinds of change – growth and diminution (change in quantity); locomotion (change in place), change in quality (alteration) and "generation and corruption", (coming to be and passing away). Change towards and in old age may be viewed in changes in the various quantities (i.e. the length of telomeres) of our bodies. Or it may refer to changes in the quality of our bodies and minds as itemized by the changes observed in the aging process. As one underappreciated philosopher, (Scott Buchanan, *The Doctrine of Signatures*) has suggested, the visible qualities of old age are "symptoms" or *signatures* of changes in our biological systems and in the habits of character responding to those changes. Aristotle's change "by corruption" may be the most appropriate change characterizing aging, since it is linked with the notion of passing out of existence. The losses of old age are inextricably linked to our eventual extinction.

2. *Time*

Since change takes place over time and old age losses take place in time, a brief philosophical discussion of the nature of time is useful to an understanding of these losses. The history of thought, oversimplified, suggests three major approaches to time-objective time measured by clocks and calendars, internal or "subjective time" and eternity, time which is deemed to extend forever or exists outside the ordinary movement of time. Objective time orders the activity of our lives and the stages of our lives. Objective time is a resource which, in old age, is running low. At the other extreme is eternal time. In Edward Waller's poem cited below, I left out its final lines,

The Soul's dark cottage, battered and decayed
Let's in new light though chinks that time has made;
Stronger by weakness, wiser men become
As they draw near to their eternal home.
Leaving the old, both worlds at once they view
That stand upon the threshold of the new.

which advert to the arrival of eternal time in the losses of old age. Despite all the objective measures of the time of old age, I believe that the subjective, inner time in old age is more important. In this view, we share in time and time is part of us. For the German philosopher, Immanuel Kant, time was an intellectual category of the mind through which we perceive the empirical world. For modern phenomenologists, time is encountered through memory and reminiscence, interpretation of our experience, critique of history or participation in the social world. Without trying to describe all these views of inner time, I (and I hope the reader) are content to simply observe that our old age sense of time may be composed of our memory and reminiscence of the past, the viewing of our old age in history, reflection upon our sense of time in our everyday old age lives, and our awareness of the world of social time. I shall describe these kinds of time more concretely in the final seven chapters where I describe the losses in detail.

Loss as Detachment of the Goods of Life

I have stressed that, unlike many everyday losses at earlier stages of our lives, old age losses are inevitable, irremediable, cumulative, irretrievable, and final. Some of the losses are losses of "external goods", the loss of income, deceased friends and loved ones, and the loss of opportunities and time to engage in many life projects. There are also the losses of "internal goods" we once possessed—such as internal capabilities, motivation, and energy. Our biological decline results in losses of the capabilities of agency—the capacities to initiate, continue, and complete action. For example, the irremediable loss of work in retirement often results in a gradual loss of the capacities such work demanded. These capacities are not recovered later in old age. And each loss may compound and accumulate with the other losses. The loss of work may impede ambitions; the loss of biological capacities may impede self-sufficiency, which in turn, may lead to increased dependency. All of the losses are predecessors to death.

To understand the nature of goods lost in old age, I draw upon Aristotle's *Nicomachean Ethics*. Aristotle viewed our entire human life and its projects as "aiming at some good". When defined, that good was not any grand metaphysical good, but simply the moral and intellectual excellences, found in the capabilities unique to the human character as well as the activities stemming from such excellences. These capabilities and their exercise were to be sufficient for a good life, although supported by a modicum of external goods including friends, an appropriate political community, and good fortune.

We deem these capabilities and their functioning to be good because they are part of what is meant by being truly human. Like the ancient Greeks, we recognize the excellence of the performance of these capabilities and we honor this excellence. The classical or, for that matter, the modern "perfectionist" understanding of man is a "rational animal" whose happiness is marked by the excellent exercise of the capabilities which lead to a kind of fulfillment. The classical view assumes that the essence of our lives is the acquisition of unique excellences, "virtues" of action and thought ordinarily reached and expressed in middle age. Perhaps the deepest reason for regarding old age as tragic is our unconscious adherence to the ancient Greek assumption that only at the peak of the arc of life can the excellence of bodily and mental functioning which is the essence of humanity be achieved. This excellence is lost in old age. Thus, the moral virtues of justice, courage, temperance, liberality, and wisdom don't fit easily into the reality of old age. (Perhaps this "lack of fit" explains Plato's and Aristotle's shabby treatment of the elderly. In the discussion of justice in Plato's *Republic*, the old man, Cephalus, leaves the dialogue on justice to make sacrifices instead. The assumption is that serious dialogue about justice is not a task for the elderly. They are not capable of it. Aristotle himself painted a starkly negative picture of the elderly when describing them as a potential audience to be addressed with the arguments of rhetoric. Plato and Aristotle recognize that the capabilities of character may be lost in old age).

One might mistakenly imagine goods to be like beads on a bracelet, to be plucked off by the passage of time. But these goods of life are not a disconnected mélange of goods, but rather an embedded part of our body, our character and our entire life's narrative. The modern French philosopher, Henri Bergson, captures the subtlety of such a process of loss. He rejects the belief that "...growing old can be nothing more than the gradual gain or loss of certain substances...." Growing old is part of our *duration*. In Bergson's words,

> My mental state, as it advances on the road of time is continually swelling with the duration which it accumulates; it goes on increasing –rolling upon itself as a snow ball on the snow.

Central to Bergson's understanding of life is notion of duration - the continuity of the movement of time.

> Life does but prolong this prenatal evolution...in short, what is properly vital in growing old is the insensible graduated continuance of the change in form" and despite the reality of organic destruction, ...the evolution of the living being, like that of the embryo, implies a continual recording of duration, a persistence of the past, and so an appearance, at least, of organic memory."

Once old age losses are viewed as part of a continuous life, these losses can only be understood in light of duration. *The goods of old age and their loss are time-bound.* They can only be understood as Jean Amery, in his recent work *On Old Age,* has described. For Amery, time is, in part, an inner sense: "time is *always* within us". The aged are aware of this inner sense of time and they experience it as irreversible, although some engage in the hopeless wish to reverse time. For Amery, when we are young, we are oriented to space – the world around us. but when old, we *become* time.

"The more definitively we recognize ourselves as aging persons

> the more we experience time in its irreversibility…the more intimately we belong to it. It is everything that we still are: we can no more give it up than we can give ourselves up, even though we know that we will lose it and ourselves…We are saying that an aging human being is a bundle of time or a stratified mass of time…."

The very definition of most of the losses in old age implies the passage of time. We experience many of the signs of biological decline as the fruits of our past life. Our eclipse of the past and the foreshortening of the future are obviously time related. Our abandonment of our faith in the progress of history is a giving-up of belief in a certain pattern of time. Anticipation of death and sense of waiting is fraught with awareness of time. Amery is correct to label us "a bundle of time".

One unique loss experience in old age is the loss of the self. Growing old may accentuate a sense of threat to our sense of self as we retreat from interest and participation in the social world. But also, as we understand old-age losses to tear at the fabric of our lives, the integrated part of a continuous thread of life. As a consequence, over time, these losses may contribute to a broader loss of the self. Three notions of the self can be found in the history of thought- the self as embodied life, as a conscious and thinking being, and as an identity. Each loss in old age may contribute to the erosion of one of these selves.

Biological decay affects the self as embodied life – the self, which the ancient philosophers identified as "the soul", a principle of life which includes "self- movement" of nutrition, growth, and locomotion. Such biological decay may also interfere with our self-conscious and thinking activity selves. (Perhaps the frequently observed lack of shame in the elderly may be signs of lack of self-consciousness). If we believe the self to be a form of personal identity, then the eclipse of our memory of the past cuts off the personal narrative which helps to make up such an identity, while the foreshortening of the future weakens our impetus for undertaking future projects, an impetus which often defines who we are.

Other losses have a similar impact. The growth of dependency inhibits the personal autonomy which is part of our identity. Our retirement removes some social roles by which we and others define us. Another loss in old age, a declining faith in the progress of history, may undercut our ability to be part of a shared political faith, which, in the past, had been part of our social identity. Of course, death promises the extinction of the self, however defined. Despite these assaults, we may hold onto some form of permanent self in old age, at least in early old age. We may reach the same conclusion as Edmund Waller in his poem "Old Age":

> The seas are quiet when the winds give o'er;
> So calm are we when passions are no more.
> For then we know how vain it is to boast
> Of fleeting things, so certain to be lost
> Clouds of affection from our younger eyes
> Conceal that emptiness which age decries.
> The Soul's dark cottage, battered and decayed...

In sum, the losses are the "chinks that Time has made". (In fairness to Waller, as I pointed out earlier, the poem's final lines suggest that eternal light will shine through such chinks). Each of these losses are seen as necessary and integral part of a complete human life accumulating into an old age self and accentuating it's sense of time.

The Acceptance of Old Age Losses

In a well-known poem, Dylan Thomas advises us "Do not go gentle into that good night", since "old age should rave at the close of day". Here I suggest a "grudging" acceptance of old age losses and that, indeed, we should "go gentle" and accept the losses of old age. In order to accept them, we must recognize, describe, understand and accept them. Contained within our acceptance of old age is an assent to the necessity of loss and a consent to the remainder of our lives being ordered in light of such necessity. Fortunately, at least for many of us, old age is long enough and losses are gradual enough to give us time for such acceptance.

Recognition involves a special awareness that the losses are old age losses that they truly exist and that these losses are irretrievable and final. Such recognition grows out of our experience and is both intellectual and emotional. Based upon such experience, we can identify and describe the loss both for ourselves and others. But understanding such losses – why they originate, what form they take, and what purposes they serve in our lives and in the world– is more difficult, and it is the classic works which help us with such an understanding.

Other classics may make a somewhat different contribution to our understanding of the losses of old age. These classics may assume a perspective in which we simply detach ourselves from our own personal experience and impartially scrutinize "the facts" of old-age loss. Francis Bacon, in his *Essays*, offers a delightfully objective account of aging, along with advice on how to live long. (Bacon himself died of pneumonia as a consequence of his experiment of freezing chickens to determine if freezing might lengthen life.) Nor does an objective account need to be an optimistic one. The account set forth in Sherwin Nuland's *How We Die* is hardly an hopeful picture! From another perspective, a "revelatory perspective", the Bible and Dante's *Divine Comedy* both view human loss at any age as part of God's divine plan for man (his punishment or, perhaps, as in the story of Job, a test of faith). To adopt another perspective, many of us moderns believe that these losses simply reflect the decay of the underlying mechanical workings of our physical structure, as viewed through the modern scientific disciplines. Aristotle, Galen, Lucretius, Charles Darwin, and August Weismann offer accounts of old age through the sciences of biology and physics which describe that underlying structure. There is no reason why all or any of these perspectives cannot be embraced in our understanding of the losses of old age. Such understanding prepares us to detach ourselves from the losses and find consolation for them. In the Chapters 3 and 4, I shall describe this detachment and consolation in general. In the final chapters of this book, I shall devote eight chapters to the recognition, description and understanding of the eight specific old age losses.

Recognition, description and understanding of old age losses prepare us for an informed if reluctant acceptance of them. This acceptance of losses requires our *assent* to their reality and their necessity as well as our demanding a willing *consent* to rearrange our old age lives in light of that reality. John Henry Newman, in his *Grammar of Assent,* distinguished between notional assent and real assent – the former is the apprehension of propositions, the latter is direct apprehension of concrete reality. It is this real assent to the concrete reality of our old age losses which is required for our acceptance of them. Whatever general understanding we reach regarding old age losses, whether through the classics or the sciences, when we accept these losses, we are *acceding* to their reality and necessity as part of our own personal aging process. Newman recognized that such assent had to be an assent to the particular subject and he suggested a specific faculty of understanding or "illative sense". According to Newman, such an illative sense operates in the professions of law and medicine when applied to particular clients or patients.

In addition to the recognition and understanding of specific losses, assent must extend to assenting to the necessity of those losses as well as their permanence and finality. It was the ancient Greek and Roman Stoics who first taught us to willingly accede to such necessity. As the Greek slave, Epictetus stated: "There is only one way to happiness and let this rule be ready... not to look at things out of the power of our will...." Extending this insight, we can only exercise freedom within our assent to the necessary losses of old age.

Conclusion: Accepting the Losses

In addition to such *assent* to the necessity of old age losses, we must also *consent* to order our lives in light of these losses and their necessity. Such a consent is an agreement- in dictionary terms, a willing yielding" – a voluntary act of free will of acceptance to the reality and necessity of old age loss; (after all, even if we assent to the necessity of death, we have the power to consent to Senecan suicide, or "the Dylan Thomas option" of raging against the dying of the light or, perhaps some more tranquil response). Part of the freedom in our response to the necessities of old age loss is the little recognized fact that such losses, even if necessary, *leave us other choices as to how we choose to live our lives.*

CHAPTER II

Emotions of Old Age Loss:

A tepid languor enervates all my faculties. The spirit of life is gradually dying out in me. Only with difficulty does my soul any longer thrust itself out of its decrepit wrapping . . .

—Rousseau, *The Reveries of a Solitary Walker*

. . . I should have lost a gesture and a pose.
Sometimes these cogitations still amaze
The troubled midnight and the noon's repose.

-T.S. Eliot, *La Figlia Che Piange*

In old age, I find myself frequently sad. A certain lassitude has set in—with late rising in the morning, evening vacuity in front of the TV, aimless inactivity throughout the day. I find myself increasingly irritated at minor affronts to my own sense of importance (although that importance has certainly disappeared with old age). I idly research my own history and write articles which recapture some past events in my life—events I barely remember or care about. My awareness of any extensive personal future dampens enthusiasm for long-term projects. My cocktail of old age melancholy is mixed a dash of regret, anger, nostalgia and alienation.

I am now convinced that the history of the world does not march to any measures of meaningful progress, and I find it difficult to get excited about politics any longer. The death of myself or my wife seems a vague possibility, but as each friend or acquaintance of my age dies, that possibility grows less vague and more real. Yet the sadness I feel is a tranquil one, a melancholy which is almost pleasant. Perhaps it is unreal—an old-age conceit.

Introduction: The Emotions of Old-Age Loss

Since I seek an understanding of old age through the framework of elegy in which losses are sustained, sorrows felt and mourned, detachment grows, and consolations found, I explore each of these elements of elegy in turn for them. In this chapter, I examine the old-age sadness, regret, nostalgia, anger and alienation which result from such losses, although I regard sadness as the central emotion of old age. I am painfully aware that these losses are only a few of the myriad of feelings encountered in old age: grief, despair, despondency, fear, anger, shame, remorse, repentance, loneliness, dread, anxiety - to name but a few. I have selected those which are most often mentioned in old age literature, which I have experienced, and which seem related to many of the other emotions listed.

Rousseau's old-age reveries quoted in the epigraph, teach us (if we needed teaching) that the losses which culminate in old age have deep emotional consequences. In old age, Rousseau lost his friends, reputation, wealth and security and his reveries reveal moods of melancholy, regret and nostalgia. Whether such diffuse moods or more specific emotions attach to old age losses, (perhaps both!), we elders must understand and evaluate them in order to determine the role they play and should play in our old age. After such understanding and evaluation, we must respond, whether to encourage and embrace such emotions, prevent or suppress them, distract ourselves from their presence, or find a proper place for them within our character and way of life.

The Specific Emotions and Moods of Old Age

Although the dominant mood of old age is sadness, each old age loss brings in its wake a unique set of emotions. Our physical and mental decline, with its accompanying lack of energy, may produce frustration, anger, fear and regrets of all sorts ("Why didn't I take better care of myself?"). Our retirement from work may produce a sense of momentary freedom and exhilaration, but it is followed by alienation, including a sense of powerlessness, purposelessness, normlessness and loneliness ("Why don't they consult me more?"). The eclipse of the past leaves us feeling empty, as if our personal history is no longer relevant. ("Don't they remember that I did that first?"). We also regret that the past does not contain any of our hoped-for or historic victories, thus securing our memorialization ("Why didn't I receive that award?"). The foreclosure of the future eliminates a sense of purpose and initiative. ("I need to find a new purpose in life!"). The loss of ambition for oneself and one's community produces a lassitude and sense of impotence ("Should I really enjoy getting up so late? I should help out!"). Old-age dependency may create embarrassment and shame ("You know, I'm fat now but I used to run marathons!"). Old age poverty may breed envy and anger. ("I worked hard all my life; it is not fair that I should be poor at the end of my life!). The abandonment of faith in the possibilities of individual improvement or progress in history yields a sense of hopelessness ("One can't really change things!") or indifference ("Who cares?"). The proximity of an inevitable death produces withdrawal and a vague anxiety and fear for one's loved ones. ("Who will take care of them after I die?"). Thus, each of the losses suffered produces its own unique feeling: the alienation in retirement, the regret in consulting one's past, the pain of losing possibilities for the future, the frustration of disability for oneself and one's loved ones, the hopelessness when contemplating the future, the envy and shame of old age poverty, the quiet anxiety at the approach of the loss of our own being.

These emotional reactions, when experienced in the supposed tranquility of old age, combine to create a general mood of a melancholy and regret, softened upon occasion by nostalgia, blunted by alienation and pierced by anger keep us company in our final years. This sorrow and other feelings are not only the result of the slow accretion of specific losses. Sadness and alienation result from the fact that each specific loss we encounter in old age contributes to a gradual loss of the entire self, and we mourn the loss of that self. The loss of self is the loss of the capacity for initiative, which we once exercised in a place which supports our talents, and which expresses our identity – an identity based upon a solid sense of our past and our ambitions for the future, not only for ourselves but for our community.

To be sure, there are some who suggest that the sadness and other emotions felt in old age is not serious, either because the old-age losses are counterbalanced with wisdom or, at least, because the sadness of loss is lightened by old-age delights or other "remains of the day" enumerated in Chapter I. In Browning's "Rabbi Ben Ezra," the poet invites us to "Grow old along with me. / The best is yet to be, / The last of life." Matthew Arnold's "Old Age" answers Browning and suggests that feeling becomes "frozen" in old age, overwhelming any of Browning's delights. Arnold's words are,

> And feel but half, and feebly, what we feel
> Deep in our hidden heart
> Festers the dull remembrance of change
> But no emotion . . . none . . .

There may be an explanation for Arnold's response to old age. If emotions are the outgrowth of instincts and their physical correlates, as suggested by the psychologist and philosopher, William James, perhaps in old age there is a weakening of our instincts for self-preservation or, as suggested by Freud, an ominous growth of the death instinct. Or, to seize upon another explanation, if emotions are not simply instinctual but are desires which hover near a reason which shapes their content and meaning, With the loss or weakening of desire, it is understandable that the old age range of emotions would be limited and we find ourselves "frozen". Whether or not some of us become frozen in old age, sadness is very real for many of the elderly. Such sadness is a permanent part of the lives of many who are old,.

The Nature of Sadness of Old Age

If the dominant mood of old age is a diffuse and tranquil sorrow, sadness, or melancholy which accompany the cumulative losses of this stage of life, such sadness is distinct from grief, despair, depression, desolation, gloominess, and acedia. Many accounts of the emotions through the ages seek to reduce the range of emotions, including sadness, to some primal emotions, such as desire and grief. To be sure, this feeling, "the sadness of old age," is related to, but distinct from, the normal grief we feel when our loved ones die. Roland Barthes wrote movingly about such grief at the death of his mother in his *Mourning Diary*. In one entry, Barthes captures it:

> Sad afternoon. Shopping purchase (frivolity) of a tea cake at the bakery. Taking care of the customer ahead of me, the girl behind the counter says "voila." The expression I used when I brought Maman something, when I was taking care of her. Once, toward the end, half-conscious, she repeated, faintly "voila" (a word we used to each other all our lives). The word spoken by the girl at the bakery brought tears to my eyes. I kept crying quite a while back to the silent apartment. (Mourning Diary, Oct 26,; September 15, 1979)

Although our old-age sadness lacks the intensity and focus of Barthes's grief for the death of a loved one (a frequent occurrence in old age), we aged find ourselves mourning for the loss of our own past selves which seem to have died—the lost persons that we ourselves were in the past. As a result, we may find ourselves preoccupied with our youth, searching for it in furtive ways. We may feel angry and silently protest its disappearance, while, at the same time, we regret that we did not make more of the possibilities, whatever they were, in our past lives. Like depressives, we may find ourselves with diminished interests, insomnia, loss of energy, lethargy and fatigue, feelings of worthlessness, and thoughts of death, although, unlike clinical depression, these symptoms of sadness may be mild, pervasive, continuous, and permanent. Unlike intense grief or clinical depression, there may even be a touch of pleasure in old-age sadness, pleasure which is captured in the sadness we take from elegiac poetry and in old age nostalgia.

Since I have chosen to approach old age through the framework of elegy, it is not surprising that I turn to elegies to capture the sadness felt upon old age loss. The most famous ancient and early English elegies are, of course, expressions of sadness at the loss of a loved one; but poets have extended the elegy to all modes of loss, including the loss of deserted farmhouses and villages, the past ways of life they symbolize, and even the loss of the poet's own youth. In the words of one such elegy, "Tears, Idle Tears," by Alfred Tennyson:

> Tears, idle tears, I know not what they mean,
> Tears from the depth of some divine despair
> Rise in the heart, and gather to the eyes,
> On looking on the happy autumn fields,
> And thinking of the days that are no more.

Tennyson's elegy is the expression of a general sadness at old-age loss. The elegy of old age is not merely an intellectual recognition of the loss of the "days that are no more," or a rational recognition of the diminishment of our capabilities and the loss of all the possibilities of our previous life, described in the previous chapter. An elegy is also the literary expression of sadness—the mourning of that loss. Elegy expresses the sadness or melancholy as well as a range of related emotions we feel as we experience and meditate on loss. Poetry and novels do not merely describe these emotions; they help the reader to feel them. Sadness is also found threaded within biographies. For example, James Boswell, in his meticulous biography *The Life of Samuel Johnson*, describes Johnson in his last years, still mentally acute and approaching death with a religious fear and reluctance, but also laden with illnesses (asthma) as well as sleeplessness, weariness, and incontinence. In Johnson's own words, "I live too much in solitude and am often deeply dejected"; in the same letter, after cataloging his complaints, he concludes, "This is my history, like all other histories, a narrative of misery." As we learn from Boswell, Johnson's history was much more than that, but we cannot help feeling sad as we read the final words of this biography.

In this modern age, dominated by the pursuit of happiness and, equally important, the ideal of the pursuit of happiness, we moderns, with the help of modern psychiatry, are likely to regard permanent sadness, even the sadness of old age, as abnormal depression. However, Freud, in his *Mourning and Melancholia*, while recognizing that sadness might be abnormal if too intense or if not recoverable over time, might also be quite normal. As we learned in the last chapter, Freud wisely found mourning the many losses of life, not only the loss of loved ones but the loss of entire civilizations or cultures, to be part of the inevitable transience of life.

One way of understanding old-age sadness is to distinguish it carefully from other related, less welcome feelings. Sadness, if not depression, is not despair. The medieval theologian St. Thomas Aquinas distinguishes sorrow from despair; for him, sorrow is one of the prime emotions, based upon a perception of the loss of goods—an obvious aspect of old age. But Aquinas associates the condition of despair with a loss of hope of a specific good, that is, a loss of salvation based upon an unbelief in spiritual goods. In the medieval mind, such despair is often accompanied by acedia, "the monks' disease," which was often seen as overcoming monks in the sixth hour of their day. Acedia (often translated as "sloth) is a condition of deep torpor, an oppressive sorrow leading to the neglect of spiritual goods. Modern psychologists such as Erik Erikson appear to find a secular equivalent to acedia in a despair due to the absence of hope in old age, when one fails to secure an integration sought in this stage of life. In Erikson's account, despair is the feeling that one's life has not been successful but time is short—too short to attempt to start another life to seek alternative roads to integrity. Thus, Erikson's goal of the integrated personality "replaces" the medieval notion of faith in the salvation from God. But neither Erikson's despair nor Aquinas' acedia is the same as sadness due to the losses of old age.

Other conditions, such as desolation, may come with old age, but being desolate is not quite the same as experiencing sorrow; in fact, the word "desolation" connotes a complete emotional collapse—not a healthy, sustained, and permanent old-age sadness. To be sure, "desolation" is also used to describe landscapes which have been destroyed, and one might in some ways regard the "landscapes of old age" as destroyed or barren. Like desolation, the condition of being "forlorn" might also be associated with sadness. When one is forlorn, one is often consigned to loneliness or isolation. There is a loneliness and sense of isolation in old age, but as I shall discuss below, such isolation is simply one of many dimensions of a particular kind of loss in old age.

Thus, sorrow, melancholy, or sadness—not despair, acedia, desolation, or forlornness—is the condition of old age, and, just as the classics help us understand the nature of emotion and distinguish various emotions, they help us better understand this old-age sadness.

Anger, Fear and Alienation

Fear, anger, and alienation are often felt and expressed in old age-anger towards those deemed responsible for the losses, fear that the losses may deepen and multiply and a sense of isolation when seeking to cope with these losses. Aristotle's description of elderly men found them cowardly, always anticipating danger, with sudden fits of anger and shameless, feeling contempt for what people may think of them

Each of these emotions has been defined and redefined through the history of the classics. Thus, the Roman Stoic Seneca offers an extensive treatment of anger in his *De Ira*. Lucretius devotes his entire *De Rerum Natura* to soothing the fears of the aged and others. Alienation is first described by the monks of the Middle Ages who claimed to experience what they called "the noonday demon". Hegel, Marx and Durkheim captured the notions of meaninglessness, normlessness, powerlessness and self isolation. More recently, Simone de Beauvoir offers descriptions of the alienation of the elderly in her *Coming of Age.*

The Different Perspectives of Old-Age Melancholy

Portraits of sadness or melancholy as well as regret and nostalgia may be found in many of the classics, each of which has its own unique perspective on these old age emotions. As we have seen above, in Roy Shafer's discussion of regret, these moods may be given very different meanings through the different perspectives by which they are approached. To illustrate, since I regard sadness as the most pervasive and fundamental of old age moods, I shall identify four very different perspectives of sadness. The first perspective is the deeply *personal perspective* found in much literature, such as the novels of Dickens and Balzac, but also the essays of Montaigne. The second perspective is *a disciplinary perspective* in which sadness is viewed through the perspective of some academic discipline. The classics illustrating this perspective are the theological/philosophical work of Aquinas, and the psychological work of Freud, and James. A third approach is that which seeks an *objective perspective* of sadness as illustrated by Burton's classic work on melancholy. The fourth perspective is a *revelatory perspective* in which the classic views emotion through the perspective of revelation. Miguel Unamuno offers such a revelatory perspective. The following is a quick review of these approaches which lays the groundwork for concluding that one may take different approaches to understanding sadness and hence responding to it in different ways.

1. Personal Perspectives

One of the most moving personal accounts of sadness is found in Montaigne's *Essays.* Montaigne, when mourning the death of his dear friend Etienne de La Boetie, tells the reader of their deep friendship. The ostensible purpose of one essay is to describe friendship in general, a category that includes "lower" relationships between men and women,

ancient Greek homosexual relationships, and other friendships of
convenience and mutual advantage. However, in the most moving
part of the essay, Montaigne recounts the meeting of his friend, their
mutual interests, and the love they had for each other. After four years
of friendship, La Boetie died, and, in Montaigne's words,

> Since the day I lost him . . . I only drag on a weary
> life. The very pleasures which come my way, instead
> of consoling me, redouble my grief for his loss. We
> went halves in everything, it seems to me that I am
> robbing him of his share. . . I was already so formed
> and accustomed to being a second self everywhere that
> only half of me seems alive now. . ..There is no action
> or thought in which I do not miss him, as indeed he
> would have missed me.

Montaigne's sadness at the loss of his friend was not the sadness of
old age, although he claimed that the sadness of his loss in early life
permeated his entire life, including his old age.

A more specific example of old-age sadness, discussed above, can be
found in Rousseau's late-age mournful diary *The Reveries of a Solitary
Walker*, which he viewed as a continuation of his *Confessions*. As we
saw in the epigraph to this chapter, Rousseau writes that his condition
is one in which "a tepid languor enervates all [his] faculties. The spirit
of life is gradually dying out in [him]." Rousseau describes his solitude
and isolation as, in part, voluntarily sought, and in part imposed upon
him by his "enemies" and accepted by him. In old age, Rousseau viewed
himself as having lost many things, but most important, he lost his
reputation and the truth about who he was, what he did and stood
for. He believed he had lost the respect of the public, his capacity to
associate with former friends, and, at the very end, his physical and
mental health. His fundamental loss was the loss of a "justified past"
in which his past deeds and accomplishments were called into question
by his "enemies," thus attacking his entire identity.

Of course, this identity was in part composed of a series of great works, including his *Discourse on the Arts and Sciences*, *Discourse on the Origin and Basis of Inequality Among Men*, *The Social Contract*, and *Emile*, all of which were restored as classics in the public's mind only after his death and which then continued to influence modern thought. These works, however, were part of a life which Rousseau sought to live. Consequently, in the *Reveries*, for the most part, Rousseau does not seek to justify his life by appealing to his past works (which he sought to do in previous publications such as the *Dialogues*). Instead, Rousseau writes an old-age work in which he "moves on" from his previous work and deeds to describe the last two years of his life. Despite sporadic protestations regarding his happiness (for the most part found in the reminisced-about happiness of the past) and "contentment," the following excerpt from the Second Walk captures a different mood.

> ...I gradually turned away from these minute observations so as to give myself up to the no less charming, but more moving, impression which the whole scene made on me. A few days before, the grape gathering had been completed; strollers from the city has already withdrawn, even the peasants were leaving the fields until the toils of winter. The countryside, still green and cheerful, but partly defoliate and already almost desolate, presented everywhere an image of solitude and of winter's approach. Its appearance gave rise to a mixed impression, sweet and sad, too analogous to my age and loss for me not to make the connection. I saw myself at the decline of an innocent and unfortunate life, my soul still full of vivacious feeling and my mind still bedecked with a few flowers—but flowers already wilted by sadness and dried up by worries. Alone and forsaken, I felt the coming cold of the first frosts, and my flagging imagination no longer filled my solitude with beings formed according to my heart. Sighing I

said to myself: "What have I done here-below? I was made to live and I am dying without having lived….

To be sure, Rousseau's sorrows were in part uniquely wrapped up in his own regrets about his individual misdeeds, such as having placed his children in a foundling home, and his old-age sadness seems dominated more by his anger at his rejection by the public at the end of his life rather than by the old-age losses which I have identified above. Perhaps the regret and anger which Rousseau feels is an example of the eclipse of the past in old age, which I have identified above and will discuss in more detail below. Nevertheless, his sentimental nature and his desire to express his feelings in the *Reveries* give us a firsthand description of the sadness of this philosopher in old age.

2. A Disciplinary Perspective

One of the most analytic treatments of sorrow is found in Aquinas's *Summa Theologica*, which views sorrow through the discipline of theology; in fact, Aquinas views all the emotions in the context of this complex discipline. Theology as set forth in the *Summa* focuses upon how God enables man to seek natural and divine happiness through both faith and reason. Humans have the intellectual powers of reason and will to pursue happiness, but he encounters emotions, that is, "passions" which "affect" both himself and other animals, and which influence his subsequent actions. The four dominant passions are joy, sadness, hope, and fear. Due to his belief in its importance, Aquinas discusses sadness or sorrow extensively. He views sorrow as one of the passions which is "concupiscent," or growing out of desire, and, as stated above, he carefully distinguishes it from despair and sloth, which deal with spiritual matters. For Aquinas, sorrow is the interior pain resulting from the loss of goods desired in the present or past. When a loss is in the past, as is frequently the case in old age, such sorrow is experienced "in repose." The source of such sorrow is frustration of the desire for the acquisition of some good in unity with the self. As the contrary of joy, sorrow represents a withdrawal or shunning of such a loss since, although the good is or has been the object of desire, its very loss constitutes the presence of evil. (Aquinas defines evil as simply the privation of good.) Applying this concept to the losses of old age, Aquinas would find its sorrow to be the painful result of the overwhelming power of biological aging resulting in the loss of goods possessed in past life. This loss is experienced in repose, but stimulates a reaction of withdrawal.

For Aquinas, passions, including sorrow, are neither good nor evil in themselves, but are good only insofar as they conform to reason; correspondingly they are evil if they conflict with reason. Reason finds expression in the acts of the will, and hence passions, to be good, must be in accord with the will. Thus, for Aquinas, our old-age sorrow is a passion subject to being directed by the natural power of the will. In turn, that natural power of the will may be directed by faith. Presumably, for Aquinas, sorrow would be good to the extent that it is based upon or conforms with our reason, which recognizes the inevitable biological losses from aging; such a reason informs our faith and actions in accordance with that faith.

More recent psychologists and psychoanalysts continue to adopt a disciplinary approach to the study of the emotion but their discipline differs from Aquinas. It is William James, pragmatic philosopher and psychologist at the end of the nineteenth century, who, in his *Principles of Psychology* (1895), followed in the footsteps of Burton. James views psychology as a science in which the psychologist sought his reality through a study of the thought (including the thought's object and the psychologist's reality), through introspection, to be tested and corrected through experimental work, and/or by a comparative method. James regards emotions as outgrowths of instincts, ones which "mingled with instincts." Although James does not address sadness, he supplies an extensive physiological description of grief, and proposes his now well-known theory of the source of emotions as "following upon bodily expression." He documents the bodily expressions of grief and the other emotions, suggesting that such bodily expressions are the immediate result of perceptions; these bodily expressions then give rise to the emotions. For James, such a theory of emotion explains the vagueness of its boundaries and definition: "If we fancy some strong emotion, and then try to abstract from our consciousness of it all the feelings of its bodily symptoms, we find we have nothing left behind." In James's physiological account of the feelings of grief, the sadness of old age would be the emotional reaction to physical weariness, heaviness, innervation, and contraction of blood vessels. Removal of such sadness would require physiological changes, perhaps, as with Burton, through diet, exercise, or medicines.

It was only two decades after the publication of the *Principles of Psychology* that Sigmund Freud wrote his own account of sadness in his monograph *Mourning and Melancholia* and his essay "Transience." In the first, Freud points out that mourning comes with loss, and he expands the notion of loss to embrace not only the grief at the death of a loved one, but also "the loss of some abstraction, such as one's country, liberty, an ideal and so on." This expansion of the range of losses which may provoke sadness is important since, as I have suggested in the chapter on losses, old age is a source of many losses and hence old-age sadness may be the cumulative effect of many losses. By recognizing the variety of losses in old age, one may be better able to detach oneself from the losses which are important in one's own life.

In *Mourning and Melancholia*, Freud distinguishes between "normal mourning" and clinical depression; the former is less intense and temporary than the latter. Normal mourning appears not to require treatment, while clinical depression does require psychoanalysis. If old-age sadness, at least in many cases, is normal, what is its source? Freud supplies the answer in his beautiful little essay entitled "Transience," written (as was *Mourning and Melancholia*) during the First World War, (discussed above). In the essay, Freud speculates upon the destruction of the war and the losses it created. Talking to a poet friend, Freud argues that the transience of objects we value does not remove their value—indeed, the very temporariness of the objects enhances their value, as "transience value is scarcity value in time." Freud seems to reject arguments that "somehow, this loveliness must be able to persist and escape all the values of destruction," but he suggests that "all this beauty and perfection is determined only by its significance for our own emotional lives." Freud's arguments to his friend are unsuccessful, he believes, because the friend was "mourning." In Freud's explanation,

> We possess, it seems, a certain amount of capacity for love—which we call libido—which in the earliest stages of development is directed towards our own ego. Later, though still at a very early time, this libido is diverted from the ego onto its objects which are thus in a sense taken into our ego. If the objects are destroyed or lost to us, our capacity for love is once more liberated; and it can then either take other objects instead or can temporarily return to the ego. Why it is that this detachment of the libido from its objects should be such a painful process is a mystery to us.

Freud finds it not surprising that in such losses, we then cling to what is left with greater intensity: "When it has renounced everything that has been lost, then it has consumed itself, and our libido is once more free (*in so far as we are still young and active*) to replace the lost objects by fresh ones equally or still more precious" (emphasis mine). Thus, though Freud views with optimism the normal mourning process, he exempts the old and inactive from such optimism!

3. Objective Perspectives

If, for Aquinas, James and Freud, sorrow must be understood by means of a discipline, whether theology or psychology, Robert Burton's study of melancholy avoids relying upon any one discipline and simply seeks to study melancholy objectively. Robert Burton, was a English country clergyman of the seventeenth century, who sought to construct an objective and comprehensive account of melancholy which embraces all manner of sadness. Writing during the transition from the Middle Ages of Aquinas to the cusp of the Enlightenment in the 1600s, Burton, who himself suffered from melancholy, committed his life to its study, reporting his results in a three-volume work, *The Anatomy of Melancholy*.

And what a work it is! The first volume dissects melancholy, its nature, symptoms, and causes; the second volume suggests a myriad of remedies; and the third devotes itself to the melancholy of love and religion (the latter, perhaps, because Burton was a parson by occupation). Burton defines melancholy as a dotage (feebleness of mind), accompanied by fear and sorrow, and categorizes it as either a disposition or habit of the head, or the body overall, or parts of the body. Perhaps influenced by the ancient Greek atomist Democritus, or the ancient physician Galen (whom he frequently cites), and with a nod to his contemporary physicians, Burton offers a complex anatomical account of melancholy which envisages interactions between the mind and body; he finds the sources of melancholy in a wide variety of physical "inward" and "outward" causes, ranging from a blow on the head to an innate humor or a "hot brain." In this sense, Burton is remarkably "modern" in his materialistic explanations, if not in his precise diagnoses.

Burton finds old age to be one of the causes of melancholy, since, according to him, both age and melancholy are "cold and dry." Other causes of melancholy, which often accompany old age, are solitariness, poverty, and a variety of other losses, especially the losses of friends and loved ones. To arrest the operation of these causes and mitigate melancholy, Burton recommends a wide variety of remedies, among which are diet, exercise, and drugs. Although Burton offers an account analogous to the modern medical account of the symptoms, causes, and remedies of melancholy, he comes too early in Western intellectual history to carefully benefit from the more modern disciplinary medical experimentation which distinguishes among the variety of proper remedies for depression. Moreover, Burton approaches his topic with a sturdy Englishman's common sense. Thus, while suggesting religious remedies for religious despair, he also suggests at the end of his magnum opus a remedy for sorrow: "Be not solitary, be not idle."

3. Revelatory Perspective

When discussing sadness, the authors above focus upon the losses and emotions of this world. Miguel de Unamuno's approach is different.

In his *The Tragic Sense of Life*, this modern Spanish philosopher gives sorrow a very different and more central role in the religious life of all humanity, not just the elderly. Unamuno finds human tragedy to begin in the ineradicable desire of flesh-and-blood human beings for some form of immortal life. However, for Unamuno, this desire for immortal life, an expression of life itself, conflicts with the reality of human mortality. Hence, such a desire for immortal life is an impossible desire, and hence, such an unrealizable desire engenders sadness. Unamuno finds the human efforts to secure immortality through exercises of reason (such as the creation of philosophic systems) or science or medicine to be futile. In Unamuno's view, those who rely upon reason to secure immortality will discover that old age is simply a time when we become aware of the incompatibility of the forces of life. These forces are our desire for immortality and our realization that human reason is unable to satisfy this desire.

Regret and Nostalgia

Like sadness, regret and nostalgia are frequent companions to old age sadness. It is the emotion which accompanies the retrospective awareness of mistakes we have made or possibilities we have failed to take advantage of. The spirit of regret is captured in these verses from T. S. Eliot's "Burnt Norton," from the *Four Quartets*:

> Footfalls echo in the memory
> Down the passage which we did not take
> Towards the door we never opened
> Into the rose-garden. My words echo
> Thus, in your mind.
>   But to what purpose
> Disturbing the dust on a bowl of rose-leaves
> I do not know.

Regret may accompany each of the losses of old age. With decline, one may regret the failure to care for one's body. With retirement, one may regret the failure to work harder or pursue other ventures. With the eclipse of the past, one may regret the forgetting of one's triumphs or the remembrance of one's failures. With the foreshortening of the future, one may regret not using one's past time well. With the advent of dependency, one may regret one's past failures to help the vulnerable or one's inability to learn how to give and receive love. With the abandonment of commitment to individual or community progress, one may regret not having been more committed at an earlier stage of life when it might have made a difference. When facing death, one may regret the way in which one led one's life.

A contemporary psychoanalyst, Roy Schafer, has suggested that the classics describe different attitudes toward regret. The romantic attitude, as set forth in Dickens's *Great Expectations*, regards past failings, although regretted, as simply part of a heroic quest in which one has struggled and conquered adversity. The comic view, as illustrated by Henry James's *The Ambassadors*, views the past objects of regret as simply uncontrollable absurdities, often rectified by circumstances, leading to a happy resolution. The tragic view, illustrated by Shakespeare's *King Lear*, finds regret in internal failures and unconquerable external circumstances, leading to catastrophe. The ironic view, as set forth in Virginia Woolf's *Mrs. Dalloway*, recognizes the regret of misdeeds and missed opportunities, but regards these in a detached manner, which comes from reflecting upon both the benefits and burdens of these past events.

This analysis suggests the conclusion that emotions do not have univocal meanings and that one may, at least to some extent (depending upon the degree of flexibility in old-age character and the press of external circumstances), experience or adopt one or another perspective in facing the regrets of one's old age. Such an analysis may apply to sadness as well as regret, suggesting that we may recognize old age against one of these background perspectives. Seen in a comic perspective, sadness may be the prelude to happy outcomes. Seen in a romantic perspective, old-age sadness is simply part of some heroic quest in life. (But happy or romantic outcomes in old age are difficult to imagine, if only because this stage of life ends in death!). It might be argued that old-age sadness should be seen as tragic; after all, such losses may lead to the loss of self and ultimately death. Yet, tragedy involves unique, intensely calamitous events, either created by the person suffering the events or happening outside the control of the person. At least in some versions of tragedy, such events inspire pity and fear in their beholder. Ordinary old-age sadness does not rise to the level of such tragedy, perhaps because it is not unique or because it is part of the normal arc of life. Perhaps old-age losses and the sadness they inspire are more appropriately regarded in an ironic mode, best viewed in a detached manner, with the recognition of their mixed consequences. Perhaps Arnold's poem on old age was itself an ironic expression of a not-yet-old man, perhaps making fun of Browning's enthusiastic celebration of old age!

A third emotion accompanying old age loss is nostalgia which is often expressed in elegy. Thus, there is a touch of yearning for the loss of the past in Gray's *Elegy in a Country Churchyard*. Often nostalgia is identified as a feeling of melancholy at the loss of a home and the longing to return to that home. Perhaps old age nostalgia can be viewed as in the Eugene Field poem, *Over the Hills and Far Away* - a sad poem in which the narrator remembers of the lost home of youth and its goods. Not only poetry but public memorials of all kind recapture in present nostalgia the events otherwise eclipsed by the past. Unlike sadness and regret, nostalgia often joins both the pleasure of remembering and the pain of awareness of loss.

Nostalgia may be restorative or reflective. As restorative, it seeks to restore or return to the past in some way, although "restoration" may involve the creation of the past by present "memory". Or nostalgia may simply be reflective, in which one ponders the loss of the past in recognition of the permanency of that loss. In Chapter 16 "Eclipse of the Past", I shall review in more detail the ways in which the classics can assist the efforts to simply reflect upon the past or restore it. Nostalgia is a theme running through the classics from Odysseus' nostalgic remembrance of his compatriots at the battle of Troy to Proust' s delicate remembrance of the Madeline cookie! Nostalgia is captured by Dickens' account of aged reminiscence in his description of Mr. Lorry in *The Tale of Two Cities*, but it takes a very different as "antiquarian history" rejected by Nietzsche in his *The Uses of the Past;* he prefers a history that grasps the present and future forces of life - a history of youth and not old age.

Anger and Alienation

Two other emotions are frequently found in the accounts of old age: anger and alienation. Aristotle described anger in his *Rhetoric* as "a desire, commingled with pain, to see someone punished and which is provoked by an apparent slight to the angered person or to something or someone that belongs to him, when that slight is not justified." Portraits of old age anger can be found in ancient, early modern, and more recent literature. Aristophanes' *Wasps* offers the view of an angry old man, jailed in his own house by his family, since they believed he was obsessively committed to joining the Athenian jurors (the wasps") who were always bent on punishing someone. Shakespeare's *King Lear* opens with the wrath at his youngest daughter, who refused to vow complete love to her father, thus foiling his plans to neatly dispose of his kingdom into three parts to his three daughters. And Dylan Thomas, in his well known poem "Do Not Go Gentle into that Good Night" urges the dying to "rage, rage against the dying of the light". Kubler-Ross, in her *On Death and Dying* finds anger to be the second stage in the dying process.

Another emotion frequently allied to old age sadness or contained in descriptions of old age suicide, is alienation. (I shall discuss this emotion in more detail in my discussion of retirement). Alienation is described as having a sense of purposelessness, powerlessness, without guiding norms, estrangement and lack of involvement with others. The work of

Jean Amery in *On Aging* and *On Suicide* captures vividly the subjective alienation of the old; Simone de Beauvoir, in her *Coming of Age* describes it objectively and many painters of the elderly have captured their sense of alienation.

Conclusion

We learn from the classics that old age sadness, regret, nostalgia, anger, and alienation may be understood in different ways. As a consequence, many different responses to these emotions, our assessment of them, and their role in our path of life, are available to us as we consider our emotional responses to loss. The most radical approach to extirpating such sadness may be to remove its' cause, whether through suicide, as Jean Amery proposes or reducing or postponing the losses giving rise to the emotions through such measures, for example, as avoidance of retirement or extreme health inducing measures to extend health and life in old age.

At the other extreme, one might accept the losses and embrace the emotions. Just as the devotees of Dionysus welcomed the passions of Eros in celebratory rituals, and Nietzsche welcomed the emotions of tragedy in Wagner's music, we, as old age romantics, might welcome the emotions of old age, including sadness, regret, nostalgia, anger and alienation. Of course, a welcome of such emotions might be part of a therapy, if, as Freud urges, the sadness is too deep and unwavering, requiring psychiatric treatment of some sort. If Burton and James are correct and sadness is physiologically generated, their nostrums which include hot baths (endorsed by Aquinas as well!) and exercise might be undertaken. Such remedies aim at the more physiological causes of melancholy or offer simple distractions of their effects.

Perhaps one of the most interesting treatment is suggested by Aristotle's view of the emotions which, as outgrowths of instinct and desire, are shaped by habit and reason, the latter helping to define the ends of life and select the proper means though deliberation in specific situations. Seneca makes similar recommendation in outlining the proper response to anger. For these philosophers, "control" of our emotions, whether in old age or otherwise, is the result of an educated character which is formed to cope with loss over the time of our lives.

However, I suggest another route for coping with the losses and their consequent emotions – detachment from the losses and emotions and seeking consolation for the losses through deliberation about the "avenues of solace". The next two chapters deal with detachment and consolation.

CHAPTER III

Detachment: The Power of Distance

A free man chooses flight by the same strength and presence of mind as that by which he chooses battle

—Spinoza

The harder his position became and the more terrible the future, the more independent of that position in which he found himself were the joyful and comforting thoughts, memories and imaginings that came to him.

—Tolstoy

Detachment marks key moments in my life. I would curl up in a library chair and detach myself from my everyday life—into the world of Oz, the American westerns of Zane Grey, or the innumerable celebratory World War II stories. In my first year of college, I detached myself from the Catholic community and its faith, when, upon reading about ancient Greek religions, I found the very rudiments of my Catholic faith in the rites of primitive rural Greek rituals. I renounced my inherited faith, proudly announced my apostasy to my parents, and, since then, have held onto a detached view of religion. My study of philosophy at university reinforced this detachment. At the University of Chicago, we studied each system of western philosophy without any commitment to one system of thought, reinforcing a belief in philosophical pluralism – the conviction that all philosophical systems harbored some significant truth. (In my old age, upon reading Walter Watson's The Architectonics of Meaning, I more fully understood and embraced such a detached pluralism).

After college, a certain attitude of detachment continued. During my work life as an attorney, I both participated in and remained partially detached from the reforms that I and others were promoting, able to critique each reform in turn: the urban renewal effort, the anti-poverty program, new town development, and the environmental movement. I found myself reading and writing about the nature of the city, the conditions of poverty, community theory, and the emerging science of ecology. This reading and writing helped me to detach myself from any full involvement in these reform efforts. ! Even my desire to retire was a conscious decision to seek detachment from the work world. Now, old age is the almost-final destination of my detachment. I have socially withdrawn from most of my colleagues and most civic activity, remain in the solitude of my home library and read and write about the history and thoughts of others who have pursued a solitary life. Through a reflective meditation on the classics, I approach old age with intellectual detachment. .

Introduction

I urge detachment from the losses of old age and the sadness they bring. I consult the classics, since the beginnings of such detachment is found in the classic poetry and prose of elegy. Peter Sacks, in his study, *The English Elegy*, demonstrates that writing the elegiac poem itself is the poet's method for achieving detachment from the death and sadness of his or her loved one. For example, consider one of my favorite Yeats's poem "Those Dancing Days are Gone." The last stanza reads,

> I thought it out this very day,
> Noon upon the clock,
> A man may put pretence away
> Who leans upon a stick,
> May sing, and sing until he drop,

Whether to maid or hag:
I carry the sun in a golden cup,
The moon in a silver bag.

Yeats's old-age abandonment of pretense and absence of shame at singing (or writing poetry) is based upon his old-age ("a man . . . who leans upon a stick") detachment by singing with a vision of the cosmos ("the sun in a golden cup"; "the moon in a silver bag".) The earlier stanzas of Yeats's elegy recognizes old age loss of a loved one as a time of witnessing the "foul body" wrapped in a rag, and her children interred "under a marble flag," - a time of loss and sadness. The poem embodies a detachment in which the old can sing in a poetry which contemplates death and the workings of the universe. Such an elegy exemplifies my view of old age which I seek a detachment secured through the very writing (and reading) of this book.

Detachment as part of elegy provides, in the felicitous words of Amanda Anderson's *The Powers of Distance,* a "power of distance," which enables us to reach "the house of ideas" – a quiet and comfortable home occupied by the furniture of interconnected ideas; these ideas have a rich and complex architecture and history by which one can both gain understanding and consolation for our old age To undertake an exploration of this architecture and history of ideas of old-age loss and sadness requires detached inquiry separating oneself socially, imaginatively, and intellectually drawing upon the intellectual resources of the classical tradition. These classics, as texts and works of art, are themselves expressions of authorial detachment which require, in turn, our old age activity of reading books and appreciating works of art. Thus, the classics are tools for a detached understanding of old age. As we shall see in the next chapter, this detachment leads to different kinds of consolation.

To be sure, detachment is not all good. Denial of old age loss through escape and permanent residence in the "house of ideas" may become a denial of reality. Such escape must be temporary and one must return to reality from the comfort of such ideas. There is also, as I describe in Chapters 5-8, a false form of detachment. In these chapters, I will set forth mistaken efforts to deny old age—efforts to scientifically extend life, create an afterlife in religious faith, focus upon the hedonic delights of old age, or launch into unthinking and meaningless activity in old age. All of these false forms of detachment do not accept old age and its losses; they are the result of what I believe to be mistaken efforts at detachment.

Not only are there fundamentally mistaken denials of old age *but the classical tradition contains a variety of literary devices or "genres" which approach old age with detachment, but only to deny its losses and consequent sadness.* These overlapping genres include irony, satire, parody, and comedy. Beyond surface meanings, irony leaves unsaid whatever truths contrary to the superficial meaning of the words. When, in Plato's *Republic,* self-satisfied old Cephalus abandons the search for the meaning of justice and leaves the scene of the Socratic to make sacrifices to the gods, Plato may have intended that the reader to ironically recognizing that old Cephalus is giving up the search for truth in dialogue for the unthinking pursuit of conventional religious beliefs. A more obvious example of irony is Socrates' famous speech in the *Apology,* where he asks the jury to reward rather than punish him. However, such Socratic irony is insufficiently explicit to assess whatever truth is hidden.

Whether offered by the ancient Greek dramatist, Aristophanes, the Roman poet, Juvenal, or later renaissance and enlightenment figures, Erasmus, Voltaire, and Swift, satire employs descriptive portrayals, sometimes exaggerated, to criticize the subjects of the poem, story or essay. Thus, Voltaire, in his *Candide,* uses the story of the hapless Candide, beset by all kinds of disasters, to satirize Leibniz's philosophical argument that, despite apparent evil, this world is the best of all possible worlds. When Aristophanes, in his play, *The Clouds,* describes the ridiculous "Thinkery", he is making fun of Socrates, through his portrait of the futile efforts of the old man who, seeking to make money, promotes his son's and his own education at the "Thinkery". To grasp the criticism of satire, one must search for unspoken meanings; the satire often does not give directly the reasons for its implicit criticisms. A third genre which seeks detachment from the losses of old age is comedy itself which, as applied to old age, deals with the losses as simply laughable incongruities. Thus, in Aristophanes' *The Wasps*, the playwright draws a portrait of an old man with an uncontrollable desire to participate in Athenian politics. Or, in a comic moment within Shakespeare's tragedy, *Hamlet*, we see the aged foolish Polonius, spouting obvious platitudes with the tacit, but obviously ridiculous claim of old age wisdom. The resulting humor does not offer argumentative content for the criticism.

More important, these genres, unlike elegy, fail to take seriously the loss and sadness of old age. In their humor and reticence to explicitly address the losses of old age, they fail to accept the seriousness of these losses and the emotions which these losses excite. Only elegy and tragedy address these losses and sadness head on. But the losses in tragedy deal with uniquely serious matters, demanding the purgation of the pity and fear they engender. Elegy supplies a more tranquil detachment and consolation for an acceptance of losses which are susceptible to such remedies.

The Nature of Detachment

If satire, comedy, irony and parody are not proper means of detachment from old age, what is the proper means of detachment? As elegy teaches us, genuine detachment in old age is that form of physical, emotional, and intellectual separation resulting in self-reflection on our loss and sadness. Such separation removes us from the intensity of immediate experience of old age loss and bestows "the powers of distance" by means of entertaining a cluster of ideas enabling us to behold that old age experience in universal terms.

Such distance may include a social detachment in old age, an old age solitude in which one withdraws from many of the activities and acquaintances of earlier stages of life. Based upon such social withdrawal, imaginative and intellectual detachment take place. These social, imaginative, and intellectual detachments are interrelated; together they "separate us" from the losses of old age and the sadness and other emotions we experience from these losses. Such detachment may be consoling in itself, but it is also a preface to finding consolation in old age. In the previous chapters, I have discussed the need to assent to old-age losses and understand the sadness they generate, and, in the next chapter, I shall discuss the nature and kinds of consolation available in old age after such detachment is secured . In this chapter, I shall focus upon detachment itself.

1. Social Detachment

A well-known mid-twentieth-century study of aging, *Growing Old*, purports to find a process of "disengagement" of the elderly, in which the elderly withdraw from the social system—not only from work, but also from extensive contacts with family members, friends, and others. The authors of the study suggest that this withdrawal brings in its wake both a qualitative change in those contacts that remain and an altered purpose in whatever social interaction takes place in old age. Since the study supporting these conclusions was published in 1962, there have been a variety of critiques of it; some have suggested that a "new aging" takes place in which the elderly undertake (or should undertake) all kinds of new ventures when freed from their work worlds. Such critiques of withdrawal are answered in the work of Simone de Beauvoir, who, in her classic, *The Coming of Age*, recognized, on the one hand, that the solitude of the poor elderly may be imposed by economic circumstances, but that, on the other, many other elderly, including famous literary and political figures, voluntarily withdrew and embraced solitude in their later life. In my readings, I have found that withdrawal in old age was experienced by Plotinus, Petrarch, Montaigne, Rousseau, Jefferson, Churchill, and Erikson. In the words of Rousseau's, in *The Reveries of a Solitary Walker*,

> The fact is that I am growing old, that my activities
> are diminishing, and that I withdraw a little farther
> from the world every day. Since my bereavement I
> find it hard to be interested in anything but my own

fate . . . the vitality of these friendships dwindles. . . . I soon grow tired; every evening I reach the limits of my powers; I need a great deal of sleep and quietness; my days are short and even spring does not lengthen them. I am obliged to conserve my strength, to draw myself in, and to concentrate upon these two strangely incommunicable worlds that I now bear with me— the immense, deserted world of my past, in which I wander some of the time, and the shrunken limited world of the present, cut to my measurements. . . . I am building myself a little cottage in the roaring   forest of the world."

Although Rousseau's "acceptance" of his social withdrawal is reluctant, there is a western tradition of valuing solitude as a way of life. This tradition began with the Hellenistic philosophers, some of whom followed ways of life which honored solitude. One of the best rationales for social detachment lies in the Stoic recognition of our limited control over our environment—a recognition which is accentuated in old age, a time when we may gradually lose actual control over that environment and, in some cases, our own body. In Epictetus's advice: "It is the part of a wise man to put a high value upon that alone which is placed within his possession; and not to sigh after those things which lie beyond his reach." From this point of view, social detachment in old age is a way of recognizing our limited control over our environment—our limited ability to ensure the perpetuation of our friendships and our relationships with loved ones, increase our wealth, pursue our political and other ambitions, and maintain our vitality. Hence, like the Stoics, we reduce our demands and dependence upon our environment by withdrawing from it. A more modern version of such withdrawal may be found in Voltaire's *Candide*, whose foolish hero, after many disastrous attempts at doing good, retired to cultivate his garden.

The ideal of solitude was articulated in different ways by the Roman statesman and philosopher, Seneca, the Christian saints, the early Renaissance humanists such as Petrarch, the French essayist, Michel de

Montaigne, the American Transcendentalists, Henry Thoreau, modern monks, such as Thomas Merton, and contemporary essayists such as May Sarton and Paul Auster. The objectives of such solitude ranges from facilitating prayer and contemplation, attunement to nature or oneself, supporting reflective and literary meditation and self-healing, undertaking solo adventure, and fostering creativity. Many of these purposes seem uniquely suited to an aged way of life, especially to its activities of imaginative and intellectual detachment.

2. Imaginative Detachment

We all spend a significant portion of our time in life in daydreams. Surveys of the elderly reveal, not surprisingly, that they spend as much as two or more hours a day watching television. Whether in daydreams or television viewing, we are engaging in a form of detachment from our personal situations, leaping, with the help of imagination and modern communications, into a different world. Reading the classics, especially histories, and biographies, introduces us to this different world—one which may be real or imagined, but even when it is real, as in the case of history and biography, it is, at least in part, the product of the author's and reader's imaginations.

Poetry, novels, music, and the other fine arts can have a similar effect. Poems such as "The Cumberland Beggar" and novels such as *Don Quixote*, *The Leopard*, and *Old Goriot* supply us with vivid images of other old-age lives. The French nineteenth-century novelists, such as Hugo and Balzac, seemed particularly interested in describing the lives and characters of the old, and they crafted many remarkable portraits. The biographies of Samuel Johnson or Thomas Jefferson or the autobiography of Henry Adams carry us imaginatively into different worlds at different times and, in so doing, allow us to begin to imagine alternatives to our own lives and our own old age. Pictures and sculptures can have a similar effect.

Ordinarily, philosophers are not viewed as authors of imaginative works, but certainly their works contain imaginative content and suggest remarkably different ways of life than our own. Pierre Hadot, in *Philosophy as a Way of Life*, beautifully describes the way of life pursued by the Hellenistic philosophers. John Cooper in his recent *Pursuits of Wisdom,* expands Hadot's work to present six ways of life of ancient philosophy, (Socratic, Platonic, Aristotelian, Stoic, Epicurean, and Skeptic). Although these philosophic portraits also call upon the intellectual detachment of the mind through argument and ideas, they also ask us to *imagine* specifically different ways of life pursued by philosophers from Socrates to Plotinus.

Imaginative detachment is not limited to the writings of ancient philosophers. Amanda Anderson, in her fine study of Victorian literary figures, documents the ways in which the Victorian imaginative literature and criticism of Bronte, Dickens, Arnold, George Eliot and Oscar Wilde impart lessons and portraits of cultivated detachment, whether expressed as disinterestedness, playful restlessness, objective realism, critique, cosmopolitan distance or ethical stances. To be sure, none of these works are elegiac treatments of old age loss. For elegiac detachment, we must turn to innumerable examples of poetry and prose, in which the actual or implied author achieves detachment in the face of a wide variety of losses. To take but one example, let's look at Hardy's poem, *Going.*

Why did you give no hint that night
That quickly after the morrow's dawn,
And calmly, as if indifferent quite,
You would close your term here, up and be gone.
Where I could not follow
With wing of swallow
To gain one glimpse of your ever anon.

Never to bid good-bye,
Or lip me the softest call,
Or utter a wish for a word, while I
Was morning harden upon the wall
Unmoved, unknowing
That your great going,

Had place that moment, and altered all.

Why do you make me leave the house
And think for a breath it is you I see
At the end of the alley of bending boughs
Where so often at desk you used to be.
　　　　Till in darkening dankness
　　　　The yawning blankness
Of the perspective sickens me.

　　　　You were she who abode
　　　　By those red-veined rocks far West
You were the swan-necked one who rode
Along the Beetling Beeny Crest,
　　　　And, reigning night me,
　　　　Would muse and eye me
While Life unrolled us its very best.

Why, then, latterly did we not speak,
Did we not think of those days long dead,
And ere you vanishing strive to seek,
That time's renewal? We might have said,
　　　　"In this bright spring weather
　　　　We'll visit together
Those places that once we visited."

　　　　Well, well! All's past amend.
　　　　Unchangeable. It must go.
I seem but a dead man held on end
To sink down soon...O you could not know
　　　　That such swift fleeing
　　　　No soul foreseeing-
Not even I - would undo me so!

The loss of his wife, the sadness and regrets he feels and evokes, and the consolation he seeks in his own imminent death are three of the four "standard" central elements of elegy. But the fourth, detachment, is less visible; *it lies in the poem itself.* Hardy gives his sadness, regret, and the consolation he seeks a poetic form – one which carries with it the poet's detached control through formal stanzas, as well as repetitive rhythm and rhyme. In addition, a certain detachment can be found in the poem's musing interrogation of his dead wife about the speed of her death, her failure to say good bye, the yawning blankness left, and their joint failure to "think of those days long dead" before she died. And finally, detachment is found in accepting the unchangeable past making amends impossible. Perhaps the final lines, "O you could not know/ that such swift fleeting/ No soul foreseeing – /Not Even I- should undo me so!" breaks though the detached musing.

By calling such detachment "imaginative," there is a danger of thinking of it as trivial and ineffective. Not so! Montaigne, in his essay "On the Power of Imagination," documents the power of imagination in understanding medical diseases and their cures, the practices of religious beliefs, and even sexual behavior. Such imaginative detachment in old age can have a similar power, helping us to imagine the different ways of life to be pursued in old age, and even if we don't adopt those imagined lives, an imaginative account of them clarifies our own way of life. Thus, as the philosopher, John Kekes has observed, in finding these lives within novels, we are introduced to a romantic, moral, gentlemanly (applicable to both men and women), skeptical, inwardly reflective, political, and/or exuberant and sensual style of life. Each way of life is illustrated by a classic author and his works: Mishima (romantic), Cato (moral), gentlemanly (Trollope), skeptical (Hume), inwardly reflective (Montaigne), political (Cicero), and exuberant (Cellini). These different ways of life view the losses of old age differently. For the romantic Mishima, such losses would be simply passive harms to be overcome by romantic thought and action. For Cato, the losses are minimized through the adoption of strong moral standards. For Trollope, losses are to be borne with gentlemanly integrity (that is, coherence of character, attitude, and actions). For Cicero, these losses are impediments to be overcome by the continued pursuit of gentlemanly farming or continued links to a political life. For Montaigne, the losses are the subject for inward meditations. For Hume, they are the subject for moderate philosophic skepticism regarding their causes. For Cellini, the losses are to be drowned in the exuberance of life.

Of course, our choice among these alternative ways of life in old age is limited by the fact that by reaching old age, we have already acquired a fixed character, less able to choose different ways of life which are inconsistent with that character. Nevertheless, the imaginative re-creation of these ways of life permits us to clarify our own way of life, determine the extent to which it matches or differs from the alternatives we imagined, and perhaps modify our own way of life with such information.

3. Intellectual Detachment

Social and imaginative detachment may include or be accompanied by an intellectual detachment which enables us to understand the essence of the goods we are losing in old age, the nature of the losses which take place, and the quality of the emotions which collect around these losses. Such an intellectual detachment abstracts and reworks the materials of sense, memory and imagination pertaining to old age loss, and enables us to reflect upon such loss in light of clusters of ideas, some of which are organized into complex systems of thought. It is these clusters of ideas which are expressed in the many forms of the classics – poetry, novels, philosophies, literature, histories, science as well as fine art.

The ancient philosophers found such intellectual detachment to be a many-splendored activity. The Hellenistic philosophers labeled it "aposprotheia"—securing a "view from above." For some, such detachment takes the form of "askesis"—a kind of asceticism which constitutes independence from the demands of custom and law. For others, the balanced "ataraxia" of the skeptic is to be achieved by a detachment from the partiality of one's and others' biases and arrival at a balance among conflicting opinions. Another kind of detachment is found in "enkratia"— a sense of autonomy and self-control, in which one is detached from the power and control of others. Detachment, of course, may connote"apatheia"—the freedom from the emotions themselves. Even "phusikai"—a conformity to nature, a kind of "going with the flow" rather than fighting against nature, may suggest a kind of detachment from efforts to control or master nature. Thus, at least for the ancients, a detachment in old age means viewing the world "from above," expressing itself in contempt for social convention, adopting a lofty neutrality among warring people and passions, harboring a sense of autonomy and self-control in face of pressure, and seeking conformity with nature - all to achieve emotional serenity.

How does one achieve such detachment in old age? This is where the classics are so useful since they offer a rich variety of pathways in which detachment may be sought and reached. Reading, appreciating, and meditating on such classics enables one to analyze losses, understand the emotions they generate, enable detachment and self-reflection which lead to consolation. The initial resting place is the arrival at the cluster of ideas pertaining to our own old age: "The House of Ideas".

The House of Ideas

Perhaps the best-known classical description of intellectual detachment from concrete experience is Plato's account of the detachment needed to find love in *The Symposium*. For Plato, love is the desire of goods, particularly beauty, and detachment to find such love is achieved as follows:

> In the first place, indeed, if his conductor guides him aright he must be in love with one particular body, and engender beautiful converse therein; but next he must remark how the beauty attach to this or that body is cognate to that which is attached to any other, and that if he means to ensure beauty in form, it is gross folly not to regard as one and the same the beauty belonging to all; and so, having grasped this truth, he must make

himself a lover of all beautiful bodies and slacken the
stress of is feeling for one by contemning it and counting
it as a trifle. But his next advance will be to set a higher
value on the beauty of souls than on that of the body,
so that however little the grace that may bloom in any
likely soul it shall suffice for him for loving and caring,
and for bring forth and soliciting such converse as will
tend to the betterment of the young; and that finally
he may be constrained to contemplate the beautiful as
appearing in our observances and our laws and beyond
it all bound together in kinship and so estimate the
beauty as a light affair. From observance he should be
led on to the branches of knowledge, that there also he
may behold a province of knowledge, that there also he
may behold a province of beauty, and by looking thus
on beauty in the mass may escape from the mean a,
meticulous slavery of a single instance, where he must
center all his care, like a lackey, upon the beauty of
a particular child or man or single observance; and
turning rather towards the main ocean of the beautiful
may be contemplation of this bring forth in all their
splendor many fair fruits of discourse and meditation in
a plenteous crop of philosophy until with the strength
and increase there acquired, he decries a certain single
knowledge connected with a beauty which has yet to
be told.

Plato's approach is not the only method for finding ideas.
Nevertheless, for the moment, I shall follow the insights of Plato, and
seek detachment from the particular losses in old age, ascending from
the experience of such losses to a cluster of universal ideas, which, in
turn, may yield meaning to those losses. I begin the ascent from old age
losses to the "House of Ideas" by placing them within the framework
of elegy. By choosing the literary genre of elegy as the framework of
detachment, I have assumed that elegy provides an "imitation of old

age"—a mirror to hold up to old age to be viewed as a series of specific elegiac losses and ensuing sadness. Viewing old age through the lens of elegy and its elements – loss, sadness, detachment and consolation- enables me to begin to regard the losses of old age with detachment. *The literary concept of elegy is my mirror for the study of old age, allowing me to step back, pause, and detach myself from our specific experience of the losses of life and its sadness.*

Here is a summary of "the house of ideas" which I shall discuss in more detail in the following chapters. My effort to understand the general notion of loss in the first chapter stimulates awareness of the ideas of *goods, time* and *change.* In Chapter II, the discussion of the emotions consequent to old age loss raises the ideas of *sadness, regret,* and *nostalgia.* This present chapter on detachment explores the notion of *idea* itself, and the following chapter will explore the idea of *consolation.*

To understand my notion of "the House of Ideas", it is necessary to understand the notion of "idea" itself. Philosophers have viewed ideas as objects of thought, (immediate data of sense-experience, memory, imagination, pure concepts of reason, or eternal forms) or as concepts through which some form of reality is apprehended. If objects of thought, such ideas originate from divine illumination, or innate mental endowments, or acquirement though perceptions, intuitions, and reflections, or recollection by the mind upon its own contents, or a reworking of the material of sense and imagination, abstraction from sense data, or the derivation of transcendental ideas through reason.

I adopt the notion of ideas as concepts abstracted from experience *through which* the reality of old age may then be understood. First, I shall turn to specific ideas suggested by the particular losses and emotions of old age. With each of the specific losses reviewed below in Chapters 13- 20, a series of different ideas emerges. For example, when reviewing the loss of biological decline in old age, I explore the notions of *health, equilibrium* and *natural cycling.* Reviewing the loss resulting from retirement leads me to the ideas of *labor* and *leisure.* The notion of old age poverty leads me to ideas of *equality* and *justice.* The old age eclipse of the past leads to ideas of *memory* and *history.* The foreshortening of the future suggests the ideas of *ambition, honor,* and *legacy*. The growth of old age dependency leads me to the ideas of *autonomy, dignity* and *love*. The abandonment of faith in history leads to the ideas of *progress, regress, historical cycles,* and *paideia*. The anticipation of death leads to the ideas of *life* and *non-being*.

All these ideas emerge out of the analysis of old age elegy and the specific losses in old age; ideas are amplified in the classics whose plots and arguments express or address the ideas in question. Seeing these ideas in the context of the classics reveals their own complex architecture. Take, for example, the classic treatment of retirement in the works of Emile Durkheim, Adam Smith and Karl Marx. In their discussion of retirement, the concept of *work* carries the subsidiary notions of *labor* and *effort, production, occupation, job, position* and *trade*, compared with concepts such as *rest, inertia, unproductive activity, leisure, alienation* and *unemployment*. These subsidiary ideas are arranged to establish the architecture of the major ideas of work and leisure. Viewed historically, the internal architecture of ideas changes over time their meanings. When viewed against a history of ideas, such ideas are seen to be ambiguous, although they share some limited common meaning over time. This common meaning of each idea provides the threads which bind the tradition of classics and permits one to talk about ideas in the abstract. In Wittgenstein's famous phrase, there is a "family resemblance" of ideas from one classic work to another.

Here is an example of some of the historical changes in the meaning of the idea of death- one of the losses encountered in old age. Viewed through the lens of Stoic detachment, death is simply part of the impermanence of all life. Viewed through Plato's eyes in the *Phaedo*, "death" is simply part of a radical discontinuous sequence of eternal universals of death and life. From Aristotle's ethical perspective, death is the end of a biography—the end of the narrative of the way in which one's life has sought happiness for oneself and others. For one of Tolstoy's novellas, death is the opportunity for subjective understanding of the acceptance of love. From the perspective of the psychologist William James, death is simply the cessation of consciousness. For Heidegger, death is simply "being-toward-death." Identifying these general ideas of death sets the stage for a more detailed examination of each meaning of death and its different losses: the ebbing of life, the extinction of consciousness, the end of a biography, a movement toward love, transition from the universals of life to death, and the presence of the prospect of non-being. All of these ideas and the classics in which they are found help us to understand the multifaceted idea of death.

The cluster of ideas surrounding each of the losses of old age occupies the House of Ideas. Or, put another way, as we reflect upon these ideas which are relevant to our old age losses, we have intellectually detached ourselves from the losses and entered the quiet and peaceful House of Ideas. But we cannot stay.

Conclusion: Leaving the House of Ideas

In Plato's *Republic,* after his best people receive an extensive education to prepare them as guardians, and after they have beheld the idea of the Good, Socrates requires that the guardians must return to "the cave" of everyday life to guide those left behind in the cave. In other dialogues, Plato requires his protagonists to test the truth of their ideas either in dialogue or the creation of a community which tests the truth of the ideas in question. While not adopting the grand vision of the *Republic,* I do believe that, in old age, one must leave the "house of ideas" and return to reflectively meditate about one's own losses with the help of those ideas and the classics in which they are found. In Chapter 12 below, I shall outline the steps of such a meditation.

In the brief remainder of this chapter, I wish to emphasize the different way in which ideas are understood when one leaves the detachment achieved in the house of ideas. The notion of the "house of ideas" peopled by ideas treated as *objects of thought* is not a sufficient response to old age and its losses. Whatever understanding is obtained about such ideas does not yield an understanding of one's own or the readers' *particular losses* In the house of ideas, we are simply left with a detached knowledge of a series of interesting universals. We do not understand how these ideas apply to us, nor, do these ideas, in the abstract, give consolation. As W. H. Auden wrote about ideas in the late 1930s, when England faced the imminent prospect of the war with Germany:

> Goodbye now, Plato and Hegel
> The shop is closing down.
> They don't want any philosopher kings in England
> There ain't no universals in this man's town.

Now Auden is not quite correct. There are indeed universal ideas, (which may or may not "exist" independent of the human mind), and, as philosophers through the ages, such as Plato, Schopenhauer, Whitehead and Russell have recognized, we cannot function without such universal ideas. However, the real problem with simple detachment into a house of ideas is that such detachment treats ideas as if they were only *objects* of knowledge, rather than ideas *through which we know reality*. As Aquinas has stated: "a concept is not what is actually understood, but that *by which* the intellect understands." According to this approach, we learn about the realities of old age loss *though the ideas*. If, for example, we find alienation to be an aspect of old age retirement, we might study the idea of alienation in the history of thought, but we still must look to the actual experience of old age in light of this idea to determine whether that idea is "true" to our experience of old age retirement. *The source of that truth lies in reflection upon our own personal experience, accounts of old age experiences found within the classics, and empirical studies of aging and retirement.* Once these sources are consulted, the truth about old age alienation is determined by whether the elements of old age alienation can be clearly and distinctly identified, whether these ideas fit within the more general experience of retirement, whether they originate from sources related to retirement, and whether the realities of such alienation correspond to the idea itself. This search for the truth of ideas arising out of old age loss will be further explored in the Chapter IV on consolation, Chapter XIII on reflective meditation and in the Conclusion of this book.

CHAPTER IV

Avenues of Solace: The Consolation of the Classics

…many philosophers…. conclude that the whole …is… ordered with perfect benevolence… [and] every physical ill… makes and essential part of this benevolent system…. You would surely more irritate than appease a man lying under the racking pains of gout by preaching up to him the rectitude of these general laws…These enlarged views may please…the speculative man, who is placed in ease and security….

David Hume

This book has been the result of my search for consolation in old age. I have come to deeply value old age as a time of leisure in which I can seek understanding of my life and its losses, with the help of the classics and the ideas they supply. Reading these classics fosters detachment and consolation, both parts of "the elegy of old age". The classics help to bandage up the wounds of physical decline, (including gout!) help me to recover or recreate my forgotten past- a kind of reaffirmation of the self. Reading and writing about these classics supplies material for creating my own "legacy" by means of my admittedly temporary participation in their permanent ideas. These classics and their ideas have helped me to give up my personal ambitions, hopes for historical progress of my country and my own future personal improvement. I found within some of these works the guidance for compassion for my aging wife before her death and self-consolation for myself. I anticipate death to be near - setting the necessary limit of the arc of my life, the end of my consciousness, and the reality of my non-being. Through these works, I am now content simply to witness and quietly accept of the cycles of nature, history, and thought. I'm hoping my loved ones, friends and other readers can find comparable consolations.

Introduction

In previous chapters I have suggested that the elegiac story of old age is the story of loss, sadness, detachment and consolation. The losses are serious and the sadness real. Total removal of these losses and erasure of their emotional consequences are impossible; these losses must be acknowledged and accepted. But I have found that some intellectual and emotional detachment from them, although difficult, is possible. Such detachment is some consolation, but, in addition to detachment from these losses, other forms of consolation are possible. In this chapter, I suggest that not only do the classics supply a measure of detachment from the many goods we lose as we grow old, (as described in the previous chapter), but also, these works supply their own unique forms of consolation. And hence, it is important to better understand the nature of consolation within the traditions of classics before turning to the specific avenues of solace which such works provide.

The Tradition of Consolation

The classics supply several special traditions of works of consolation including poetic elegies, and consolations taken from scientific, philosophic and works of fine arts. To console himself in prison before his death at the hands of the Nazis, Bonhoeffer read and wrote about a range of classic works and clung on to Plutarch's *Lives* to the very end. Words of consolation, beginning with the ancients, both secular and religious, are found with the works of the Hellenic and Hellenistic philosophers, the Bible and medieval Christian thinkers and attain full expression with the humanism of Petrarch and other Renaissance thinkers. Modern philosophy continues the consolatory tradition in such works as Spinoza's *Ethics;* some contemporary philosophers such as Pierre Hadot in *What is Ancient Philosophy?* have sought to recover the ancient consolatory tradition. Modern consolations have also taken new forms, including the psychotherapy of Freud and his followers and the popular essays of William James, Ralph Waldo Emerson and Henry Thoreau. These works are supplemented by modern novels, poetic elegies, and writings by those in prison or facing imminent disease and death. These works set forth many different "avenues of solace", both intellectual and emotional, among which we may select for our own old age.

The question remains: how do such works offer solace? How do works of philosophy, rhetoric, scientific discussion, novels and poetry, music and other fine arts provide consolation? For whom? As one author asked: how do just words have the power to offer consolation? Let me anticipate the following prosaic answers which will be further spelled out below. These works offer four principal means by which consolation may take place: (1) the offering and receipt of love; (2) the reaffirmation of the self and its' virtues; (3) the bandaging of the wounds of loss through the rearrangement of the environment; (4) the transformation of the self through therapy, reflective meditation, philosophy and religious faith. In this chapter, I shall discuss consolation in general. In subsequent chapters, I shall discuss consolations for each specific loss in old age.

First, the works of consolation may express a faith-informed or a natural love. Emotions may be stimulated from reading, listening or appreciating classic works. Although consolation is most often animated by love of family, friends and colleagues, (although it may be extended beyond those close to us), certain classic works may enable three kinds of love: sympathy or compassion for oneself or another, empathy or identification with another's losses, or union with another in a loving relationship. Each of these kinds of love have their own traditions of thought which delineate their power in the work of consolation.

Second, the classic works of consolation often urge the reaffirmation of the self and its virtues in time of loss. The notion is that old age is not a totally separate stage of life, but a stage within a continuous life which, to a greater or lesser degree, has equipped the old person with a range of virtues by which to cope with old age losses. Cicero and others have identified these virtues, defined their nature, and the applied them to different losses.

Third, consolation, although animated by love, and met with strength of character, may simply provide bandages for irremediable wounds in old age. On a prosaic level, consolation may simply provide help by giving the sufferer access to external circumstances needed for comfort and solace. Such circumstances may range from simply being present to the one needing consolation to a variety of actions which facilitate ease and comfort. Such actions may also include the mitigation of a person's condition, (palliative care extended to all old age loss), diversion of the sufferer's attention by means of the humanities, art or music, as well as a variety of rhetorical techniques. Such works offer bandages for the wounds of loss or, in Boethius's works "poultices".

These classic works not only suggest ways of simply comfort with the rearrangement of the environment, but also, they may help to familiarize the-soon-to-be-old with the losses before they occur; for example, Montaigne suggests a variety of rhetorical maxims borrowed from the ancient Stoics and Epicureans aimed at helping the person, to familiarize him or herself with death while still young! (He retreats from this approach in his later essays!). In short, the classic works offer accounts of how such external circumstances may contribute to old age happiness at the time of loss.

Fourth, in addition to expressions of love, reaffirmation of past virtues of character, and rearrangement of external conditions of comfort, the classics may provide deeper "therapies" for the sufferer, helping him or her to achieve the capacity for self-consolation. Self-consolation takes place by means of therapy, including a corrective emotional experience, or catharsis, or fundamental change through reflective meditation, philosophy or religious faith. For example, listening to *the Faure Requiem* may produce a catharsis which changes the listener's life. The classic plays, such as Shakespeare's *King Lear,* may stimulate and purge feelings of old age fear, sadness and regret. Tolstoy, in his remarkable novella, *Death of Ivan Ilyich* invites the reader to transform himself from a man of conventional ambition to one who, when dying, can give and receive love, as the protagonist did in the story.

These classics also may transform us by putting the losses in perspective; Lucretius, for example, offers us the opportunity to contemplate disease and death of the plague in Athens, but he portrays this plague only after viewing it against the larger context of the motions of elements in the universe. Such transformation may enable *us to* substitute a different way of life for the one we have lost. In his *Confessions,* Augustine found a religious faith to substitute for his futile and frustrating early life. The classics, especially philosophical works, may remind us of *the* necessary truths of our existence, as Heidegger has done in *Being and Time.* Some truths discovered in classic works, when experienced in old age, enable us to forge a final symmetry in our lives, re-creating an arc of our life and its history. I shall explore below how the classics are able to produce these consolations later in this chapter. However, first, it is necessary to explore the nature of consolation itself.

The Nature of Consolation

Consolation may be from extended from the author or artist of a classic work or the work itself to the specific audience of a work, (as in the case of the reader of a consoling letter) or the "bystander appreciator" who reads the letter, even though it is not intended for him or her. Consolation may set forth the author or protagonist's consolation extended to a family member or friend. In ancient Rome; the well-educated Romans used to send letters of consolation to their relatives and friends upon the occasion of death, exile or other serious losses. There was an ancient and medieval literary tradition of "consolatio" letters. These letters may be seeking to offer consolation for the letter writer or another. For example, one of these letters was from the Roman Stoic, Seneca, who, in his letter to his mother – "Letter to Marcia" – adopted the novel approach while in exile by sending a consolation letter from himself, the one suffering exile, to the one who was mourning his exile, seeking to console her.

Consolation is not limited to letters; it finds expression in books such as *Boethius's Consolations of Philosophy or* in works of art such as Michelangelo's late Pieta of Nicodemus or the Faure, Mozart or Bach Requiems. The classic consolation may the author's description of his own self-consolation – a consolation which, indirectly may offer comfort to others as in Boethius's *The Consolations of Philosophy*. Also, the consolation maybe a request aimed to God, perhaps in the form a prayer, or simply to oneself as a form of self-consolation in which the writer or artist is both the producer and the receiver of the consolation.

(*I regard this book as an exercise in self-consolation.* In this book I include the different kinds of consolation in my discussion, "sending" this book as a "letter" of consolation for old age to friends and family, while hoping that the book may be published for bystanders to read. At the same time, as I write it, I seek to console myself as I encounter the losses of old age. Thus, such an exercise may console all the readers who may be mourning the actual or anticipated losses of their as well as my own old age. In doing so, the book serves consolation for all of us).

The great German sociologist, Simmel has offered a rich definition of consolation:

> ..."man is a consolation-seeking creature. Consolation is something other than help – even an animal seeks help – but consolation is the remarkable experience that not only allows one to withstand suffering but so to speak elevates suffering into suffering. It pertains not to misfortune Itself, but to its reflection in the deepest level of the soul. Man by and large cannot be helped. Therefore, he has cultivated the wonderful category of consolation that not only comes to him *from the*

works that people speak for that purpose, (italics added) but which he also draws from a hundred factors in the world."

Two Kinds of Consolation

Before reviewing the tradition of the classics of consolation, I should like to recognize an important distinction in the meaning of consolation. One kind of consolation, frequently associated with the Stoics and those who, like Cicero, adopt, at least in part, Stoic beliefs, is "hard" consolation which urges a denial or a "standing up" to the losses encountered. The final book of Cicero's *Tusculan Disputations is* one example of "hard" consolation which urges a Stoic virtue (specifically bravery) in encountering loss. This "hard consolation" assumes the possibility of "hardening one's character" to cope with the slings and arrows of old age.

Such an appeal to "hard" consolation is often assumes the that the person extolled is virtuous, especially possessing the virtue of courage. However, as Aristotle and many others have recognized, character is the product of habits acquired over time. One of the tragedies of old age is that character is pretty much fixed or at least there may be limited time to develop anew the virtues in old age! I have acknowledged the possibility of hard consolation in my discussion of the reaffirmation of the self and its virtues in old age.

On the other hand, there is the "soft" consolation which permits, indeed encourages and ministers to the expression and open acceptance of grief and sorrow, allowing for the possibility of the occasional transformation which takes place in old age. I shall not choose between these two kinds of consolations; obviously both are desirable. Even if one has acquired the virtues of courage during his or her lifetime, other consolations may be required when one encounters loss in old age. However, before a deeper discussion of the kinds of consolation, I wish to identify the different traditions of consolation found in the classics.

Traditions of Consolation

1, Ancient Consolation: Philosophy and Rhetoric

Consolation has a rich tradition of specific formulations, especially within the ancient classics. Plato's Socrates, in the *Phaedo,* consoles his friends, by appealing to the eternal ideas, before taking the poison. In the *Tusculan Disputations,* the Roman philosopher and rhetorician, Cicero finally finds the consolation for many ills in the cultivation of virtue early in life, but he also recognizes that consolation can be something different - a form of solace - not a cure, but a comfort. Thus, he acknowledges the losses be treated in a new way, recommending the bandaging of their wounds, just as Boethius, in his *The Consolations of Philosophy,* recommends "poultices". Cicero adopts the several approaches to consolation to be employed in anticipation of death, the feeling of pain, or the experience of disease, grief, or distress. He recognizes that different ancient philosophers- Stoics, Epicureans, Peripatetics, and the Cynics - take different approaches to consolation. In his *Tusculan Disputations*, he reports that he has employed them all when seeking consolation for the death of his daughter. He spells out, (not unlike the modern lawyer!) the various ways of coping with suffering, i.e., denying death and its' severity, recognizing the loss, seeking to stop the progress of sadness, diverting attention from the loss or simply giving into it.

After Cicero, the Stoic, Seneca, with his many consolation letters mentioned above as well as within several essays, suggests a variety of intellectual techniques. Many of his letters of consolation illustrate the usual versions of the Stoic consolation (i.e. noting the fact that all men must die, there is no need to grieve for the dead since they feel nothing and that time will ease sorrow but reason can do so first). Montaigne was to repeat many of these nostrums as I shall describe below.

Boethius' late ancient *The Consolations of Philosophy* is one of the major consolation classics, but he takes a somewhat different tack than either Cicero or Seneca. Facing certain death in captivity, he minimizes the importance of the external goods he lost upon his imprisonment and, after receiving the ineffective "poultices" of music and poetry, turns to "Lady Philosophy". Like Seneca, Boethius finds consolation in the recognition of how small a part he plays in the grand cyclical motions of the whole universe and, despite facing torture, claims to find happiness in God. Boethius, however, is not willing to simply consign his fate to necessity. Despite the evil of his situation, he seeks to establish the fact of human freedom and dignity in the face of the natural necessities of the universe and the Providence of God - necessities which appear to constrain him and will ultimately result in a painful death. Although Boethius finds consolation in the God's providence based upon His eternal knowledge and, he asserts the belief that man is not the victim of divine necessity. Exemption from natural necessity, tor Boethius, is based upon a recognition of a human dignity, founded upon the capacity of human choice in this temporal world. Such a capacity makes humans responsible for their choices and hence subject to punishment or praise in the eyes "of [his] prince". For Boethius, it is this fundamental human dignity based upon human choice which is the ultimate consolation in a world in which one does not have complete control over all natural or human events.

2. *The Christian Tradition*

There are two Christian traditions which offer consolations for selected sorrows of disease and death. One tradition views these sorrows as punishment for human sin, testing our faith and finding consolation in Christ's forgiveness, his resurrection, and promised afterlife in Heaven. This approach mirrors the Stoic approach advanced by Cicero, urging the sufferer to hang tough! In its extensive history, such a Christian belief not only appeared to give a special meaning to one's suffering, (as the justified punishment of God), but also encouraged the Christian to bear the suffering as a test of faith with courage. It began with the Bible stories such as the suffering of Job, whose faith was deliberately tested by a God who designed all forms of misfortune for Job. A similar tough-minded approach was taken by Augustine who thought that if faith were firm, no other consolation was needed. Later, the expressions of Christian faith began to soften with a distinction made between natural suffering to be endured and theological suffering deserving consolation; this distinction led to a gradual acceptance of the suitability of consolation for misery in general. Although consolation was accepted, and elaborate clerical manuals were prepared in the later periods of Christian thought, the view of suffering as a test of faith was extended to more recent times and is set forth in Thomas More's *Dialogue of Comfort,* and C.S, Lewis's *The Problem of Pain.*

Thomas More's *A Dialogue of Comfort Against Tribulation* was written while More was in prison for refusing to endorse Henry VIII's divorce of Catherine and marriage to Anne Boleyn, while declaring himself the head of the Christian church in England. More argued that God was the source of all comfort, that tribulations were God's test of man's faith, encouraging him to repent of past sins and avoid future ones. Only one who has suffered tribulation can enter the Kingdom of Heaven. Unlike the ancients, More and, following More, C.S. Lewis don not find suffering meaningless in itself, but rather claim, if Christian faith is embraced, that suffering is a meaning punishment in this world, to be rewarded in the next one.

According to a second tradition, one may understand Christian consolation in light of its more general ethic of a supernaturally inspired love and charity. Here, an important biblical text is the Good Samaritan's parable, extending through the works of the early apostolic fathers, the meditations of Bernard, Richard, and Bonaventure, culminating in the extended discussion of Aquinas in the *Summa Theologica* followed by extended debates among Catholics and Protestants through the ages. To take one example, religious consolation originating in God's love can supplement natural love. St. Thomas Aquinas In the *Summa Theologica* suggests the following relief of pain and sorrow:

When one is in pain, it is natural that the sympathy of the friend should afford consolation… since the sorrow has a depressing effect, it is like a weigh whereof we strive to unburden ourselves; so that when a man sees others saddened by his own sorrow, it seems as though others were bearing the burden with him, striving, as it were, to lessen its weight; wherefor the load of sorrow becomes light for him, something like what occurs in the carrying of bodily burdens.

St. Thomas continues to suggest that it is the love of a friend, (in addition to sleep and a bath!) which helps to assuage the sorrow and pain. It is perhaps the recognition of this power of love which constitutes the greatest contribution of Christian thought to an understanding of consolation. For a contemporary instance of such Christian love as consolation, Dietrich Bonhoeffer's *Letters from Prison* captures his efforts to console his family and friends in part through discussions of the lcassics.

3. *The Humanist Tradition*

The most extensive humanist treatment of consolation, a product of both Christian and ancient influences, is found in the writings of Petrarch, often viewed as the father of the Renaissance. In his works *Secretum* and *The Solitary Life*, he sets forth a program of self-consolation. In his letters, including his letters in old age, he offers the consolations of friendship. And, in his major *Remedies for Good and Bad Fortune*, he addresses a myriad of remedies for the public. Petrarch had good reason for his remarkable work on consolation, since he confronted uncertainty in his own life, the heinous living conditions of the city, the advent of the plague. He extended that consolation not only for the occasions of death, but also for distress (including accidie), sickness, exile and old age through dialogues, treatises, letters and manuals. Just as I offer classic works in response to old age, he asserted the importance of rhetoric, theology, and solitude to purge the emotions of suffering and strengthen his own character in the face of distress. In his letters to friends, he exhorted them to tranquility and fortitude. In his two volumes work of remedies for the public, he sought to focus his advice to counter the emotions of desire, pleasure, fear and grief, urging among other things, the importance of reading and the humanities, which he claimed would provide powerful words for sickness, pain and death. Like Boethius before him and Pico della Mirandola after him, he appealed to the dignity of man as the ultimate answer for human suffering.

A later humanist, Michel de Montaigne, in his *Essays,* repeats the classic Stoic arguments for self- consolation in his essay on "That to Think as a Philosopher is to Learn to Die" and he adds many more arguments, all in pursuit of becoming "familiar" with death. He recommends thinking each day is our last; repeating the thought that "no man is more frail that another, no man more certain of his morrow"; asking yourself "why, in so short a life, make so many plans?" ; recognizing how small a portion of life remains for the old; remembering that "as our birth brought us the birth of all things, so will our death the death of all things"; taking comfort in the thought that mortals live mutually dependent and pass on the torch of life and that we are merely guests so that when we have visited enough, it is time to depart; accepting the sad fact that our fathers saw no other things, nor will our sons behold anything different; "we turn, every one enclosed, in the same circle"; do not expect that "in true death, there will be no other self, which, living and standing by our prostrate body, can mourn to thyself, thy extinction"; and remembering that, wherever your life ends, it is all there. Many of these consolations appear to apply to old age as well as death. On the other hand, in his later essays, after Montaigne had experienced the impact of the plague and war, He appeared to admire the unthinking Stoicism of this neighbors facing death and, in his final essay, he appears to find consolation in living within the immediate present moment.

4. The Modern and Contemporary Traditions of Consolation

Although modern philosophers, Kant, Hegel, Mill and others have penned accounts of human sympathy for those who suffer, these accounts do not rival the attention to personal compassion and consolation which earlier Christian and Humanist thinkers have written. One exception is the German philosopher, Schopenhauer, who, while offering a mixed estimation of the happiness and misery of old age, advanced an argument for recognizing the general misery of mankind, and, hence, he was known as the "philosopher of pessimism". As consequence, he offers an interesting modern analysis of the need for consolation as compassion. However, in doing so, he encountered a problem; his starting point was the subjective individualistic perspective of Descartes and Kant; hence he had to explain how the individual could reach out to console others in their misery. (This problem is called "the problem of empathy" and it has preoccupied many modern thinkers). Schopenhauer, (borrowing in part from Eastern thought) argued that altruism was possible by "identifying with" the sufferer, (although he created considerable confusion about the nature of this "identification").

A second modern philosopher whose entire work, in some ways offered consolation for the miseries of life was Benedict Spinoza. In his *Ethics* which sets forth a comprehensive philosophy, he concludes by seeking to demonstrate that the perception of individual and events in light of an intuitive as well as a deductive and knowledge of God's nature can offer a profound sense of peace in response to all the emotions encountered in life including, of course, those which are consequent to loss.

More contemporary efforts to think seriously about and provide consolation include the works of essayists such as Thoreau, Emerson, William James. Efforts of modern psychology and eastern meditation have also sought to offer accounts and methods of consolation. One recent effort is the work of Pierre Hadot who has sought to resurrect the ancient Hellenistic notions of philosophy as a unique "way of life" with "spiritual exercises" to designed to cope with life's problems. These exercises included meditation, reading, thinking of death, and viewing oneself from above.

Rather than the efforts of modern philosophers to explain how compassion is possible, it is the modern poetic elegy which captures the most intense expression of sadness at loss in old age, and which offers some of the most moving expressions of consolation. These modern elegies were preceded by a rich tradition of ancient elegies and myths, such as the story of Orpheus and Eurydice, which tells the story of love, loss and consolation. The early English elegies are well known; Tennyson's *In Memoriam* and Wordsworth's *The Cumberland Beggar* are classic evocations of the sadness of age and death. In Tennyson's defensive words,

"…What hope is there for modern rhyme

To him that turns a musing eye,
On songs and deeds and lives, that lie
Foreshortened in the tract of time?
…But what of that? My darkened ways
Shall ring with music all the same,
To breathe my loss is more than fame,
To utter love more sweet than praise…."

One well known old English elegy is Gray's *Elegy Written in a Country Churchyard,* not because of poetic subtlety, (which it lacks), or its religious conclusion, (which is trite), but because of the sad mood it evokes with Gray's own contemplation of the churchyard, a contemplation in which many of us have engaged:

"…Beneath those rugged elms, that yew-trees shade
Where heaves the turn in many a mouldering heap,
Each in his narrow cell forever laid,
The rude foregathers of the hamlet sleep…."

Within that melancholy mood, he finds ironic consolation for the dead in the notion that the fate of these obscure country folks is no different from the rich, the famous and the powerful; ironically, unlike the latter, the poor, without grand ambitions and accomplishments, did not have to commit great crimes before their death. But Gray goes beyond such concerns of class. He suggests that the poor were lucky that, In the course of their lives, they may have had time to savor the quiet beauty of the countryside, which Gray describes so well. (A modern commentary on English elegy felicitously labels it the "placing of sorrow" in nature and several modern nature works have rediscovered this theme, including Kohak's *The Embers and the Stars*).

It is the elegiac poetry of T.S. Eliot which is most moving for me. Even his first poem ("The Love Song of J. Alfred Prufrock") anticipates the concerns and regrets of old age, ("I grow old, I grow old, I shall wear my trousers rolled"). I have already mentioned above Eliot's *La Figlia Che Piange,* which, if not a poem of old age, is nevertheless a poem of elegiac regret of lost love, ("I should have lost a gesture and a pose"). Losses are echoed in the *Wasteland,* "breeding lilacs into the dead land", "the wind crosses the brown land unheard", and "the river's tent is broken; the last fingers of leaf clutch and sink into the wet bank". Eliot describes the dead state of Phlebus, as "a current under sea picked his bones in whispers." Almost despair is felt. "Where are the roots that clutch, what branches grow out of this stony rubbish?" As for old age: "I Tiresias, old man with wrinkled dugs, perceive the scene and foretold the rest- I too awaited the expected guest". To my mind, (and, in the opinion of some modern critics), the *Wasteland* is not only a cultural commentary, but a deeply personal poem evoking the distinctive mood of much of Eliot's poetry – a sadness, regret, nostalgia, "mixing memory and desire", all of which capture the elegiac mood of old age. Not only does Eliot voice the loss of an entire culture but also personal losses of his own failed marriage. Sadness from such loss finds its way into his poetry.

There is elegaic detachment there as well. Such detachment is, after all, Eliot's specialty, whether achieved through irony, humor, or simply the learned references within his poetry. Hence, when Eliot begins to get serious either about his or civilization's losses, he veers off skittishly into a "...o o o o that Shakespearean rag, it's so elegant, so intelligent...." mocking himself. If loss, melancholy and detachment may be found in Eliot's poetry, some suggest that Eliot offers little consolation in the *Wasteland.* But, within the poem, moments of past memory, the savoring of nature in the form of lilacs, (unwelcome, to be sure), warm winds and protective snows, and, despite the dry rock, an imagining of water pools, and the projection of the eternal movement of the Thames river gives some comfort. Eliot even calls upon his youthful study of Indian philosophy to end his great work with "Shantih, shantih, shantih", (which he translates in his notes as "the peace which passeth understanding".

Another equally moving modern consolatory masterpiece is Rilke's *The Duino Elegies.* In the first elegy, Rilke begins by pointing out the fundamental loss of all humanity: "If I cried out, who would hear me among the angelic orders?" Part of that loss comes with death and

Rilke places the reader into death: "... of course it is odd to live no more on the earth, to abandon custom. You begin to get used not to give meaning to roses and other such promising things in terms of a human future." Such loss results in profound sadness: "I choke back my own birdcall, my sobbing. Shouldn't these ancient sufferings of ours finally start to bear fruit? ...we who can sometimes draw from the wellsprings of sadness...how could we exist without them?" And yet, in elegiac fashion, he greets such loss and sadness with detachment: "throw armfuls of emptiness out to the spaces that we breathe -maybe the birds will sense the expanded air" and "you try to make up till slowly, you start to get a whiff of eternity... the drift of eternity drags all the ages of men... you can be weaned from things of this world". So we seek consolation: "who can we turn to in this need? Not angels, not people. We aren't especially home in this deciphered world...Is the old tale pointless that tells how music in the midst of mourning made emptiness vibrate in ways that thrill us, comfort us, help us now?" These and other elegiac works, in Simmel's words, "elevate suffering into suffering..." as consolation.

As John B. Vickery has documented, the literature of contemporary consolation is not limited to poetry nor its subjects reserved to the loss of death; it extends to prose works, which find losses which range to the loss of family, loss of self, loss of cultures and civilizations John Bayley's *Elegy for Iris* supplies one such example, This is the author's story of his love for and marriage to Iris Murdoch, an Oxford philosopher and novelist. The story reveals Iris an academic woman, absorbed in her work, accepting the love of Bayley, but not above a playful promiscuity, at least early in their marriage. Since both were Oxford Dons, a placid picture of Oxford life emerges, with the success of both their careers. Then, Iris begins to fail due to Alzheimer's Disease and Bayley becomes her protector and caregiver. A sadness suffuses the account as we witness the decline of a remarkable mind. But Bayley's continued love for her as recounted in his somewhat detached account leads the reader, the author, and Iris to a consolation at the end with, an ordinary Christmas walk in the park, a Sunday breakfast, a Sunday nap and the listening to Christmas carols. It is clear to the author and the reader alike that this peaceful moment is not the end, but merely a welcome interlude in the coping with the trials of Alzheimer's and her imminent death. As the *Elegy for Iris* and other contemporary works reveal, the expansion of the loss, emotions, and consolations or other endings in modern elegies suggest that, when elegy is applied to an understanding of old age, the ranges of losses, emotions, and possible resolutions in old age may be much greater than simple awareness of one's mortality, sadness and some form of comfort. Modern elegy changes our expectations about old age.

What then is the lesson of this sketch of a history of the literature of consolation? On the one hand, the history suggests that consolation has many different meanings throughout the ages. Such a history widens our notion of consolation, embracing the emotions of sympathy, altruism, compassion and love, "applying" these emotions to a range of losses sustained by oneself, one's loved ones and perhaps even others, On the other hand, the history reveals common themes of "avenues to solace": expression of love, arranging the external conditions of comfort, reaffirmation of the self, and transformation. Now I shall turn to these consolatory "avenues of solace".

Avenues of Solace

The brief history of consolation above reveals that not only poetic elegies but other works, such as letters, natural science, philosophy, rhetoric and the fine arts also offer solace. That history indicates the many purposes of such consolation and outlines its' methods. A common theme in many of the historical accounts of consolation is its origin in the expression feelings of love, in the form of sympathy, compassion and empathy. Second, such love and compassion may be expressed through rhetoric and the arts, but also simply the prosaic arrangement of external comforting conditions. Third, such consolations may rest in the reaffirmation of one's "fading self" by reasserting one's freedom and identity. Finally, solace goes beyond such efforts to salve the losses of old age by including philosophical or religious justifications for accepting them - an acceptance which may result in some form of cathartic transformation of the sufferer as well as the one offering consolation.

1. Love at the Core of Consolation.

The history of consolation continually refers to its origins in love. In the *Phaedo,* Plato, facing death, finds consolation in the love of philosophy and its eternal forms recoverable through his beloved dialectic. In the Old Testament, the love of God allowed Job to withstand the sorrows and losses imposed upon him. The New Testament bids us to love our neighbor as ourselves and the parable of the Good Samaritan illustrates such love. The love of God animates Boethius in his final meditations on consolation in prison. For Aquinas, the virtue of charity is a remedy for the sorrows consequent to loss. Even the humanist Petrarch, in his remedies for himself in the *Secretum* and for others in the *Remedies* appeals to the power of love.

Although a benevolent love grounded in religious belief is a central principle of Christian faith, the history of consolation, especially modern writings, appeal to a secular natural love as the writings of Schopenhauer, Bayley and Yeats indicate. Such a love may simply be a natural tendency of human desire. The kind of love expressed within consolation may be one of sympathy in which we believe we feel similar losses to suffering in general, or a compassion directed to specific loved ones, or identification in which we empathize with the unique losses of the sufferer or participation within the unity of a relationship of love and friendship. Although fueled by desire and emotion, these feelings may be guided an intellectual or imaginative judgement valuing or granting esteem directed at the suffering person. Perhaps the ultimate form of loving consolation is one in which we participate in the unity of a relationship of friendship or love.

2. Bandaging the Wounds: Arranging External Conditions for Comfort

In Cicero's famed essay *On Old Age*, he recommends the old age activities of gentleman farming and political consultation; Boethius found initial consolations in music and literature; Aquinas recommended hot baths; Petrarch sought solitude, Rousseau indulged in wandering through nature. Although all offered other remedies as well, they also presumed or recommended various external arrangements to mitigate the losses, ease the sorrows, and supply consolations of old age and approaching death, whether friends, palliative care, a comfortable ambience. Some of the ancient Stoics as well as humanistic philosophers of the Renaissance urged the cultivation and practice of moral virtues, since reliance upon external circumstances without such virtues subjected them to the whims of fortune. Moral virtue, they urged would secure autonomy and control over their lives. However, scholars who have studied the lives of Stoics have found them to make such stringent recommendations from the relative comfort of their wealth.

It was Aristotle who confronted the difficult relationship between virtue and prosperity in our lives. Although he suggested that virtue should govern the elements of happiness in our lives, he did not exclude other important goods – health, friendships, and a moderate degree of wealth. Such external goods were seen to be both goods for their own sake, and possible instruments for the cultivation and practice of virtues, (although Aristotle was quick to recognize that the undue pursuit of these external goods might interfere with the development and practice of the virtues).

How might these external goods be relevant to the losses, sadness, detachment and consolation of old age losses? With old age losses of biological decline and the prospect of death, the virtue of courage is made relevant; such a virtue is cultivated, at least in part, by the subjecting the young to challenging circumstances as part of their education. As for the loss of an expanded future in old age, the virtue of temperance is particularly appropriate since it limits the desires and ambitions unsuited to old age. Increase of dependency in old age calls upon the virtues of love and friendship for oneself and others. An important part of the cultivation and practice of such virtues is the presence of favorable external circumstances which facilitate such virtues. Aristotle was realistic enough to recognize that unfortunate situations can overwhelm the happiness of even those possessing moral virtue. The modern philosopher, Simone de Beauvoir documented this reality in her portrait of the poverty of the elderly.

Moderate prosperity enables the rearrangement of the external conditions which, in turn, permits the substitution for the goods lost during old age. Elsewhere in this book, I have suggested that, upon retirement, when consulting Aristotle, Horace, Petrarch and Montaigne, I found their recommendations for a "pastoral leisure" and solitude to be a happy replacement for the time previously occupied by my productive work. The replacement, however, was not automatic. I have described below in the book that a process of reflective meditation must take place leading to the conviction that, indeed classical leisure can replace the loss of previously satisfying compensated professional work. Such leisure is not merely the "free time" of a work- oriented society – an old age free time of pleasures to compensate for the years of work. Such "free time" continues to assume the values of a work-oriented society, in which freedom is defined in terms of the work it has escaped.

The turn to classical leisure to compensate for lost work is an example of redressing loss through substitution. Another example of substitution, may take place when our biological decline leads to dependency, requiring us to be supported through others' sympathy or compassion or living within the welfare state with the receipt of state supported pensions and health care. Such "institutionalized compassion", substitutes public resources for private charity. Beveridge, in his outline of the principles of the welfare state and Martha Nussbaum, in her *Political Emotions* indicate how welfare state can substitute, at least in part, for the personal compassion for the vulnerable, including the elderly. Sigmund Freud, in his short elegant essay on *Transience* suggested that the sadness of loss would be compensated over time by substitution by an ongoing life. Writing in 1915, Freud clearly had in mind the rebirth of civilization after the destruction of World War I.

As the future dims or contracts for the old, thus stunting ambitions and weakening any drive for self-improvement, I have suggested that one way of facing a diminished future is to construct "legacies" which substitute for the "legacies of ambition" which are lost in old age. I did not find the legal legacy of transferring property to loved ones, nor pursuit of a legacy of a long-lived reputational honor, (which few attain), nor even the legacy of being part of "a family tradition", to be personally satisfactory, although I do not deny the satisfactions of such legacies for others. *For myself, I found that legacy in reading the works or Aristotle, Plato and Aquinas, and other classics and hence to be part of participation in the eternal ideas found within their works, as part of a continuing legacy of western thought.* My library and its books are the external expression of such a legacy.

My own substitution for work in retirement is primarily the solitary intellectual activity of reading, appreciating major works, and writing, primarily for myself. This substitution did not take place over night. It began with my retreat into the library to read when a small boy. It was cultivated in an education which permitted me to read and write in Chicago coffee houses, on the London strand, and the park benches of many cities. There were many moments in the flurry of my adult life when I could and did retreat. Now, sitting on my terrace in Vermont summer day, or sitting in front of a fire during Vermont's quiet winter, I don't have to seek solitude. It is here. The rewards of such solitude are the freedoms to reflect upon nature, the world, my family and life with the help of the classic works. I have found intellectual support for my solitary life, when I read Petrarch, Montaigne, or Thoreau, and more a more solid emotional support from my wife before she died. Of course, I am under no illusion that it is a life suited to everyone. Yet, there are many older persons who lead solitary lives and who may find my approach to old age suited to them as well.

3. *The Reaffirmation and Reconstitution of the Self- Self Consolation*

I have suggested throughout this book that the many losses in old age may accumulate to a loss of the self. Loss of the capacity to initiate action, eclipse of the past, physical decline may result in the "fading" of the identity of the very person who pursued life prior to old age. Yet, despite such losses, the consolation classics often recommend the reaffirmation and recover of the virtues previously possessed in order that a capacity for self-consolation may take place. For example, as noted above, Cicero, after reviewing all the possible consolations for life's distress turns to invoking virtues such as courage and temperance to meet the fears and other emotions aroused by old age loss. In doing so, he is following in the footsteps of the Stoics who assume that the "hard consolation" constituting a detached denial of the very importance of the losses encountered is possible given a character which has familiarized itself with the losses in advance. We saw above that Montaigne tried to prepare for such losses earlier in his life by familiarizing himself with the losses he might encounter later in life, but there is no indication that such an effort helped him to acquire the character he needed once old age arrived.

The central problems in looking to self-consolation for the losses encountered in old age are that the appropriate virtues constituting character may not have been cultivated earlier in life and even if they were, the losses of old age may weaken or eliminate them! If so, these appropriate virtues may either have to be reaffirmed in some way or new ones substituted. I suggest below that such a restoration requires a transformation in old age either by means of therapy, reflective meditation, philosophy or religious faith. The classics pay a central role in each of these methods of transformation.

4. Transformation of the Aged Self

Finding solace in the giving or receiving of love and rearrangement of the circumstances of our lives are not the only consolations in old age. Restoring the virtues and character of our former selves we once possessed may be possible, a least somewhat. But perhaps a more radical transformation is necessary. Exposure to the classics, whether religious or non-religious classics, may stimulate a kind of personal transformation which helps us to cope with these losses. To be sure, many of the classic portraits of old age do not guarantee that any transformation will take place. Quite the contrary. The view of the elderly, whether by novelists such as Balzac, poets such as Arnold, or philosophers such as Aristotle, playwrights such as Aristophanes, offer a depressing portrait of old age character growing more rigid, selfish and less attractive with each passing day. One notable exception is Tolstoy's *The Death of Ivan Ilitch* in which the dying government official gradually gains new insight into the meaninglessness and triviality of his past life and the importance of the love he had missed giving and receiving during his lifetime. Tolstoy's other short stories about old people carry a similar message about the need for transformation and the discovery of love.

There are several ways for seeking transformation of the wounded self of old age: the practice of therapy, reflective meditation, philosophy, and religious faith. The classics, as identified below, play a central role in describing and prescribing each of these methods of transformation

Therapy

Classics may function to encourage and purge feelings which may indicate ways to transform oneself in old age. Of course, the modern psychoanalytic works of Freud, Jung and Erikson and their followers may lead us to seek therapies which help us to come to terms with our old age. In addition to psychotherapy, there is literature which evokes catharsis - the elegies of old age, as well as tragic and comic dramatic works. We may regard ourselves with pity and face our old age with fear. It is precisely the exposure to the major works of sadness, pity, compassion, and fear through which we may experience and "purge" our own comparable feelings. It is Aristotle's *Poetics* which suggests that tragedies elicit feelings of pity and fear from an undeserved reversal in the fortune of significant protagonist- one with we can identify our own lives. Although our own lives may not have the neat plots of tragic dramas, nor may our lives assume the significance of tragic heroes, nevertheless, our old age may mark the end of the story of a life, a kind of drama. Although the harms encountered in old age are often gradual, rather than quick tragic reversals, these harms, like those of tragic drama, may include the loss of "external goods" of wealth, honor, and power through aging. Although the recognition of these losses may not be the dramatic discovery of an Oedipus or King Lear, there is a stage of gradual recognition of loss in old age and that recognition may evoke emotions similar to those within the tragic drama – pity, compassion, and fear, often for ourselves. Cathartically experiencing them in drama may prepare us for our own experience both the losses and their emotions in old age.

Catharsis is not limited to beholding tragedy. Walter Watson, in his recreation of Book Ii of Aristotle's *Poetics* suggests that the laughable can also result in a catharsis. The plays of Aristophanes are often aimed at laughable events, circumstances and characteristics related to the elderly. Blind and greedy ambition of the elderly father for his son, and the exaggerated meddling in political activities by the aged are lampooned in *The Clouds* and the *Wasps*. There are a myriad of good jokes pertaining to the elderly and their vulnerabilities.

Another ancient means of therapy is rhetoric by means of emotion-laden argument, which incite new emotions to displace or transform the emotions of the listener. Aristotle's account of a deliberative rhetoric suggests that such changes may be produced if properly adapted to the character of the speaker and listener, the nature of their relation, the occasion of their interaction, the specific kinds of rhetorical argument and the nature of the emotions involved.

Reflective Meditation

Old age is not a completely new world. We carry many of our virtues (and vices!) into this last stage of life. To the extent that we carry the virtues of courage, temperance, justice, liberality, capacity for friendship, love, and practical wisdom into old age we may employ them in coping with old age loss. Since many of these virtues acquired and exercised in the past within the context of work or the family, we may have to reaffirm them in our old age and reapply them in the context of our old age. To reaffirm and reapply them requires reflective meditation – a systematic meditation on classics pertaining to each loss. In the later chapters of this book, I shall undertake such a meditation.

Although I am no paragon of virtue, let me offer here one such example – my losses which took place due to retirement. A moral and psychological vacuum was left in my old age when I gave up work and whatever ambitions for riches, honor and even professional self-improvement, Retirement created the opportunity, (a rearrangement of the circumstances of life), to pursue the classical ideal of leisure in which the pursuits of reading and writing for its own sake operated as a substitute for previous employment. Upon reflection, I realized that I had entertained an affection for this ideal throughout my life. Upon retirement I turned to a reading of justifications of such an ideal and accounts of its practice by others. In classical leisure, the aged may either pursue a civic leisure turning to political or community activity and, in the process, may acquire new political virtues, which they may or may not have had in the past. I had been active in civic activities most of my life, and was not attracted to this form of leisure. Instead, I turned to a "pastoral leisure" which is occupied by more solitary intellectual pursuits. These pursuits have helped me to acquire new capacities, such as the enjoyment of solitary study and the capacity to read and contemplate a variety of subjects pertaining to my past life and the study of old age. Exercising these capacities of leisure in old age consoles me for the loss of work and its driving ambitions. I believe I have experienced a fundamental transformation of myself from one the seeking to change the world and, in the process receiving honor, wealth, or success. I changed myself into a "leisured being" able to pursue intellectual activities for their own sake.

My old age experience exemplifies consolation of loss through substitution, I have suggested that the recovery and reconstruction of one's autobiographical history can supply a substitute for that which has been eclipsed through the passage of time. Augustine and Rousseau's *Confessions*, John Stuart Mill's *Autobiography,* and Henry Adams in his *The Education of Henry Adams* provide models for such an effort. I shall describe in greater detail below how such a recovery and reconstruction can take place in later chapters.)

Philosophy

One avenue to consolations in old age is to acquire a detached philosophic understanding of its losses and provide recommendations for responding to such losses. Such understanding may place the losses in perspective, familiarize the soon-to-be-aged with the prospect of old age, and recognize the inevitability and finality of old age as part of the larger workings of nature and society. Such a consolation tacitly accepts that it may not be possible to find substitutes for the losses we encounter in old age, such as irremediable losses of health and strength in old age. There may be no substitutes for such losses, but, when reading natural philosophers (Lucretius) and modern biologists, (Darwin, Weismann), we might accept that the decline of health and vigor is part of a natural process of an organism's natural biological decline – a decline which, in turn, is part of the ancient recognized cycles of nature or the modern recognized pattern of evolution. Such a wholistic perspective may operate to minimize the significance of the old age loss we encounter.

Montaigne's essay, *To Think as a Philosopher is to learn to Die, is* a collection of intellectual techniques borrowed from Lucretius and Seneca and designed to provide consolation in the face of death, but many of its arguments, may apply to old age as well, (simply because death is an important loss ending old age and anticipation of it may suffuse throughout the time of old age). Montaigne, arguing for a life aimed at the delight resulting from tranquil virtue, and urging a gratitude for the life already lived, suggests a variety of techniques for familiarization with death, the recognition of death (and old age decline), acknowledgement of its' inevitability, finality, and universality, and acceptance of its unimportance when measured against one's life before birth and after death. Montaigne suggests that old age and its completion in death leaves no self behind to mourn the loss of future plans so he asks why mourn them before death? (Montaigne's questions are part of more comprehensive philosophic systems of Epicureanism and Stoicism, which may be studied on their own. If they are so studied, old age and its losses may be understood in the context of these systems of thought).

Religious Faith

Another kind of transformation which may help us to cope with our losses in aging is religious faith and belief. Although I shall identify later the limitations of religion in relation to old age, I cannot deny that such faith can produce transformations is recounted in Augustine's *Confessions* where Augustine finds himself transformed upon reading a phrase in the Bible. Such Christian faith emphasizes the role of love in providing consolation:

> "Thou shalt love the Lord thy God with all they heart, and with all thy soul and with all thy mind. And second is like unto it. Thou shalt love they neighbor as thyself. On these two commandments hang all the law and the prophets"

The grand intellectual analysis of compassion is set forth in Aquinas's discussion of charity in his *Summa Theologica*. Charity for Aquinas is one of the theological virtues, along with faith and hope, all three of which are closely connected. Charity is love for another so as to wish good to him. Although, for Thomas, perfect charity is only in the next world; in this world, there is an imperfect love between God, angels, and humans. This love is not dependent upon the virtues of its recipients, but extends to all, even the aged. Since it aims for the good of another, it may entail self-sacrifice. Such as love, even if not animated by a Christian faith, seems suited to the situation of old age in which the sufferings of ones' loved ones and friends may be prevalent; it is these sufferings which call forth compassion. Finally, as our discussion of Thomas More revealed, Christian doctrine also offers a theological justification of the losses encountered in life as punishments for our past sins, deterrence for our future ones, and incentives in the form of a heavenly afterlife – all of which may result in transformation of our behavior and character.

Conclusion

In summing up this chapter, the nature and origins of consolation, as avenues to solace in old age, are found in the love to and from others. The means of pursuing such solace are the rearrangement of the external circumstances of our elderly lives, the effort to hang onto or recover past virtues required to cope with old age losses and the transformation of the self by means of therapy, the reflective meditation, philosophy, and religious faith. The classics may introduce us to these possible "instruments" of consolation.

In Part I: Chapters 1 to 4, I have reviewed the major elements of an elegiac understanding of old age: the recognition and acceptance of loss, the feeling of sadness, regret as well as other emotions, the securing of a detachment from old age loss and its' emotions, and the nature and means of consolation in old age. In Part II, Chapters 5-8, I turn to a discussion of what I regard to be mistaken ways of coping with the losses of old age- the pursuit of biological immortality, the burying oneself in a "busy" life, the futile hope for an old age life of delight, and the adoption of a blind religious faith. These mistaken ways of old age life fail to recognize *the essential elegy of old age* and hence, I call them, "the enemies of elegy". I shall now turn to explore what light the classics can shed upon such enemies of elegy.

CHAPTER V

Religion's Denial of Old Age

Once the aging realize that they are only just time and will soon be removed from space, a number of illusionary comforts appear to them, besides even the greatest and most beguiling illusion of all. Religion.

Jean Amery, *On Aging*

In childhood, I was preoccupied with eternity. This preoccupation was a gift from the Catholic Church. The Catholic nuns recounted to us the horrors of hell—illustrating its pain with the description of an eternally lighted match engulfing our entire young bodies. Little wonder that I prayed penitently to the upraised host—a prayer which my missal promised would secure seven years off my time in Purgatory. Little wonder that I felt the purifying sense of relief after confession for the remission of my trivial sins. And yet, the joys of the world remained—the secret happiness at stealing chocolate milk from the rectory, the thrill at first touching the neighbor girl's freckled breasts, the excitement at stealing a case of beer from a union picnic. Since childhood, my religious faith has waxed and waned. At one time in my life, I seriously contemplated entering the priesthood. But in college, the church's social positions against contraception and my discovery of the remarkable similarity of Christian beliefs to the early Greek mystery religions cooled my ardor. When I enrolled in the philosophy department of the University of

Chicago, I found in philosophy and its eternal ideas to offer the substitute for religion and now, I seek any eternity within its discipline. In old age, my Catholic faith has long since disappeared and along with its disappearance has gone my faith in its promise of eternal bliss, and yet, what remains is my belief in the importance of the eternity of ideas shared by both the underlying elegy of religion and the classics, both contributing to an understanding of old age itself.

Introduction

Old age often yields a heightened sense of time. Shakespeare captured it in the following Sonnet lines:

> When I have seen by Time's fell hand defaced
> The rich-proud cost of outworn buried age;

And Jean Amery has found time to rest at the core of old age consciousness. "Time is always within us, just as space is around us... We find time in aging, even if we do not …entertain the poetic illusion that we have …place it in suspension, and thereby insinuated ourselves into eternity…."

Obviously, the losses of old age take place over time. They are often gradual, and their consequent sadness is often delayed. Detachment from the losses and whatever consolations are to be had also are experienced over time. The importance of time to old age is obvious upon reflection. One's time of life is almost over. It is probably no accident that late in life, Augustine appended his discussion of the nature of time to earlier completed autobiography, *The Confessions.* A sense of the passage of time hovers over the deterioration of one's biological functions, the sense of an eclipse of the past and the foreshortening of the future and the exile of retirement. Abandonment of belief in progress, and anticipation of death heightens our awareness of time's passage.

Some suggest that the sense of time passing is but a fleeting awareness among with everyday activities of old age. This lack of awareness my be the result of the variety of ways which many of the elderly have adopted to cope with the anxiety and sadness which old age may produce as it contemplates the passage of time. These "denials" of the passage of time are the subjects of the next four chapters. The elderly may look to religion, or seek to extend the time available to them with the help of medical technology. They may indulge in an old age hedonism, seeking moments of delight, beholding flowers in the rubble of old age. Or they may simply stay busy, to convince themselves that time is not passing since nothing in their lives has changed.

Fortunately, just as the classics shed light on the elegiac elements of old age, they also explore these conventional approaches to coping with the time of old age.

Consequently, I shall draw upon these classics to shed light upon these responses to time in old age.

Classics and The Religious Response to Time's Passage

One of several responses to the losses encountered in old age is the turn toward religion – its experiences, beliefs, practices and institutions. Thus, like the denial of morality in the scientific effort to extend life, or ignoring aging by remaining "busy", or by finding "delight" in old age pursuits, religion may be regarded as an alternative avenue for coping with time in old age. The imminent approach to death associated with old age may argue for the suitability of religion to this stage of life. Since historically, the stage of old age was limited to a short period before death, it may have made sense in the past to associate religion with old age. However. due to increases in longevity, modern old age is a more extensive period of time, at least for many people, and hence, it is less obvious that religion, with its attention to death and afterlife, is suited to modern old age. Moreover, when carefully examined, religious doctrines have surprising little to do or say about old age! Since, in the eyes of religion, old age is merely the realization of mortality, a quick transition to death, and an entry into a promised afterlife, it fails to provide attention to the gradual process of loss in old age nor provide consolations for those losses.

Such observations might suggest that religious beliefs do not offer a significant alternative to the classics for an understanding and consolation of the passage of time in old age. But such a hasty conclusion rests upon a false dichotomy between religion doctrines and the religious classics. Of course, many of the classics themselves are intimately associated with religious beliefs and practices. The *New and Old Testament, the Koran,* Augustine's *Confessions,* Dante's *The Divine Comedy,* Aquinas's *Summa Theologica,* Calvin's *Institutes,* are some of the works advancing religious beliefs. Other classics such as the works of Freud, *The Future of an Illusion,* Marx, *Capital,* and Nietzsche *Twilight of the Gods* articulate critiques of religion. A third category of classics, which neither promote nor attack religious beliefs, includes a myriad of other poems, histories, philosophies, novels, and social science works, in which religion remains an important topic in one way or another. For example, religion plays a role in Aristotle's *Metaphysics,* Chaucer's *Canterbury Tales,* Rabelais' *Gargantua and Pantagruel,* Descartes' *Meditations, and many other works.*

Consequently, it is not possible easily to separate the classics from religion.

This linkage between the classics and religion is not accidental, since there is a deeper link between religion, the classics and old age. *This linkage is found in the shared elegiac perception inherent in many religious beliefs, religious classics, and the experience of the passage of time in old age.* Just as old age may be characterized as a period of loss, sadness, detachment and consolation, religious beliefs, especially those of the revealed religions such as the Judaism and Christianity, also exemplify elegiac patterns which may be uncovered in the classics themselves. By exploring the treatment of the passage of time in the loss, sadness, detachment and consolation that one finds in the religious classics, we may understand better the passage of time in old age itself. Thus, despite the apparent irrelevance of religion to old age, the underlying elegy and the passage of time which characterizes old age echo within the central beliefs of the major western religions of Judaism, Christianity and the Moslem faith. These religions tell the elegiac story of loss, sometimes implicit in the concept of sin. Loss as well as a deep sadness is evoked in the story of Adam and Eve's disobedience, the trials of Job, and the crucifixion of Christ. The revealed religions seek and find a form of detachment, i.e., a transcendence through faith, prayer, ceremony and meditation. For the Christian believer, consolation is found not in old age, but in the love of his neighbor, God and the prospect of afterlife in heaven. Hence, the stories in the classic texts and works of art inspired by revealed religion echo a form of the loss, sadness, detachment, and consolation, (even though in these religions, these elegiac elements are not limited to the stage of old age).

Once the elegiac content of revealed religion is recognized, the religiously related classics—loss in Milton's *Paradise Lost* and the story of Job in the Bible; sadness in the punishment of Adam and Eve in Genesis and Unamuno's *The Tragic Sense of Life*; transcendence in the biblical accounts of Christ's ascension, Augustine's conversion and Aquinas' contemplation; and consolation in Dante's account of heaven in *The Divine Comedy*—may lead us to better understand the elements of old-age elegy. Indeed, the story of the entire Christian faith – the story of loss in sin, sadness in the face of our mortality, transcendence in faith, and consolation of the afterlife – fits old age. Despite the fact that *religion's understanding is not aimed at comprehending old age and coping with the experience of its passage of time,*, the religious classics can provide help us to explore the extent to which religion can conquer the passage of time which is part of the elegy of old age.

The Classics and the Nature of Religion

A recent comprehensive review of the idea of religion as set forth in the classics, (Sullivan, *The Idea of Religion),* reveals a minimal definition of religion covering most formulations of the nature of religion itself – "the reverence for transcendent goodness". (This definition may not be completely adequate since some philosophers, e.g. Spinoza, Bergson, and Whitehead, claim to find God to be immanent in life or the processes of nature. Nevertheless, even within these religious statements, God or, more generally, goodness is distinguishable from nature, and hence "transcends" the brute facts of nature and life. Nevertheless, to accommodate these views, one might broaden the definition to be "reverence for immanent or transcendent goodness"). According to such a definition, religious belief finds some form of goodness in the face of our awareness of a passage of time which contains the losses and consolations of old age.

The Kinds of Religion

In order to explore the relationship between religion as reverence for goodness and old age, it is necessary to make our understanding of religion more concrete by means of identifying six major kinds of religion found within the classics: ceremonial, moral, mystical, revealed, secular and immanent. (In this list, I have relived upon Sullivan, but added the immanent category, which he treats as "atypical religion"0. According to this classification, to be religious may offer prayers and sacrifices to the gods to secure their beneficial intervention in our lives, (ceremonial); do good to one's fellow man in conformity with some moral exemplar (moral); seek unification with the one true reality, (mystical); respond with faith, obedience, prayer and ceremony to the one revealed God who may offer us divine help, (revealed religion); cooperate with the realization of an ideal humanity gradually revealed in history, (secular); or appreciate a divinity found within the creative processes of life and nature, (immanent). The classics have articulated each of these views of religion in some detail, but since none specially address the unique natural losses of the aged, including the passage of time, not the need of consolation for such losses in light of these religious approaches, I shall endeavor to do so. How might these different kinds of religion find relevance in our world of old age loss?

Ceremonial

The view that religion is principally ceremonial is set forth by Plato and Cicero. In Plato's *Republic*, when Socrates wanted a serious dialogue about the nature of the republic and justice, he permitted the old man, Cephalus to leave the conversation in order to make his sacrifices to the gods, (presumably thanking them for his "successful" life). The ancient Greeks and Romans were great believers in ceremonial religion. The implication is that old age is a time for attending the ceremonies of religion, not philosophical dialogue. The Platonic treatment of Cephalus mirrors the contemporary attitudes and practices of many toward religion. Surveys of religious practices in the United States suggest, not surprisingly, that the old rather than the young are likely to claim that religious ceremony is important to them. In my trips to the European cathedrals, I found only old people, mainly women, sitting and praying in the pews. Perhaps the presence of the old in churches is simply an indication of a declining social practice, rather than old age and religious ceremony are indissolubly linked. The purpose of a ceremonial religion was to secure beneficial interventions of the gods in our lives. Given the losses in old age, it may not be surprising that many would seek the help of the gods in coping with such losses.

Since Cicero writes explicitly about old age and religious beliefs, how might he view how religion might cope with the passage of time in old age? At one level, as set forth in his essay on old age, the losses of old age with the passage of time, for Cicero, is, filled with non-religious activities which are suited to the time of life of the old. Thus, political consultation, active exercise, temperance, moderate enjoyment of selected sensual pleasures, farming, friendships and teaching are among the activities Cicero recommends. All of these are adjusted to the natural time of life, in effect "conforming to nature". The anticipation of death apparently does not bother Cicero, although he metaphorically "extends his life" through his anticipation of the personal glories and immortality in another world. This somewhat common sense and conventional approach based upon a tentative belief in the pagan gods of the state, as well as belief in their intervention into this world, partly at behest of the prayers of humans.

Moral Religion

The moral view of religion is offered by Rousseau and Kant who sought in religion a moral exemplar, either real (Rousseau) or ideal (Kant). The notion might be that if one could identify and define such an exemplar, one might pattern one's moral life after him (her) (it). For example, Kant appeals to "holiness, mercy and justice" as the qualities of his moral exemplar, but he does not commit to the exemplar's existence. At the very least, despite its admitted vagueness, such a religious view would urge the aged to find appropriate moral exemplars to help them respond to their aged losses in a morally satisfactory way. In a sense, these exemplars are timeless, guiding our transitory old age lives.

Revealed Religion

We are most familiar with revealed religion of the major religious beliefs: Christianity, Judaism and the Moslem faith. Revealed religion is set forth in many western classics including Augustine's many works, Aquinas's *Summa Theologica,* Dante's *The Divine Comedy* and Milton's *Paradise Lost and Regained.* Revealed religions, although including appeals to moral exemplars and engaging in ceremonial practices is primarily unique in its belied in a God who reveals himself to us and intervenes in this world.

As suggested above, there is the paradox: even if old people are more likely to take religion seriously, that fact doesn't mean that religion takes old age seriously. Not at all! For Western religious beliefs, old age is merely a transition time to another life. Western revealed religion, whether Christian, Jewish, or Muslim, is, after all, reverence for some form of transcendent goodness. It is this transcendent goodness which makes possible another life in an eternal time which dwarfs in importance the passing moments of old age, that is, "elder time," the period at the end of our natural lives.

This religious "back of the hand" to old age is confirmed by the fact that little attention is paid to old age in the Bible. Even if some of its main figures, like Job and Moses, become old in the biblical stories, their old age is not a central concern. The central stories of the creation—Adam and Eve in the Garden of Eden, the flood, the story of Job, Moses and the commandments, the exodus of the Jews to the "promised land," and the birth, life, and death of Jesus—contain little serious mention of old age, and when old age is mentioned, it is not in a complementary way. Let's face it—Jesus died young.

Another sign of the insignificance of old age for religious belief lies in Catholic practices, in which there are no significant sacraments attached to old age. Sacraments are attached to birth, puberty and youth, marriage, entry into religious orders, penance, and extreme unction at the time of death. The period between marriage and death is not accorded any sacrament. There is no gold watch in Catholic belief. According to Aquinas, the sacraments were designed to perfect man in relation to God and to cure his defects, either in this world or in preparation for the next. Religion identifies defects as "sins" which are spiritual shortcomings to be cured by penance, not the irrevocable losses of old age requiring solace in this lifetime. In short, religious practices have little to do with old age as such. Old age is largely invisible to the dominant religious beliefs of the West.

In the case of revealed religion, it is true that, from time to time, old age is recognized as a unique stage of life. In the words of the Old Testament, "…a time to be born and a time to die…." It is also true that religious belief addresses many key problems faced by the elderly—loss, suffering, death, the hope for an eternal legacy. But even when religion identifies some of these problems found among the aging, religion does not address them *as the unique losses of old age to be experienced and consoled within old age.* For religion, the focus is on suffering and death, whether taking place in old age or not, and hence old age, *as such*, is not particularly important to the religious believer. Nevertheless, the importance of love of and for God and charity towards one's neighbors espoused within the Christian faith suggests one important response to the old age losses of others. Equally important, the very activity of love and the objects of love carry with them an implication of eternity.

There is a good reason why religion has little to do with finding one's way of life in old age. This reason is found in Thomas Aquinas's *Summa Theologica*—a central statement of theology for the Catholic Church. The end of man for Aquinas is happiness, and although *imperfect* happiness can be found in this world, *perfect* happiness is to be found in God in the next world. That happiness is perfect in part because it is secured in eternity through faith in God's incarnation on this earth through Jesus Christ and his sacrifice for our sins, (including the original sin of Adam and Eve), in this world. In contrast to this eternal happiness, the temporal happiness which takes place during our lives in this world and includes the happiness to be sought during old age, is imperfect in every way. Thus, for revealed religions, the gap between eternity and the "elder time" of this world appears unbridgeable. Becoming aware of the very notion of eternity in religion highlights the fact that when, as in this book, we attend the transient losses within old age, we accept the importance of time in this world, seeking eternity only in eternal ideas.

Secular Religion

If revealed religion does not accord old age special attention, does a secular religion which projects an idealized humanity as an end of the progress of history? August Comte, Feuerbach and, more recently, John Dewey set forth such a secular religious perspective. The objective of such a religion is a form of idealized humanity to be realized eventually through the progress of history. It is true that belief in such a secular progress may inform belief in the extension of life or the hope in a gradual mitigation of old age biological decline though scientific progress, (both are discussed in the next chapter). On the other hand, an important old age loss – the loss of belief in progress - conflicts head-on with this secular religious perspective of a historical movement toward an idealized humanity. (This old age abandonment of belief in progress is discussed in Chapter 19 below). Since old age loss is the abandonment of belief in historical progress, the central belief of secular religion is not appropriate to old age.

Despite my rejection of the core belief in the secular religion of progress, I do not reject a secularized understanding of old age itself. As I shall argue in the chapters that follow, understanding and valuing old age are essentially based upon the secular understanding of the transiency of perceptible things against a background of eternal ideas. I shall suggest that our old-age experiences within the flux of time acquire their meaning within the secular an awareness and understanding of eternal ideas. If there is one canonical author who best grasped the value of our transient lives, it is Shakespeare in his sonnets. The proof is in Sonnet 73:

> That time of year thou mayst in me behold
> When yellow leaves, or none, or few, do hang
> Upon those boughs which shake against the cold,
> Bare ruined choirs, where late the sweet birds sang.
> In me, thou see'st the twilight of such day
> As after sunset fadeth in the west;
> Which by and by black night doth take away,
> Death's second self that seals up all in rest.
> In me thou see'st the glowing of such fire,
> That on the ashes of his youth doth lie,
> As the death-bed whereon it must expire,
> Consumed with that which it was nourished by.
> This thou perceiv'st, which makes thy love more strong,
> To love that well, which thou must leave ere long.

Here there is the nostalgia of age: the facing of death, memory of the last stirrings of a consuming passion of the past, and the eternal idea of a final love before goodbyes.

Mystical Religion

Mystical religion involves an inner quest for an ineffable unity with a deeper reality beyond the transitory nature of our everyday lives. . The classic authors who appeal to such a mystery- Plotinus, (*Enneads*) and Gabriel Marcel, (*The Mystery of Being*) do not single out old age for special attention, but another "author" of mystic religion, Sankara (*Vedanta*), adopts the Hindi view of the cycle of time and the stages of life, and old age is the fourth stage (ashrama) which is an ascetic non-materialistic wandering stage of life, prefacing death and a new cycle of life. However, the transitory time of old age is merely part of a larger unity of the cycles of life and death, without any special meaning which I seek to uncover in this book.

Immanent Religion

Immanent religion finds God, not simply as transcendent, but as immanent in the otherwise secular workings of life, nature and reality. Henri Bergson, (*The Two Sources of Morality and Religion,* Pierre Teilhard de Chardin, Alfred North Whitehead, (*Religion in the Making*) and Benedict de Spinoza, (*Ethics*) exemplify such an approach. All of these immanent religions, in different ways, find the eternal *within* the natural processes rather than beyond them. Thus, for example, Alfred North Whitehead find "eternal objects" which make their way ("ingress") into never beginning and never-ending process of nature.

In so far as old age is a distinct part of the processes of nature and life, it may be possible for these immanent religions to view it within a religious framework. Thus, for example, Bergson finds the origin of religion, in a consciousness of death, frustrating the impetus of nature, leading one to adopt a belief in life after death. He might have added (but did not) that such consciousness is likely to arise most often in old age. Whitehead may view old age as part of the deterioration that takes place in the process of nature and, perhaps, the loss of possibilities which remain within God, since God, for Whitehead, is the repository of all the possibilities which the natural process may or may not realize. As In an old age poem I have cited elsewhere, "…it is the loss of possibility which claims you bit by bit…" Such a poetic line, in expressing the sadness of old age, also reflects a metaphysical truth with which Whitehead would agree.

Old Age Elegy and the Religious Classics.

Despite the fact that religious belief does not treat old age seriously and although the canon contains numerous so-called "anti-religious" works, religion offers a kind of elegy of loss, sadness, detachment, and solace for its believers and this religious elegy may be helpful in our approach to old age. We may regard the religious elegy as an echo (or a model) of the central secular elegiac experience of old age. As a consequence, we may be able to learn about the central elegiac elements of old age from reflections upon the elegy of religious classics. To search for the meaning of this religious elegy, we must turn to the religious works in the classical canon. Some of these works reveal a reverence for some form of transcendent good. Thus, there are the basic texts, the Bible and Koran, and theological classics, such as those of St. Augustine, St. Thomas Aquinas, Calvin, Luther, Pascal, and Barth. There are the philosophical works of Plato, Plotinus, and Kant, which ultimately appeal to transcendent entities. Other philosophical authors find "transcendence" operating within the workings of the world itself—Spinoza and Whitehead in the West and the Chinese classics, such as the *I Ching*, the *Tung Chung-shu*, and the *Lotus Sutra* of the East.

The canon, however, is not merely a set of books for a course in theology and philosophy. In some great poetry—Homer, Dante, Milton, Blake—religious belief is central. The power of religious retribution in Dante's hell or the immense attraction of the love of God in his heaven exemplify the importance of religious belief in some canon works. Similarly, in novels, religious beliefs may play an important role, as in the writings of Cervantes, Goethe, and Joyce. In poems and plays from the Greeks to Ibsen, religion plays an important if somewhat terrifying role. In sum, the canon supplies an immense reservoir for understanding religious elegy and its applicability to old age. To gain such an understanding, we must turn to the more specific elements of elegy.

The Anti-Religion Classics

Even if religion can, in some way, introduce an eternal element into the transitory losses of old age, anyone who is committed to the classics must not base her conclusion upon simply a selection of religious classics. When one looks to the classics for consolation in old age, a second paradox emerges as we explore old age and religion through the tradition of a wider selection of the canon works. This paradox results from a finding that there are many classic works which regard religious belief with skepticism or downright animosity. The ancient nihilism of Lucretius, the early modern skepticism of Montaigne and Hume, the historical criticism of Christianity by Gibbon, the animosity of Nietzsche toward Christianity, Freud and Marx's reduction of religion to "an illusion" or "an opiate of the people", and the rejection of Ireland's Catholicism in Joyce's *A Portrait of the Artist as a Young Man* are but a few of the denigrating views of religion found in the major works of Western civilization.

In addition to such anti-religious works, there is a rich tradition of scientific works, some of which have given rise to a scientific positivism which implicitly appears to deny the importance of religion or, at least, any role of knowledge in religious reasoning. These anti-religious and scientific works require any thinking person, at any age, and especially a thinking old person, to confront the challenges they pose for adherence to the kinds of religions. These challenges extend beyond the debunking of miracles or claimed historical facts pertaining to religious figures. Even if one does not embrace the alleged anti-religious implications of modern science, one must recognize, along with Gibbon, Marx and Freud, the vicious role and modern cruelties perpetuated by institutional religions in the course of history. Along with Freud, Marx, and Max Weber, we cannot help but note the apparent social, economic, and psychological sources and functions of some religious faiths – sources and functions which, when recognized, can lead to the questioning of religious beliefs.

Let's tale Freud's *Future of an Illusion* as an example. Freud suggests that religious beliefs arise in response to the need for consolations in the face of uncontrolled and uncontrollable risks posed both by nature and other humans. However, according to d Freud, the truths of these religious beliefs are not established either by blind faith nor sophisticated philosophy. In short, these beliefs are illusions. Nevertheless, they are adhered to because they fulfill "the oldest, strongest and most urgent wishes of mankind" Freud asserts:

> …the benevolent rule of a divine Providence allays our
> fear of the dangers of life; the establishment of a moral
> world- order ensures the fulfillment of the demands of
> justice, which have so often remained unfulfilled in human
> civilization; and the prolongation of earthly existence in
> a future life provides the local and temporal framework
> in in which these wish-fulfillments shall take place….

Freud notes what he believes to be the modern loss of these "illusions" and, despite recognizing that they reflect a history of deep repression which, if removed, might result in lack of human controls over irrational behavior, he urges their abandonment, as science gradually takes hold in modern society. Whether one sides with some form of religious faith or with Freud's faith in science, both Freud and the religious beliefs described in this chapter, share a pattern of elegiac thought in which losses are felt, detachment, whether through science or religious faith, follows and some form of consolation is hopefully achieved. A similar pattern of elegiac thought is found in Marxist beliefs. The lesson learned from both the religious and anti-religious classics is that they share a common elegiac perspective – one which is uniquely applicable to old age.

Learning from the Religious Elements of Elegy

1. Loss

Like the elegy of old age, the experience of loss permeates religious thought—Adam and Eve's being forced to leave the Garden of Eden, the losses of the Jews in Egypt, the disaster of the Flood, the catastrophes striking Job, and the death of Christ are but a few such instances. Of course, the meaning of these "losses," just like the losses in old age, remain to be found and explained. Two different views of these losses are set forth in Milton's *Paradise Lost* and the story of Job. In the words of Milton:

> Of Man's First Disobedience and the Fruit
> Of that Forbidden Tree, whose mortal taste
> Brought Death into the World, and all our woe,
> With the loss of *Eden,* till one greater Man
> Restore us and regain the blissful Seat.

The ultimate loss in the Christian religion was Adam and Eve's expulsion from the Garden of Eden—a loss which was the product of disobedience and a prideful desire for knowledge of good and evil. The punishments for this original sin are visited upon everyone through time and include man's mortality, woman's pain in childbirth, the loss of innocence, and the need to labor. In a religious version of detachment, All of the old-age losses I have identified can be linked to the punishment of Adam and Eve and hence these losses are part of divine justice for human disobedience. Perhaps there is some satisfaction in believing that the old-age losses we encounter are the result of our own doing, and that all of us are subject to these punishments. In a sense, from this point of view, the losses are deserved.

I prefer a different biblical account of human loss in the story of Job. Satan and God propose to test Job to determine whether he is faithful simply as the product of his affluence or, in God's words, "a righteous man.". Job loses everything—his wealth, his children, his status, and his reputation. His old friends tell him that he must have sinned, but he remonstrates with God, claiming that the misfortunes seem unfair. A young friend suggests that he concentrate upon the undoubted beneficence of God, rather than accusing God of injustice. God finally talks to Job, telling him of his great powers, and asks,

> Where were you when I laid down the foundations of the earth . . . who laid its cornerstone, when the morning stars sang together and all the sons of God shouted for joy? Or who shut in the sea with doors, when it burst forth from the womb; when I made the clouds its garment and thick darkness its swaddling band . . .Have you commanded the morning since your days began and caused the dawn to know its place that it may take hold of the skirts of the earth . . .

God's answer seems to be that the losses Job suffers are not the product of his sin, but are the fateful result of irremediable contingencies created in the workings of a magnificent universe created by God. According to this view, our old-age losses are simply the result of the necessity and contingency of nature and fate—not the punishment for our sins. In this view, unlike in the story of Adam and Eve, old-age losses are not subject to cosmic justice—these losses, to a lesser or greater degree, mark the limits of human control and perhaps also God's control of a contingent universe.

2. The Sadness of Loss

In a previous chapter, I discussed the sadness consequent to old-age loss and identified St. Thomas Aquinas, among others, as offering a deep discussion of sorrow. Religious beliefs, however, identify despair as the most central form of religious sorrow. For Aquinas, such despair is the ceasing to hope for a share in God's goodness. It may be based upon a failure "of appetite" or of belief, or both, and is closely related to sloth (acedia), a spiritual weariness. A second religious account of sadness is offered by Miguel de Unamuno in his *The Tragic Sense of Life*. For Unamuno, our sadness or tragic sense derives from our mortality and the consequent realization that we cannot achieve all the desires in our lives. Such sadness rests not in the loss of God, but in the recognition of our own human limitations.

Such religious accounts hold lessons for a secular understanding of old-age sadness. Like Aquinas, we moderns recognize that despair is only one dimension of sorrow, not to be confused with the sorrows we experience at the loss of human goods—our health, our past, our work, and our future. Second, like Aquinas's account of despair, we recognize that some old-age sadness may border on despair in that it signals the loss of hope. In the poet Kelly Cherry's words, old age is "the loss of possibility." But for moderns, as for Unamuno, the sadness lies in the recognition of human limitations, not the loss of God. The modern psychologist Erik Erikson captured this notion of old-age sadness in his modern notion of its "despair," which "expresses the feeling that the time is now short, too short for the attempt to start another life and to try out alternative roads." In sum, the religious classics, or at least some of them clarify the meaning and possible source of sadness, sorrow and despair.

3. Transcendence

Most religions appeal to an ultimate and transcendent good. Such a good presents itself through some form of revelation and is deemed to constitute a reality present beyond the ordinary transient experience of mankind. In the Western faiths, transcendence is implicit in the acceptance of a variety of more specific religious beliefs, including the immortality of the soul, the sacredness of the universe, the possibility of impersonal perfection, the notions of a supreme being, and the claim that religious texts are, in some sense, the word of God; in Eastern faiths, the notions of nothingness and nirvana may offer similar ultimate realities. The Western religious faiths seek to document transcendence through stories, such as the appearance of God to Moses and the ascension of Christ after his crucifixion. In several of the Western faiths, the principal means for access to transcendence is faith. In one of many definitions of faith, it is "a habit of the mind whereby eternal life is begun in us, making the intellect assent to what is non-apparent." In some of the Eastern beliefs, a specific kind of meditation may be the means to transcendence, hence the term "transcendental meditation."

Secular detachment from the losses and sadness in old age parallels the fundamental truth of transcendence claimed by religion—that the mind may grant intellectual assent to eternal life within us. However, for the secular detachment, the eternal life is found within those universal ideas to which we have access through processes of abstraction through consultation with the canon and other works. What the canon works contain are *ideas*—universal conceptions through and about which we think, know, feel, and act. The ideas in the Western canon include good and evil, change, chance, being, infinity, soul, and many others which may or may not have religious significance. In addition to the specifically religious ideas such as God, holiness, reverence, transcendence, ultimacy, faith, love, finitude, hope, suffering, eternity, immortality, and religion itself, many other ideas, less associated with religion eternal in their own way, may be found in the canon; ideas such as animal, astronomy, constitution, democracy, evolution, labor, logic, medicine, oligarchy, reasoning, and so forth.

In addition to these Western ideas, a scholar of the Eastern tradition, Theodore de Bary, has suggested that Eastern thought offers a number of different important ideas which are difficult to classify as either religious or not, including emptiness, sacrifice, sage, heart, mysticism, and enlightenment. These Western and Eastern ideas bridge the gap between religious and secular thought and hence are starting places for both understanding the canon and finding the eternal dimensions in the interpretation of old age in light of the canon.

In both Eastern and Western traditions, many somewhat different meanings are given to ideas over time, (although a common threat is maintained). These meanings are found in texts at different stages of history; the meanings are the products of the different historical contexts in which they appear. Each idea also has a complex internal architecture. Moreover, many ideas are tacitly contested by other ideas within the canon; for example, the ideas of aristocracy, democracy, tyranny, and oligarchy don't sit well together within the different political theories presented in the canon.

Equally important, throughout of the history of thought, various definitions have been given to the very notion of "idea" itself. Thus, ideas have been seen as eternal forms, conceptions by which the mind thinks or knows, pure concepts, or even the unity of existent qualities. I do not propose to engage in an elaborate inquiry into which of these views of ideas is correct. Nevertheless, despite their different meanings and their internal and external complexity and conflict, all of these ideas offer permanent markers - "topics" or "places" which stand within the history of canonical texts and which have persisted in some sense throughout the history of these texts. This permanence has led some ancient thinkers (Plato) and modern ones (Whitehead) to find in ideas not only universal meaning, but also eternal content. Al though enmeshed in the reasoning of specific philosophies, the plots and characters in specific novels and poems, the theories and observations within specific scientific reports, and at certain times within the movements of history and everyday life, the meanings of these ideas can be reached through abstraction. Thus, such ideas can be drawn from the discussion of old age, the science of aging, the history of old age, and the everyday experience of age. These ideas, after abstraction, give meaning to the transient losses of old age or the accounts of such transient losses and the emotions they produce.

How then can these universal and permanent ideas help us to understand the particular transience of our own old age? The modern philosopher and mathematician Alfred North Whitehead sought to explore precisely this question in his great works: *Science in the Modern World*, *Religion in the Making*, *Process and Reality*, and *Adventures in Ideas*. He has traced the universal ideas of science, education, religion, and others to help us understand the workings of these ideas in history and nature. Let me summarize briefly one of Whitehead's works.

In *Religion in the Making*, Whitehead traces the moving history of the idea of religion as a transcendent important activity capable of transforming our lives. He finds its' transformation through ceremonial, mythical, and sociable phases of its history until in modern times it becomes rationalized in either the Asiatic concept of an impersonal order, the Semitic concept of a personal God, or the pantheistic belief of the identity of God and the world. For Whitehead, a modern religion must be founded upon metaphysics defined as "the general ideas that are indispensably relevant to everything that happens" in the world. This world has a character of temporal passage to novelty. It is made up of "actual occasions" which exemplify the realm of ideal entities or forms. These actual occasions and ideal forms are part of the order of nature, and, in Whitehead's suggestive works, these ideas "ingress" into the actual occasions of change. He writes,

> the order of the world, the depth of reality of the world, the value of the world in its whole and in its parts, the beauty of the world, the zest of life, the peace of life, and the mastery of evil are all bound together— not accidentally, but by reason of this truth: that the universe exhibits a creativity with infinite freedom and a realm of forms with infinite possibilities; but that this creativity and these forms are together impotent to achieve actuality apart from the completed ideal harmony which is God.

How might Whitehead's discussion of ideas apply to our understanding of old age? As aging human beings, we are part of the flux of nature. When we think about our old age, we necessarily bring into the equation a whole host of ideas, including time, change, animal, human, life, and soul. These ideas, when initially abstracted from particular experience, can achieve universal eternal meanings which, at the same time, may change in their applications and consequent meanings as they are "applied" in our knowledge during the course of history. I understand my aging only by employing the ideas of self, time, and change which I find to be implicit in the process of aging. The idea of time itself is found within the notion of change which takes place in or through aging. This change may be the impermanence of time in the body, possibly in contrast to the permanence of a self, (or soul or mind).

For Whitehead, these ideas of time and change are "eternal objects" (his words) which enter into ("ingress") the flux of time to become part of the momentary experience which make up our lives and we may, in turn abstract them from that experience. Thus, some poets talk about ageless beauty, some theologians about an ageless God; philosophers talk about ageless truths; they recognize a dimension of eternity in the ideas of beauty, God, and truth. Others, like Shakespeare, as evidenced in the sonnet above, recognize beauty in change itself. Change becomes an eternal idea in Shakespeare's sonnet.

Whitehead's insight into the ways in which ideas enter into the flux of time provides a way in which we can draw upon the canon of classics to understand old age. For example, consulting the notions of soul from the religious texts helps us moderns to understand the change in the process of aging measured against the background of a "permanent self." Even the notion of religion itself, if taken from the canon to be a reverence for the eternally transcendent, may enter into and become part of our passing lives if we entertain the ideas of "reverence" and "eternal" as eternal ideas, momentarily "ingressing" in our lives and understanding.

At the end of his essays and his life, Montaigne captured this sense of the "eternal now" in the immediate experiences of life:

> When I dance, I dance; when I sleep, I sleep; yes, and when I walk alone in the beautiful orchard, if my thoughts have been dwelling on extraneous incidents for some part of the time, for some other part, I bring them back to the walk, to the orchard, to the sweetness of this solitude and to me. . . . We are great fools. "He has spent his life in idleness," we say; "I have done nothing today." What,,have you not lived?

Thus, Montaigne captures the transience of our lives which may be abstracted and measured in the "eternal now" of the very idea of transition, as exemplified in Montaigne's appeal to life ("have you not lived?") which includes "dance," "sleep," and "solitude."

4. Consolation

Religions are a means of consolation. Western religions find such consolation in the afterlife, the prospect of which, in one way or another, consoles us as we face the losses of this life. The Catholic faith offers the vision of an afterlife of heaven, hell, and purgatory, which rewards us for our virtuous acts, punishes us for our major sins, and helps us make up for those minor transgressions during our life.

Dante, writing at the climax of medieval thought, offers us an incredible and moving portrait of the afterlife in his *The Divine Comedy*. As Virgil escorts Dante through hell and purgatory, he gives him a vision designed to guide him from error and expiate his sins. The vision of hell in the *Inferno* portrays eternal punishments fiendishly designed to precisely fit the sin of the person in question. Thus, the souls of the sellers of ecclesiastic favor who made fun of the baptismal founts were turned upside down in the equivalents of the founts and, rather than submerged in water, their feet were burned. In the *Purgatorio*, Dante captures the long and difficult journey required by even minor sinners, who must exercise their free will to expiate their crimes. In the *Paradiso*, Beatrice leads Dante to a place among the moon and stars where the love for God and God's love will envelop all.

Even if we moderns abandon the detailed Catholic faith that inspired Dante's *Divine Comedy*, we are nevertheless left with principles which can animate our own lives. Dante was in middle age when escorted by Virgil, and hence his journey allowed him time to mend his way of life. Speaking broadly, the three regions of Dante's afterworld are governed by three eternal principles. The principle which animates the *Inferno* is retributive justice—that kind of justice which we are thought to deserve for our major evil actions. The principle animating purgatory is the need for renunciation of our sins and self-improvement through the slow removal of the sinful aspects of our selves. The ideal animating heaven is the love of God and man, an awareness of God's love of us and the hope that we may be deserving such love. All these principles and ideals can help to guide some elderly lives, providing consolation in the thought that if we follow them, our lives will be better.

However, old age and its losses pose special problems for such a vision. In old age, most of our life is behind us and hence we have little opportunity left for just actions. The elderly are seldom motivated to undertake grand projects for self-improvement and, upon reflecting on their lives, may be pessimistic about the success of such projects. Whether we love God and deserve his love is probably already determined by the amount of faith we have found in the course of our lives. These problems inherent in old-age loss suggest the need to find other consolations in old age. I shall discuss such consolations in later chapters.

Conclusion

In this chapter, I suggest that religion is not seriously concerned with old age since, at least in most religions, old age is regarded as merely a temporary period preceding our entry into eternity. The prospect of such an eternal afterlife dwarfs the importance of seeking the understanding and appreciation of old age. At the same time, one cannot deny that many of the classics, which I have suggested hold the key to an understanding and consolation of old age, are animated by religious belief and many contain extensive discussions of religious subject matters. Since I have proposed to deal with the canon works as they shed light upon the elegy of old age and its losses, and since the canon contains many works which attack religious belief as well as many that embrace religion, I must identify how religious and ani-religious works might contribute to an understanding of old age. I suggest that at least some religious and anti-religious classics embrace an elegiac vision which includes a variety of eternal and universal ideas through which we can gain both a secular understanding of the old age. In the chapters which follow, I shall discuss those classics and their ideas as they supply that understanding and consolation of specific losses in old age.

CHAPTER VI

The Dream of the Fountain of Youth

"I accept my three score and ten years. If they are filled
with usefulness, with mercy, with goodwill: if they are
the lifetime of a soul which never loses its honour and
a brain that never loses its eagerness, they are enough
for me, because these things are infinite and eternal... "
George Bernard Shaw, "Back to Methusala"

*Now I am 88 years old. I keep myself going with a variety of medicines for
high blood pressure, elevated cholesterol, and a growing prostate. The knee
pains are growing more serious, but don't prevent walking but they prevent
running and tennis- two of my favorite sports. My late wife before here recent
death, had two artificial hips and two mechanical knees — replacements
of her aging joints, which has left her with problems of balance. She has
recently had a bout with cancer from which she has fully recovered. A series
of minor strokes led to the big one. Despite all of this medical help- the
result of modern technology, for which I am profoundly grateful, I remain
ambivalent about our society's new medical efforts to extend life beyond
its "normal limit", (whatever that is!), but I do fully support science and
its efforts to maintain our quality of life within that "normal limit" of an
acceptable old age. One of the tasks of old age is to define one's life, not in
terms of its number of years but in terms of its biography – its beginning,*

middle and end - as a work to be proud or ashamed of or at least to be aware of.

Introduction

Modern science and its hand maiden, medical technology, are devoted to the cause of extending life, perhaps at all costs. Our modern society's quest for bodily immortality is symbolized in the story of Spanish explorer, Ponce De Leon, who, allegedly sought the Fountain of Youth and allegedly found it in St Augustine, Florida — now one of the centers of the aging population of America. In St. Augustine, there is a tourist attraction — the Fountain of Youth - memorializing Ponce De Leon's search. (There is irony in the fact that the St. Augustine's municipal authorities advise tourists not to drink the water. Perhaps there is a lesson there).

The Fountain of Youth story has a long and venerable history, beginning with ancient myths. One of the earliest versions is the story told by the Greek historian, Herodotus, in his delightful *Histories.* According to Herodotus, spies of Persia went to Egypt and found there a spring with water the scent of violets. They came away believing that when bathers washed in the fountain, they achieved a life of 120 years. Ironically, Herodotus ignored the climate and fish eating habits of these early Ethiopians. Now, the life expectancy of Ethiopians is low by modern standards – perhaps the result of periodic famines and the impure water which no longer smells like violets.

The modern American version of the Fountain of Youth story is a different story. In this story, there is the dramatic mission of the Spanish explorer, Ponce De Leon, who searches and discovers a magic fountain which will yield perennial life. The quest for such a fountain captures our imagination and fuels an overweening pride — a pride fed by the successes of scientific technology. That scientific search for immortality began in early Enlightenment, when we began to treat our body as our "self", giving up a philosophical or religious belief in the soul. Equipped with science, technology and a body, some of us are prepared to deny what Jung calls "the arc of life", with its beginning, middle, and end, and are ready to embrace the effort to extend life indefinitely. (I am not one of them!) Thus, the modern obsession of extending human life is the product, at least in part, of a millennial decline in the belief of the soul and growing confusion about the nature of the self.

(Below, I shall identify another kind of medicine – one originating in ancient history, lost over the centuries, but recently rediscovered. This other kind of medicine accepts the normal span of life and seeks to assist its healthful functioning. But I am getting ahead of my story).

The problem of seeking the Fountain of Youth is not limited to its subtle erroneous assumptions such as replacing the body for the self. The Fountain of Youth story illustrates a more fundamental obstacle to thinking seriously about old age and death. *By focusing upon the prolongation of life, belief in the Fountain of Youth and its modern equivalents rest upon the denial of the distinct form of a complete life.* Such a life is understood not by an experimental and mechanical biology, but by both a unique biology and a biographical literature, psychology and history.

If life has a beginning, middle and end, the meaning of life's end is two- fold: a purpose and completion. The purpose of an entire life underlies the activities in which we engage, even if we are unaware of such a purpose underlying those activities. In fact, we may only discover that purpose through reflection late in life or it may only be discovered by others long after we live. For most, such a purpose of life is hopefully supported by a healthful functioning throughout our life span; its completion is found in its biological and biographical old age and death which is part of its narrative. *Old age and death end our lives and complete their meaning.* The meaning of this life is found through the interpretation of a reflective biography of our entire life. The disciplines of biology, literature, psychology, psychoanalysis, and philosophy help in the task of interpretation. Those who focus upon the Fountain of Youth to extend their lives fail to properly view them through this range of humanistic disciplines which make up biography.

The modern effort to extend bodily life is based upon a third erroneous assumption. In addition to mistaking body for soul or self, and failing to view life through the disciplines of biography, a third defect in the Fountain of Youth mentality is that it is narcissistic, focusing only upon the individual self. In fact, our individual lives can only be fully understood by the modern disciplines of ecology and history. *Ecology and history enable us to see ourselves as part of a larger whole – either nature or human history.* Ecology sees our lives as a discrete part of an entire system of nature and its functions. Those committed to prolongation of an individual life simply view old age and death as setting the physical limits of an animal's life; they fail to see life (including our own), within the cycles of the whole of nature. Darwin saw life and death as part of the necessary processes of nature. Modern ecology has expanded his insights, enabling us to see ourselves as parts of the cycles of animate and inanimate nature. Our bodies are cycled through nature serving succeeding forms of life. This cycle of life is also part of a larger course of human history. When we view our lives as part of history, we can benefit from the kind of biography which sees an entire individual life as part of a more comprehensive history of a family, a community, or some chosen discipline. Plutarch's *Lives,* St. Augustine's *Confessions*, and Thomas Mann's *Buddenbrooks* exemplify such stories of complete lives as parts of social and political history, religious faith, and family lineage. By contrast, those who seek to promote the extension of life, whether through scientific experimentation, cosmetic surgery, the replacement of body parts, steroids, or growth hormones abandon the interpretive understanding of completed lives as part of nature and history. They *replace a narrative of the arc of life with some pallid vision of perpetual youth. In doing so, their attention is diverted from careful recollection, reflection and meditation of the quality of our lives in old age —including its old age losses and consolations.*

Fortunately, some of the earlier central texts of western civilization anticipated and rejected modern appeals to perpetual life and early experimental medicine. Aristotle, Galen, Bergson, and their modern counterparts suggest a biological alternative to an experimental medicine devoted to life extension. Thomas Aquinas anticipates and critiques the modern narcissism underlying life extension projects. Malthus and

Darwin see our lives in the broader context of nature and society which set limits on life as part of the process of nature and history.

The great biographers of all ages offer the narratives of completed lives.

Not only do the great works of history celebrate the discrete limits of life. They also suggest the dangers of extending such life. Medieval philosophers and modern dramatists suggest that prolongation of life might promise an eternity of boredom of acedia, a mixture of boredom, melancholy and alienation from God. Whether one turns to Chekov's plays with their accounts of the long boring days in the Russian countryside, or to the delightful insights of George Bernard Shaw picturing Adam's dread of the prospect of eternal bliss in the Garden of Eden in *Back to Methuselah,* or to Balzac's sad description of *The Centenarian,* literary cautionary flags are waved to warn those who believe that life's prolongation is a blessing.

The Embrace of Mechanical Medicine

One kind of medicine – experimental medicine – which draws upon a physiological understanding of the body and its genetic structure - offers us help to find out why our bodies stop living and devise how they might keep on living. The roots of this modern scientific effort of experimental medicine to prolong life lie in the Enlightenment period of our western civilization. To understand the contributions of the Enlightenment, it is useful to look at the early Enlightenment figure, Francis Bacon, lawyer, judge, and an important early proponent of the scientific method. This sixteenth century philosopher carefully cataloged the factors contributing to long life in his *Natural History of Life and Death.* He applied his "scientific method" even to the prolongation of life by engaging in various experiments to extend life. Ironically he died after catching cold in an experiment seeking to freeze a chicken in order to extend its life. If he and his chicken did not live on, his philosophy did, and that philosophy when combined with the subsequent history of medicine dictates how many moderns approach the problem of old age and death through scientific medical experimentation.

Bacon believed traditional learning unduly emphasized a focus upon words, studied trivial subjects, and practiced deception when it claimed that knowledge was animated by a reverence for the past studies of men! In *Novum Organum,* he describes "the idols of the mind" — idols of the tribe, the den, the market and the theatre. These are the influence of custom and popular opinion,(tribe), individual bias,(den), distortions of language, (market) and systems of philosophy, (theatre). (Bacon would have very little sympathy for this book which seeks to explore the traditional ideas found in the western canon to understand old age, although, to be fair, he did suggest other arts, including a "method of tradition" which would seek to recreate an account of the inquiries followed by earlier thinkers) .

Bacon's vision was later taken up by Rene Descartes, who applied his "method of understanding", among other things, to the analysis of organic matter. Relying upon his own anatomical dissection, (as well as having read the work of Harvey), Descartes describes the mechanical operation of the heart. His vision of the warm body as mechanically heated is beautifully captured in his remark that God "...kindled one of these fires without light [the soul] which I did not conceive as in any way different from that which makes hay heat when shut up before it is dry..."

Thus, for Bacon and Descartes, the essential kind of knowing is an early form of scientific experimentation. Knowledge was the power through empirical experiment to control nature. In many of his writings, he outlined how such experimentation might take place. *It is this concept of scientific experimentation which underlies the modern search for bodily immortality.* After Bacon's work, the extension of life became a goal of a new medicine which employed the scientific method. This new approach to medicine is best illustrated by the work of Claude Bernard. In his nineteenth century *"An Introduction to the Study of Experimental Medicine,* Bernard urged that such an "experimental medicine" could separate clinical medicine,(the observational treatment of patients), from the physiological study of the physics and chemistry of, (in his words), *"the functioning living machine."* The modern laboratory biologists and chemists who are seeking to manipulate cells in an effort to find the key to aging are following in the tradition of Bernard's experimental medicine. Thus, Bernard conjoined scientific experimentation and a mechanical view of the body in the discipline of experimental medicine.

Since the work of Bernard, modern experimental biology and medicine has proceeded to find at least some of the possible causes of aging at the cellular level. It has suggested that the bombardment of free radicals, the built-in limitations of cell division, the accumulation of cell waste, and the loss of functional cells may all contribute to the aging process. In consequence of these discoveries, techniques for lengthening life — calorie restriction and selection of foods, exercise and rest, avoidance of environmental toxins, and the taking relevant vitamins, especially antioxidants are now understood in terms of their possible impact upon preserving cellular health. More radical interventions such as organ repair and replacement to extend life beyond its normal span may soon follow from this deeper understanding of our cellular life.

Thus, Francis Bacon, Rene Descartes, Henri Bernard, and their modern followers seek to prolong life based upon a kind of science which is different from the traditional understanding of nature and humans. Extending life through the manipulation of genes, repair of organs or even by means of an abstemious diet - all as applications of experimental science - is established on and assumes a mechanical view of our health and our lives. This mechanical view sees the workings of the body as movements of material, as an extension of physics and chemistry and susceptible to explanation based upon quantitative measurement alone. Such a view regards the quality of our bodies and our lives as simply secondary expressions of more fundamental natural processes.

It is interesting that modern physicists such as Albert Einstein, and modern scientifically and mechanically sophisticated philosophers such as Alfred North Whitehead suggest that "a new physics" rejects such a mechanical approach. Equally important, many of us believe that such scientific view does not provide the full understanding of our entire lives nor the quality of those lives. Through experimental medicine we are unable to view ourselves as unique self-reflective beings experiencing a finite arc of life. To be sure, the quality of this life may emerge from the conditions of our cellular and sub-cellular life, but the biophysics of cellular manipulation which understands that life does not pretend to offer full comprehension of the nature and value of our own biography.

One literary view of modern experimental medicine is found in Mary Shelley's *Frankenstein*. Mary Shelley's *Frankenstein, The Modern Prometheus* is well known and has struck such a chord in our culture that it has been repeated in different forms and through different media in the last two centuries. In the much retold story, Dr. Victor Frankenstein created a life by running electricity through many body parts. The resulting creature was horrible to behold and rejected by society, doomed to live a life of criminality — last to be seen in the ice flows of the Arctic. The epigraph of the book, (taken from *Paradise Lost)*, was as follows:

> "Did I request thee, Maker, from my clay
> To mold me man? Did I solicit thee?
> From darkness to promote me ?"

Perhaps a similar question might be asked of those modern cell biologists intent upon extending life.

The Eclipse of the Self

In addition to the transformation of modern medicine into a mechanical experimental science, another historical development accompanies the present preoccupation with the "scientific" prolongation of human life — the decline of belief in the self as a unified soul. Of course there has been a modern secular rejection of the religious notion of the soul and modern skepticism regarding the very notion of the self as a scientifically validated object. Historians and philosophers have documented the rise of secularism and the growth of atheism underlying the rejection of the notion of the soul. But there has also been an attenuation in the contemporary belief in a unified self and this decline has been documented in many histories of the idea of the self. I shall not repeat that history here. Instead, I shall turn to one principal philosopher who contributed to this decline — David Hume. David Hume was one of the great 18th century philosophers, author of the monumental *Treatise on Human Nature.* (He was also well known for his *History of England,* and his agreeable personality.!) By the way, that personality was reflected in the nature of his death — a death well documented by Adam Smith and James Boswell. Hume died peacefully, while reading Lucian's *Dialogues of the Dead.* In posthumously published essays, Hume argued against the immortality of the soul asking the question: " But what arguments or analogies can we prove any state of existence, which no one ever saw and which no wise resembles any that was ever seen? " He regarded his own annihilation with equanimity since, as he said, he hadn't worried about his non-existence before he was born, why should he now worry? Hume leveled an even deeper attack on the notion of the self in his *Treatise* where he argued that he could find no underlying "self" to bind the myriad of impressions and ideas he studied in the *Treatise.* Such arguments have resonated in the works of philosophy since Hume.

With the decline in the belief of the immortal soul as well as the growing eclipse of the notion of the self, the hope for our immortality either of the soul or in self appears to collapse. With this collapse, at least some are motivated to extend their bodily lives in this world, drawing upon modern experimental medicine, which, as described above, ignores the phenomenon of the self. Extending our bodily life through experimental medicine becomes one way of holding onto ourselves based upon the underlying assumption is that our selves are our bodies.

The Narcissism of Life Extension

If the rise of experimental medicine and the decline in belief in an immortal soul lie behind the new search for the prolongation of life, what is the fundamental impulse which is given for such a venture? Why bother prolonging bodily life? The fundamental rationale for the modern prolongation of life rest in a deep love of the bodily self. If the ancient story of Fountain of Youth offers a parable for the hope of experimental medicine, the myth of Narcissus offers a similar parable for understanding the motivation for understanding modern bodily self- love. Narcissus was unable to love the nymphs who loved him. His punishment was to fall in love with his own image in a pond and unable to realize that love, he pined away to death. A happier variant of the self-love theme is the myth of Pygmalion, the sculptor, who did not like women, but who fashioned a beautiful statute of one. He fell in love with the statute, and upon his request, Venus allowed the statute to come alive in the embrace of Pygmalion. The modern playwright, George Bernard Shaw portrayed self-love in the form of Pygmalion as the artificial designer of biological mechanisms of the future, but self-love is a theme which traverses all of western intellectual history. Self-love can easily be seen as part of the romantic era; self-love's most ardent defenders were Rousseau, who offered a system of education to develop such love and Nietzsche, whose self-love found he expressed through honoring the principle of life, embodied in Zarthustra – the creation of himself as the "ubermensch" .

Neither Rousseau nor Nietzsche offer any in-depth analysis of why we should love ourselves. Although anticipated by Aristotle, offers the deepest defense of a *proper* self-love was provided by St. Thomas Aquinas who argued that proper self-love is the love of that *which is good within us.* The good that is within us, however is not primarily our body, (although St. Thomas finds some good in all existence). Rather the good is to found in the *fullness* of existence which, in the case of humans is embodied in the virtues, both secular and theological. For Aquinas, those virtues include not only the ancient virtues of courage, temperance, wisdom, and justice, but also the theological virtues of faith, hope and charity.

What is important for our inquiry is the fact that St. Thomas's account of the practice of these virtues does not suggest the importance or goodness of prolonging bodily life. And Aquinas is correct. If one adheres to the notion of virtues or excellences as a basis for self-love, (and, to be sure, many moderns do not), it is difficult to see how the extension of life has anything to do with these virtues. Some virtues, i.e. courage, depend upon running the risk of death, and, indeed, some of the theological virtues, such as faith and hope imply the acceptance of death in this world in anticipation of a future life after death. The important conclusion to be taken from St. Thomas is that bodily life and its extension does not offer a sufficient rationale for its own value.

An Alternative Tradition of Understanding Life

There is an alternative tradition to understanding life and its value. This tradition begins with Aristotle and extends through the works of Hippocrates and Galen, the ancient medical doctors, whose work was accepted but modified by Harvey in his discoveries of the heart's role in the circulation of the blood. This "alternative view" of life is recognized by the authors of modern non- medical classics such as Charles Darwin and Henri Bergson. It has been resurrected in contemporary thought by such Henderson,

The appeal to the value of life as a defense of the prolongation of life requires one to define what life is. An alternative tradition to that of Bacon, Descartes and Bernard found in western carries out a long exploration of the nature and value of life without looking to mechanical explanations based upon experimental science. Theorists such as Aristotle found life in vitality of the body — a "soul' which was characterized by the form or organization of the body – such organization making it capable of self-movement and growth, as well as a variety of higher biological functions, including thought. (In more recent versions of such an approach, life has become identified with the capacity of self-organization).

The ancient doctor, Galen, applied Aristotle's insights to the medical treatment of the human body. Medicine was envisaged as cooperating with nature to restore health. Health was the proper functioning of the body. (Insofar as the body declined in aging, cooperation with nature requires an adjustment from the treatment of those in the prime of life!). Tissues made up organs which were "faculties" which, as part of physiological systems, had the power of serving bodily functions, e.g. nourishment, locomotion, etc. These, in turn, constituted utilities for the body as a whole. This body, in turn, function in the larger context of nature and society.

The one theorist who best captured this nature of life as part of a larger natural world, was Charles Darwin, the author of *The Origin of the Species* and *The Descent of Man.* Although he did not offer any grand theory of the nature of life itself, the great nineteenth century biologist studied life in all its variety and particularity, formulating the principles of its evolution. At first glance, his theory would appear to support any effort to prolong life since he recognized the importance of an instinct for self-preservation and a struggle of all life for continued existence. But a deeper examination of his theory suggests another conclusion. Darwin, along with Malthus, anticipated the ever-increasing population of living things. Darwin recognized that such an increase would outstrip the resources immediately available to particular lives and described these constraints of the environment, including predators, and competing organisms which served as limits to population growth. Such limitations thus placed constraints upon any efforts to prolong the lives of individuals. It is these constraints which operated to naturally select the most adaptable organisms to survive. The variety of organisms with different capacities in the struggle of existence result from both mutation and acquired characteristics. The successful adaptation of some organisms operates to select them for continued existence and reproduction, hence operating as the engine of evolution. The flip side is that those who are less adaptable die, and extinguish their lines of potential maladapted organisms.

Darwin, the scientific originator of evolutionary theory, did not trace the philosophic implications of his theory. This task remained for others,including the French philosopher, Henri Bergson. Bergson, at the turn of the twentieth century sought to capture the radical philosophic implications of Darwin's thought. In his classic *Creative Evolution,* he characterized life as movement and activity — the evolving product of a fundamental impetus expressing itself through a variety of different directions of evolution. Organisms, which are channels of energy in evolution, are organized to "endure". "The past, in its entirety, is prolonged into its present and abides there, actual and acting". Time is part of living. "Wherever anything lives, there is, open somewhere, a register in which time is being inscribed". It is this "inner cause" of evolutionary time which persists despite the destruction of any organism. Thus, according to Bergson, we understand life, not through the scientific intelligence alone, but through intuition, based upon intelligence and instinctive participation in the whole process of evolution itself.

Aside from the value of living itself as reflecting a vital evolutionary impulse, Bergson found the process of living as free creative adaptation to possess its own value. But such a value is not limited to humans, nor is it limited to individuals. On the contrary, like Darwin, Bergson accepts the inevitability of death, but views death as part of a larger evolutionary process of life.

> "Besides the worlds of dying, there are without doubt worlds that are being born. On the other hand, in the organized world, the death of individuals does not seem at all like a diminution of life in general or like a necessity which life submits to reluctantly. As has been more than once remarked, life has never made an effort to prolong the existence of the individual, although many other points it has made so many successful efforts. Everything is as if this death had been willed, or at least accepted, for the greater progress of life in general."

The Complete Life and Biography

The conclusion of the alternative view of life leads to a new understanding of life itself. Aristotle set forth the biological notions of "a life span" and a "complete life". That life, according to Galen was, in part, health: the functioning of the powers and faculties of the body.

The purpose of medicine was to cooperate with nature and support healthful functioning. That functioning involved not only the proper internal relations of organs and their powers, but also the relation of the entire body to its environment. Darwin captured the evolutionary history of the relations between the organism and its environment. The history included, indeed required, natural selection, which turn, assumed the death of organisms, including humans, as part of the selection process.

Once health is viewed as the proper functioning of the body as part of a life-span completed in death, it is possible to understand the relations of medicine and health to old age. Old age is part of the complete life span, in which, due to the aging process, the functioning of the body changes as part of a unique stage of life. Such change is recognized by modern theorists such as Erikson, who linked the biological changes to psychological stages of life. A "Galenic" medicine, which is to "cooperate with nature" must thus "cooperate" with the natural processes of change through time – a "gerontological medicine" which recognizes the aging process.

Health, as the functioning interaction of the body with the environment over time, is part of a more general interaction of the body with its environment. For example, not only medicine, but temperate habits in life may contribute to a healthful life. In short, medicine is not the only route to health. More important, as most of the classic writers recognized, health was not the only part of the good life. To be sure, the healthful functioning of the body may yield pleasure, but pleasure was not the only purpose in life. The healthful functioning of the body provides support by which a range of goods might be sought throughout a complete life, ranging from the activities of friendship, intellectual activity, moral excellence, as well as food, sex, and other delightful goods. And these activities, may, in themselves produce pleasure. *The fundamental fallacy in the life extension effort is the mistaken identification of life extension with health. Even if extended life in some instances may coincide with health, health itself is not the end of life, but simply the support for a range of goods to be realized in a complete life.*

The disciplinary study of particular complete lives is the literature of biography and autobiography, such as Boswell's *Life of Johnson,* and Augustine's *Confessions* or Joyce's *Portrait,* fictional novels, such as Balzac's *Centurian,* Eliot's *Middlemarch,* or Mann's *Magic Mountain,* essays, such as Montaigne's *Essays,* and plays, such Shakespeare's historical works or Chekhov's vivid portrait of life in the Russian countryside . These literary disciplines seek to recount the variety of ways in which we seek to lead our lives.

Conclusion: Acedia and Prolongation of Life

One more Greek Myth: the myth of the Goddess of Dawn, Aurora, who loved mortals and her favorite mortal was Tithonus. She prevailed upon Jupiter to grant him immortality, but forgot to ask for him to have perpetual youth. She grew anxious as she watched him grow old. At length he lost the power of his arms and legs and then his voice grew feeble. Finally she shut him up in his chamber and turned him into a grasshopper. This lesson for the prolongation of life is a sobering one. But perhaps the cost of a long life is better portrayed by the 19th century Russian dramatist — Anton Chekhov. In his remarkable play *Uncle Vanya,* Chekhov illustrates how one such work illuminates old age in a way which diets and vitamins never can. (I must confess a special love for the play and, perhaps, a bit of uneasiness from its story, since I, like one of the characters of the play, am an old professor retired in the countryside).

Uncle Vanya takes place in the Russian countryside. The story is a simple one, at least on the surface. The retired scholar Serebrykov has arrived at his country estate, accompanied by his young wife, Yelena. He dominates the life of the estate with complaints over his health and his sense of self importance. Uncle Vanya, the brother of the Professor's first wife manages the estate along with Sonya, the daughter of the Professor's first wife. A frequent visitor to the estate is Astrov, a doctor and an avid conservationist. In much of the play, the characters are preoccupied with dullness and boredom of countryside life. The time of this uneventful drama is filled with the gradual revelation of the relationships of these people: Vanya's anger and contempt for the old professor; Vanya and Astrov's love for the Professor's young wife, Yelena; the love of Sonya for the doctor. The climax comes with the Professor's announcement that he wishes to sell the house, thus threatening to ruin the lives of Uncle Vanya and the others who live and work permanently on the estate. Vanya goes into a rage, expresses his contempt and hatred of the Professor and attempts to shoot him, but misses. In a sad final Act, the Professor and his young wife leave the estate. Astrov also decamps after learning that the young wife has no intention of leaving her husband for him. Vanya and Sonya return to the unfinished work of the estate with Sonia expressing her final hope that in another world both she and Vanya will find happiness.

Uncle Vanya offers a savage portrait of old age in the person of the Professor. He is pretentious, whining about his elderly maladies, insensitive to the people around him, ungrateful for those who have worked for him, simply expecting those around him to care for him and his estate, and unable to recognize the poverty of his own past academic life — a life without any permanent accomplishment. According to Vanya, he taught art without understanding what art really is. Even Serebrykov knows that he is washed up, finding himself to be old, repulsive, "a corpse".

There is a deeper lesson about aging to be discovered in the play. At one time or another in the play, the doctor, Vanya, and even Yelena and Sonya see themselves as "old" or "almost old". The doctor exclaims, "how could I help ageing? Besides the life is tedious, stupid, squalid." Vanya philosophizes: "everything is old...I grumble like some old fogey". Yelena, in response to the complaints of her husband, says: "Wait a little, have patience! In five or six years I will be old too!" The sense of age comes from the time-laden life they lead — a life of boredom and tedium and one with an unfulfilled loves or the lapse of commitment to long term goals. Thus, Chekhov portrays the conservationist doctor as seeing himself in the woods, but with no light to guide him out. In the final speech, Sonya says:

"Well, what can we do? We must go on living! We will
go on living, Uncle Vanya. We will. I've lived through
a long long succession of days and tedious evenings, We
will patiently suffer the trials which fate imposes on us."

and, looking to the next life, she ends the play with " We will rest!"

Chekhov gives us an understanding of aging and old age very
different from those seeking the fountain of youth. Chekhov offers a
view of old age as part of a *story of various lives*. The story of our lives is
ultimately the shape of our entire lives and cannot be disconnected from
the complete story. Chekhov believes that understanding of aging comes
from the experience of living and loving within a normal life span, ("and
then we will rest"), not from the drinking from the Fountain of Youth
nor the manipulation of genes. Our old age should reflect or express
the history of our deepest desires and, hopefully, the old age holds onto
some of our best capacities within the limits of a life span given to us
by nature. It is that understanding of old age and the acceptance of its
losses and limits and the sadness which accompanies them which we
shall seek to describe in this book through a reading and discussion of
the central texts of our civilization.

CHAPTER VII

The Mirage of Old Age Delight

"We should cherish old age and enjoy it. Fruit tastes most delicious when its season is ending. It is the final glass which pleases the inveterate drinker..." - Seneca, *Letters from Tranquility*

"Peace and tranquility, the pleasures of the countryside, the serenity of the heavens, the murmur of the fountains, and ease of mind can do much towards causing the most un-productive of muses to become fecund and and bring forth progeny which will be the marvel and delight of mankind" -Cervantes, *Don Quixote*

My mother, a frustrated English teacher, rewarded me with her approval when I would read through the summer months. The high point of my young life was my award from the town library of a hideous plant for having read during the summer the most books of any child in the town. And yet, I don't remember the books, except perhaps for the Wizard of Oz! I remember the sheer delight of riding my bicycle, running off to the Lake Michigan beach, playing with my friends, savoring the green beauty of my Lake Forest home. I took that love of nature's beauty with me to college in Colorado and left it there. Despite the beauty of the campus and the mountains at its edge, it was the reading lists to which I gradually turned again. I and a friend resolved to gain all the knowledge in the world and began to read the first volume of Encyclopedia Britannica with the intent of plowing through all twenty six volumes. Needless to say, we did not get very far, but my commitment to books was solidified. I soon left the beautiful campus in Colorado for Chicago and an even more intense pursuit of knowledge. I left the delight of nature behind. So now here I sit - a retired old law professor, trying to make sense of old age, in part with the help of all these books. These delights now extend to the memories of my beloved wife, long telephone conversations with my children, the occasional company of a few friends, the enchanting beauty of Vermont, and a fine old home (filled with bookcases), in a lovely small town. I continue to read and I really love the experience of reading. I have my old age project - making sense of the world of old age though the ideas gleaned from the works of the western and eastern canon. Most important, I have the leisure of old age and time to meditate on what, if anything, a life adds up to. But is all of this simply a mistake? Should I be seeking simply to expand the quiet Epicurean pleasures of an old age without seeking to read another book? Should I begin to pay more attention to the foreboding signs of our advanced old age? What is likely to be the effect of the slow physical decline I am experiencing? My gradual loss of a sense of the past? My increased dependence? My sense of a shortening future? My abandonment of any commitment to a faith in history's progress? Is death near and should I better "prepare myself for it"?

Introduction

After we give up the effort to prolong the sheer quantity of our years and refuse the siren religious promises of eternal bliss, we can adjust our expectations and begin to look at the *quality* of old age in our lives as a whole. Seneca, in the first epigram to this chapter seems to regard old age as the final glass of wine. Browning went one step further: "Grow old along with me/The best is yet to be/The last of life, for which the first was made".

Examining the quality of our lives in old age is not easy. Some of the delights of old age are obvious. There are many such delights. Old age offers more than few select moments for which there is time to savor and hold Burke's "un-bought grace of life". There is some escape from the time-bound responsibilities of adult life - work and family duties. This escape provides a kind of perverse freedom which enables us to be more aware of our past and the decisions which have shaped us. Such reminiscence may be a delightful experience. There is time for a kind of re-weaving of the narrative of one's life. The freedom of old age extends beyond simply a retired life of leisure. We elders can avoid many of the intense passions and actions of everyday life -passions which may give a richness to life; such passions, as Thoreau argued, lead to harried "lives of quiet desperation". The decline of such desperation may reflect the decline of our ambitions for ourselves and the world. Finally, retirement, when combined with the slow passage of time, can produce a calm detachment - almost a kind of indifference - which the ancient Stoics and Epicureans sought in their lives. Let me review each of these delights in a little more detail.

1. The Delights of Nature

The pleasures of old age are likely to be transient quiet ones, which come to one, almost accidentally, and which are rare and pass by quickly. They must be grabbed and sucked dry in the moment. Two such pleasures for me are my work in the garden and my long walks Preparing the soil, planting flowers and vegetables, cutting grass, weeding the beds and raking leaves offer a deep sense of satisfaction and continued acquaintance with the cycles of nature. Long walks permit the time to look at nature in detail; my walks around Occam pond nearby, or in the pines along the Connecticut River allow me to monitor the seasons of the pond, and its occupants, including the bloom of gold fish and the advent of the Heron in the Spring, and the occupation by skaters in the winter. My walk on "the two mile loop" near town has enable me to see both deer and fox, the latter up close, with the added bonus of yielding a view of my town from a nearby hill.

I used to think that I inherited from my childhood days my liking for the natural beauty of the gardens, fields and forests. But my reading of Epicurus' letters and Lucretius' poem, led me to discover something else. Lucretius, the Roman poet, in his *Rerum Natura,* seized upon the insights of Epicurus and placed them in a grand poetic portrait of the cycles of nature- the ceaseless movement of atoms and the consequent cycles of life and death. Recognition of such cycles is strangely comforting and some of us can wring a few moments of pleasure or detachment from this recognition. For Lucretius, it was not these few moments of pleasure at the beauty of nature which were valuable, but rather the quiet contemplation of the cycles of birth, loves, battles, disease, and even death in nature. These cycles of the gardens, their initial growth, full flowering, the generation of fruit, and their decline, death and decay - all embodying the very passage of time have given me the most pleasure, accompanied by the sad thought that I might not witness that cycle for much longer. But nature's cycle will continue after my own death and I shall become part of that cycle.

Thus, the slow passage of time along with an awareness of nature's cycles serve to sharpen the pleasures of the present in old age. The ancients knew this well. When Epicurus and his spokesman, Lucretius, began their description of the flux of nature's atoms, and drew from that flux a vivid description of the cycles of nature, they held on to the human delight in philosophical contemplation and the poetic description of nature. This description is now found in the remarkable poetry of Horace. In Horace's words:

> "Snows gone away: green grass comes back to the
> meadows; and green leaves back the trees, as
> the earth suffers her springtime change...
> Yet be warned, each year gone round, each day-snatching
> hour
> Says -"Limit your hopes: you must die.
> Frost gives way to the warm west winds; soon summer
> shall trample spring and be trodden in turn
> Under the march of exuberant, fruit spilling autumn,
> then back comes
> Winter to numb us again. ..

2. The Escape from Responsibility

A second of the momentary delights upon coming to old age is the escape from responsibility. To be sure, there remain the responsibilities of daily life and practical preparations of old age decrepitude and death. But, in old age, one leaves behind the duties of raising a family, earning a living, and frantically pursuing civic activities. These activities, no matter how worthwhile, operate to hide from us the passage of time in our lives. Suddenly in old age, we wake up. A yawning gap of unencumbered time suddenly confronts us with an exhilarating feeling of freedom. The demands and expectations of the "outside world" are muffled. We do not need to go to work, pick up the kids, or save the world. Of course, such freedom can inspire dread since our jobs or family duties are no longer guides for choosing who we are or should do, nor can they fill the time of our days. In understanding this freedom, I find a rereading of existentialist thought to be most helpful. As Sartre notes in *Existentialism is a Humanism,* our preexisting human nature cannot guide our lives and we must decide who we are for ourselves. We do not have a human essence which can help us decide. Rather, we create ourselves through our decisions. We must create our old age, even if we failed to create the rest of our lives.

A sixteenth century Spanish author Miguel Cervantes led a colorful life which included imprisonment, poverty and fame. Cervantes claimed to write the story of Don Quixote in order to satirize the many tales of chivalry which were then popular. Don Quixote (a name acquired for purposes of knighthood), was an elderly Spanish gentleman, who after collected and read many books in his retirement, including many romances about chivalry. He became so enamored by his reading these books and he read so much that he went completely out of his mind. Later in his story, the curate, believing his insanity came from his books, committed most of them to the flames.

After reading these books, Don Quixote decided in his old age to leave his country estate and pursue the profession of knight errant to restore the ideal of chivalry. He equipped himself with a helmet, lance, and broken down horse, Rociante. As a knight errant, he chose a neighbor farm girl as his lady to be protected and named her Dulcinea del Toboso. In his early adventures, he found an inn keeper who could dub him, "the knight of the woeful countenance". He soon acquired the squire - a hapless poor neighbor farmer, Sancho Panza, who liked the old man and who was promised great things by the Don. In Quixote's first sally across the plains as a knight, he "[strung] together (in his mind) absurdities, all of the kind that his books had taught him..." As a consequence, many adventures followed in which Don Quixote battled windmills as giants and flocks of sheep as armies. In his apparent delusions, Quixote believed he was rescuing the enslaved or punishing the evil knights, all on behalf of his loved one "Dulcinea". Others, both friends and enemies laughed at him, but they sometimes helped him, even though they thought he might be mad.

A certain ambiguity lingers throughout this tale. Despite making fun of him, some who encountered the knight on his adventures felt ennobled by his courteous treatment of them. In another ambiguity, we read that from time to time throughout the adventures, Don Quixote appears to recognize that he was not a knight. Was this merely an act, and, if so, to what purpose. Perhaps the ultimate ambiguity comes at the end of the story, when he returns to his estate rejecting the chivalrous life he has led: he appears to recognize that his adventures were those of a madman. In an added ambiguity, Cervantes' entire story seems to blur the relationship between fiction and non-fiction. Contained within Quixote's library is another volume, an actual volume written by Cervantes and during the destruction of his books, the curate claims to know Cervantes. Even the authorship of *Don Quixote* remains uncertain. Cervantes claims that he received the tale from a wise chronicler, Sid Hamete, who, at the end of the tale, supports Cervantes effort to discourage the romances about chivalry. Ironically, after the first part of *Don Quixote* was written, a person other than Cervantes wrote a sequel. Cervantes incorporates mention of this incident in his second part of the book.

Quixote makes his peace with the church and dies. (Perhaps he was not unlike St. Thomas Aquinas who apparently, on his death bed, rejected his own writings as "mere straw".) Don Quixote returns to his

Catholic beliefs and leaves a will which conditions a bequest to his niece, conditional upon her not marrying anyone who has read the books of chivalry. His old age quest is over - whether it was a quest to embody the ideals of chivalry or an ironical tale making fun of the ideals is left to the reader.

Quixote is the patron saint of my book - the book you are reading. Like the old Spaniard, I too have moldered in libraries too long and I suspect I too am mad. Both of us retired to our country estate. Both of us are under the undue influence of the books we have read. Quixote believed in the ideal of chivalry; I believe in the canon. Both beliefs are sadly out of date. Quixote has the weapons of his trade - his armor, horse, helmet, and squire. I have my Britannica, The Great Ideas and the Synopticon, the Great Books of the Western World and a good selection of eastern classics. The noble knight went out into the countryside to fight the dragons, armies and enemy knights. I propose to use my weapons to fight the problems of old age - retirement, an eclipsed past, decay, death and the securing of a legacy. Each of us is creating a world - for Quixote, the world is a world of chivalry - battles with shiny swords on behalf of courtly loves.

3 The Freedom of Decrepitude

Despite freedom from work and family in old age, there are other conditions of old age which save us from an unbounded freedom, and, in so doing, offer another delight. That delight is found in the experience of the degraded condition of our old age - a condition which protects us from temptations which haunt younger people - the temptations of sex and ambition. In old age, we are "jailed" by our biological condition, which keeps us from repeating our past passionate follies. Such old age protects us from ourselves- from the opportunities to once again commit our irresponsible actions. Thus, a pleasure to be found in "the prison of old age"; it is the pleasure of momentary safety – a security of life given by the absence of overweening intense passions and the opportunities to act upon them. Through the sheer passage of time and biological decay, by witnessing the price paid for uncontrolled passion in our past lives and the lives of others, and with the help of old age friendships, reading or meditation, we experience the slow ebb of our strong feelings, or find ways to mitigate or redirect them, or strengthen milder emotions to replace them. The pleasure results in a sense of self-control or at least continence.

In this regard, it is the reading of the some classical authors in whom I find such comfort. Not so much Plato or Aristotle, but rather the "Hellenistic philosophers", especially Epicurus, Lucretius, and Seneca - all of whom seem to have grasped the importance of the passage of time in human lives. They are the philosophers for old age since they explicitly address problems of old age and death. One of my special delights in old age is to read the writings of the French philosopher, Pierre Hadot, which along with the work of other Hellenistic philosophers, advise us in how to read their books as "spiritual exercises" preparing us to lead a meditative way of life.

4. *The Delight of Detachment*

These authors appeal to a variety of stances with which to confront our condition. Each ancient philosopher offers a unique recipe. The skeptics urge us to recognize that intellectual conflicts cannot be resolved and hence we should embrace an "ataraxia" which is the tranquility in the acceptance of unresolved conflicts. The Stoics, such as Marcus Aurelius urge "autarkia" - a sense of autonomy and self-control. Seneca, especially in his letters, offers a powerful case for tranquility in such self-possession. The Epicureans recommended "apatheia" - a freedom from feeling. Epicurus and Lucretius, found contentment in the recognition that the forces of nature - the movements of the atoms and the remorseless cycles of nature - permit a quiet freedom which through a philosophical therapy can detach ourselves from our natural passions and permit us to enjoy the quiet enjoyment of nature. The Cynics offered a recipe of frugality and simple honesty which is especially useful in old age.

Although all of these Hellenistic philosophers suggest ways in which pleasures may be found or held onto in old age, it is the Epicureans who are the philosophers best suited to explain the delights of old age. Lucretius, in his Epicurean poem – *The Way Things Are* – identifies each of the kinds of pleasure – sensational, intellectual, emotional, artistic – and traces them to the movements of atoms. Lucretius recognized some of the emotional fears of old age –fears of death and the punishments of afterlife - and sought, both in his poetry and the message it contained, to alleviate those fears. When one views one's death as simply the dissolution of atoms and after life as simply the continued eternal flux of atoms, fear subsides. A certain intellectual pleasure is found a system of the mind which views the pains of life as simply the product of the movement of certain kinds and shapes of atomic matter. Artistic pleasure, "honey", in Lucretius words, is derived both from the poetry which presents the physical system of nature and the beauty of nature itself, all of which, according to Lucretius, dwarfs the pains of our lives and death.

All of these Hellenistic philosophers recommend a kind of "apospatheia" - a detachment from emotion- a viewing of things from above. This detachment may spring either from our recognition of our lack of certain knowledge and the inevitability of uncertainty, or our acceptance of an ultimate lack of power over external events, or simply the ability to view "the way things are", an old age detachment which enables us to see ourselves and the world around us. Old age marks a recognition of the cycles of life, the decline of entangling passions, an escape from many daily responsibilities, and the detachment necessary for such an assessment.

With the freedom and irresponsibility of old age, Don Quixote read abut a world of romantic chivalry and created that world for himself. So too, with a similar freedom, we modern oldsters may find or create a world beyond ourselves. Surely, savoring natural beauty or our friendships, with the realization that both are subjected to the cycles of nature, we recognize a world beyond ourselves. A sense of detachment enables us to see the world rather than simply the momentary day to day tasks with which most people occupy themselves.

Don Quixote encountered a reality within his world - the windmills, the sheep, the barber's basin, the run down inn, the chain gang of galley slaves and so on. As he met them, he transformed them - at least momentarily - to fit within his imaginative adventure.

In doing so, he also, at least from time to time, also transformed the "real world" and the people he encountered. Thus, he gave freedom to the galley slaves and dignity to Dulcinea, whether either deserved such treatment.

The Challenge of Matthew Arnold

Despite Browning's enthusiasm for the benefits of aging and my expansion of his accounts of the delights of old age, something is missing. Perhaps the place to begin to search for what is missing in Browning's account is in Mathew Arnold's answer. Matthew Arnold answered Browning in his poem *Growing Old* finding old age to be the loss of "the glory of the form... the lustre of the eye ...to feel each limb grow stiffer ...not to have our life mellowed and softened as with sunset-glow...not to see the world as from a height...nor feel the fulness of the past..."

> *"It is- last stage of all-*
> *When we are frozen up within, and quite*
> *The phantom of ourselves*
> *To hear the world applaud the hollow ghost*
> *Which blamed the living man.*

The different responses of Browning and Arnold may be simply the individual and cultural differences in the way in which old age is experienced. It may even be possible for one person to have both responses. Old people are ...well ...old, meaning that they have experience of the mellowing of life, while, at the same time, feeling each limb grow stiffer. Part of Arnold's pessimism surely must come from high expectations in and from old age. Perhaps Browning simply has more modest expectations either of life in general or old age in particular – expectations which may soften the impact of aging. Or, perhaps, each is suggesting a different stage of old age- early old age when health may be relatively good and old age when infirmities begin to accumulate.

Simone de Beauvoir, in her *Coming of Age,* may be interpreted to suggest another explanation for these different views of aging. Although she recognizes that old age for most is a sad and lonely time of life, she suggests that at least some of the delights experience in old age may be traced to the rewards of class privilege of the rich; she documents in detail the travails of the aged poor. I will freely confess that many of the delights I have experienced in old age are due to affluence – not only a past affluence which enabled me, my wife and family to secure an education, but also a present affluence and a fortunate escape from debilitating illness, which enable all of us to live in comfort.

Despite the joys of an affluent and fortunate early old age, accompanied by an optimistic temperament, there remains a foreboding in old age. This foreboding is captured in the essays of Jean Amery's *On Aging: Revolt and Resignation.* Amery summarizes it as follows:

> "…In aging we become the worldless inner sense of pure time. As aging people, we become alien to our bodies, and at the same time, closer to their sluggish mass than ever before. When we have passed beyond the prime of life, society forbids us to continue to project ourselves into the future and culture becomes a burdensome culture that we no longer understand, that instead give us to understand that, as scrap iron of the mind, we belong to the waste heaps of the epoch. In aging, finally, we have to live with dying, a scandalous imposition, a humiliation without compare, that we put up with, not in humility, but as the humiliated…."

The delights of old age identified above are colored by these qualities of aging. Our delights of nature become limited as "the sluggish mass" of our bodies interfere with walking and other natural pursuits. The escape from some responsibilities is cut off by the arrival of new responsibilities to care for ourselves and our aged loved ones. Our delightful stage of irresponsibility is limited by our inability to project ourselves into the future. Our detachment is tested by the reality of living with dying. To be sure, Amery may overstate matters. His melancholy response was undoubtedly conditioned by his torture and imprisonment in Auschwitz concentration camp and shortly after he completed his next book, *Suicide*, he took his own life. But his description of the deep problems in the experiences of aging tests any blithe faith of Browning's "the best is yet to be".

In this book, I have taken up the challenges of old age which Amery identifies and I identify them as necessary losses of that stage of life. These challenges, which I shall discuss in more detail below, include exile from the work world, eclipse of one's past, decay of our bodies, loss of a future, growing dependence upon others, a diminished faith in progress in the world which goes on without us and death. Our retirement rudely reminds us that we are part of a larger social and economic world which is impervious to our needs: "on the waste heaps of the epoch". The eclipse of our past suggests that we gradually lose that small part of history which begins before our lives and extends to their end. The decay reminds us that we are part of a biological and physical world: "alien to our bodies and their sluggish mass". And the approach of dying and death promises not only the humility of recognizing the promise of our non-being but also the humiliating way in which we realize that promise. In short, all of these challenges, in one way or another, suggests to us that we are part of a world, however, defined.

My contention, unlike Amery, is that like Don Quixote, there are books which help us to define this world of old age. Don Quixote "found" his world in his books. He donned his armor and sallied forth to encounter, in a variety of adventures, the world he desired to establish, interpreting that world to fit his own reality as best he could. But, eventually, he returned to his home and to another reality. Perhaps in telling the tale of Don Quixote, Cervantes wished to criticize not only the readers of the romances of chivalry, but also all those who find their worlds in books, and who try to adjust their experiences to these worlds. (If so, he was not the only great author to do so. Voltaire, in *Candide* tells the story of a fine young man, who began his life tutored by the philosopher Pangloss, who believed, along with the real philosopher, Leibniz, that this world to be the best possible world. He made his way in the world only to encounter natural disasters of storms, plagues, earthquakes and human evil of war, crime and slavery - all of which eventually convinced him to retire and simply cultivate his garden without philosophical discussions. Thus both Quixote and Candide eventually turn their backs upon the life lessons of books.

As I and my older reader consult the canon works, find our world in the western and eastern traditions of thought, and "sally forth" to encounter its quiet adventures, will we too have to adjust to the realities we encounter, perhaps modifying or jettisoning the grand ideas we have discovered? Will I subject myself and the reader to the same ridicule Quixote received? Paradoxically, Cervantes *Don Quixote* and Voltaire's *Candide* are part of the very tradition of great works which I propose to consult in my old age. As a consequence, I begin my adventures in the world of old age being warned that a too great faith in the great texts may lead to the kind of foolishness that Quixote and Candide experienced.

Conclusion

What conclusions may be taken away from this meditation on the delights of old age? On the one hand, there are without doubt a number of identifiable delights which accompany old age, whether they are limited to an early stage of old age or to certain more optimistic individuals. But, as Arnold, de Beauvoir and Amery have shown us, deep problems with this sunny view of old age. In fact, many of the old age infirmities identified by these authors may uncut the possible delights we otherwise might experience. One reason for this may be that, as Aristotle and others recognized, pleasure is an outgrowth of the proper functioning of the mind and body and aging interferes with such functioning.

At the very least, aside from the delights, the deep losses of old age must be recognized and accepted as part of growing old. I shall explore these losses in more depth below. I will suggest that only the recognition and acceptance of such losses can consolation be found for them. And here is where Jean Amery and I part company. Amery has written his powerful book, *On Aging, Revolt and Resignation,* to reject consolation. In Amery's words:

> "Specifically, as I felt my way forward, step by step, I have to give up the hopes always evoked by the aging: I had to invalidate consolation. Whatever there is in consolation that is recommended to the aging- how to come to terms with one's decline and fall, even if possible to gain assets from it, nobility of resignation, evening wisdom, late tranquility – it all stood before me as vile dupery, against which I had to charge myself to protest with every line...."

The last lines of Amery's book are:

> "...Have A. done something to disturb the balance, expose the compromise, destroy the genre painting, contaminate the consolation? He hopes so. The days shrink and dry up. He has the desire to tell the truth."

The reasons for Amery's rejection of consolation are both deep and complex. I cannot explore them here, except to suggest that Amery argues that in aging, we have become our past time, without a future necessary to provide consolation for us. We lack an identity by which to receive consolation and others have become strangers to us, making their consolation impossible. We are estranged as well from the culture around us which is no longer our culture – new systems of thought and art, which we do not understand, offer no consolation. In aging we have to live with dying and death which is, of course, no consolation. As

Amery suggests in his last lines quoted above; we must choose between consolation and the truth.

The question I leave this chapter with is: *does the recognition of the brutal realities of aging recognized by Amery, comparable to the losses in aging which I have identified and will discuss below prevent the possibility of any consolation?*

CHAPTER VIII

Pragmatism's Folly

"Her [pragmatism's] only test of probable truth is what works best in the way of leading us… what fits every part of life best…" William James

…"it is contemplation, nevertheless, which lays peculiar claim to the office of the investigation of the truth.…" Augustine

When I left the University of Chicago, a Midwestern pragmatism propelled me from philosophy to the study of law. At Chicago I had studied the works of John Dewey which prompted me to seek the study of law and public policy at the London School of Economics, Yale Law School and Brandeis University. These institutions were preoccupied at the time with the issues of inequality and social welfare – poverty, race discrimination and the decline of the city. Yale, in particular, was a hot-bed of a pragmatic approach to the law, having embraced the tradition of legal realism and its successor jurisprudence of law and policy. It prepared me well for my future career in urban development, anti-poverty work, and environmental law. Upon entering the work world, given my past history of pragmatism, I was ready to fashion a pragmatic response to the problems of the city and the environment. This career in turn led me in later life to teach law and planning – a planning deeply imbued with pragmatic principles. But further reflection on old age has suggested to me that there are fundamental problems with pragmatism and especially with a pragmatic approach to old age.

Introduction

The denials of old age – technological efforts to extend life, turning to the afterlife of religion and exaggeration of old age delights – are easy to unmask and refute. But one denial is more subtle - the placing of old age in the framework of practicality. According to this approach, old age is simply a challenging problem which can be resolved through a wide variety of actions, designed to "resolve" the problem. This pragmatic approach is well suited to the national character of Americans. As de Tocqueville tells us, we are a pragmatic people tackling problems, including problems of social reform, with optimistic inventiveness, ingenuity and especially mechanical ability, often in pursuit of economic wealth. Unfortunately, a history of anti-intellectualism often accompanies this pragmatism. In de Tocqueville's words:

> "...Nothing is more necessary to the culture of the higher sciences
> Or of the more elevated departments of science than meditation
> And nothing is less suited to meditation than the structure of
> Democratic society...."

This practical bent in our national character has given rise to one of the few original American philosophies – pragmatism – originating at the end of the 19th century with the work of Charles Pierce, John Dewey, and William James, but spreading throughout the 20th century in various guises to innumerable American thinkers. I shall outline this manner of thought in more detail below.

In this introduction, it suffices to assert that a pragmatic approach to old age losses transforms these losses into problems to be resolved in one way or another, by one action or another. With this pragmatic focus, the old age losses are not seen as inevitable losses in the arc of human life, nor are they viewed as irremediable. The meaning of these losses and their consequent sadness are unnoticed, in favor of actions designed to remove the losses and soothe the sadness. In effect, action operates to deny the losses and their consequences, while leaving the image of successful coping with old age. Such a practical approach ignores the task of clarifying the meaning and purpose of such actions when facing such a loss. In a sense, these pragmatic actions, without meaning or goals, are profoundly unethical since it is their meaning and purpose which supply their ethical justification. Equally important, the actions are ultimately not successful in addressing the losses; these actions leave an irremediable residue of loss to be addressed in some other way.

The Pragmatic Approach to Old Age Loss

Before delving more deeply into American pragmatism, let me explore the pragmatic approach to old age. Such a pragmatic approach will identify its problems – retirement, biological decline, eclipse of the past, a foreshortened future, growing dependency, historical pessimism, and anticipation of death – and prompting devise actions to rectify them. In response to retirement, the securing of adequate financial support, (whether public or private), the search for new activities to replace work and fill the time, and the replacement of friends of the workplace, now lost with retirement. The prospect of physical and mental decline suggests the need for adequate health insurance, preventive health measures of diet, mental and physical exercise and preventive drugs, and adjustments in expectations of one's own and one's spouse's physical performance. The eclipse of the past may spur the effort to recollect and remember the past, including engagement in specific memory exercises, and attendance of reunions and commemorations. Coping with a foreshortened future may suggest the need to reduce ambitions, created legacies extending beyond one's life and promoting one's longevity. The prospect of increased dependency may require health and home care insurance, transitional care arrangements, and adjusting one's way of life to fit this dependency. A decline in the faith in the ideal of progress may require the diminishment of political and civic participation, an increased attention to natural and social conservation, and increased attention to the present or "a-historical" values. Anticipation of death may lead to practical steps to arrange for a painless or "good" death either through arrangements with hospice or public end of life arrangements, living wills, organizing one's affairs, and making cemetery arrangements.

Indeed, many of the problems – the leisure of retirement, the reducing expectations of one's physical performances, the freedom from the burdens of our past, the caring required from a growing dependency, the planning for an infinite future with a reduced ambition, the comfort of a newfound old age conservatism, and even the tranquil anticipation of death are not to be ignored. But undertaking actions without meaning or purpose will not yield their satisfactory solution.

Nevertheless, The identification of the problems of old age and the taking of appropriate action to resolve them without extensive attention to meaning and purpose fits well the American temper. A survey of the characteristics of national character throughout history in the *Annals of America* documents extensively both "the American emphasis on the practical: inventiveness, ingenuity, and mechanical ability" as well as "anti-intellectualism" in religion, business and politics and education.

Perhaps the best known historical description of this aspect of the national character of Americans comes from a visitor to this country in the early 1800's– Alexis de Tocqueville, who at the beginning of the second volume of his classic *Democracy in America,* concludes about the "philosophical method of the Americans" as follows:

> "...To evade the bondage of system and habit, of family
> maxims, class opinions and, in some degree, of national
> prejudices, to accept tradition

Only as a means of information and existing facts only as a lesson to be used in doing otherwise, and doing better; to seek the reason of things for oneself and in oneself alone; to tend to results without being bound to means; and to strike through the form to the substance...."

De Tocqueville divides science into three parts: theoretical principles, general truths and methods of application; he finds the Americans to "admirably understand" the practical part of science while paying careful attention to general truths. He argues that the American culture of practicality is due to "the social conditions and the institutions of democracy which prepare them to seek the immediate and useful practical results of the sciences ". He concludes that such practicality will thrive in a democratic age.

Joined to this focus on the practical is the American optimism – the faith in human progress throughout history. Like the *Annals of America,,* de Tocqueville views the Americans as a nation exemplifying the inevitable progress of equality, optimistic that such progress will take place in the future, but restless and unsatisfied with the present. According to de Tocqueville, this optimism about progress extends beyond simply the conditions for equality. He concludes that "this equality suggests to the Americans the indefinite perfectibility of man." As castes disappear and classes draw together, and manners and laws vary, with the "tumultuous intercourse" of men, as new facts arise, new truths brought to light, ancient opinions dissipated "the image of an ideal but always fugitive perfection presents itself to the human mind.' According to de Tocqueville, this ideal of human perfection, along with a constant design to grasp fresh gratifications leads to a restlessness in the midst of prosperity, because "they are forever brooding over advantages they do not possess.

If the *Annals* and de Tocqueville are correct about the American national character, it is perhaps not surprising that the philosophy of pragmatism originated in the United States and is ascribed to Charles Sanders Pierce, John Dewey and William James. Charles Sanders Pierce, a little known American philosopher writing at the end of 19th century is credited with originating pragmatism. In his 1878 article, "How to Make Our Ideas Clear", he concludes that after simply finding obvious meanings and exploring the definition of ideas, we should trace the practical implications of the idea in question:

> "…It appears then that the rule for attaining the third grade of clearness of apprehension is as follows: consider what effects, which might conceivably have practical bearings, we conceive the object of our conception to have. Then our conception of these effects is the whole of our conception of the object.…"

Applying this simple rule to an old age term like "retirement", we can trace its effects in terms of the increase of "free time", the decline in work related income and the loss of work related friends. These practical effects become the "meaning" of the term "retirement".

Following Pierce, William James is often credited with coining the word, "pragmatism" and, in 1907 he wrote a book entitled *Pragmatism,* in which he credited to Pierce the principle of the pragmatic method (which "interprets each [metaphysical] notion by tracing its respective practical consequences").

> "…But if you follow the pragmatic method, you cannot look on any word as closing your quest. You must bring out of each work its practical cash value.…"

To test of the "cash value" of an idea:

> "…means that ideas (which themselves are but parts of our experience) become true just in so far as they help us to get into satisfactory relation with other parts of our experience.…"

Thus, the truth of the idea of retirement rests in our recognition of how it fits with consequences which are other parts of our experience (e.g. increase in free time, loss of work friends, diminished income).

Although William James was well known as a psychologist and philosopher, it was the American philosopher, John Dewey, who, during the early and mid-twentieth century, most thoroughly set forth the philosophy of pragmatism and its implications for all the areas of philosophy. Dewey most explicitly placed pragmatism in the context of a theory of inquiry set forth in *Logic: A Theory of Inquiry* and a readable little book, *How We Think*. In these books, he outlines the pragmatic method of thinking - beginning with an unsettled or indeterminate situation or one in which there is an obstacle to ongoing action, the identification of the situation as problematic requiring inquiry, the searching out of the constituents of the problem, the posing of possible ideas, at first vague, and later more specific for resolution of the problem, the examination of the idea for its possible contribution to resolution, and the "operationalizing" of the idea in order to test its' "fit" to resolving the problem. Such an approach, as applied to "the problems" of old age would encourage a detailed examination of the constituents of old age problems. For example, if lack of income is a constituent in the problems of retirement for a specified person or persons, an inquiry into the sources and need for income for these persons might follow along with suggested actions for either securing more income or minimizing need.

The pragmatic approach to old age begins with the premises of pragmatism itself. These premises start with the assumption that we are organisms in interaction with our environment. As Darwin has demonstrated, such organism both shape and are shaped by this interaction, and hence there is no fixed human nature which is not reshaped by the environment. We seek truth as an instrument of the good – to fit well within the environment. As a consequence, thought emerges as we, as organisms recognize and encounter problems within the environment which, in some way impede our activities. We identify the constituents of these problems and ideas are suggested as to how the problems would be resolved. The ideas in question are simply hypotheses or suggestions upon which action is taken. To the extent that these hypotheses are verified in action to fit with the environment, they may be said to be true. Thus, for example, if declining health in old age is the problem, we may identify its constituents in terms of adequate healthful living and sufficient preventive and remedial health care. Hypothetical ways of promoting healthful living are suggested and we may act upon them. To the extent that we have successfully removed or mitigated declining health through such measures, we may be said to have found something true about old age, i.e. that it is the product, in part, of unhealthful living as defined by the specific actions we successfully undertook to prevent it in the future.

If the pragmatic philosophy of these American philosophers were simply a brief passing phase in the complex and difficult history of philosophy, it would not be worth mentioning them, since common sense alone finds such pragmatism appealing. But not only have the works of these philosophers become part of the western canon of thought, but, in addition, pragmatic philosophy has continued throughout the twentieth century. The more recent works of George Herbert Mead, C.I. Lewis, Sidney Hook, O.W. Holmes Jr., Harold Lasswell, B.F. Skinner, Nicholas Rescher and Richard Rorty, (although differing among themselves), attest to the continued strength of this mode of thought not only in philosophy but in other fields including the social sciences and law. More important, such pragmatism mirrors the pragmatism with which many approach old age. But, as I shall seek to demonstrate below, despite the continued strength and attraction of pragmatism and its adoption as a strategy for approaching old age, it suffers from serious limitations, which are illustrated when we examine carefully how it is applied to the losses of old age.

The Errors or Omissions of Old Age Pragmatism

If we examine more carefully the principal assertions of pragmatism we encounter serious difficulties. First, pragmatism challenges our common sense views about the nature of reality and its capacity of being known. Second, pragmatism, by implication challenges the very notion of human nature – a human nature which is fully revealed to the aged. Thirdly, pragmatism fails as a method of ascertaining the truth. Fourth, pragmatism's optimistic and future oriented attitude conflicts with the realities of aging. Let me briefly explain these criticisms.

1. *Pragmatism and Reality*

Pragmatism appears to reject the acceptance of a reality independent of our own knowledge and deny the commonsense assumption that an independent reality can exist in a knowable form. For the pragmatist, reality is only found in the interaction of organisms with their environment and it is this interaction which reveals knowledge. Such a view is compatible with viewing knowledge as only the product of experimentation, especially scientific experimentation. Old age, however, heightens our recognition of an independent reality, as we become more aware of the cycles of nature which we cannot fully control.

2. *Pragmatism and Human Nature*

Not only does pragmatism reject the notion of an independent reality, but it also subtly attacks the very notion of a human nature. It does so by attacking the notion of form and substance.

Once the pragmatists dispose of form and substance, they are able to similarly attack the notion fixed human nature with distinct powers and capacities. Even the pragmatist, John Dewey, who wrote a little book entitled *Human Nature and Conduct,* spends most of book arguing for the power of habit, the plasticity of human impulse, and the absence of separate instincts and separate intellectual powers by which to define human nature. Thus, pragmatism ignores the biological basis of the natural human capacities which wax during our lives and wane in old age.

3. *The Pragmatic Method of Truth*

As a consequence of its premises, pragmatism rejects the notion that our knowledge can, in some way, represent an independent reality in order to form truth, i.e. judgments which are tested by their conformity with such a reality. The philosophy of pragmatism, with its imitation of the methods of scientific experimentation, taken as the sole avenue towards reaching truth, mistakenly turns to action alone to find and "test" the truth of our beliefs. In doing so, it appears to echo David Hume's famous conclusion:

> "When we run over libraries, Persuaded of these principles, what havoc Must we make? If we take I our hand any volume...let us ask *Does it contain any abstract reasoning concerning quantity or number? NO.* Commit it then to the flames: for it can contain nothing but sophistry and Illusion..."

By drawing upon pragmatism's antecedents in Darwinism, in which "experience" is constituted by the interaction of an organism and its environment, the pragmatic "test" proposes to appeal only to "the fit" of the proposed knowledge, (in James' words), *not its conformity with reality.* Such a pragmatic test of truth is at best ambiguous and unworkable; *at worst it ignores the essential nature of truth as conformity of knowledge to an independent reality.*

4 *Pragmatism's Optimistic Attitude Toward the Future*

Implicit in the first three characteristics of pragmatism is a dangerous optimism. The denial of an independent reality and a fixed human nature appear to remove ordinary obstacles encountered in the losses of old age. For the pragmatist, reality, whether external or internal, no longer stands in the way of human endeavors. The resulting pragmatic mode of seeking truth optimistically envisages successful actions aimed at finding a future "fit" with the on-going ways of life of the truth seeker and his community

Old Age Refutations of Pragmatism

The experience of old age leads to conclusions which contradict the premises of pragmatism. In contrast to pragmatic beliefs, experience of old age leads to a deep recognition of one's own (and others) decline and imminent death. The immediate prospect of death in old age dissolves any idealism which finds human reality only in the ideas of the mind to be followed by testing them in action, since decline and death confront the old with the ineluctable presence of an independent reality outside our own soon-to-be extinguished consciousness and ultimately resistive to our manipulation. The experienced reality of decline and the prospect of death are part of a growing old age awareness of the limits of a human nature characterized by predictable stages of flourishing and decline. This awareness of the "seasons of our lives" and human mortality at the end of the season is an awareness which also confronts the presence of an independent reality. This reality will continue to exist after death and its presence challenges the fundamental premises of a pragmatism which denies a fixed human nature and an reality independent of human effort which sets limits to every human life.

In short, the pragmatic optimistic attitude towards the future contradicts the dominant reality of old age with its losses, sadness, detachment and consolation. Understanding of these facts of old age elegy is not to be gained through pragmatic action, whether scientific experimentation or other actions but only through reflection upon common sense experience, including the elegiac experience of loss, sadness, detachment and consolation. A pragmatic focus buoyed by an optimism for the future hardly comports with the present losses of old age, the sadness which results and the very limited future which it faces.

These general philosophical observations which question a pragmatic approach to old age can be best explained by examining the applicability of such pragmatic actions to the specific problems of old age. Drawing upon one of many pragmatic actions in response to the problems listed above, i.e., retirement, let us suppose that, in retirement, I proceed pragmatically. As one of the constituents of retirement, I identify the loss of work-place friends. Immediately, the idea may suggest itself that I seek to replace these lost friends from the workplace. Consequently I join a "men's group" which meets sporadically to talk about the world at large. In addition, when appropriate, I continue to attend meetings or conferences at my place of work, which continues my contact with workplace friends. I also continue joint research and writing projects with past colleagues. I increase my contacts with past friends. In the past, we sporadically attend a seminar dealing with issues arising in my late wife's profession sponsored by her friend and colleague.

These actions are intended to replace the losses of work friends in retirement, but to assess the extent to which these measures succeed in "fitting" the situation and resolving the problems requires one to interpret the precise *nature of the loss experienced* and the *kinds of friends* chosen to replace that loss. Such interpretation requires not merely the action of securing new friends*, but knowledge of the form and purpose of friendship itself.* To understand friendship, one might explore the idea of friendship by turning to an exposition of its nature within the classics. Thus, the works of Aristotle, Rousseau, Austin and Shakespeare, among others, may help in the exploration. The idea of friendship, along with its "fellow traveling" idea of love, fills the pages of many of the classical works, both ancient and modern. For example, Aristotle identifies friendship as a reciprocal relationship of affection based upon mutual enjoyments, or shared advantage, or mutual moral and intellectual stimulation aimed at improving one another. In modern work situations, most friendships are either ones of mutual enjoyment or advantage. Whether one seeks to replace these friends in old age depends upon whether such kinds of friends are still desired or whether old age signals important changes in the capacity and desire for the particular kinds of friends from a previous life.

In considering the old age loss of friends in retirement, there is another important consideration. There is a substantial literature, anecdotal and scientific which suggests that a process of social withdrawal may take place in old age. (I shall suggest below that such a withdrawal may be mirrored by the detachment from the losses and sadness found within the elegy of old age). Such detachment may have implications for the seeking or keeping of friends. This topic will be explored below.) Although the research about old age withdrawal is contested, such research, if valid in its claim to find withdrawal raises the question of the need for continuing friendship in old age. Accepting for a moment, the status quo of modern work situations and making the assumption that, upon retirement, the old person continues to desire friendships, the question becomes whether the proposed "replacement friends" adequately serve the purposes of old age friendship. Although it may be relatively clear that such replacement friends serve the purpose of mutual enjoyment, it may be less obvious as to whether the undertaking of joint projects or shared conferencing serves the mutual advantage of both parties. Since the retired person may receive little if any career or economic advantage from such joint projects and conferences, and since the other non-retired friends may not "need" a retired friend in order to pursue their own continuing careers, a mutual advantage may not be present to support such a friendship.

On the other hand, it is my contention that modern work conditions yield few opportunities for the activities of deep friendships - friendships characterized by deep emotional ties and aimed at moral and intellectual reciprocity. As a consequence, retirement from work may not result in any loss of such friendships, since such friendships are not present in work. Of course, there may be such rare friendships that may occur during work life and, of course, they should be preserved. But even if one does not find true friendships during one's work life, old age may lead to the desire to find such friends in retirement. To find such moral and intellectual reciprocity in friendships during old age, unless based upon past long term friendships, (many of which are fragile and transitional in old age), may require some shared interest and circumstance, such as the sharing of old age with its losses and sadness. Without exploring the idea here, perhaps a new unique form of old age friendship may be erected upon the mutually shared losses of old age; I shall return to this notion in my discussion of consolation.

All of these concerns about the nature and purposes of friendship suggest that even if the pragmatists are partly correct and the practical actions undertaken to replace lost friends in retirement may be desirable, such actions, to be undertaken successfully, require that one understand the very meaning of friendship in old age. It is not the blind *act* of finding new friends upon retirement which resolves this common problem of retirement. It is a *reflection upon the circumstances and meanings of old age loss as well as a detached inquiry into the more specific nature and purposes of friendship which enable one to find truth, guide and inform the activities of friendship, and thus achieving the various goods of friendship.* Contrary to pragmatism, action is not enough. Detached reflection is required to find the meaning of the appropriate action and understand it as part of a continuous activity, before, (i.e. deliberation), during, (reflective awareness) and after, (i.e. evaluation), the activity takes place.

That reflection is informed by the forms of knowledge of old age and friendship, and this knowledge is found not only in experience, but in reflection upon the classics of psychology, philosophy, and literature. In sum, if one attacks the problems of old age simply in a pragmatic manner, one denies the importance of the search for meaning of friendship in the elegy of old age.

Conclusion: The Pragmatic Denial Of Ideas in Old Age Loss

It is now useful to retrace this chapter's discussion in light of the argument of the book. I have maintained above, old age is viewed elegiacally as a stage of life of loss, sadness, detachment and consolation. As we have seen in past chapters, the response to old age may be to deny its' elegiac nature by pursuing religious beliefs, life extension through medical technology, or a quest for old age delights.

This chapter claims that the most subtle denial of old age loss comes from an often found practical approach to old age – an approach which has, as its philosophical equivalent, philosophical pragmatism. This pragmatism is consonant with American culture and it has enjoyed 100 years of continuous philosophical inquiry during the past century beginning with the work of Pierce, Dewey, and James and extending to the modern work of many contemporary philosophers. It views the search for truth as beginning with problems, seeking their resolution by treating the ideas stimulated by these problems. These ideas, however, are treated as merely suggestions or hypotheses to be tested in action. The test of these ideas lies in their practical consequences and the "fit" of these consequences with the rest of life.

Pragmatism, as applied to old age, means approaching it with the identification of generic problems, including biological decline, retirement, etc. Once such generic problems are identified, their more specific constituents are delineated. For example, in the case of retirement, the constituent problems may be the securing of adequate financial support, the searching for ways to occupy one's newly found free time, and adjusting to the lost friendships of work. The circumstances of each of these problems suggest ideas to guide one to their solution. Thus, loss of income suggests the need for non-work related *welfare,* (whether through pensions, public assistance or family assistance). The search for ways to occupy free time in retirement suggests the need to explore the idea of *leisure.* The loss of work related friends stimulates an inquiry into the nature of *friendship.*

However, pragmatism is content to posit actions to resolve the problems identified above. Thus, one might seek increased income through retirement work, volunteering to fill one's time, and reaching out to find new friends. However, to truly resolve the problem of retirement, these actions undertaken must be meaningful. The meaning of these activities is customarily found in their purposes, which continually inform the activities as they are taking place and are implicit in the activity. Thus, for example, old age friendship finds its meaning in the purposes of friendship; if the purpose of the friendship is mutual enjoyment, such enjoyment should be found in and guide the activities of the friendship. Similarly, the purposes of welfare and leisure will inform the activities of financial support and the occupation of free time in retirement.

Thus, to understand the meaning of these activities requires an exploration of the meaning of the ideas of welfare, leisure, and friendship- ideas which set forth the form and purposes of the activity in question. These ideas remain at the heart of any consideration of the meaning of old age retirement and similar meanings underlie the understanding of the other losses in old age. Only though reflective meditation can one such meanings.

Unfortunately, the pragmatic treatment of old age, by reducing old age to problems to be resolved through action based upon ideas functioning as hypotheses, ignores the fact that ideas are not merely hypotheses for action. They are concepts with intellectual content which rest at the heart of understanding both these losses of old age, their elegiac consequences and any consolation for those losses. Detached reflection upon the losses of old age with the help of these ideas is necessary in order to achieve an understanding of the losses and sadness, achieve detachment from these losses, and guide activities undertaken to secure some degree of consolation.

CHAPTER IX

The Tradition Of The Classics

What are the classics but the noblest recorded thoughts of man. They are the only oracles which are not decayed. –Thoreau

"The Foundation [of conversation] must be laid by reading. General principles must be had from books, which, however, must be brought to the test of real life." - *Samuel Johnson*

When I was a child, I was tutored in the children's classics by my Mother. I was a bookish child who delighted in reading, in part, no doubt to please her. At my first undergraduate college, the library portico was emblazoned with Cicero's saying – He who knows only his own generation remains always a child". When I went to the University of Chicago, I found a university, inspired by Robert Maynard Hutchins which believed in and taught the great works and their important ideas. The curriculum was based upon the ordered study of the great works in the humanities, the natural and social sciences, mathematics, and languages. After undergraduate work, I pursued the study of philosophy, primarily through the study of the great philosophical works. After Chicago, I studied Marx, Weber, and other social thought at the London School of Economics. In the later non-academic years of my life, I took time out to teach the great books and study the works of

Hegel and Whitehead. Upon returning to academia later in life, I once again embraced the study of both environmental classics and jurisprudential works. Late in life, I read Walter Watson's The Architectonics of Meaning, *and Mortimer Adler's Syntopicon, which demonstrated how a pluralism of principles shaped the classic texts and perennial ideas established their relationships –* one *to another. This insight governs my view of the tradition of classics. I ended my academic years in the study of selected ancient authors and their relationship to modern law, editing books on Plato, Aristotle, Cicero, Augustine and Aquinas and the modern legal commentaries on their works. Now, in old age, I read the classics, both ancient and modern and explore their relationship to my old age.*

Introduction

In his old age, the Roman statesman and orator, Cicero, retired to write a series of works on the Greek classics to introduce them to the Roman public. These books canvassed the various views of the good life, *(De Finibus),* the universe and God, *(De Natura Deorum),*and death and pain, *(Tusculan Disputations).* He also wrote a short and perennially popular essay on old age, *(De Senectude),* urging a very modern agenda for coping with the travails of old age. In this latter essay, he found that activities, such as agriculture or philosophy are best adjusted to the more limited physical powers of the aged, that more modest and intellectual pleasures are embraced with old age decline, in part due to our lessened capacity to enjoy physical pleasure. Fear of death is allayed in old age by carefully considering, (in part by reading the Stoic philosophers), the limited pains of dying and the lack of pain after death. Cicero also suggested that the loss of power which comes with retirement need not prevent the elder from offering wise counsel on public affairs. Unfortunately, the ambitious old Cicero could not keep from meddling in the political affairs in late Republican Rome. As Plutarch tells the story in another classic, *The Lives,* Cicero, later in life, intervened in the Roman civil wars, attacking Anthony in his famed series of orations – *The Philippics*. Anthony's henchmen traced Cicero back to his seaside country- house.

"...But, in the meantime the assassins were come with a band of soldiers...Find [ing] the doors shut, they broke them open...a youth, who had been educated by Cicero in the liberal arts and sciences, informed [them] that [Cicero's litter] was on its way to the sea....Cicero, perceive [ing] [the assassins] running in the walks, commanded his servants to set down the litter; and stroking his chin, as he used to do, with his left hand, he looked steadfastly upon his murderers, his person covered with dust, his beard and hair untrimmed, and his face worn with his troubles. ..And then he was murdered, stretching forth his neck out of the litter... [Anthony] commanded his head and hands to be fastened up over the rostra where the orators spoke..."

Such a story should give anyone pause in drawing wisdom from the classical works including those works written by a great Roman statesman! But to ignore Cicero's classic works would be to ignore someone who faced up to his old age by consulting the classic works. Thus, Cicero consulted the works of prior Greek philosophers including the Stoic, Epicurean, Peripatetic, and Academic philosophies about serious problems facing old age including the ends of life itself and the meanings of pain and death. His work not only deeply informed the later works of Christian thinkers such as Augustine and Aquinas, but his ideas on rhetoric helped to shape one branch of liberal education throughout the ages . The Founders of our American constitution read his works and benefited from them in the adoption of the constitution. Even in the midst of his own personal and political troubles, Cicero was able to detach himself, if only for the moment, with the help of the Greek classics. Like Cicero, I freely admit to being an enthusiastic supporter of the importance of classic works, ("the best that has been thought and said in the world..."), and, hence, It is not surprising that I believe that rather than Augustine's deep religious faith, or Bacon's robust endorsement of science or Epicurus' quiet delight in the calm pleasures of old age, (all of which I discussed in the previous chapters), the calling upon the tradition of classics offers a deeper understanding of old age and better solace for the experiences of loss during that old age.

The Tradition of Classics

By the tradition of classics, I do not mean only the writings of ancient Greece and Rome or a carefully delineated list of "Great Books". I am comfortable with extending the tradition of the classics to the significant important writings of the western tradition, the important works of fine art and architecture, and the accounts and monuments of influential practical accomplishments in western history and its' thought. Unlike some, such as Harold Bloom, who appear to limit the list of important works to the humanities, I believe that the classic works include the works of the natural and social sciences, as well as the humanities. In fact there are marvelous presentations of those scientific works, such as Hawkings, *On the Shoulders of Giants,* social sciences, such as Donald Levine's *Visions of the Sociological Tradition,* law, such as Ephraim London's *Monuments of Law,* and art and architecture in Giorgio Vasari, *Lives of the Painter, Sculptors and Architects.* When I first thought about "the classic" as a source for wisdom about old age, I ignored fine art works, but when I remembered my thrill of first hearing the Faure Requiem or beholding Michelangelo's statute of Nicodemus in a late Pieta, I knew I must include the fine arts in the tradition of classics important to old age. Despite the belief of some that the fine arts cannot and should not be reduced to ideas, these works do provoke feelings and corresponding ideas, both of which may be deeply relevant to old age, its losses, and its consolation. Moreover, in viewing the accomplishments or reading accounts of statesmen and lawgivers, whether ancient, such as those reported in Plutarch's *Lives,* or modern political works, such as the Constitution and *The Federalist Papers,* I have found a similar measure of greatness and so I include both the works and biographies of great statesmen.

Reluctantly, I have excluded from my definition of the classic tradition the major works of the East and Middle East as well as important works of most minorities, not because I judge them to be inferior, but simply because I am not familiar with them, and hence, they do not operate to assist my detachment and consolation in my old age, and I suspect that many of my readers do not know them either. Even with my omission of Eastern and Middle Eastern classics, the list of western classic works is formidable. One of the best known recent set of such written works is the Encyclopedia Britannica's *Great Books* which includes not only sixty odd volumes but also a huge well organized bibliography of other major works in the western tradition. Encyclopedia Britannica has also published 25 annual supplementary volumes (*The Great Ideas*) containing all or part of up to 75 other works) as well as a "Gateway" to the great books which includes shorter works by major authors. A myriad of other collections and lists of classics have been published over the centuries.

Of course, there is no complete agreement on what should be included or excluded from these lists although there is more overlap in the lists than one might imagine; fortunately, my task is not to prepare such a list, but rather to draw upon those books which appear to shed light upon the elegy of old age. Obviously, all of these works cannot be consulted and a degree of arbitrary selection is inevitable. When one is young and beholds such a list, it may be inspiring since one imagines that one might read them all in the course of one's life. On the other hand, in old age, such an extensive list may be profoundly depressing since there is little time or energy to master any but a few of parts of few of these works. But, when one accepts the importance of the vast number of works in question, a sense of relief and humility arrives with the realization of the limits of one's actual and possible knowledge. Such a realization is especially vivid in old age!

To identify classic works, some understanding of the criteria for selecting and reading or appreciating in Yeats' language, such "monuments of unaging intellect". These works may be the product and expression of key historical eras or events in western history. They may be intellectually influential in history or seminal in the history of thought, art and action. As a consequence they are a cumulative part of our culture and education. They have stood the test of time, and have been valued over the course of different periods of history. They also stand the test of time in one's own life, since they may be read and reread with profit and enjoyment throughout one's life. Their success may be due to their suggestibility of a rich variety of meanings, as well as their profundity and depth, constituting models of thought central to an understanding of systems of thought, academic disciplines, or as artistic formulations which touch our feelings of humanity in deep and permanent ways. They may supply sophisticated and complex arguments which expose the complexities of their ideas. They may deliver universal truths and instances of remarkable beauty.

These classics are part of a continuous tradition of diverse works, and are often shaped by the works preceding and following them. Within that tradition, they often refer to one another, deriving meaning from each other, but often fighting with one another as well. They are often original, but in their originality, they may incorporate the ideas of past works within their creativity. This tradition of past works is shaped by individual works with incommensurable principles. Nevertheless, despite their diversity and frequent conflict, these classics contain permanent truths as well as remarkable accounts of scientific experiments or other methods of discovery, and different examples of how beauty may be found in art.

These works have been an integral part of liberal education in ancient, medieval, and modern times. In *The Great Conversation*, Robert Hutchins, President of the University of Chicago and Editor of the Great Books set forth in bold terms the case for a university curriculum for the classics and for publishing the classics. Writing in 1952, he suggested that there was a western tradition of great works important for a liberal education within democracy. This tradition includes political, social, economic, natural science and humanities works from ancient Greece to the twentieth century, which, until "recently", were central to education in the West. Hutchins opined that a liberal education in these books operates to clarify basic problems in any age, facilitate the learning of the liberal arts and provide a basis for more specialized education. While including the experimental sciences in the classics and liberal education, Hutchins rejects the application of the scientific method as appropriate to all fields of knowledge. Hutchins also rejects the pragmatism of John Dewey and the economic realists who argue that every citizen cannot benefit from a liberal education. Hutchins suggests that the modern economy can support the leisure necessary for all to secure a liberal education. Hutchins concludes that the classics begin to equip citizens to cope with what will be world problems and, to create eventually a world republic of law and justice which will embrace both eastern and western traditions.

In his fine little book, Hutchins invites us all to participate in an education which was informed by the western classics. The notion of a continuous and chronological tradition of significant works is important for reasons articulated by Edmund Burke. Such a tradition links the past generations to the present and future generations, broadening our vision through time. In Burke's language, society is "a partnership in all science; a partnership in all art; a partnership in every virtue, and in all perfection" … not only between those who are living but between those who are living, those who are dead, and those who are to be born". Such a partnership suggests the need to preserve that tradition through participating *within* it. That tradition, as described by T.S. Eliot, is formed by the existing monuments which have both a temporal and timeless dimension. At the same time, individuals, in their work, draw upon that tradition and, in doing so, become aware of the how that tradition affects them and how their work is part of a greater whole. In the process of writing this book, I have become aware of how it is part of an extensive tradition of works extending back to ancient times.

In the modern age, at least until recently, the tradition of classics was respected in academic circles, although some philosophers, such as Francis Bacon or John Dewey, argue for a more science oriented approach to all knowledge. In the past, the classics were often taught either in pedantic exercises of translation of Greek or Latin works or in predigested textual summaries. (The curricula of the University of Chicago, Columbia and St. Johns College were notable exceptions). In the late 20th century, a variety of historical forces and intellectual developments has fueled an intense "anti-canonism". Such "anti-canonism" is supported by appeals to a range of philosophical and literary theories which attack "the canon" for masking the realities of social, economic and political power – power which determine which works were to be included in "the canon" itself. More important, these anti-canonists claimed that the canon appeals to spurious universal themes (such as human nature) and these universals mask particular social and political realities resting "underneath" of the classic tradition and hidden by it. As applied to my efforts to understand old age through the tradition of the classics, these "anti-canonists" would suggest that my old age might be very different from the old age of an ancient Greek aristocrat or a poor uneducated modern resident of a nursing home. One of the most famous modern treatments of old age in poverty is written by the Marxist informed existentialist, Simone de Beauvoir, who, in *Coming of Age*, describes the "objective" social reality of oppression and poverty to underlie the subjective experiences of old age for many. But Beauvoir also recognizes the shared subjective existential experience of aging in all classes and times. Without denying that my efforts to give or find meaning in old age through the classics may be prejudiced by my own education, affluence and good health, (at the moment!), I will suggest and seek to demonstrate that there are certain universal losses in old age which apply to all of us, whether rich or poor, and awareness and understanding of these losses are available to many of the aged through at least some of the classics.

Ironically, the canon includes the classic works of many who would argue against the canon itself! The contemporary anti-canonists seek to impose a limited number of current fads of thought: Marxist, existentialist, structuralist, deconstructionalist or feminist philosophies- all of which assume that the classics must be understood only through the lens of these particular philosophies. But the tradition of the classics is much broader than the works of Marx, Foucault, Derrida, Sartre or others, although indeed, their works, in their power and depth, should be included within the list of classics. The tradition of classics embraces a broad pluralism of works ranging from Plato and Aristotle to John Dewey and William James, from St. Thomas Aquinas to Karl Marx, from Cicero to Spinoza. These classic works embrace a variety, diverse and conflicting assumptions and principles. It remains to all of us, including the old, to choose among this rich variety offered by the tradition of classics to find "a fit" with our age and its problems

The selection of classics in old age and exploring their meanings for the understanding of old age provide a series of criteria by which I may choose among the myriad of great works. First, I am content simply to indicate that I have found and chosen some significant works which I have loved to read and reread and which seem especially relevant to an understanding of old age based upon their content and my own experience. Second, I have further extended my selection of works by including elegiac writings, since I have organized and framed my discussion of old age based upon the central insight that old age may be viewed in elegiac terms. Third, I have also included works which address the elements of elegy – loss, sadness, detachment, and consolation.

1. Significant Works Dealing Directly with Old Age

My selection of works to those dealing with old age either directly or indirectly. Fortunately, two thoughtful scholars reviewed all of Britannica's *Great Books* as well as a selection of French classics to identify almost 400 significant references to old age. Perhaps such scholarly efforts are not needed. For example, anyone familiar with ancient plays can pick out Sophocles' *Oedipus at Colonus* as a remarkable portrait of old Oedipus. Two millennia later, Shakespeare drew a very different portrait of a old king in *King Lear*. If one turns to philosophy, in Plato's *Republic,* the old Cephalus begins the dialogue, but soon leaves to make his religious sacrifices; in Plato's *Laws* one can find oldsters sitting under a tree in Crete, engaging in an extensive discussion of the drafting of legislation for the new colony. Novels, such Mann's *Death in Venice*, or Balzac's *Pere Gorgio* come to mind as well. To demonstrate these works are not simply isolated examples of the treatment of old age, I have discussed many other works in this book and appended to this book a list of works in which I believe the theme of old age is important.

Listing works which explicitly deal with the subject of old age does not begin to plumb the depth of relevance of the canon to old age. The canon deals with old age obliquely as well. For example as I have suggested above, understanding old age requires an understanding of the stages of a whole life. But many biographical, e.g., Boswell's *Life of Samuel Johnson, LLD.)* biological, (Weismann's *The Duration of Life*, psychological (Erikson's *Identity and the Life Cycle)* and philosophical (Aristotle's *Nicomachean Ethics*) works deal with the topic of a whole life and its development in stages. Such treatments shed light upon old age as part of the life cycle. Other works dealing indirectly with matters relevant to old age may adopt a religious perspective on old age rather than viewing it as simply a transition station on the way to an afterlife. The description of the after- life, as provided by Dante in the *Divine Comedy*, may hold significant Implications for understanding one kind of religious view of old age as the completion of an person's entire life filled with sins which which merited assignment to hell for punishment, purgatory for purification or even the proximity to God in heaven.

2. Elegy and the Tradition of Classics

As the introduction indicated, the central theme of this book is that old age is best understood within the framework of elegy. The idea of elegy helps to select the relevant works and ideas pertaining to old age. The classic elegies compose a rich history in western poetry and prose, which I did not detail in the introduction. The ancient works of Ovid, as well as the English elegists, Spenser, Shakespeare, Milton, Gray, Shelley, Tennyson, Swinburne, Hardy and Yeats are part of any classics of western literature. Modern poets, such as T.S. Eliot, Pound, Auden, Stevens, and many others have continued the tradition of elegiac poetry. There is even a scattered selection of modern old age elegies including works by Spender, Penn Warren, Brogan, Van Doren (Mark) and others. Modern prose works by Agee, Woolf, Joyce, James, Hemingway, and Faulkner have broadened the elegiac tradition, finding new occasions of loss in form of family disintegration, withdrawal of love, breakdown of marriage, the fading of ideals, the eclipse of a culture and the disintegration of the self. Many such losses are experienced in old age. Given this extension of the elegy from the poetry for the death of a loved one to the prose of losses of all kinds, a further extension may find the "elegiac temper" in histories, such as Huizinga's *The Waning of the Middle Ages* and philosophies, such as Unamuno's *The Tragedy of Life*.

3. The Elements of Elegy

The classic works also shed light upon each of the elements of elegy: the nature of the goods lost, the nature of the processes of loss, the efforts to prevent the loss, the state of the old person after loss, the emotions resulting from specific losses, the efforts to detach from loss and the consolations sought or found for such losses. The goods which are lost in old age are both external goods – friends and access to the world – and internal goods - the capabilities of adult life. The classics shed light upon both sets of goods – works on the nature of external goods such as friendship and political participation, and works on internal goods such as health, moral virtues or intellectual activities. The classics address each of the kinds of losses within old age offer themselves up to conceptual analysis. The losses pertaining to retirement are understood through a probing of classic works which deal with the ideas of work and leisure. The biological works of Aristotle and Darwin have importance for understanding the biological decline we undergo. The psychological works such as William James' *Principles of Psychology* address the loss of mind and memory. The eclipse of the past and the foreclosure of the future in old age stimulates an exploration into the notion of time itself. Thus, selected classics may be related to each of the specific losses in old age.

The elderly person is less capable than his earlier self, more vulnerable and more dependent than earlier in life. There is one residual emotion - sadness or melancholy - which dominates old age. Such a feeling of sadness is captured in the letters of Ovid, the poetry of Donne, Yeats, Shakespeare, and T.S. Eliot, the essays of Montaigne, the biography of Johnson by Boswell, the novels of Cervantes, Aldous Huxley, Hemingway, Lampedusa, Beckett, as well and the magnum opus on melancholy by Robert Burton. The discussion of melancholy can be found or experienced in many of the many elegiac authors listed above, and, as we might expect, modern theorists of "melancholy" and mourning extend to from Aristotle to Derrida. The western tradition of thought including the works of Plato and Aristotle, the Stoics and Epicureans, Augustine and Aquinas, Hume and Spinoza, Freud and Jung suggest different theories of the nature of emotions, including sadness, and their relationship to reason, One recent work, Eva Brann's *Feeling Our Feelings* supplies a remarkable account and interpretation of these theories. Although understanding the full scope of these theories is beyond this book, some of the authors identified by Brann may be judiciously selected to help us understand the nature of our feelings in old age. Not only do the classics supply different views of the nature of emotion as such, but they also supply a variety of descriptions and analyses of a variety of specific emotions we experience in response to the specific losses in our old age. For example the poet, Ovid, supplies us with vivid description of his sadness at his exile- an exile not dissimilar to involuntary and even some voluntary retirements. A social and economic analysis of the alienation experienced in some retirement is set forth in the works of Durkheim and Marx. The feeling of shame may accompany the increase of our dependency in old age.

I have identified in the previous chapter some of the classics which shed light upon the nature of detachment in confronting old age loss and sadness. With the help of classics, I described a process of detachment which may take place Imaginative literature, with examples such as Thoreau's *Walden* which offers descriptions of social withdrawal and the classic philosophies of detachment and solitude, and Petrarch's *The Solitary Life* and Montaigne's *Essays* which become important to understanding intellectual detachment. But since I have not yet addressed consolation of old age, let me turn to this final element in elegy – anticipating a more detailed treatment in the final chapter below. In an elegiac account of old age we seek consolation for the losses we encounter. We begin to find such consolations from the elegiac works of mourning which occur not only for the dead, but also for those experiencing other losses. With such losses of old age, we elderly seek substitutes for what we have lost - calm pleasures to replace the lost passions of our younger days, sedentary activities which fit our limited physical capabilities, thus, replacing the more intense exercises of our youth, a newly constructed history to make up for our fading memories, invented legacies to leap over our limited future, even the reformulation of our death – not as nothingness, but as the end of a hopefully rich and full life or, at least, a final escape from a painful one.

The Classics and Detachment -The Role of Perennial Ideas

How then, do the classics facilitate the process of detachment from the losses of old age? First, each classic exhibits a unique perspective which may differ radically from our own view or, if it mirrors our own views, expresses them in a way different from our own view . For example Montaigne sees the world in a subjective and personal manner which may be different from our own more objective point of view. Or vice versa. Spinoza may adopt an objective view of the universe, while we may wallow in our own personal views of our world. The nature of the reality which a text or other work expresses may differ from our own view of reality. Thus, while we, like Shakespeare, may regard reality as a passing parade of appearances, others, such as Marx or Freud, find reality underneath everyday appearances, in the substrative workings of economic relations or psychological forces. In addition, the author of a classic may think in ways very different from us. Thus, some classics are framed around conflict, such as Milton's *Paradise Lost*, while others purport to be strictly logical, such as Descartes' *Discourse on Method*. These differences between our own perspectives, realities and manners of thought compared to those of the classic works we encounter can jog us out of the immersion in our own way of thought allowing us to abstract from our ordinary way of thinking.

Second, the classics supply an abundance of universal ideas and principles through which we may view reality, including the reality of old age. In the works of Mortimer Adler:

> "The great ideas are not simple objects of thought.
> Each of the great ideas seems to have a complex interior

structure…[they] are also the conceptions by which we think about things. They are the terms in which we state fundamental problems; they are the notions we employ in defining issues and discussing them. They represent the principal content of our thought. They are what we think as well as what we think about…."

In this book, I have looked to the idea of loss of *good,* the *emotion* of sadness, the defects of *religion,* the limits of old age *pleasure,* the failure of *science,* the meaningless of old age *action,* the possibility of old age *freedom,* the nature of *detachment* with the help of the *classics.* All of the italicized ideas have a tradition of meanings found in the tradition of the classics. In the future chapters, I will explore the nature of *liberal education, adult education* and old age *reflective meditation.* In the final chapters, I shall employ the ideas of *leisure, health, time and history, the future, dependency* and dignity, *progress,* and *death.* The conclusion will discuss *consolation.* In short, with these classics, we are supplied with the universal ideas and principles which enable us to study old age and its losses and meditate with detachment on its consolations.

Aristotle's Questioning of the Benefits of the Classics

Aristotle would not accept my praise of the classics for old age, partly because they are not suited to old age, partly because books and art do not promote virtue. Aristotle did not have a very high opinion of the elderly populace, if his remarks in the *Rhetoric* are to be accepted. In laying out arguments for the kind of emotions one should appeal to in rhetorical argument, he found the elderly audience :

"…have lived many years; they have often been taken in, and often made mistakes; life on the whole is a bad business. As a result, they are sure about nothing and "underdo" everything. ..They are cynical, that is they tend to put the worst construction on everything.

Further, their experience makes them distrustful and
therefore suspicious of evil ...they neither love warmly
or hate bitterly. ..they are small minded because they
are humbled by life; their desires are set upon nothing
more exalted than what will keep them alive... they
are not generous...they are cowardly...they love life,
the more when their last day has come...they are too
fond of themselves...they guide their lives too much
by what is useful and too little by what is noble...they
are shameless...they lack confidence in the future...
they live by memory rather than by home...their fits
of anger are sudden but feeble... their sensual passions
have either altogether gone or have lost their vigor...they
are slaves to the love of gain...old men feel pity... out of
weakness...they are querulous. ..."

This observation not only reflects Aristotle's poor opinion of the
elderly but also the belief that it is character, shaped in part by habit
which guides our lives. Let me summarize the *Ethics*. In the work,
Aristotle suggests that all of the activities of life, (and, by implication,
life itself), pursue some good, and, for humans, that good is happiness
or fulfillment. Happiness of Aristotle is not a static state or "a product"
(hence possession of wealth, property, acquisition of academic degrees in
itself does not make up happiness). Rather, for Aristotle, happiness is a
uniquely human activity conducted in accordance with the excellences
which humans may possess. More specifically, these excellences are
states of self-sufficient character which include developed capabilities -
the product of nature, custom, education, and the past choices we make.
Ordinarily these excellences are referred to as "virtues" (but without the
connotation of chastity!) These virtues are both moral and intellectual
capabilities acquired by the deliberative choice under guidance. The
actions taken according to these virtues are set by a mean, (the famous
"golden mean") between extremes, according to the circumstances.
Thus, a courageous act would be one between a rash and a cowardly
act according to the circumstances. The moral virtues include courage,

temperance, liberality, magnificence, proper pride, moderate ambition, friendliness, good temper, truthfulness, ready wit, proper shame, and justice. The intellectual virtues include science, art, practical wisdom, intuition, and philosophic wisdom. Friendship was also deemed to be an important condition for a happy life. Aristotle was realistic enough to recognize that many of us pursue pleasure and he was no prude. For him, pleasure emerged out of the practice of virtuous activities and the immoderate pursuit of pleasure constituted either vice or an incontinent life. On the other hand one might be continent, leading what appears to be a virtuous life but not possessing fully the character of virtue. Finally, Aristotle found the highest form of happiness to be found in speculative activity in which only human thought may achieve identity with the highest forms of being.

Thus, Aristotle's view of the elderly as quoted above suggests that he regards their character to be already shaped by their past lives and present circumstances. Aristotle defines the virtues and their practice according to "a mean" in relation to the circumstances; old age may be one such circumstance which changes the mean by which the virtues are realized. The virtues of old age may have to fit the circumstances of old age perfectly well – courage in the face of pain and death in old age, temperance in living habits, good temper and ready wit in the face of old age losses, proper pride for one's past. These are virtues which the elderly may be expected to exercise and which fit their condition. But such virtues depend, not upon the old age reading of classics, but rather the acquisition of a kind of character. That character is itself developed through experience and practice. In the words of Aristotle,

> "Now character, as the word itself indicates, is that which is developed from habit; and anything is habituated which, as a result of guidance which is not innate, through being changed in a certain way repeatedly is eventually capable of acting that way…

The emphasis upon habit and repetition might suggest that the virtues needed to confront the losses of old age are simply aspects of character formed by routine habit early in life. But the actions for forming habit require" guidance". Such guidance helps the learner to perceive the moral dimensions of the situation, assists him with the assessment of the purposes of the action and promotes deliberation and judgment in the choosing the action in question.

The classics, especially literature and history, help with the learning of moral perception, understanding and judgment, since these works recount examples of such perceptions. The purposes of action are explored in the ethical, social, and political literature; deliberation for achieving the means to achieve such purposes is assisted by the full range of knowledge found in the classics as well as accounts of prudence are found the classics. Hence, Aristotle's account of ethical action allows for a contribution by the classics and hence we can learn from Aristotle's own classic work and "apply" it to old age. Aristotle's conclusions may carry other implications which argue against undue reliance on the classics to cope with old age. It is clear that the sources of virtue, whether in early life or in old age, are not found in the reading of books but in the inculcation of right habits and the formation of a good character. From this point of view, Aristotle's own canon work argues against simply relying upon the reading of great books or the appreciation of fine arts as a precursor to living a virtuous old age. Aristotle's *Ethics* is a warning about the limits of "bookishness". Thus, Aristotle supplies an answer to the contradiction between Cicero's old age wise words based upon his reading of the classics and Cicero's own actions leading to his murder. Reading is not enough and Cicero may have lacked the other virtues necessary for a safe old age.

Despite some permanent truths which may be found in Aristotle's *Ethics,* more recent works have reinterpreted, supplemented or rejected all or parts of Aristotle's *Ethics*. This is one reason why *the tradition of classics* is important; it contains earlier or later works which operate as a check upon our understanding of apparent truths taken from the first classic we consult.Thus, after reading the *Ethics*, one might review the Stoic account which recognizes the important role of fortune and will power within our lives – roles which may modify the impact of culture and character. Later works might include the Christian addition to

Aristotle's work by St. Thomas Aquinas who fleshes out a fuller and richer view of the eternal objects for contemplation at any age, the utilitarian critique by John Stuart Mill who suggests a more important role for pleasure in the pursuit of happiness at any age, and the idealist critique of Immanuel Kant which seeks to explain how we might achieve freedom despite the apparently deterministic force of our past character. In modern times, there have been many efforts to interpret, correct, or refute Aristotle's *Ethics.* All of these works shed very different lights upon the relevance of the classics to old age

Conclusion

The argument of the first nine chapters of this book has now marched to the present conclusion: old age is a time of loss and sadness, for which detachment and consolation are needed. One instrument of detachment, (but not the only one), is a reverential reading and appreciation of classics, "the best that has been thought and said" and the appreciation of great art and historical accomplishments. Reverence for the classics is a love based upon recognition that they are not merely a meager list of great books nor a set of works of art, but part of an extensive educational and cultural tradition which exerts its fluctuating but cumulative influence and authority upon our lives and society. These works facilitate detachment from the immediate wounds of old age loss and console for that loss by supplying the transparent bandages of universal ideas through which we can view those losses and take distance from them. The classics facilitate detachment from our losses. Many of them regard old age and its losses in different ways than we might experience them, thus enabling us to observe with detachment our losses as reflected in the narratives and theories of these works. Moreover, these works supply universal ideas pertaining to old age, ideas through which we are allowed to find significant meanings in our old age.

A great educator of the twentieth century, Robert Maynard Hutchins, argues persuasively that over time all citizens may benefit from a liberal education which enables every adult to gain access to the classics. But in the near term, many of the aged living today, whether because of inadequate past education or economic and social constraints, will not have the time, desire, or capacity to seek detachment and solace in the classics. On the other hand, in the United States today, approximately one third of the adults are college graduates who presumably are equipped to read or appreciate at least some of the classic works or to engage in adult education courses which can equip them to do so. It is among this group, along with those presently in the educational pipelines and who are destined to grow old over the next 30 years to whom this book is addressed. In the following three chapters, I shall set forth the kinds of liberal education in the classics which equip them to enjoy the garlands of repose in old age.

CHAPTER X

The Beginnings of a Liberal Education

"I must reiterate that you can set no store by your education in childhood and youth, no matter how good it was. Childhood and youth is not time to get ready to get an education. The most we can hope for...is that we shall set on the right path of realizing our human possibilities through intellectual effort and aesthetic appreciation..." Robert Maynard Hutchins

At different stages of my life, I have participated in ventures in liberal education. I taught an urban studies course at Connecticut College, an environmental law course at Dartmouth College and a legal ethics, torts and jurisprudence courses at Vermont Law School. In all of these courses, I sought to introduce the reading of relevant classics into the assignments and even compiled two books Green Justice *and* Torts: Classics Lite. *These efforts were only partially successful. But I also participated in a Great Books program, both as participant and leader and this experience was much more successful, in part because we were a small discussion group focusing upon a given text, in part because our attendance was voluntary and in part because mature adults attended. It was this experience along with my early liberal education which converted me to a deep belief in the value of liberal education though the study of the classics.*

Introduction

A liberal education, before and during old age, is necessary to reaching an understanding of our whole life and its final stage of old age. Old age is a unique stage of life in which, if we are likely, we are enabled to look back over our life and its history. At the same time, old age, as a stage of life is characterized by loss, sadness, detachment, and some consolations. The classics can help us understand this "elegy of old age", especially enabling our detachment from the losses and providing the means of quiet consolation for them. Liberal education helps us to gain access to the classics. This liberal education normally takes place in liberal arts colleges for the youth, but it is or should be preserved, tested, and strengthened by adult education as well. In adulthood, we hopefully integrate the ideas and principles of the education of our youth. In old age we meditate upon the ideas such classics offer to understand our old age as part of our entire life.

In this regard, the example of Jefferson is worth noting and I shall often cite his life and old age since, he exemplifies my ideal of a liberal education. As a youth, he studied Greek and Latin, the ancient classics, history, science, law, ethics, philosophy and most of the other subjects of a traditional liberal education. This form of liberal education was outlined by John Stuart Mill almost a century later in his inaugural lecture to *St Andrews* and I shall discuss Mill below. (In the next chapter, I shall recount how, in middle age, Jefferson drew upon that education, especially his reading of natural history and the legal classics, to write his *Notes on the State of Virginia* and how, in old age, he drew upon that education, which was continuous throughout his adult life, to recommend the curriculum for the University of Virginia and to conduct extensive communications on all manner of subjects with the intellectual and political leaders of his day). Jefferson's life is important since it suggests that a liberal education, in youth and during adulthood is desirable for an understanding the middle years and the final stage of our lives and, perhaps, the coping with the losses of old age.

In the previous chapters, I suggested that the classics are the primary instruments for achieving detachment from the losses in old age. However, understanding and appreciating the classics and their implications for old age depends upon our acquiring the knowledge, habits, and disciplines necessary to read and understand these classics. A liberal education introduces us to these classics and during our college years, exposes us to the means of obtaining the habits and disciplines needed to understand them. Developing habits and disciplines requires time, indeed, an entire lifetime, and testing the truth of the classics also requires the experience of adulthood and old age. Hence, liberal education must take place over a lifetime. *Exposure to liberal education in our youthful college years, followed by perfecting of the disciplines and testing the conclusion of the classics in our adult life, and finally meditating upon our entire life in old age in light of the classics are the three necessary stages for composing a lifetime liberal education.* Ideally, this lifetime education would be supported by a learning society which provides the leisure, culture and kind of education necessary to pursue such an education. The outline of a "learning society" was first portrayed in Werner Jaeger's portrait of ancient Greek society in his three-volume work, *Paideia*. A modern discussion is sketched by Robert Hutchins in his classic work, *The Learning Society*. But Hutchins, writing almost a half century ago, discerned an unfortunate evolution of our educational system towards a centralized national system promoting primarily the goals of economic development and national defense and the disappearance of liberal education. Thus, if Hutchins is correct, anyone pursuing the desire to acquire the capabilities bestowed by a liberal education in youth and adulthood, will have assume control for his own education. To do so requires the becoming an autodidact, picking up from college and from elsewhere the skills necessary for such an education. (Mortimer Adler, in his *Guidebook to Learning,* offers one such guide). In order to sketch my view of this lifetime education, this chapter will concentrate upon a youthful liberal education, i.e. high school and undergraduate college education. The next chapter will discuss adult liberal education, and a third chapter will discuss reflective meditation – a unique form of education in old age.

Objections to Liberal Education for Old Age

There are five major objections to the claim that a liberal education can help one in old age. First, there is simply the fact that most old people are not suited to engage in the activities demanded by a liberal education. Second, to the extent that some old people are suited to such activities, they are a small minority "elite". Third, it is suggested that old people don't need a liberal education; they hopefully have the experience of a lifetime and a natural wisdom. A fourth objection is that an early college liberal education is erased by a lifetime of forgetting. As Woody Allen, the comedian, has pointed out, most of us remember one line from each of the college courses we took. A fifth objection suggests that a liberal education, valuable as it might be, will not assist in coping with the deep losses of life including the losses in old age. I will address each objection in turn.

First, the grand claim for an important role of liberal education in old age is rejected by those who view old age as only a stage of physical and mental decrepitude. We know elderly who fit Aristotle's savage description in his *Rhetoric*. A more extensive discussion of Aristotle's approach is set forth in the previous chapter.

> Elderly men...have often been taken in and often made mistakes and life on the whole is a bad business...They are small minded because they have been humbled by life...They are cowardly and are always anticipating danger...They are not shy, but shameless rather...they live by memory rather than by hope... Their fits of anger are sudden but feeble...They guide their lives more by reasoning than by moral feeling...they are querulous....

While there is little doubt that physical and mental decline is an eventual companion of old age, liberal education can help us cope with these problems of decline of mind and body as well as the other losses in old age although I shall be the first to recognize that when the deep stages of debilitation arrive, liberal education will probably be of little use.

In a second argument against the proposition that a youthful liberal education is useful for the old, (perhaps in response to the example of Jefferson discussed above), some will argue that a liberal education is a rare commodity for anyone and hence my appeal to an education from which few will benefit reeks of undemocratic elitism. To be sure, such elitism can be found in the works of the originators of the idea of a liberal education – Plato and Aristotle. Aristotle did not believe that all the elderly would benefit from a liberal education because he believed that only a few of any age would benefit. He thought that a liberal education required that educable children would have to possess a natural temperament, which would provide the basis for the practice of a variety of moral virtues. These virtues were required to benefit from a proper education over time. Since not all children have such temperaments nor do all develop moral virtues and few, whether because of lack of motivation or opportunity may be motivated to pursue such an education. Even when the student possesses a good character and is motivated, there remains the need for individual and societal resources to support further education.

In the classic Greek view, a liberal education would be the exercise in political or intellectual activities pursued for their own sake within a state of leisure: that is, freedom from the necessity of work to support oneself and the opportunity to learn for its own sake. Only those who had leisure could benefit from such an education. For the ancient Greeks, such leisure was based upon a society in which slaves, artisans and farmers provided the economic support for an aristocracy which might pursue learning or political activities. If Aristotle is correct, only a few might benefit from liberal education for and in old age. In fairness to Aristotle, he envisaged the possibility of the mechanization of labor which might replace slavery, but even with this change, the educational and political principles he advanced, which accepted at least a partial inequality "by nature" in the political community meant that a minority only would be able to benefit from a liberal education.

Since the time of Aristotle, and especially in the last century, there has been a significant increase in schooling, including a liberal education for thousands. There has also been an increase in free time for many, especially during old age. For many old people in the United States and Europe, the retirement years are blessed with good health and adequate economic support whether through savings, homeownership, private pensions or social security. As a consequence, liberal education, as a leisure pursuit of learning for its own sake, seems uniquely appropriate to the lives of the modern educated elderly, who are freed from work, and in relatively good health. To be sure, the free time of many of the elderly is presently devoted to family and recreation, but many of the elderly pursue, albeit fitfully and in an ad hoc manner, the study and practice of liberal activities. *This book is primarily directed to these elderly who received a liberal education and hence are equipped to gain access to the classics or perhaps those unique few who desire to secure such an education late in their lives and can benefit from this education in old age.*

With a third objection, some reject the notion of the importance of liberal arts in old age because they believe in natural old age wisdom. It is true that some old people appear to have the natural wisdom of their years, whether through temperament or a lifetime of experience. A liberal education, whether early or late in life may not be needed by such elderly persons, but surely most of us do not fit this description of the naturally wise and require help from whatever source! As I shall argue below, the fruits of a liberal education can supplement any old age wisdom we aged may have.

The fourth and perhaps the most telling criticism of relying upon a youthful liberal education for old age is that the effects of such an early education wear off before old age arrives! Any elderly person wishing to engage reading or experiencing classic works in old age is likely to have attended a liberal arts college or a liberal studies program within the university during his or her youth. Although our society does not assume that such a liberal education is necessary either to earn a living, to pursue the obligations of citizenship, or to elevate friendships, most people assume that if liberal education is pursued, a limited four year period is sufficient for a lifetime. Of course, this assumption is mistaken, not only because it takes a longer time than four years to gain liberal capabilities, but also since the beneficial effects of an four year liberal education may be forgotten or erased by experiences in later life as illustrated in Erich Remarque's novel, *All Quiet on the Western Front.* In the novel, the protagonist soldier, Paul Bohne, a man of good education and literary expectations, returns home, having experienced the horrors of front line combat and revisits his room with its books he once loved:

> "In my room... stand the bookshelves with my books...I bought gradually with the money I earned...Many are secondhand, all classics...I read them all with laudable zeal...I want the quiet rapture I used to feel when I turned to my books...I know them all still. I remember arranging them in order. I implore them with my eyes: speak to me- take me up - take me...nothing-nothing. My disquietude grows. A terrible feeling of foreignness suddenly rises in me..nothing stirs. Then I take one of the books, intending to read and turn over the leaves. But I put it away and take down another...Words, words, words, they do not reach me. Slowly I place the books back on the shelves. Nevermore. Quietly, I go out of the room..."

Our German soldier had experienced war at the front; all of us do not suffer from such horrendous events. But the work, family life, and other events over the time of our lives may separate us from the books of youth and whatever classroom knowledge we might have had. At the time of the impending Second World War, the English poet, Louis MacNeice cynically summarized the world England was facing after many of its college educated youth, including MacNeice, had received a classic liberal education at Oxford or Cambridge. In his poem: he writes:

"Goodbye now to Plato and Hegel:
There ain't no universals in this man's town.
They don't want any philosopher kings in England
The shop is closing down…"

Even if one's early liberal education is not erased by subsequent adult experiences such as world wars, this early education may not last through a lifetime because it often is merely an introduction to the classics and the liberal arts which make up such an education. When liberal education goes beyond simply the gathering of information and extends to an acquisition of the capacity to undertake the methods of the arts and sciences, let alone understand the significance of those arts and sciences, much more time is needed. Most thoughtful proponents of liberal education recognize that such an education must continue in old age. In the educational classic, *The Education of Henry Adams,* the author describes briefly his haphazard liberal education at Harvard in the 1800's and labels the remainder of his life "an accidental education" which he describes in detail and which seemed to him to be the most important part of his education. Similarly, John Stuart Mill, in his *Autobiography* recounts that long after his intense childhood liberal education, he encountered personal crises in his adult life and both a new relationship with Harriett Taylor and a new exposure to Coleridge's works helped him out of that crisis.

Adams and Mill, (and Jefferson!) may be the exceptions. Even if a youthful liberal education is a good one and it is reinforced during our adult years, such an education will not necessarily prepare us to engage in an organized and purposeful practice of the liberal arts in old age. One can realize the truth of this observation by inspecting the present practice of liberal education for the aging. Such a practice of liberal arts consists of the ad hoc enrollment in one or another course for the elderly, attendance at lectures, fine arts events, and participation in occasional book groups, (some of which read serious books). To be sure, such courses are multiplying and many are valuable. But matter how edifying these activities might be, such a liberal arts education fails to enable oldsters *to systematically confront the major losses of old age and, with the help of the classics, firmly detach themselves from these losses and find consolation for them.*

These observations lead to perhaps the fifth criticism of liberal education by its foremost champion and theorist, Cardinal Newman. Newman, in his *The Idea of a University* and other writings argued that although liberal education has immense benefits (which I will describe below), it will not be able to enable its beneficiary to cope with the crises of life, including the losses in old age. In his famous essay, *The Tamworth Reading Room,* Newman argued that secular education cannot equip its students for virtue. Virtue must be sought in "graver and holier place than in libraries and reading rooms". Thus, although Newman believed that reading literature was of great value, he also believed that it separated feeling from action and failed to involve the reader in a way that religious texts which require faith and action might. In my discussions of reflective meditation and consolation below, I shall seek to answer Newman's argument.

In the meantime, in the next three chapters, I shall suggest *an admittedly utopian program* of three stages in a liberal education - youthful attendance in a demanding liberal arts curriculum, adulthood in which this education is expanded and integrated within one's life, and finally, a meditative liberal education in old age, when the learning of a life time is synthesized and employed to confront the major losses of old age. This chapter, Chapter X, will be devoted to liberal education for young people. The next chapter, Chapter XI will describe liberal education in adulthood. Chapter XII will describe a "reflective meditation" appropriate to old age. In all three chapters, in order to understand how liberal education might find detachment and consolation in old age, I shall turn to a selection of works within the tradition of western texts. The works of Plato, Aristotle, Confucius, Aquinas, Montaigne, Hegel, James, Dewey, and Whitehead among others treat the subject of education in general and liberal education in particular. These works pose difficult questions about the nature and purposes of education, the different kinds of education, and even the limits and detriments of education. In this chapter, I shall concentrate on primarily the intellectual aspects of liberal education as treated in the works of John Stuart Mill, Cardinal Newman, and Robert Maynard Hutchins.

The Disciplines, Purposes and Materials Of Liberal Education in Youth

Liberal education for the young adult is a systematic introduction to "the liberal arts and disciplines", their methods, principles, and applications as embodied in the central works of western and eastern thought. Learning these disciplines and their application to the central intellectual and practical problems confronting our civilization is the task of the student in liberal arts colleges. The liberal disciplines, originating in ancient Rome and Greece gained definition in the Middle Ages when they were identified with the "trivium" – grammar, logic and rhetoric – and the "quadrivium" – geometry, arithmetic, music and astronomy. (Grammar was broadly conceived to embrace literature, a rhetoric which was gradually extended from oral to written works, and, by the beginning of the enlightenment, the quadrivium embraced mathematics and the scientific method). In the medieval university, these subjects were preparatory to theology, philosophy, law and medicine. These liberal disciplines have evolved over the centuries and been redefined by many authors. My favorite recent author is the twentieth century philosopher, Richard McKeon who categorized the liberal disciplines for modern purposes as consisting of *the arts of invention and discovery of facts, the interpretation of experience, an understanding and mastery of the methods of inquiry and proof, and the placement of disciplines within systems of knowledge and action*. McKeon's reformulation reflects the fact that since the time of the trivium and quadrivium, the modern reformulation of the liberal arts has incorporated the rise of modern science and technology, an expansion of the arts of interpretation of texts, (beyond the Bible),, and a new understanding of natural and cultural histories, contexts and systems of thought.

Those who hold onto some common ideal of the liberal arts through the ages share the assumption that the present structure of college liberal arts education consists of an introduction to the liberal disciplines to the adolescent and young adult. Such an assumption might find its justification in the appeal to an inherited tradition, but others suggest a sociological rationale for a modern liberal education, namely, that such liberal disciplines or "powers of the mind" are a needed response to the making sense of "modernity". Alternatively, Erik Erikson provides the material for psychological rationale according to which the youth are seeking to define their own identity and their relationship to the world and liberal education is part of this effort. Rather than turn to these modern views, (and there are many of them!), I choose to select three classic visions of liberal education by John Stuart Mill, Cardinal Newman, and Robert Maynard Hutchins who explain how such an education can enable the powers of the mind and forge an identity for youth as well as "prepare" for old age reflection.

1. *The Disciplines of Liberal Education*

John Stuart Mill, a famous philosopher of the 19th century and a beneficiary of a thorough liberal education in childhood set forth the modern view of liberal education in his *Inaugural Address to St. Andrews*. Mill identified the liberal subject matters and disciplines to include Latin, Greek, and foreign languages, science and mathematics, logic, physiology, psychology, ethics and politics, jurisprudence, political economy, history, literature and the fine arts. Mill did not merely define these subjects, but indicated their purposes and methods as well as their limits. Mill not only defined the nature of these subjects, but also the specifics of the subjects to be learned and the resulting capacities acquired in the learning of them. Take, for example his description of history:

> "Education may also introduce us to the principal facts which have a direct bearing ...on the different modes or stages of civilization and the characteristic properties of each...The leading facts of ancient and modern history should be known from his private reading..."A professor

of history has to teach...the meaning of those facts...to help the student in collecting from history what are the main differences between human beings and between the institutions of society at one time or place or at another...in picturing to himself human life and the human conceptions of life, as they were at different stages of human development; in distinguishing between what is the same for all ages and what is progressive, and forming some incipient conception of the causes and laws of progress"

Mill includes the more specific knowledge of our political and civil institutions as part of history, and, in a general way, the institutions of other "civilized" nations - a knowledge which he deems essential to citizenship. But he seeks a more general understanding as evidenced in the following:

"The object is to make him take interest in history, not as a mere narrative, but as a chain of cause and effects still unwinding before his eyes and full of momentous consequences for himself and his descendants, the unfolding of a great epic or dramatic actions to terminate in the happiness or misery, the elevation or degradation of the human race...

He also envisages not merely a detached view of history, but an account of good and evil powers, in which "...even the smallest cannot escape from taking part...." To anticipate the implication of this for old age, by learning this history in our youth, we are prepared in old age, to look back upon our past, with the help of the discipline of history as envisaged by Mill, we can see our lives as not only part of history's patterns and drama, but also how we participated in history's good and evil.

Like history, all of these liberal disciplines are appropriate for the understanding of the losses experienced in old age. The Latin and Greek authors, whether in their language or in translation, offer many insights into old age, as Cicero's *On Old Age* illustrates. The natural sciences, especially medicine and physiology, contribute to our understanding of our own biological decay. History helps us to recover not only the specifics of our past but the patterns of the past. History and political economy may be pertinent to thinking about our legacy Philosophy and literature may assist when death approaches.

2. Liberal Education as Knowledge For The Sake of the Entire World

If liberal education consisted of a discrete group of disciplines, this might be sufficient to justify its practice. But as Mill and others recognized, it is expected to be something more.

Mill suggests:

> "...What every pupil should be taught here ...is to methodize his knowledge; to look at every separate part of it in its relation to the other parts, and to the whole, combining the partial glimpses which he has obtained of the field of human knowledge at different points into a general map...of the entire region; observing how all knowledge is connected, how we ascend to one branch by means of another, how the higher modifies the lower and the lower helps us to understand the higher; how every existing reality is a compound of many properties, of which each science or distinct mode of study reveal but a small part, but the whole of what must be included to enable us to know it truly as a fact in nature and not as a mere abstraction...."

This vision of liberal education as *the seeking of knowledge as an interconnected whole to be studied for its own sake* was advanced by Cardinal Newman in the middle 18th century when he delivered a series of lectures on university teaching, collected in his classic, *The Idea of*

The University. When these lectures were delivered at the founding of a Catholic university in Ireland, Newman was anxious to make room within the university to allow for both the secular study of science and literature, as well as theology but, as suggested above, he did not hold the expectation that such studies would promote virtue or the useful arts. Newman's rationale was that each study abstracted only part of the knowledge of a whole world, and hence many studies were required to limit their competing brethren disciplines and to enable the student to see the whole of reality. Philosophy was to allocate the appropriate place of the individual studies in question, but theology held a unique position as "completing and correcting" the other sciences. The unity of the liberal arts was to be found primarily in the mind of the student and the result was the production of "gentlemen" marked not by social status, but by intellectual excellence. Although, according to Newman, liberal education does not promote the major virtues, it promotes an intellectual excellence reflected in "a cultivated intellect, a delicate taste, a candid, equitable, dispassionate mind, a noble and courteous bearing in the conduct of life".

For Newman, the subjects of a liberal education which are the fruit of human reason, are to be studied *for their own sake.* In Newman's own words referring to liberal education

> "...Its direct business is not to steel the soul against temptation or console it in affliction...; be it ever so much the means or the condition of both material and moral advancement, still taken by and in itself, it as little mends our hearts as improves our material circumstances...."

Rather, Newman views liberal education as the grasp of the interconnected whole of knowledge, without justification in utilitarian, moral, or consoling functions contradicts in many ways modern expectations for a liberal education, in which the modern student might hope to find some utilitarian purpose for his education. Since the days of Newman, not only has the scope of knowledge vastly expanded, and the ways of organizing knowledge into a whole have multiplied, but also, there is no widespread modern belief that philosophy or theology or, for that matter, any other discipline has the capability and authority to allocate the branches of knowledge in any systematic way. To be sure, some modern university curricula have sought to introduce the student to organization of the major branches of knowledge and review the different ways in which these fields might be organized, but such efforts are rare. For the most part, universities in the western world are roughly organized into conventional divisions of science, humanities and the social sciences without a great deal of justification offered for the division.

Not only does Newman's hope for a liberal education which places before student the branches of knowledge as part of an interconnected whole now seem impossible, but also, Newman's view of liberal knowledge *as its own end* appears to contradict the general approach to all education in the modern world which views such an education in utilitarian terms. (To be sure, Newman is careful to reserve the purity of liberal education as its "direct business" but he recognizes its other uses in describing liberal education's *indirect* business). Despite the modern embrace of utilitarian goals for education, there remains an important core of truth in Newman's insight that education is for its own sake; that truth is important for an old age which as described earlier, requires a detachment to cope with its losses. Liberal education, by initially studying the bodies of knowledge and the great works which embody them "for their own sake," initially taking them on their own terms and seeking to fully understand them as presented, serves as an apprenticeship in detachment. Thus, by seeking knowledge as its own end, students can begin to secure the degree of detachment needed when later such detachment is needed in confronting the losses of old age.

3. *Liberal Education as the Study of Great Works*

Liberal education is not only an education in these disciplines for their own sake and an exploration of the organization and unity of these disciplines. Liberal education pursues or should pursue these disciplines through the study and appreciation of the great works, including an interpretation and discussion of the central works of western and eastern civilization - some within their original language, others in translation. These great works are themselves the best examples of the liberal arts at work; they are works of history, political economy, philosophy as well as the fine arts. In the words of Hutchins, they are the "means of understanding our society and ourselves" and, I would add, the universe and perhaps God as well. There is no comparable repository of wisdom. These works are recognized to be important over the ages and when revisited in old age, they reveal their depth and truth. These great works as part of a lifelong liberal education require careful repeated analytic reading, listening and observing, as well as disciplined discussion beginning in college. Unfortunately, these activities are often not taught in secondary schools and many colleges. Yet they are necessary to secure an interpretation, understanding and evaluation of the texts, reports or reproductions of experiments and works of art. Works of history, rhetoric, political theory and science and economics are helpful in guiding future civic actions as well. Since these works exemplify the disciplines which Mill identified to be essential to a liberal arts education, exposure to them facilitates the learning and understanding of the disciplines.

Careful study of these works reveals the principles and ideas which are part of these works. For example, a careful reading of the few excerpts of Mill cited above reveal that when he formulates his description of history, he assumes as principles in history some kind of essential human nature, and a historical progress in stages of human or societal development. For Mill, this progress is one which incorporates a struggle between historical forces of good and evil. By studying this struggle in the march of progress, the student gains a knowledge which enables him to engage in democratic participation, (not unlike Mill himself). Thus, Mill's basic principles and ideas of human nature, the struggle of good and evil and progress, inform his description of the nature of history and its study.

The basic assumptions illustrated by Mill's approach to history exemplify the kind of ideas and principles to be uncovered from a careful reading of all texts. Such principles, once uncovered, must then be studied and critiqued as part of a liberal education. (Thus, we might ask Mill: is there an essential form of human nature? Is there progress in history? If so, in what does it consist? Is history a tale of the struggle of good and evil? Will knowing history in this way really help us effectively participate in political activities?)

It is this study of principles and ideas which makes liberal education a "general education". As Newman was deeply aware, in liberal education, we teach or learn general principles and ideas, as well as *the disciplines and studying the specific great works*. But both he and Hutchins recognized that ideas are conceptions *by which* we think about things; they are the notions *by which* we define issues and discuss them. They represent the principal vehicles *through which* we approach reality in our thought and speech. But such ideas are not simple, since they have a complex order of parts which elaborate their meanings, they evolve over time and they are part of diverse systems of thought contained within the great works. These systems of thought and their ideas and principles are often opposed in one way or another to one another, and this opposition creates basic issues and the consequent development of ideas within the tradition of works. (Newman was especially interested in that development of ideas and traced the development of the Christian doctrine).

It may be tempting to simply teach the disciplines, e.g., economics or physics, or the ideas, e.g. democracy or God, without the great works of Adam Smith, Galileo, John Stuart Mill, or St. Thomas Aquinas. Yet it is the *great works which supply the specific or concrete context for these disciplines and ideas and, when studied chronologically, these woks set forth the development of ideas and conflicting arguments about them*. Newman in particular was deeply aware of the necessity to "concretize" our knowledge of ideas and he viewed it essential that the general ideas and principles of the Christian faith be concretized by the story of Christ. Similarly, the classic works, whether religious or secular, can operate to concretize our knowledge of ideas and principles.

For example, understanding the notion of "progress" as adopted by Mill's approach to history in the *Innaugural Address* on liberal education is not a simple matter. Progress, as an idea may refer to some form of temporary or permanent advance of humanity or to selected human beings, as part of (or separate from) a more general advance of a community; moreover, such an advance may be due either to the laws of history, more general laws of nature, or the choices of men and communities. Mill's notion of progress can only be limned from a knowledge of his other works which embrace, among other things, the march towards representative democracy, (including Mill's own political participation in the conflicts over electoral reforms of the 19th century in England). Thus, Mill's notion of progress is one view of progress, part of a larger tradition of an enlightenment belief in progress advanced by some of the great works in western thought dealing with the notion of progress. This history may be documented in histories of ideas such as Bury's *The Idea of Progress,* or more recently, *Van Doren's The Ideal of Progress,* but Mill's notion of progress may also be usefully compared to other works, such as those by Condorcet, Spengler or Toynbee, which contain different notions of progress or reject notions of historical progress altogether. Only a careful reading of Mill's writings along with other works on history will yield an understanding of his concrete notion of progress and its more general validity or invalidity.

The modern mathematician, physicist and philosopher, Alfred North Whitehead and the scholastic philosopher, Mortimer Adler, have recognized the importance of ideas in thought and reality. Whitehead, in his *Adventures in Ideas* and *Science in the Modern World,* has traced the history of ideas in science, religion and other fields and offered an explanation of how ideas enter into the process of a changing reality. In his *Syntopicon,* Mortimer Adler has presented a variety of ideas, traced the location of these ideas in many of the great works of the western tradition, and identified some of the issues pertaining to those ideas. Adler's Institute of Philosophical Analysis, has explored in great depth the ideas of freedom, happiness, justice, progress, religion, equality, beauty and education as expressed in the works of western thought. The works of both authors offer examples of how ideas and principles might be understood in relation to the great works. These ideas, as we shall see, have particular relevance to an understanding of the specific losses experienced in old age.

But it is not enough to study and learn ideas and disciplines abstracted from the works out of which they arise. And the graduate of a liberal arts college should bring with him not only an acquaintance with the disciplines and a habit of mind for applying them, but also a solid knowledge and memory of the classic works themselves. It is the knowledge of these works which will make possible the use of their ideas and principles when confronting the losses of old age.

The Modern Attack on Liberal Education

The authors I have chosen wrote their praises of liberal education in the distant past. One of them, Robert Hutchins, although a champion of such education, wrote in his *The Great Conversation* about the "decline of liberal education". Hutchins saw the decline of liberal education due to a "vocationalism", in which education is deemed to serve the individual and nation's economic aims, the subtle effects of a "scientism" according to which the only valid form of knowledge is the scientific method, and a "specialization" of subjects of study reflecting a division of labor in knowledge and the influence of science and technology. All of these trends are reflected in the demands that liberal education give way to more study of science and mathematics, confined to more narrow subjects, i.e.,"majors", and in practically "relevant" courses. Of course, Hutchins and other thoughtful educational commentators, recognized the importance of science, technology and practice, and specialization. Their argument is that science in part of a liberal education and that specialization follows after a general education.

The decline of liberal education, and the growth of the undue influence of the scientific method, technology and vocationalism have significant implications for old age. As pointed out in a previous chapter, one response to old age is based upon science and technology-seeking to extend lives through the benefits of the techniques of modern medicine and related biological specialties. Such an emphasis, however, will be unfortunate if it excludes attention to the ways in which the liberal disciplines can assist in response to the losses of old age.

Contributions of Modern Liberal Arts
To Reflective Meditation in Old Age

Among the many reformulations of liberal education in recent years, a renewed awareness of the personal perspective, a related sensitivity to a narrative understanding, and a reaching out beyond the western classics are three major modern changes which have significant implications for the study of liberal education in youth as it might bear upon old age reflective meditation.

1. The Personal Perspective

In recent years, within the academy, there has been a revivification of attention to students as members of groups, such as Blacks, Asians, Latinos, Gays and Women, or of having a unique sense of self. This attention has promoted the notion that the curriculum should provide opportunities for such students and their classmates to explore the implications of membership in these groups for their studies and college life. To be sure, such attention is not unique to recent years. The availability of counseling and therapy, especially Freudian therapy to students in past generations allowed them, as part of their therapy to focus upon themselves and understand their college life through the spectacles of their personal problems.

Although it may not have been made apparent, many of the classic works studied in the liberal arts also adopt a personal perspective. Thus, in their writings, philosophers such as Descartes, Kierkegaard, Nietzsche, and James adopt personal perspectives, as do poets such as Walt Whitman, essayists such a Montaigne, and even novelists such Dostoyevsky. These personal perspectives lead the reader to appreciate the uniqueness of the persona presented in the text by the author and, in so doing, may stimulate the reader to also ask who he, (the reader), is and what his own personal perspective is. An awareness of this personal perspective fits well the situation of those of us in old age. We are "old people" who see the world as old people do. Classics with personal perspectives ensconced in the text provoke our own recognition of the importance of our own personal perspective as old people and stimulate us to think how our personal situation affects how we view ourselves and how we think about our world.

2. A Narrative Understanding

Closely connected to the personal perspective is the currently popular narrative approach – the placing of characters, thoughts, and events in the narrative of history, or in the story found in literature, or in the account of an experiment, or in the course of evolution of bodies and minds, or the time related steps of a philosophy. The French philosopher, Lyotard, sees narrative as a form of knowledge in his account of the "post-modern condition" and believes it to be one of the major forms of legitimate knowledge in the modern university. But narrative is not simply a modern form of thought discovered by contemporary French philosophers. Hegel and Marx embraced a narrative of history, Shakespeare tells stories in his plays and sonnets. Galileo's dry report of science hides the story of his controversial experiments. Darwin gives a story of evolution and Henri Bergson tells us how the duration of our lives fits into the historical process of that evolution. The Bible tells many stories including, of course, the stories of Moses and Christ. St. Augustine tells us the story of his own life as well as the history of Rome and Christianity. Dante tells us the story of man's damnation and salvation, Chaucer offers us tales told by a group escaping the plague. Goethe tells the story of the old scholar, Faust. Plato tells great stories in his dialogues. There are narratives behind the apparently static works of fine arts as well.

As a legitimate object of knowledge, narrative in its many forms should be consciously introduced in the curriculum of a liberal education. By doing so, such narratives not only introduce the notion of imaginative possibilities into our lives, but they also introduce us to the dimension of time, hence foretelling the period of old age reflection in which we gain an acute sense of time due to the fact that time is at the core of the very being of old age. When, in old age, we read the classic narrative works, we are reminded of "the time of our lives", and are prompted to see our lives as stories shaped by the passage of time. When we tell ourselves and others these stories of our lives, we find that such a narrative gives a unity and form to our lives.

3. A Global Vision

In the 21st century, perhaps as an aftermath of the world wars in the last century, perhaps the result of television, communication and transportation, we are now acutely aware that our nation is part of the world. To be sure, many of the "western" classics of the ancient past – Homer, Herodotus, Maimonides and, in the more modern era- Claudel, Dewey, Whitehead, Schopenhauer, and many others - reveal an awareness of other "non-western" parts of the world. Today, universities are adding classics from the East to their list of Great Books and scholars are recommending a revised "Great Conversation" which includes the voices from the East. New translations and new interpretations of eastern classics have been prepared in recent years. Martha Nussbaum, in her book, *Cultivating Humanity,* reports on several interesting undergraduate liberal arts colleges which are not only promoting an educational program consisting of visits to European and non-European countries, these programs are studying ways of carefully comparing modes of thought and interactions among them in the East and West. The Eastern classics may have special relevance to old age. For example, several of the eastern classics advance an exposition of "the sage"– presumably an elder individual with special wisdom acquired over time, whether through the limit of desire, meditation or "quiet sitting" or a variety of rituals. The portraits of an Eastern wisdom which includes methods of meditation or quiet sitting may be particularly relevant to those of us who are old.

Conclusion: The Contribution of the Liberal Arts Tradition to Old Age Detachment and Consolation

Liberal education, both classical and modern, enables the youth to begin the acquisition of the capability of detaching oneself from loss and finding consolation in old age. As Newman clearly recognized, the liberal disciplines are abstractions from the world and hence, hopefully, such disciplines can help the elderly to abstract from their losses. Modern study of personal narratives assists the student in relating the classics to the student's life. The study of the relationship of the disciplines, one to another, as recommended by Newman, permits an integrated reflection upon old age. The extraction from the classics of principles and ideas in liberal education will be "tested" in adult life and reflected upon in old age. But these ideas and principles are made useful only through a remembrance or re-acquaintance with the works in which they are found. Thus, the collegiate study of the classics for their own sake lays the groundwork to enable the liberally educated elder to detach from the weight of old age loss and sadness. In short, the great works – the books, monuments and fine arts – first studied in youth, revisited and tested in adulthood, and returned to in old age – will yield worlds of ideas and principles which can permit a detached view of old age loss and consolations for the losses encountered there.

CHAPTER XI

Integrating Liberal Education
Into Adult Lives

"For this reason philosophers admonish us not to be satisfied with learning only, but also to add study and then practice" - Epictetus

"Never stop sculpting your own statute"- Plotinus

At each stage of my life, some book captured my imagination and guided my life at the time. Upon completion of graduate studies, it was Aristotle's Nicomachean Ethics *an ethical system which has given direction to my life. During the 1950's after my stint as a caseworker in the Chicago slums where I visited welfare applicants each day, I attended the London School of Economics, studied Marx and began to understand the class system in the West. During the 1960's when I worked in the program to renew the physical and social structure of New Haven, Connecticut and later, to participate in the building of the new town of Columbia, Maryland, I read Lewis Mumford's remarkable* Culture of Cities *and the "community classics", (Tonnies et al.) which inspired my thoughts and writings about our efforts to recreate the urban community. When I "enlisted" in the environmental movement in the 1970's, I was inspired by Charles Darwin's works and Eugene Odum's* Foundations of Ecology *which helped me understand environmental problems as the results of human interventions into a larger ecosystem. In the 1980's when directing the Environmental Law Center at Vermont Law School, I found St. Thomas Aquinas's* Treatise on Law *to be one of the best statements of the relationship of law to nature and I returned in later years to co-edit a book of modern legal writings on Aquinas, one of several edited books on classical philosophy and modern law. In my teaching of tort law, I compiled a book of excerpts from legal classics dealing with torts; in population law, I required the students to read Malthus and Darwin, and in environmental law, I co-wrote a book,* Green Justice, *as a text which sought to relate the classics to the study of environmental law. During this middle age, I took courses in Whitehead's philosophy at the New School of Social Research, and Hegel's philosophy at Connecticut College. In the 1990's, near retirement I stumbled upon Walter Watson's* The Architectonics of Meaning *and Mortimer Adler's* Syntopicon *from which I learned about the incompatible variety of principles which inform the different philosophies and perennial ideas I had studied earlier in life. In this last decade, in retirement, I have turned to the work of Alfred North Whitehead, who, I believe has best grasped that the truth is found through the workings of ideas within the flux of a changing reality. All of these books did not offer a blueprint for each stage of my adult life, but they accompanied my life and my work, often resonating with the events of the day, informing my actions and broadening my understanding in many ways. After reading these classics, as history moved on, the ideas contained in these books have been modified and my understanding of them in light of more recent time has changed. Nevertheless, these works are now a fundamental part of who I am.*

Introduction

Despite the roseate glow which surrounds the memory of a youthful liberal education and the myriad of books which describe and praise it, we would be wildly optimistic to believe that such an education results in a coherent view of the world, to be remembered and acted upon in middle or old age. Even if modern liberal education is proven to encourage the students' whole hearted commitment to lifelong liberal learning, the high price for such an education discourages many from seeking it. In addition, the daunting prospect of having to earn a living upon graduation will discourage many students from seeking such an education when they arrive at the university.

Although there are limited classic writings on adult liberal education, there are opportunities for encountering the classics in middle age. The proof lies in the fact that there have been some remarkable individuals in the past who do secure a thorough liberal education and hold onto it throughout their lives. To be sure, we might expect ancient philosophers such as Plato and Aristotle to pursue a life of learning. Cicero was an autodidact throughout his life, Augustine pursued philosophy before his conversion and theology after it. A life of learning was followed by some but by no means all monks in the Middle Ages. In the Renaissance and the early modern age, we have the examples of Petrarch and Sir Francis Bacon. During the early Enlightenment, Montaigne and Samuel Johnson as well as many other philosophers and scientists pursued a continuous course of learning throughout their lives. Often, we are not aware of such adult learning, since we focus upon the writings or experiments of these authors without viewing them as part of an adult education. We reserve "adult education" to institutionalized formal education.

If adult education is not limited to such a formal education, we can witness its practice in the biographies and autobiographies of many authors of the classics. John Stuart Mill, whose description of liberal education was set forth in the previous chapter was one such person. As the previous chapter pointed out, Thomas Jefferson, as revealed in his *Autobiography,* pursued his learning in many subjects throughout his life and into his old age. Of course, few can rival John Stuart Mill nor Thomas Jefferson in their accomplishments. Most of us, unlike Mill and Jefferson, (both of whom received a remarkable early liberal education complete with the study of ancient and modern languages, literature, philosophy, history, sciences and the classics), have received, at most, a partial education, deeply inadequate in its scope and depth. Yet, we can take comfort in the fact that many noted poets, novelists, historians and

philosophers also had limited early educations. For example, the great
English poet, essayist, and critic, Samuel Johnson, received a lamentably
brief liberal education, having to leave Oxford after thirteen months due
to his poverty. Nevertheless, he was able to supplement and strengthen
that education in his later years. He taught classical languages, edited
scholarly works, and translated works both from Greek and Latin, as
well as French and Italian for publishers. At the same time, he wrote
plays, poetry, and critical essays. As Boswell's biography reveals, Johnson
possessed a remarkable character and personality which exercised
its influence on the leaders of his generation. The comforting lesson
of Johnson's life is that a complete youthful liberal education is not
needed in order to pursue liberal learning during the rest of one's life.
Johnson's experience is confirmed by the life of Henry Adams, historian
and author of *The Education of Henry Adams.* Adams found his early
Harvard education to be almost worthless, yielding, at the most, an
escape from his early provincial beliefs, a love of writing and a sense of
self-possession. He concluded his chapter on his Harvard education with
the words: "Education had not begun". He found his real education to
be an "accidental education" in history, diplomacy and economics, (as
well as personal tragedy), acquired during the remainder of his life, and
recounted in his remarkable autobiography. Unfortunately, an account
of the lives of Johnson and Adams do not reveal any of the continuities
between early liberal education and later adult learning. Even in such
a utopian view, Plato's *Republic,* the guardians of the state, after a long
education, culminating in learning the mathematically related sciences,
return to the cave of everyday life and, for the next twenty years take
responsibilities for the affairs of state. During that twenty year period,
there does not appear to be any continuous learning taking place.
Perhaps a similar process occurs when the graduate of a liberal arts
college graduates meets the cold reality of experience as an adult.

Even if one has secured an excellent liberal education, upon
graduation, there is the immediate challenge of immediately coping
with life, let alone remembering, continuing and "applying" the habits
and principles acquired at an earlier stage of life. At this beginning of
adult life, there is the arrival of a more complete set of responsibilities.

Carl Jung in his *Modern Man in Search of the Soul* has pointed out that the adult stage of life is one of entry into family and vocation. I would add to Jung's list the set of community obligations which the liberal arts graduate encounters. Erik Erikson appropriately labels its crisis as one of "generativity" through work and family conflicting with the pressures of stagnation. In response to work, family, and community and the crises they create, one might reject one's past liberal education as unrealistic means for resolving them. Thus, some see liberal education as simply not fit for adult lives. In the last chapter, I quoted the verse of the poet, Louis MacNeice to illustrate the danger of failing in middle age to conserve one's early liberal education. I quote his poem again to summarize the attitude of disbelief in the value of liberal education to resolve adult problems:

> Goodbye now, Plato and Hegel
> The Shop is closing down
> They don't want any philosopher kings in England
> There ain't no universals in this man's town.

Most attendees at American liberal arts colleges and their faculty assume that liberal education of youth is the total sum and substance of students' educations – an unrelated prologue for life. At most they appeal to some vague "habits of thought" which are imparted or they are content if the education leads to the some form of later occupational specialization – such as law, medicine, business, and so forth. To be sure, many liberal arts graduates continue into some kind of specialized education, but the faculties of professional and specialized graduate schools often fail to recognize, explore or apply the contributions which the earlier liberal studies might make to the continuing education of students, let alone to their future practice of the professions and specializations. Thus, few if any professional schools offer explicit significant opportunities for their students to reach back into their prior educations and draw explicitly upon them during the learning of their professional skills. Instead, the experience of many, if not all professional schools is centered upon learning the rudiments of the profession itself.

In short, in professional and other forms of specialized education, the previous liberal education is eclipsed in favor of learning new skills and information and, unfortunately, students lack the intellectual strength derived from the liberal education to retain its benefits.

This erasure of the effects of an early liberal education is aggravated as one enters the work force with its immediate demands upon our time and energies. Similarly, new family responsibilities - marriage and the raising of children - do not appear to call upon the capabilities developed in liberal education. Perhaps the only activity to call directly upon the capabilities imparted by a liberal education are the demands of participating in community affairs, which require organizational and rhetorical skills as well as knowledge of the political system.

Nevertheless, ignoring one's early liberal education and failing to continue it during one's own adult life is a serious mistake. It is possible to demand more from a liberal education as described in the last chapter and it is desirable to explore in this chapter how that education may be extended into adult life. One should not deny the understandings and capacities which are inherited from such an education. Such liberal understandings and capabilities can make important contributions not only to the education and practice of professions, but also to the conduct of a wide variety of occupations, family life, and community activities. It also offers opportunities for use of middle aged free time, enabling one, in vacation, after working hours, or weekend, to continue one's education beyond the indulgence in the ordinary amusements of free time. Such leisure perpetuates the influence of past liberal knowledge and capabilities; to ignore these early benefits of liberal education is simply to deny an important part of oneself and one's history. *And, as I shall suggest in this chapter, the continuation of a liberal education during middle age acts as a bridge to old age, when such an education is helpful in a meditative reflection upon the losses of aging.*

Avenues to Adult Liberal Education

What are the avenues for seeking or continuing liberal education in adult life? Probably the best way is to practice a "liberal profession". A "liberal profession" is a profession which requires intellectual activity, deliberative decision-making and creativity as part of its practice. Hence professions such as law, teaching, journalism, authorship, the ministry, management, medicine, psychotherapy, and leadership roles in many institutions and communities make use of at least some of the capacities and understandings of liberal education. Samuel Johnson's occupation as author and editor enabled him to continue his liberal learning. Robert Maynard Hutchins had moments of leisure packed into his busy life as a university president - moments in which he pursued the reading and discussion of great literature. More important, he translated these activities into his work as university president and educational reformer. Henry Adams pursued liberal studies as part of the duties of diplomacy. Fortunately, modern life has multiplied occupations in which liberal skills and knowledge is required or helpful although proponents of liberal education have failed to describe and establish these linkages. As suggested above, other activities such as community participation may also call upon liberal skills although it may be more difficult to establish the connection.

Not everyone is fortunate enough in their adult years to occupy some liberal profession or establish the relationship between their early liberal studies and the middle aged responsibilities. Nevertheless, with the increase of modern leisure for some, they can, by sheer will power and habit, proceed to continue to educate themselves - a form of auto-didacticism. There are a variety of institutions which support the effort to educate oneself, by offering materials to enable one to supplement one's earlier education in the adult years. One modern proponent of such an autodidactic adult liberal education is Mortimer Adler who wrote a *Guidebook* for auto-didactic adult learning; he and his colleagues prepared a *Propedia,* which, perhaps unrealistically seeks to help the reader through a selected reading program within the articles of the 15th edition of the Encyclopedia Britannica. Adler also authored a *Syntopicon* f central ideas of western thought and the classic *How to Read a Book* - both of which were designed, at least in part, to help the adult learner.

In addition to materials for auto-didacticism, there are a variety of programs aimed at adult liberal education. In the mid twentieth century, the Great Books program was formed to assist adult learners to read and discuss the canon works; the program continues a half century later but, unfortunately is no longer a vibrant force in American education, (if it ever was). More recently, in the quest for students, universities are beginning to open up their curricula to older students and design special liberal education programs for them. State Councils of Humanities in many states have organized ad hoc discussions of humanities topics

For adults all of these activities are relatively minor in scope even when compared to admittedly diminishing college liberal education of the youth.

Of course, the principle reason for the lack of a vibrant liberal education for adults is the American culture of leisure, which is shaped by our affluent society – our pursuit of consumer goods and a wide variety of extra work or recreation activities. But perhaps another reason for the lag in adult liberal education is the failure of any articulate method of such education suited to the pressures of occupations and family duties.

John Dewey and Learning from Experience

All of the auto-didactic efforts at adult liberal education described above were integrated with the practical experience of their practitioners. Augustine taught rhetoric and, as a bishop, prepared sermons. Jefferson had periods of leisure, (supported in part by slavery!) between his political assignments. Mill pursued political activities and editorial writing. Johnson made money by his writings. Henry Adams pursued his education within the requirements of a diplomatic and academic life. Thus, adult liberal education, if it is to be part of development of the character and its capacities during adult years is likely to be exercised and pursued as part of an occupation or set of duties or in response to the major problems unique to adult life encountered in the family and one's community.

To be sure, temperament, parental influence, friends, custom and habit, religious faith, as well as societal and government incentives, contribute to the shaping of adult character; they may shape our responses to these challenges of adulthood. Perhaps the starting point for removing the obstacles to the pursuit of liberal studies in adulthood is to promote a self-awareness of how each of these influences may shape one's adult life. One contribution of Harvard to John Adams' education was, in his words, " a negative contribution" by which he escaped the provincial influences of his past and secured a measure of self-possession. A college liberal education might require the reading of biographies and novels which recognize the integral connection between liberal learning and the demands of adult life. Biographies such as those of Cicero, Augustine, Gibbons, Mill, Jefferson, Adams and many others reveal that connection. On the hand, many of the English novels of the 18th century describe the frustration of those who had limited access to liberal education. Hardy's *Jude the Obscure* and Eliot's *Middlemarch* both offer stories which include characters yearning for liberal learning, but blocked either because of class, poverty, or gender.

Even if one becomes aware of some of the external limits to securing a liberal education, a more difficult challenge is to connect the liberal education one has received to the challenges of adult life. It was the philosopher, John Dewey who envisaged our lives as composed of continuous learning and who rejected the separation of education and experience. John Dewey's philosophy of education is best known for its description and prescription for childhood education, but he intended to describe learning at all stages of life, and I believe his insights best help us to understand liberal learning for the adult.

For Dewey, the principles of continuity and interaction are central to the understanding of experience. "Continuity" refers to the fact that "every experience influences in some degree the attitudes which help to decide the quality of future conditions. ….Moreover, every experience influences in some degree the objective conditions under which further experiences are had." "Interaction" in turn "assigns equal rights to both factors in experience – objective and internal conditions. Any normal experience is an interplay of these two sets of conditions." This interplay is exercised according to the purposes of the learning process. Such purposes are formulated by observation of surrounding conditions, knowledge of similar situations in the past, and judgment which puts together what is observed and what is recalled to see what they signify. Thus, learning is not "book learning" but rather learning from the interaction of experience. But such learning is pursued according to a method.

In *Human Nature and Conduct,* Dewey stated:

> "We compare life to a traveler faring forth. We may consider him first at that moment where his activity is confident, straightforward, organized. He marches on giving no direct attention to his path, nor thinking of his destination. Abruptly, he is pulled up. Something is going wrong in his activity. From the standpoint of an onlooker, he has met an obstacle which must be overcome from his behavior can be unified into a successful ongoing. From his own standpoint, there is shock, confusion, perturbation, uncertainty. ..But a new impulse is stirred which becomes the starting point for of an investigation...Habits which were interfered with begin to get a new direction as they cluster about the impulse to look and see. ...The momentum of activity entered upon persists as a sense of direction, of aim. In short, he recollects, observes and plans....

Dewey specifies this method in another book, *How We Think*; he suggests that the process of thinking begins with our encounter with the problem, followed by our effort to "intellectualize" it, leading to suggestions or hypotheses as leading ideas for inquiry. These ideas are elaborated and tested them in imagination or action. As we travel through our our adult lives, we encounter problems - large and small - and we think about their solutions. Thus, the way we think is immersed in our adult experience of problems and the ways in which we resolve them.

Dewey's account of experience and learning is directly relevant to the ways in which a liberal arts education in college may be employed during our adult years. In the adult years, the remembrance and continued reading of the canon works feeds the intellectual imagination and supplies ideas and principles as purposes to be tested in experience. The starting point is the adult memory of significant works studied in youth. If taught well, the memory of such works remain in adult memory. Contrary to much modern teaching, memory is an important faculty to develop since it provides materials for adult learning. Adult memory of materials learned in a college education is frequently composed of capabilities, ideas and principles learned there. It is my contention, however, that such principles should be learned and remembered as part of the arguments, plots, and characters of classic works. Thus, it is not enough to remember that the pursuit of unrealizable chivalrous goals may, despite failure, have redeeming value; it is necessary to remember this idea in the context of memory of *Don Quixote.* Such a classic offers the particular narrative which enlivens the idea, helping us to remember it and at a later stage of our reasoning test its applicability.

Both Dewey and his contemporary, Alfred North Whitehead, rejected the notion of "inert ideas" (Whitehead's felicitous phrase) suggesting that the ideas germane to a liberal education be tested in experience. It is tested twice: first, for its fit within an interpretation of the classic work from which it is drawn; second, when it is taken from that work to be employed in adult experience. More specifically for Dewey, these ideas are hypotheses to be tested by some version of the scientific method. In Dewey's words:

> "...the experimental method of science attaches more importance, not less, to ideas as ideas than do other methods... The fact that the ideas employed are hypotheses, not final truths, is the reason why ideas are more jealously guarded and tested...by the consequences which they produce when they are act

upon… [As a consequence] the experimental method
demands keeping track of ideas…a matter of reflective
review and summarizing…To reflect is to look back over
what has been done so as to extract the net meanings
which are the capital stock for intelligent dealing with
further experiences…."

Dewey expands the notion of "scientific inquiry" to recognize that
it embraces the capacity for imaginative inquiry, deliberation, choice,
action, and reflection upon that action which enables one to enlarge
the quality of experience in all stages of our lives. Imagination allows
for the consideration of different ways of looking at the world. With
such an imagination, one can imagine finding alternative actions which
correct for unsatisfactory situations, as well as enabling the discovery
and invention of future ideals and possibilities. In doing so, we make
reflective decisions about what we might do in the present, and evaluate
the consequences of those decisions.

The capacities and understandings of classics and their ideas taken
from an earlier liberal education can assist in the process of adult
problem solving, whether in our family life, our vocations, or in our
participation in community affairs. The classics we study in our college
education yield facts and interpretations of those facts important to an
understanding of these problems. For example, to understand the proper
role of punishment of our children, we may find an understanding
of the purposes of punishment through remembrance, rereading and
reflection as portrayed in Sophocles' *Antigone,* Dante's *Divine Comedy,*
Freud's *Introductory Lectures to Psychoanalysis* or Rousseau's *Emile.* The
ideas from liberal education help adults to broaden the definition of
any specific problem, supply both personal and public ideals, and help
with any imaginative inquiry into its solution. Thus, in the case of
punishment for children, we may review the classic arguments for
retribution, deterrence, and education. Early liberal education also
supplies disciplines of thought by which we "intellectualize" the
problems we face and we turn, for example, to history, ethical thought,
or literature to supply hypotheses for our thought.

However, Dewey's effort to describe how we think as adults in analogy to the scientific method is only partly correct. The relevance of classics and the ideas drawn from them cannot be tested in the same way as scientific hypotheses. Such ideas require us to interpret them and the situations to which they apply. To determine the meaning and relevance of the classics and their ideas to modern adult problems we encounter, we must revisit the canon works to discover their present relevance or analogy to our present problems. Suppose we seek to understand some of the present economic and political problems we face in the United States, and we turn to the notions of the decline of nations and empires asking whether our present nation is in decline. We may wish to turn to Gibbons' history of the decline of the Roman Empire and his account of the generic reasons for Rome's failure. (We could also consult Augustine's *City of God)*. In assessing whether such failure is inevitable, we cannot simply consult Gibbon's philosophy of history. It is necessary to also compare his portrait of the Roman Empire as set forth in his classic with the current state of the United States to determine if they are analogous. In doing so, we may conclude that his account of the inevitability of the decline of empires is not relevant to us.

Another way of thinking about how the study of classics in liberal arts college may be important for adult life is to regard such classics as good friends. One modern author, Wayne Booth has suggested that we regard the "implied authors" of good books as good friends who can supply not only useful advice, but forms of knowledge which can make us better persons. We choose these books or art works based upon the extent to which they continue to "invite" us to read and appreciate them and find them relevant to the problems we face in adult life.

The study of the canon works makes another contribution to our lives. These lives are not merely a series of disconnected efforts to resolve ad hoc problems. There is a thread to our lives - a continuous story – a plot in which we are the protagonists. This story is linked together through the interconnection of events as well as our reflection upon the ways in which our character and its ideals develop over time in response to these events. *As stated in the previous chapter, some of the canon works are also stories of lifetimes; they exemplify how such a continuous reflective process can take place during a lifetime, offering imaginative possibilities by which lives may be enlarged.* Especially in the adult stage of life, we can read and compare these works with our own live. For example, St. Augustine, in his *Confessions,* traces the course of his early education in the ancient authors, his early embrace of ancient rhetoric, his gradual discovery of the limitations of rhetoric, the embrace of the study of ancient philosophers, and finally his conversion to Christianity. The influence of this early liberal education did not stop with his conversion as can be seen in his *On Christian Doctrine* where he outlines how the disciplines of the liberal arts can assist with the interpretation of the Bible. John Stuart Mill's life, as recounted in his *Autobiography,* illustrates the liberal imagination which corrects the limits of his past education. Intensively educated by his father, James Mill, in the principles of utility, John Stuart fell into a deep depression, and turned to read deeply in the works of the romantic poets, fell in love with Harriet Taylor, and participated actively in the politics of the day. At the same time, he separated himself from his father's influence and recast the early utilitarianism he learned from his father into a new form. His most famous works on representative government, liberty and utilitarianism draw deeply on his early education. At third example is Cardinal Newman. In *Apologia Pro Sua Vita,* Cardinal Newman slowly recounts how he traced the implications of his beliefs over time, as he gradually converted from Anglicanism to Catholicism. Newman recognized that the ideas he embraces "developed" over time, partly in interaction with their historical setting and the facts of his own life. Boswell's *Samuel Johnson,* offers a detailed biography of how this great critic emerged in 18th century England building upon his early limited exposure to the classics and literature to become a poet, novelist, playwright, and author of the *Dictionary of the American Language.*

Not only biographies but also the great novels trace the development of character as the protagonists confront problems of family, vocation, and the community. Thomas Mann, in his classic novel, *Magic Mountain,* tells the story of how Hans Castorp, a young and callow engineer, becomes a patient in a TB sanatorium, and acquires a new depth of character, when exposed to the realities of sickness and death, science and medicine, love and friendship, conversation and intense political debate - all found within the sanatorium.

In many of these fiction or non-fiction works, the protagonists begin their lives with a rich liberal education. But such an education is only the beginning of their stories. They encounter serious problems in their lives and cannot simply call upon the conclusions of that early education as the only resource for resolving such problems. Upon facing the dissatisfaction with his secular life, St. Augustine reads further in the Bible and undergoes conversion. Depressed after his intense early education, Mill reads the romantic poets, engages in politics and falls in love. At loose ends, Hans Castorp determines to visit his friend in the sanatorium, only to remain for several years, experiencing sickness, death, love, and intense political dialogues. James Joyce, in his autobiographical *Portrait of An Artist as a Young Man,* leaves the rich literary education of Irish culture and Catholicism, rejecting both and escaping to write his great works abroad. In these and other stories, liberal education is merely a beginning of a more extensive adult education.

To be sure, during adult life, a narrowing process necessarily takes place. Given the pressures of our family responsibilities and occupations, we never achieve the scope of life which mirrors the breadth of a good liberal education. As we leave school, our attention to science and mathematics or languages or other subject matters may be discarded, forgotten and left by the wayside. Philosophy or poetry may no longer appeal in the face of the immediate practical pressures of life. Even in the best of minds, there is a necessary loss in the richness of our original liberal education, if that education was a solid one. Despite this narrowing process, the essentials of a liberal education continue in adulthood. These essentials are the remaining capacities which enable the liberally educated adult to engage in the activities of thought, moral conduct, and creativity. These activities are expressions of an underlying character and its capacities and they fit coherently within the pattern of a lifetime. Although these activities may grow more perfect over time, in part due to the improved character and capacity of their agent, each moment of activity is complete within itself

Thomas More and Thomas Jefferson

Two lives in particular illustrate this ideal of the continuation of liberal studies throughout one's adult life: the lives of Thomas More and Thomas Jefferson. Thomas More was a statesman, lawyer, humanist scholar, and Christian saint who lived and wrote at the turn of the 16th century. He is best known for his martyrdom due to his lack of approval of Henry VIII's effort to make himself the head of the Church. More received a rigorous classical education including demanding work in logic. He pursued his legal education and first became a practicing Barrister. Throughout his eventful life, including work as the King's Chancellor, he pursued his pursuits of humanistic scholarship exchanging his translations of Lucan with Erasmus. He taught his first wife Latin and oversaw the classical education of his children. His works such as the well-known *Utopia* were written during his official duties. Upon his jailing, later in life, he wrote *A Dialogue on Comfort against Tribulation* to cope with the conditions of his confinement and the imminent threat of death.

Thomas Jefferson, author of the Declaration of Independence, Governor of Virginia, ambassador to France, the third President of the United States, benefitted from a thorough classical and enlightenment education and a remarkably broad legal education which instilled within him a lively scientific curiosity, a love of the classics, and a reflective political mind. He had a unique opportunity to put his broadest views of government to work in his political life, not only penning key legal documents but also a remarkable study of all aspects of Virginian life. The study, *Notes on the Commonwealth of Virginia,* drew upon his extensive scientific and legal learning. He continued to read about and discuss scientific experiments of the day. In moments of leisure, between political duties or during his ambassadorship to France, he returned to reading and collecting the classics as well as studying science. His classical mind was expressed in his own architectural designs of Monticello and the University of Virginia. In later years, he organized his library, continued his agricultural pursuits and founded the University of Virginia. His final years were blessed with a remarkable exchange of political, religious and scientific views with John Adams, the second President of the United States and with many other intellectual leaders of the day.

The Spectre of Bookishness

Although in this book, I suggest that a liberal education extends to great works including fine arts and monuments, my focus has been on books. I have suggested in the last chapter than the reading of ancient, medieval and modern classics, (as well as beholding other great works), is the central task of a liberal education. In this chapter I have argued that these classics and the ideas derived from them can operate as hypotheses to be tested by confronting the problems of adulthood. Adult activity in turn can modify the ideas and hypotheses over time. For some, such an exalted role of the classics in adult life is a recipe for "bookishness", the undue reliance upon books rather than habits of mind and virtue. Ironically, it is the very classics themselves which set forth this argument. Francis Bacon attacks the reliance upon tradition and the classics as "idols of the den", relying upon repetitive and often empty books rather than a study of the nature of things themselves. Voltaire, in his delightful *Candide,* recounts the tale of a young man, captured by the tenets of Leibniz's philosophy espoused by Pangloss, who seeks various adventures including the rescue of others, only to discover that his efforts are for naught, or, in fact, do harm. Finally, he retreats "to cultivate his garden". A parallel tale is the story of Don Quixote, who, after having read too many books on chivalry, goes off as a knight in an effort to restore the chivalric ideal in Spain, only to undertake chivalric acts which bear no relation to the facts which inspire them. Quixote, in old age, apparently recovers his sanity on his death bed. Finally, in George Eliot's *Middlemarch,* Casubon, the old scholar pursues his efforts to capture all mythic knowledge in his *Syntopicon,* only to ignore his young beautiful wife and the world around him. He dies without completing the work and without the loyalty or love of his wife to continue it. All of these classics, (and many others), suggest the limits of total reliance upon books to define, occupy and guide one's life. But one learns other things from classics including the classics which appear to attack the value of the classics. In Bacon's books, we learn the experimental methods for understanding nature. Moreover, Bacon appeals to the classics, (and his criticism of them), when he sets forth his own view of natural philosophy. From Cervantes, we learn the benefits of chivalry and its fundamental ideal of courtesy, despite our amusement at Quixote's delusions. From Candide, we learn the humility which comes from undue reliance upon philosophy, and perhaps a philosophic lesson that this is not the best of all possible worlds. From George Eliot, we learn that despite the failures of many of the characters in *Middlemarch* to realize their dreams, (including bookish dreams of Casubon's wife), they learn from their failures and life goes on. Thus, if the classics identify some of the perils of an undue bookishness, they also reveal other truths useful in life and, in so doing, exhibit the very value of classics.

Conclusion

All of us face a challenge of how to perpetuate the values of a youthful liberal education in our adult years. The demands of family and work life may appear to preclude doing anything but saying "goodbye" to Plato and Hegel. However, as we learn from John Dewey that an early liberal education need not be cut off from the experience of our adult years and, indeed, may help us with solving the problems confronted during those years. More and Jefferson's lives suggest that the adult years need not be an arid stretch of time when the duties of occupation and family completely dominate, drowning liberal activity. Like More, Jefferson and the ancient Greeks, we should view the adult years as the years in which at least some of the liberal disciplines we secured in early life can be brought to some degree of perfection. Perhaps during this long period of our lives, while practicing the old liberal arts to which we were introduced in our early years, we can also learn, as did both Jefferson and More, a few additional liberal arts, to which we were not exposed in our first round of liberal education. Both the liberal education of our youth and the continuing education of our adult years can foster the activities of a liberally educated adult.

I envisage that adult liberal education can operate "as a bridge" between the liberal education of our youth and the reflective meditation of old age. This bridge is constructed by the fact that adult liberal education takes some of the classics and some of their principles and learned during the college years and employs them to help understand and resolve some of the problems of adult life. These problems of adult life are "personal" to the extent that they bear upon our personal family life, the ways in which we practice our occupations or participate in community life. Thus, adult education makes the link between the universal ideas of classics studied in college and the particular and personal challenges of adult life. As we shall see in the next chapter, when we arrive at old age, we are once again required to relate our universal ideas from our earlier life to our existential losses of old age. Thus, just as the encounter of particular adult problems moves to an embrace and employment of classics and their ideas as tools for the resolution of these problems, a similar process takes place in old age which encounters the losses experienced in old age and moves to a detachment and consolation gained through the classics and their universal ideas. But, as I shall point out below in my discussion of meditative reflection in old age, the movement from the universal ideas of our earlier liberal education to the particular losses of old age may not be aimed at resolving the losses of old age, but rather the securing of detachment and consolation for old age loss and sadness.

CHAPTER XII

Reflective Meditation on the Classics in Old Age

"Meditation is a powerful and full study for anyone who knows how to examine and exercise himself vigorously… It is the occupation of the Gods says Aristotle, from which springs their happiness and ours" – Montaigne

"All our dignity consists…in thought…" Pascal

Among the conclusions from my fifteen yearlong old age meditation is the emergence of my awareness of a pattern in my life. Summarizing that pattern, the first third was occupied with a bookish education which included twelve years of higher education. Only after law school, at the age of 28 did I enter the full time work world and the middle of my life was preoccupied with pursuit of the social reforms of day – urban renewal, anti-poverty work, new town development and environmental protection. Most of those ventures failed, or at best were marginally successful. In the latter part of my working life, I returned to initiate, administer and teach within an environmental law program. Retiring at 73, I turned to reading and rereading the classics, editing several collections of the contributions of classical authors to law, and writing this book. I note with amusement that my pattern of life is loosely parallel to the one recommended for the guardians in Plato's Republic *in which, after extensive education, the guardian returns to" the cave", only in later years to retire and engage in the study of ideas. Unlike Plato's guardians, I never reached their exalted position of rule, but like Plato' guardians, my life has been absorbed with ideas and even the years of social activism were shaped by the books and ideas of the mid-twentieth century. I remain unapologetic for such a bookish life – a comfortable life, supported in part by a loving wife - both of us benefitting from a twentieth century affluent America. I am fully aware of how fortunate I have been although I am not oblivious to the costs such a life has created for myself, other societies and other economic and social classes. Now, settled in a small lovely Vermont town, I continue to read the classics, meditate about them, and, with their help, confront the losses of old age.*

Introduction

Winter in Vermont and in one's life is a good time for meditation. With weeks of cold and snow, my world is bedded down for several months. Quiet reigns; everything rests, except the snow plow. To tell the truth, despite all of our Vermont poet Robert Frost's poetry welcoming snow and cold, I think twice about going outside. In John Updike's wise words: "To return back indoors after exposure to the bitter, inimical, implacable cold is to experience gratitude for the shelters of civilization…" Nearing 88 years of age, I believe that winter has descended upon my life as well. But my shelter of civilization for the winter of my life is the classic works upon which I meditate – day by day. Each morning, along with a steaming cup of coffee, I sit in my (admittedly pretentious) book lined living room feeling very smug indeed, as I read Augustine, Pascal, Waddington or some other work which either strikes my fancy or fits into my writing for the day. My reading in old age is a different "third kind" of liberal education – not the mastery of disciplines learned in liberal arts colleges, nor the effort to integrate my reading and its ideas into my now diminished family responsibilities, work or community life. Reading in old age is like the sugaring off of the Vermont tree sap to produce maple syrup. Now I read to find within each work a principle or idea which suggest to me some of the permanent truths to be found in the wreckage of old age, and the losses and sadness which follow in its wake.

For most of us, when old age arrives, our college exposure to the liberal arts is a faded memory. Also eclipsed by the past is any effort we might have made to build that education into our adult lives. Perhaps the most we aged can expect are distant pleasant memories of our college years, a dim sense of the moment of excitement we felt upon the discovery of some truth in the classics or disciplines we studied, and, if we are lucky, some pride at remembering one or more ways in which these classics influenced our adult years. But perhaps one should not be too pessimistic on these matters. History offers us an abundance of evidence of scholars, poets, statesmen, and others who pursued the liberal arts throughout their lives and into their old age.

Cicero, John Stuart Mill, Jefferson are examples of such continued pursuit of the liberal arts into old age. The Roman rhetorician and statesman, Cicero, convened his friends in the study and discussion of the classics throughout his life and in old age, wrote a series of works to introduce the Greek classics to the Roman public. These works canvassed the various views of the God, the universe and the good life. Perhaps the most relevant writing is Cicero's elegant essay on old age itself in which he recommends serene activities such as agriculture, (gentleman's farming) as well as the offering of wise advice on public affairs. John Stuart Mill, while serving in Parliament late in life, studied and wrote some of his best known works on liberty, representative government and utilitarianism. Thomas Jefferson planned the curriculum for his beloved University of Virginia and found some tranquility in the reading of the classics in his old age.

Of course, one should not assume that such a humanistic life guarantees happiness in old age. Plutarch in his life of Cicero reports that Anthony's henchmen traced Cicero back to his seaside country house:

> "...But, in the meantime, the assassins were come with
> a band of soldiers...find [ing] the door shut, they broke

them open…a youth, who had been educated by Cicero in the arts and sciences informed [them] that Cicero's litter was its way to the sea…Cicero, perceived the assassins running in the walks, commanded his servants to set down the litter; and stroking his chin, as he used to do, with his left hand, he looked steadfastly upon his murderers, his person covered with dust, his beard and hair untrimmed and his face worn with his troubles… And then he was murdered, stretching forth is neck out of the litter. [Anthony] commanded his head and hands be fastened up over the rostra where the orators spoke…"

The irony in this account might properly inform the accounts of the old age of the other great humanists. Thus, Jefferson was beset with serious financial and family problems requiring a state lottery to bail him out of his difficulties. And John Stuart Mill, in his autobiography, seems genuinely lost in grief for much of the remainder of his life after the death of his beloved Harriet Taylor. As Cardinal Newman observed in his writings on liberal education and libraries for the working class, there is no guarantee of happiness or salvation in a liberal education. Nevertheless, it is worthwhile to explore what such a lifetime education can yield.

The Beginnings of an Old Age Liberal Education

Unlike college liberal arts which begins with disciplines and textbooks assigned to the students and unlike the adult liberal education which begins with the problems encountered in the adult world of family responsibilities, work, and community affairs, the old age liberal education begins with a self-awareness of old age, a desire to look back, understand, and assess one's life, and the need to detach from and find consolation for old age losses. This unique origin of liberal education in old age suggests the need for a new curriculum of old age liberal arts.

1. *The Classics of Old Age*

The first stage of such a curriculum is the review of those classics which present us with a portrait, theory or aesthetic response to old age itself. Many of the classics deal with old age. The following is a select list. To demonstrate their obvious relevance to old age, the following is a list of selected works which specifically discuss or portray old age:

Lampedusa - The Leopard	Cervantes - Don Quixote de la Mancha
Tolstoy - The Death of Ivan Ilyitch	Goethe - Faust
Hemingway - The Old Man and the Sea	Yeats - Poems
Sophocles - Oedipus at Colonus	Plato - The Laws
Cicero - On Old Age	Mann- Death in Venice
Becket - End Game, Waiting for Godot	Aristophanes - Archanians, Clouds,
Arnold - Growing Old	Bacon - Of Youth and Old Age
Balzac - The Centurion, Pere Giorgio Eugenie Grandet	Boswell- Life of Johnson
Browning - Rabbi Ben Ezra	Dickens - The Curiosity Shop, Christmas Carol
Donne -Elegy 9: Autumnal	Epicurus – Letter
Johnson - The Vanity of Human Wishes	Jonson – Valpone
La Fontaine - La Mort et la Bacheron	Lucretius - The Nature of Things
Wordsworth – The Cumberland Beggar	Plutarch- Contentment
Turgenev - First Love	Tennyson - Ulysses
Shakespeare - King Lear, Sonnets	Seneca - Letters
Weissman - The Duration of Life	Rousseau -Reveries

Of course, many other great works have some implications for understanding old age. Many address the questions of life and death – questions which are central to old age. I have simply listed some which explicitly deal with the topic and I have not included examples from the fine arts, (e.g. Rembrandt's later self-portraits) or the natural sciences, (e.g. Darwin's *Origin of the Species*). In the chapters below, I shall turn to those specific works which help us to meditate on the specific harms of old age. Here, I am simply concerned with some of the more general portraits or theories of the elderly.

The listed works offer a mirror of old age to their reader or viewer. Thus, we witness the fatigue (and disillusionment) of old age in Lampedusa's *The Leopard* or in Goethe's *Faust*. We see the bold and confident hope for the elderly in Cicero's advice on old age. We sense the regret for a misspent life in Tolstoy's *The Death of Ivan Ilyitch*. We find a quiet triumph in Cervantes *Man of La Mancha* and Sophocles' *Oedipus at Colonus*. Old age contentment lives on in Browning's *Rabbi Ben Ezra,* but such hope is countered by the portrait offered by Mathew Arnold. Old age can harbor hardship, as in Dickens' *Curiosity Shop* and tragedy as in Shakespeare's *King Lear*. A sadness in old age is captured in Rousseau's *Reveries* and Mann's *Death in Venice*. Boredom and the waiting for death is captured in the works of Samuel Beckett. Decline and decay is found in Rembrandt's self-portraits and dependency and death in Michelangelo's later Pieta, in which the old Nicodemus cradled the Christ.

The variety of portraits of the elderly in the classics suggests that old age may be experienced in very different ways by different individuals or, perhaps the same elderly persons may experience matters differently at different stages of old age. Such a variegated mirror may help to diminish any simple stereotypes of old age. By comparing one's own self with these different visions of old age, one may better understand one's own old age. Such a variety of ways in which old people cope with their age may enable an old person may to choose what kind of an old person to become! However, the "pictures" of old age within the classics, whether in novels, philosophy, poetry or science are not static portraits. They are ensconced in plots, theories, hypotheses, and poetic forms. As such, the full meaning of each portrait can only be understood in the context of the work in which it appeals. For example, the regret which Ivan Ilyich experiences in the last stages of his life is followed in the story by his final embrace of love. Hence, understanding him means understanding what happens to him during the Tolstoy's complete story, both before and at the end of his dying. As such, we have the portrait of a formerly ambitious, now dying and regretful man who experiences love in his final moments; such a portrait poses the question:

can old age love remove the regret felt by those who have previously pursued a self-centered life?

In addition to the direct portrayal of old age in the great works, there is an indirect revelation of old age in the last works of many of the authors and artists in the western tradition. Sophocles' last work, *Oedipus at Colonus,* Plato's *Laws,* Cicero's *Old Age,* Aurelius' *Meditations,* Plotinus's *Enneads,* Montaigne's last essays, Yeats' last poems are but a few of such works. Although some of these works deal explicitly with old age themes, such works gain an added resonance or legitimacy when it is known that they were penned in the last years of their authors' lives.

2. *Old Age Reflection Upon One's Entire Life*

The second stage of liberal education in old age is the exploration of those works which can most assist one to look back upon one's life, seeking to find or create a coherent whole. Presumably such works will be philosophical, educational and psychological works which look at the entire life span, or historical works which supply context ones past life and possible patterns for understanding that life or biographical and autobiographical works in which the authors review entire lives, either their own or others.

One such example of a life-long focus may be taken from an eastern classic, Confucius's *Analects.* In one passage, Confucius states:

> At fifteen, my heart and mind were set upon learning
> At thirty, I took my stance,
> At forty, I was no longer of two minds
> At fifty, I realized the ming of the t'ien, (the decree of heaven)
> At sixty my ear was attuned:
> At seventy, I could give my heart and mind free rein without overstepping the mark"

Scholars have written entire books on the meaning of this, but I cite it merely to illustrate the focus upon an entire life, beginning in learning. The educational works such as Plato's *Republic* may lay out a detailed accounting of such education suited to the stages of life. The psychological works provide a theoretical structure, such as that found in the works of Freud, Jung and Erickson, by which one might view one's life whether in therapy or simply reminiscence. The biographical and autobiographical works offer examples of stories of entire lives. The great histories begin with the works of Herodotus, Thucydides, and Tacitus and extend to early modern accounts such as Gibbons, *Decline and Fall of the Roman Empire,* and contemporary works such as Huizinga's *The Waning of the Middle Ages.* The classic biographies such as Plutarch's *Lives,* Boswell's *Samuel Johnson* and autobiographies including such works as Augustine's *Confessions,* Rousseau's *Confessions* and *Reveries,* Henry Adams, *Education,* or Angelou's *I Know Why the Caged Bird Sings.*

To be sure, education works may be designed to guide the establishment and conduct of formal education and psychological works, such as Erikson's *Identity and the Life Cycle* are partly intended to guide professional therapists in the diagnosis and treatment of mental health problems. Nevertheless, these works, as Adams, Freud, Jung and Erikson have demonstrated, shed light on the interpretation of complete lives. Adams' *Education of Henry Adams* covers his entire life. Erikson in his studies of Gandhi and Luther has demonstrated the power of developmental categories in the understanding of entire lives. Similarly, old people, whether in therapy or with self-analysis can make use of the developmental categories of psychology to understand one's life.

Not only education and psychology works, but also historical works can supply a context for one's life since one's life is necessarily intertwined with the histories of communities and institutions. For example, one might study the history of the community in which one grew up to better understand the forces which helped to shape one self. But histories, especially classic histories, may also suggest that one is part of a larger historical pattern, such as the pattern described in de Tocqueville's accounts of progress towards equality in America or Toynbee's account of the rise and fall of civilizations. Patterns of progress, regress or cyclical movement in history may be suggestive of the presence of comparable patterns of the histories surrounding one's own life. Following the lead of Van Doren's *The Idea of Progress,* one might ask whether one's own life reveals or embodies such progress, if so, what kind of progress, and whether such progress is indefinite into the future or moving towards some form of plateau?

The most direct help for an old age review of one's life comes from biographies and autobiographies which contain written accounts of such lives. All these accounts suggest alternative narratives for consideration of one's own life. For example, Plutarch's account of the rise and fall of Cicero is a sobering story of the price of political ambition. St. Augustine offers the account of youthful sinning and the study of secular philosophy at an early age, both leading in different ways to his conversion to Christianity and his subsequent life as a Bishop in the Church. Mill offers a remarkable account of an intense early education dictated by his father, followed by depression and then recovery when he fell in love with Harriet Taylor, who, in one way or another influenced the rest of his life and work. In each biography, despite the complexity of events in a person's life, can be found one (or more) narrative interpretations of the life, which, when abstracted, may supply a pattern relevant, in one way or another to one's own life.

3. Addressing The Elegy of Old Age

The third stimulus to reflective meditation in old age derives from the losses encountered in old age. I have described the general nature of these losses and their consequent sadness in previous chapters and, in doing so, I employed some of the insights of the classic works to understand them. In latter chapters I shall address specific losses. These specific losses include retirement, physical and mental decline, eclipse of the past, the foreshortening of the future, growth of dependency, loss of faith in historical progress and the possibility of self-improvement, and dying and death. In the following chapters of this book, I shall take each individual loss to demonstrate how the classic works shed light upon it but before doing so, I will sketch the nature and method of reflective meditation in old age. I base this sketch partly upon my experience in the past ten years; in part I draw upon classic discussions of both reflection and meditation.

The Nature and Method of Reflective Meditation

Reflective meditation in old age is continuous, solitary, and silent contemplative thought about the elegy of old age – a meditation which focuses upon the great works of western civilization and their ideas and principles in order to trace the implication of these works for our old age and their losses within the scope of our entire lives. This meditation enables the understanding, comprehension, and appreciation of the truth of these ideas and principles derived from such classics. The meditation begins with the recognition of a loss in old age and how that loss fits within our lives.

This step in the meditation suggests relevant classic works. The meditation on such works enables an understanding of the ideas and principles in the context of the interpretation of the relevant classic works. It applies the range of liberal disciplines in order to secure such an understanding. This interpretation derives relevant principles and ideas from the classic in question. The resulting ideas and principles allow a comparison between this classic, its principles and ideas to other comparable works in the western tradition. Once such interpretation of the classic has taken place, its principle and ideas derived, and a comparison with other works completed, a process of appreciation takes place. This appreciation comes from the reflection and judgment of how these ideas and principles bear upon one's own life and old age. *The selection and Interpretation of classic works, derivation of principles and ideas, comparison with other works, leads to a final appreciation of the loss and its consequences in terms of the classic work and its principles. It also enables a detachment from the loss and the search for consolations.* (A similar process is undertaken for understanding and appreciating the emotional consequences of such losses, the process of detachment from such losses, and a final consolation).

The reflective meditation outlined above differs in fundamental ways from contemporary meditation which draws upon eastern thought. As popularly practiced, contemporary meditation does not rely directly upon written texts in the meditation process, (although the technique recommended may be the product of a wide variety of eastern texts, such as the *Upanishads, the Lotus Sutra* or the *Lao Tzu).* In contrast to such "eastern meditation", I am recommending a focus upon classic texts and their relationship to our lives as the object of reflective meditation. This reflective meditation is not foreign to western thought. Beginning with Augustine and proceeding in a long history of "ascetic reading", such reading for moral improvement embraces not only a range of Christian, Jewish and Moslem thought, but also finds early modern expression in the works of English metaphysical poetry and Descartes' *Meditations.* A parallel tradition of modern thought, originating with Horace's *Ars Poetica,* and emerging in the work of Wordsworth, Coleridge and Schopenhauer advocated an aesthetic reading relying upon the creative imagination as the first step toward the discovery of moral truths.

One author who reflects the connection between the western tradition of meditation, (as found in his frequent appeals to Plato), and the eastern tradition of meditation (meditation within himself, without benefit of dialogue with others) leading him to union with a mystical oneness, is Plotinus. The philosophy of Plotinus is set forth in *The Enneads.* Meditation is described as a process of questioning reality to find ideas within it. According to Plotinus, we participate within the realm of these ideas which are themselves part of reality. The steps of meditation lead to an exploration of these ideas; we "pasture the self" in the "meadows of truth". Tranquility is achieved when we find a simply unity in all of the ideas and their relationship. This unity is not merely an intellectual unity, but a unity characterized by the grace of love. I am not proposing adoption of Plotinus's difficult-to -understand philosophy of meditation but I summarize it here simply to suggest that there may be some more basic connection between the western pattern of reflective meditation and the contemporary eastern techniques through recognition of the role of ideas.

Recapitulation

To recapitulate, in the method of reflective meditation in old age, I envisage five steps: first, one begins with encountering loss in old age and clarifying one's "prejudgments" when approaching that loss and its consequences; recognition of prejudgments, namely, the biases one brings to an understanding of one's old age losses can assist in the selection of relevant works. Such an approach to the losses of old age requires an analysis of the nature of the goods lost, the kind and cause of change involved in the loss, one's state of "privation" after the loss and the processes of recognition and acceptance of the loss and its consequent emotions of sadness and regret. Second, one conducts, given the prejudgment and with the help of the liberal arts, a selection and interpretation of the classics helpful in understanding the dimensions of loss, its consequences and the need to recognize and accept the loss. Such an interpretation leads to an identification and understanding of central principles and ideas derived from the classic. Third, there is the process of clarification of the ideas or principles involved; this clarification includes a comparative comprehension of the idea or principle within other works of the western tradition of thought. Fourth, the implications of universal ideas or principles for one's own life and old age are explored. During this process, detachment takes place according to which one's loss is viewed in light of the universal principles derived from the classics. Fifth, based upon such an exploration, *the truth of the idea or principle as applied to one's own life is ascertained and judged.* These truths can operate as consolations for the losses. This method is that which I have employed in my exploration of my losses in old age in the final chapters of this book.

Before offering an expanded explanation of this method, let me exemplify it with a specific example. Other examples may be found in each of the chapters of this book, but especially in the chapters below, dealing with the specific losses in old age. One starting point or prejudgment in my view of old age is the awareness (or assumption) that one is entering into a new stage of life . My second pre-judgment assumes that in old age, one may look back over one's entire life. A third pre-judgment is that as part of the reflection upon one's entire life and the encounter of old age itself, one becomes aware of the presence of old age losses among which are biological decline in old age, retirement from work, the recognition of an eclipse of one's past, the foreshortening of the future, the growth of dependency, the loss of faith in progress and the consciousness of the approach of death.

Beginning with these pre-judgments regarding old age, I have identified above a number of major works which offer alternative portrayals of old age. One such work I choose Is George Eliot's *Middlemarch*. *Middlemarch* contains the unflattering portrait of Casaubon, the old scholar, who pursues the writing of a grand "Syntopicon" aimed at unifying all myths. He pursues this goal, ignoring how unrealistic it is. In the process of his scholarship, he ignores all the contemporary scholarship in the field. Equally important, in the process of pursuing his own scholarship, Casaubon ignores his young beautiful wife, Dorothea and her ambitions. He dies working till the very end, but failing to complete his work. The vision of Casaubon is not a flattering one, but it leads me to reflect upon my own continuing intellectual projects, (perhaps at the expense of my own family). This starting point with *Middlemarch* leads to my reflection upon my entire life. It introduces me to a central loss in old age – the foreshortening of the future, cutting off the possibility of ambitious projects. To what extent does my lifelong scholarship resemble that of Casaubon? What impact has such scholarship had upon my life and my old age? To what extent has my scholarship, like that of Casaubon's, pursued grand ambitions for honor and recognition at the expense of more modest accomplishments? Is this book I am writing an example of such ambition?

Thus, the beginning inquiry suggested by *Middlemarch* leads me to turn to become aware of the more specific losses of old age, and, in particular, the loss which comes from the foreshortening of the future which takes place in old age. It seems to me that the very real limits of one's personal future in old age necessarily limits the possibility of realizing one's ambitions, limiting the time available to complete new works. Time becomes the good lost in old age. That time is not the abstract time of the physicist, but the personal temporality of one's own life. Modern classics of XXX explore the nature of that temporality which is defined, at least in part, by one's biological decline and one's mortality. To recognize that personal temporality, one must recognize and accept one's own biological decline and mortality. As we shall see in the chapter discussing the foreshortening the future in old age, there are classic works which can help us to recognize, accept, and eventually, receive consolation for one's mortality.

To illustrate the second step of meditation – the interpretation of a given work to find its central idea or principle, let's again turn to Eliot's *Middlemarch*. The task of interpretation here draws upon the range of liberal arts, (much as St. Augustine drew upon these arts to interpret the Bible). Augustine suggests that the contributions of grammar, semantics, the various liberal arts and sciences such as history and the natural sciences, rules of interpretation, and rhetoric are all useful either in understanding the Bible or instructing biblical truths. It is these arts of interpretation which can be brought to bear upon any text, including *Middlemarch*.

Middlemarch is the story of an idealistic and ambitious young woman, Dorothea who, with grand ambitions, chooses to marry an old scholar, Casaubon, who is pursuing an ambitious effort at scholarship. Dorothea hopes that Casaubon will teach her and she will become his colleague. The marriage turns into a loveless one, Casaubon dies without achieving his grand scholarly goal and Dorothea turns to a younger man, with whom she has fallen in love; they live "happily ever after". This story of Dorothea's ambition is placed within the intimate social world of Middlemarch, a small town made up of a variety of people, each with his or her own ambitions; like Dorothea, most of these people are destined to be frustrated as the events in the story unfold. In fact, the Prologue and Epilogue of the novel reveal Eliot's intent to demonstrate how, unlike St. Theresa, most of us fail to reach our goals in life and have to settle for something less – something with which we may or may not be content. An idea which emerges from *Middlemarch* is the idea that ambitions are usually or at least frustrated by the reality of everyday life. A principle which emerges from *Middlemarch* is the principle of prudence in the adoption of one's life ambitions.

Once one has identified a focal idea or principle in *Middlemarch,* *i.e.* the frustration of ambitions in life and the need for prudence, a third step follows: the clarification of this principle. This clarification is necessary since, although the idea appears to be illustrated by the lives of many of the characters in the novel, it is unclear as to its precise meaning and significance, since the reasons for the failure of each life differ and the results of the failure for the subsequent life also differs. Thus, for Casaubon, his ideal was unrealizable, in part because it was inherently too ambitious, in part because he failed to educate his wife and enlist her in his venture. Both reasons were due to his pride. For Dorothea, it was perhaps her youthful naivete, her inadequate education, (the inadequate education of women at the time), her own pride and the gender inequality in marriage partners at the time. Unlike Casaubon, one might argue that Dorothea's failure appears largely due to external circumstances of the prevailing culture. The results of the failures for the two principal figures were drastically different. For Casaubon, it was failure of his project and death. Dorothea lived to find another love and gave up her exaggerated and unrealistic intellectual ambitions.

Reliance upon one classic, however, may not be enough. In this third step of meditation, such an idea and principle suggest other works with similar themes. In addition to Eliot's *Middlemarch,* the works of Cervantes, *Don Quixote,* and Voltaire, *Candide,* come to mind. In each of these works, the protagonist undertakes bold plans, only to have them frustrated by circumstance. These works are only a few of the many works which document the costs of ambition; American novels and other works, ranging from the works of Edith Wharton, Henry James, Theodore Dreiser, to the enthusiastic writings of Ben Franklin address the costs and rewards of ambition. Although many of these and European novels of Stendahl, Balzac, and Gissing may illustrate the costs of ambition, most of these works are about ambition in early life followed by fall out or disaster or, upon occasion, happiness in old age. One portrait of ambition in old age is Goethe's *Faust* in which Faust's gargantuan ambitions are realized with the help of a compact with the devil. Is the lesson here that successful ambitions in old age can only be the product of malevolent interventions from below?

When "applied" to the situation of one's old age, the lesson of *Faust* or *Middlemarch's* may recommend the abandonment of excessively ambitious projects in old age. Even Voltaire's *Candide* appears to urge a lesson of modest ambition and consequent happiness derived, in Candide's words, from "cultivating one's garden". But the lesson of *Quixote* may be somewhat different. Despite Quixote's equivocal abandonment of his knightly quest at the end of his life, (and evidence that Cervantes had intended his novel to criticize contemporaries who wrote such knightly romances), there remains within the novel something admirable about Quixote's futile quest. The reader shares the author's admiration for Quixote. Such an admiration argues against abandonment of grand and foolish projects, (if some other merit can be found within the effort!). This brief exploration of "the *Middlemarch* principle" in the tradition of great works suggests differing and sometimes conflicting interpretations of the principle, hence requiring reformulation of the principle. Perhaps grand ambitions should only be foregone if, upon reflection, they seem to have detrimental effects upon others and no redeeming consequences.

After the interpretation of the work, the derivation of its principle and its clarification in the light of similar works, a fourth step is required. The time has come to explore the implication of the principle and the works which embody it for one's own life and, more specifically, one's old age. I have labeled this stage one of "appreciation" since it involves recognition of the quality of one's own experience in light of the principles of the work in question. Thus, since, as stated above, my "prejudgment" was an awareness of the limits which old age places upon one's projects, how or in what way does the "Middlemarch" principle shed light upon that awareness? Although I shall explore this question in more detail below in the chapters dealing with the foreshortening of the future and the pessimism of old age, the Middlemarch principle makes me acutely aware of the internal and external limits of old age ambition. I shall leave open here whether in the face of such limits, one abandons such ambitions, or simply entertains them provisionally, with full awareness that they may not come to fruition in the products at which they are aimed.

Or is there another alternative which requires a change of attitude towards one's old age projects? In the chapter below, I introduce the classical notion of liberal leisure into one's old age activities and projects. Within such leisure, the activities required of the project are undertaken *for their own sake*, and are part of a timeless flow, to be *completed in the very moment of their performance;* such efforts are not mere instruments to the completion of an independent product sometime in the future. According to this view, the old age ambitious efforts should be viewed as part of an ongoing activity -complete at each moment of their performance. Such a classical notion stimulates us to return to our classics once more. *One might find an example of such a liberal activity completed for its own sake in Quixote's tilting at windmills.* To assess this alternative requires not only a deeper interpretation of *Don Quixote,* but also an exploration into the nature of ancient liberal activities and the feasibility of undertaking them in our modern age – an exploration which I shall pursue in my discussion of retirement in a chapter below.

In the fifth and final stage of my notion of reflective meditation, I conclude that any serious meditation envisages the finding of a truth at its conclusion. What then is the truth regarding the "Middlemarch principle"? Certainly, *Middlemarch* can lead one to conclude that grand projects in old age are unlikely to be successfully completed and hence should either be entertained provisionally or abandoned! Second, there may be no necessary evil with the realistic abandonment of projects in order to "cultivate one's garden". Third, if such projects are undertaken, they should be undertaken with a liberal attitude in which the activity of the project itself is realized, not the ultimate product, which is usually considered its reward. How one cultivates a liberal attitude towards one's project remains to be explored in the chapters below. In any case, *Middlemarch* may supply some truths for coping with old age's foreshortening of the future.

Conclusion

We can now summarize our conclusions before turning to meditations on the specific losses, detachments and consolations of old age in the next chapters. We began by recognizing that old age is best understood as a unique stage of life in which it is possible to reflect upon the whole of life. Reflection upon old age reveals its elegiac pattern of loss, sadness and regret, detachment and consolation. In order to cope with the loss and sadness, we must detach ourselves from them. In such detachment, we gain a certain freedom from the necessity of the aging process. But achieving detachment is not easy. It requires the help of the classic works. To obtain access to these classic works requires a liberal education in youth, adulthood and old age. Each of these forms of liberal education is different: youthful liberal education focuses upon disciplines, their organization, and exposure to the classic works with their perennial principles and ideas which exhibit the liberal arts; adult education is conducted by experiential learning in which the classic works are hypotheses for understanding and action in the adult years. Old age liberal education is a reflective meditation upon the classics. This meditation requires an understanding and comprehension of focal ideas and principles found through interpretation of the classics and appreciation of how those ideas and principles pertain to one's own old age and its losses, as well as one's reflection upon one's entire life.

CHAPTER XIII

Accepting and Compensating for the Withering of Life

"...All that I have said and done
Now that I am old and ill
Turns into a question till
I lie awake night after night
And never get the answers right...."

Yeats, The Man and the Echo

As I wrote this, before my wife died, we proudly claimed 88 and 86 years of life. We had watched each other's slow but steady decline in strength, vitality and even health. We have grown old together. Both of us were wrinkled, I more than she. My hair is graying; hers was judiciously colored. Both of us have gained weight in our old age, (not a necessary consequence of aging!). With sore knees, I have had to give up my middle-aged passion for running. Now, with a knee injury, I often rely on a walker. Mollie, despite new hips and new knees, which she had acquired in the past two decades, walked with some difficulty. Both of us suffered from mild arthritis. I have an enlarged prostate which keeps me running to the bathroom at night. Both of us have suffered from high blood pressure and her pressure might have led to her stokes and death. Mollie has some difficulty hearing in one ear and recently had here cataracts fixed. My eyesight has been weakening and recently I have experienced retinal problems. We both had grown somewhat more forgetful and less energetic. While I have been writing this book, Mollie has had thyroid cancer and her thyroid gland has been removed. This autumn she had a knee replaced and has undertaken the painful and difficult effort at rehabilitation. Given these problems of aging, before her death, we had slowly, imperceptibly altered our lifestyles. We went out much less often, drank less alcohol, (almost none!), held few dinner parties, took few trips, avoided long walks, and I no longer run or play tennis. We both took innumerable pills, and I continue to do so. At the end of her life, Mollie walked with a walker and I have inherited it. Like Immanuel Kant, I carefully measure my opportunities to drink my beloved coffee, but find it to be a drink which increasingly disagrees with me. Each of us sought to escape from old age and the decline of our bodies in different ways, Mollie through continued work and me through "classical leisure". Mollie saw her patients in her practice of psychotherapy until the day of her death. I continue to read and write, which offers a form of escape or at least allows me to detach myself from what have been minor illnesses to date. For both of us old age has been a time to help each other in our co-dependency has become a school for learning, practicing and accepting compassion.

Introduction

If the glory of peak excellence in life is best described in Homer's *Iliad,* the aching loss of strength and energy in old age is best captured in the Sophocles' play, *Oedipus At Colonus.* Sophocles was an ancient Greek playwright, best known in modern times for his tragic account of Oedipus in *Oedipus Rex.* In that play, Oedipus mistakenly kills his father and unknowingly marries his mother only to discover his horrendous deed and its resulting harm to Thebes over which he ruled. At the end of the play, he blinded himself in punishment and wandered off. Less well known, Sophocles, upon growing old, wrote a sequel, *Oedipus at Colonus,* the story of Oedipus, himself in his old age. Oedipus arrives on stage, guided by his daughter, Antigone. He comes to Athens from Thebes — "a long road for an old man" and one who is blind and tired.

Wearily sitting on a rock, near the sacred grove, Oedipus is first greeted with suspicion by a chorus of oldsters guarding the grove. In their choruses, they see him as symbolizing the status of the old - disabled, dependent upon others, vulnerable, destitute, a stranger and of little consequence. Oedipus himself faces the reality of old age which he views as part of a more general historical decline:

> "Beloved son of Aegeus, the gods alone know neither old age nor death, but all else is confounded by all-powerful time. The earth's strength wanes,that of the body is weakened, trust withers as mistrust flourishes and the spirit never stays the same, neither among men who are friends nor between cities. To some now, to others at some later time, things of joy become bitter and then once again kindly."

The chorus of old men gradually accepts Oedipus into the "alliance of the old" — and sings hymns of praise for the sacred place they guard, express nostalgia for the past and reflect upon the hardships of old age. The young vigorous Theseus, leader of the Athenians comes, and offers Oedipus protection since he recognizes in him a dignity which comes not only from his kingship, *but from his past sufferings, and his opportunity over time to reflect about and be educated by these sufferings....* This dignity and sense of worth underlies Oedipus's angry response to his son, Polyneices, who, after ignoring his father's condition for many years, comes to Athens to try to persuade Oedipus to return home. Polyneices is not motivated by filial piety, but seeks help in his power struggle with his brother. Refusing to return with Polyneices, Oedipus, despite his aged and weakened condition, declares his autonomy not only from his son, but also from the power struggles of the Athenian world. At the end of the play he retreats into the sacred grove to die.

Although Sophocles is unsparing in his portrait of the ills of the elderly, especially as expressed by the chorus in his play, he also finds in the old Oedipus, despite his dependence upon Antigone, an underlying dignity and nobility which rescues old age from its otherwise abysmal condition. That dignity is found in Oedipus's composed and serene reflections upon his own limits and failures, his sense of self and his power — based in part upon his past achievements but also his honesty in facing his present condition. The spectacle of the inevitable degradations of old age softened only by the impression of Antigone's compassion and Oedipus's dignity leads me to the question of this chapter. Can we modern old people, like Oedipus, face unblinkingly the final biological decadence of old age and the other losses it brings? If so, how?

This question is difficult to answer. After all, biological decay may impede the very human capacities of which we (and the ancient Greeks!) are justly proud: the capacities to enjoy thought, engage in physical play, appreciate art and music, exercise personal and political moral decisions, engage in love and friendship. All may be impeded in old age. In extreme cases, not even our old age memories of an earlier excellence or achievement may remain. Insofar as these activities and their corresponding capacities constitute human happiness, what is left in old age if they are lost? Insofar as these activities, capacities, and achievements are part of our selves, in old age, do we lose claim to our very selves and the possibilities of life? Under what circumstances can we retain our dignity if that dignity depends upon these capabilities? Throughout the ancient play, Oedipus relies heavily upon his daughter Antigone for help. Perhaps, ultimately, the only dignity remaining is a borrowed dignity left in the fading memories of those who knew us at our best, and the few who love and help us as we decline in old age.

The Losses in Biological Decline

Given the blindness and weakness of Oedipus, it is worth asking: what is lost in the biological decline of old age? How does the decline take place? What is left after the decline and before death? The ancient Greeks gave us the notion of "arête" – excellence - as well as a method of education to reach it–"paideia". Paideia is the educational process by which excellence is developed. Such excellence embraces health and beauty, courage and temperance, and all of the intellectual excellences displayed by Socrates in Plato's *Dialogues* and identified in a list of virtues provided by Aristotle's *Nicomachean Ethics.* These excellences have been reiterated in different forms in the history of western thought since the time of Aristotle.

The search for and recognition of this excellence, whether found in the Homeric poems, the Greek plays, the philosophical dialogues and treatises, and ancient medical writings have been an important part of the western tradition for more than two millennia. For the Greeks and the tradition which followed them, these excellences were primarily the province of the young and middle aged, with, perhaps, the exception of wisdom which was accorded to at least some of the old. (Plato, in his old age, unsurprisingly found wisdom in the aged and gave them an important public role in the colony at Crete to be founded as described in his *Laws.* But not all the old were wise. In the *Republic,* which he wrote when younger, the old Cephalus had to give up the rigors of philosophic dialogue and simply leave the discussion to make sacrifices to the gods. It is also implied in the dialogue that age had rendered Cephalus unreflective, unable to think seriously about the nature of justice).

If the ancient writings appeared to focus upon the excellences of the young and middle aged, why turn to their works when exploring old age biological decline? *Simply because the ancient Greeks recognized that these excellences in our middle aged lives are based upon sound biological functioning.* Both the Greek philosopher, Aristotle, in his *De Anima* and biological treatises and the ancient Roman physician and philosopher, Galen in his numerous medical writings outline the basic biological organs and their functions, and organize them into systems identified according to certain purposes (nutrition, locomotion, etc.); these systems are all integrated into an integrated whole. The result is the integrated functioning of the whole human organism included intellectual as well as physical functions. Given this view, for the Greeks, biological decline means not only defects within certain organs and the specific systems of which they are a part, but also deficiencies in the very functioning of the whole human organism, including, in some cases, intellectual deficiencies as well.

Many of the Greek plays reveal this Greek view of old age as a time of life which has lost its excellence. The classic Greek tragedian, Euripides painted a picture of the aged in decline in many of his plays: *Children of Heracles*, *Hecuba*, *Trojan Women*, *Phoenician Women* and others. In them, old age is seen as sorrowful, heavy, accursed, difficult bitter, hateful and murderous. There is a corresponding litany of "the signatures" of old age: gray hair, stooped backs, trembling hands and weary faces. In the plays, the entrances and exits of the old are halting and slow.

> "How steep is the climb to this house for wrinkled old feet like mine to make."

> "Aged parts of the body — aged foot, unmanly arms, sad head, trembling limbs - abound.

> The aged collapse and faint. The aged bodies are a burden — alien and heavy."

> "Old age lies upon my head a burden heavier than the crags of Aetna."

These are typical lines for the old. Vulnerable, subject to abuse, dependent upon others, unable to carry out ambitions, admiring the young - this is old age for Euripides. The presence of excellence in the young and its absence in the old suggests that the fundamental loss in old age is the loss of excellence.

The description of the aged characters of Euripides, as well as a similar portrait of the elderly in Aristotle's *Rhetoric* is painful when compared to the rich accounts of the excellences of human nature which the Greek poets and philosophers gave us. These accounts remind us of what we, in our old age, have lost. It is always useful to know what one has lost, if only to face the truth. *We are reminded that the loss of the former excellences due to biological decline carries with it a train of other losses. The loss of work in retirement, the loss of private and public memory, the loss of years left in our lives, the loss of an extended future, the possible loss of autonomy, even the prospect of the loss of our lives, and, perhaps the loss of optimism for ourselves, our community and the course of history can all be traced back, at least in part, to the biological decline we experience in old age.*

It is all of the losses which result from the loss of health and vitality which led me, in Chapter I, to assert that a central part of old age loss is biological decline, which dominates or, at least, quietly, secretly and ominously, underlies all else. In fact, gerontology — the modern science of aging — often defines aging as the normal, inherent, irreversible and progressive deterioration of biological functions. Biological decline is, at one level, obvious. I have already recounted the variety of "cosmetic changes" — the wrinkling of the skin, age spots, graying of hair, possible loss of teeth, fading of eye sight and hearing, loss of sexual drives. Many of these can be addressed by the modern miracles of cosmetics, exercise, contact lenses and so forth. But there are deeper changes which are not visible — follicles fall out, nerve cells lose their dendritic arbor, neuro-fibrillary tangles increase, morphological degeneration of striated skeletal and heart muscle cells occurs, the structural integrity of extracellular proteins such as collagen and elastin is lost as cross-linking occurs, bone and muscle deteriorates, and, illicit cross-bonding of segments of genetic macromolecules randomly take place, leading to mutation and failure of replication. These are the changes of which we elderly may be only dimly aware, but which ultimately affect our functioning in everyday life; we sense them in the gradual loss of bone and muscle strength, acuity, memory, and energy. These biological changes in functioning slowly deprive us of the excellences we once possessed (or hoped to possess) and the equilibrium of the health we possessed in our earlier years. If we do not simply wish to wallow in misery when we face (or "man up") to these changes and experience the sadness of these losses, we are forced to detach ourselves from the losses, not by denying them, but by viewing them objectively and finding some consolation for them within a broader objective understanding of the cycles of nature, biography and history.

The Sorrow of Old Age

Old age is not only a source of sorrow and pain, but also a time of delight. In an earlier chapter, I reviewed some of the delights of old age — leisure and freedom from responsibilities and the time to savor life, the absence of destructive passions, and the unique opportunity to survey one's entire life from the vantage point of its final stage. I pointed out that, paradoxically, some of the physiological declines of old age, may contribute to these delights, such as the lessening of reproductive capacities helping the aged to avoid any further duties of parenthood, and escape the demands of the passions, (whether lust, fear or anger). Similarly, our aged deficiencies may grant us a delightful freedom from some responsibilities. Even the awareness of minor age-related weaknesses may be bitter sweet reminders of the presence and importance of the body as part of our selves. Of course, delight is only half the story. Old age pain is the principal reminder and it is not so sweet. Pain, whether slight or great, may be and often is a continual companion of aging. In this regard, it is now time to repeat more of Matthew Arnold's poem, *Growing Old* captures the reality of biological aging.

> "What is it to grow old?
> Is it to lose the glory of the form,
> The luster of the eye?
> Is it for beauty to forego her wreath
>   - Yes, but not this alone
>
> Is it to feel our strength–
> Not our bloom only, but our strength decay?
> Is it to feel each limb
> Grow stiffer, every function less exact,

Each nerve more loosely strung?

...

It is to spend long days
And not once feel that one were ever young
It is to add, immured
In the hot prison of the present, month
To month with weary pain.

It is to suffer this
And feel but half, and feebly, what we feel.
Deep in our hidden heart
Festers the dull remembrance of a change,
But no emotion - none

...

This pain of aging can be the sensation of our own bodily decline - the brute immediate sensations of pain in our aging body or a sense of draining of energy. It also can be the pain of other emotions of aging — the feeling of helplessness and frustration, a sense of vulnerability with anxiety and fear. Such indirect pain can reside in the unique feeling of loss — loss of our capacities, dampening our deepest desires, and weakening our ambitions as well as dimming our memories. Indirect pain can include the pain from the loss of independence and the very loss of ourselves. We aged can even lose the world with which we were once familiar but which we can no longer fully understand nor act effectively. What, if anything, could the canon works contribute to understanding the subject of aged pain of loss, due, in part to biological decline?

One of the most thoughtful discussions of the pain of loss is found in St. Thomas Aquinas's *Summa Theologica*. Of course, Thomas recognizes physical pain of the body and realistically admits that it can interfere with the appetites of life and hence dominate our lives. But he also suggests a second kind of pain- the pain of "sorrow" which is the work of reason or imagination's awareness of our internal failure which ensues when we can no longer pursue our lives in a healthy way.

Thomas calls it "the flight of appetite". For Thomas, alienation, envy, anxiety, distress, repentance, jealousy and indignation are some of the "sorrows" which result from the loss of some good we seek. To my mind, inward sorrow is especially present in old age because, in old age, we gradually lose the capacities and desires which make up the self. In the words of Thomas

> "...Man's life consists in a certain movement, which flows from the heart to the other parts of the body; and this movement is befitting to human nature according to a fixed measure... If this movement be hindered in its progress, it will be contrary to life in respect to its species... a movement of flight or contraction...contrary to the vital movement ...such are fear and despair and, above all, sorrow which depresses the soul..."

Although St. Thomas's physiology may be out of date, the notions of life as vital movement and the "hindering" or "contraction" of the progress of man's life resulting in fear, despair and sorrow captures a very real feeling in old age.

A Detached View of the Biology of Decline

To understand our own aging and detach ourselves from its processes of decline, it is helpful to understand the nature of the physiological self which is undergoing decline and the causes and consequences of the decline. If old age brings heightened awareness of physical decline and the losses it drags in its wake, the canon supplies an objectivity which can help us to understand our decline. Obviously, the details of modern anatomy, physiology, medicine and gerontology, can assist with such an understanding of physiological decline, but these are beyond the scope of this book; I leave such a modern scientific understanding to the doctors and gerontologists. Marvelous contemporary accounts of life, decline and death can be found in the writings of Sherwin Nuland.

(*The Way We Live; The Way We Die; The Wisdom of the Body*. I propose a more circuitous route based upon the canon works which, although often dealing with scientific matters, were written to be read by the educated layman and shed light not only upon the biological decline of aging but the significance of that decline.

The canonic account offers a deep view of biological aging which, in its essentials remains largely uncorrected by recent science. These canonic works include those of Hippocrates, Aristotle, Galen, Harvey, Darwin, Weismann, Cannon, Henderson, and more recently, Schrodinger, Dubos, and Odum. Despite the fact that contemporary empirical studies have qualified or replaced some the particular findings of these earlier works, these canon works continue to supply a framework of principles for an objective understanding of the aging of our bodies. And so, in this chapter, I propose a quick and admittedly non-scientific review of some of them. These canonic works offer a comprehensive vision of our biological system – *viewing our organs and physiological systems not only as part of the body as a whole, but also part of an embodied self, situated within the cycles of life as part of the evolutionary processes of nature.*

These canon works of biology and ecology begin by establishing humans as unified organisms with limited life spans, composed of an organization of parts with various functions, both mental and physical. These parts are interrelated, achieving some form of at least momentary equilibrium, resulting in the unified human capacity for self-organization and self- movement, including growth, reproduction, locomotion as well as a variety of intellectual capacities. These capacities are the product of an evolutionary interaction and adaptation of the organism with the environment enabling the organism to continue that interaction during its life span. As Joseph Henderson has pointed out, such an interaction may reflect or result in an organism's temporary "fit" with the environment, but, as Rene Dubos has documented, the "fitness" of that species, along with its progeny, may adapt over time both internally and externally, part of an evolutionary process, reflect in its own mutations or other adjustments and changes in the natural and manmade environment. These changing life cycles of human and other organisms participate over time in the larger cycles of nature and history.

1. The unity of the human organism

The unity of the organism is assumed by most biologists, (although micro-biologists recognize that many animals including humans are colonized by micro-organisms, and hence are symbiotic clusters of organisms). Over the ages, philosophers and medical doctors have explained the unity of the human organism as simply an individual substance organized into biological parts including mental faculties, both interacting with the environment for various purposes. In addition to Aristotle, Hippocrates and Galen offered medical dimensions to the description of human biology. Before Aristotle, Hippocrates, an early Greek physician, who practiced medicine during the Athenian plague and is best known for his Hippocratic Oath and his work, *Airs, Waters and Places,* suggesting environmental sources of disease. Galen was a renowned physician born in 130 AD in Asia Minor in Pergamum, then possessing the second greatest library in the ancient world. After a liberal education in which he studied the great ancient philosophies, he undertook the study of medicine at age eighteen and devoted his life to the study and practice of medicine, but he wrote philosophy as well as medical treatises and argued for an important relationship between the two. Galen's book on *The Natural Faculties* and *The Utility of the Parts of the Body* were two of his best known treatises. In them, he joined with Aristotle and Hippocrates in suggesting that that health was the end, not only of medicine, but of diet, exercise, and temperance.

2. The Physiological Systems

As early as Aristotle and Galen, the list of bodily parts was known, and regarded as components of a series of physiological systems. For example, Galen viewed the parts of the body as having a specific utility, because they were parts of "faculties" defined in terms of powers, capacities, or potentialities. In Galen's words, "Each part has a usefulness". Thus, a stomach is part of the nutritive faculty having its utility in its capacity to digest food. Galen would conduct detailed empirical studies of the various parts and their roles to test and explain his theory. In today's view of physiology, the number of systems have multiplied to cover circulation (for heat and energy transmission), the nervous system, (to link the senses and thoughts to the parts of the body), the pulmonary system, (to secure oxygen for energy production), the skeletal and muscle systems (for stability and movement), the digestive system (for nutrition), and the elimination system (for waste disposal). The parts of these systems are susceptible to aging, which, in turn, interferes with their functioning.

3. Homeostasis

Galen's diverse "faculties" or, as we now call them " physiological systems" are united and organized in maintaining the living creature. In the words of Galen:

> "All the activities and their causes cooperate with a view to producing a single result, the maintenance of the functional unity which is the living creature
>
> ...Everything is in sympathy in the ensemble of parts and in the parts everything works together to produce the results of each of them..."

These systems are coordinated into "a homeostasis" described by Walter Cannon in his classic, *Wisdom of the Body*. This homeostasis constitutes health and enables the organism to live and function successfully in the environment. The environment itself helps these systems to function, providing them with oxygen and sustenance, well described by Hippocrates, who recognized the interaction of the organism and its environment in his works on "airs and waters", (a work which also includes an account of beneficial diets). Cannon's homeostasis or equilibrium, later called "vital balance" detailed the ways in which the systems of the body are interrelated; Cannon also documents the decline of homeostatic mechanisms of blood sugar, temperature regulation and acidity as we age. More recently, Sherwin Nuland has written another book entitled *Wisdom of the Body,* which brings Cannon's account up to date. Nuland supplies an modern scientific account of such a balance.

4. Environmental Interaction

The modern medical focus upon the human body omits the role of the interaction between the organism and its environment. But, with the help of Charles Darwin, we have re-learned in modernity what the ancients knew - that the very nature of the human organism has, in part, been shaped by its environment. According to Darwin, the environment, given a scarcity of resources and an organism with a capacity for cell mutation and reproduction, operates over time to "naturally select" those creatures whose bodily functions are best adapted to the environment. We humans are part of this evolutionary process and our very minds and bodies reflect unconsciously the history of our ancestors' past interaction with the environment. As we shall see below, with the help of Weisman, evolution plays an important role in our aging.

5 Part of The Ecosystem

Once we broaden our perspective from a focus upon an individual organism to the interaction of that organism with the environment with its consequent evolution, we are able to take the next step of viewing our health as a changing part of an evolving ecosystem. Eugene Odum, one of the founders of ecology, in his *Foundations of Ecology,* helps us to view ourselves as part of a larger population which functions within a complex biotic and abiotic ecosystem. For Odum, *our aging, death and decay become part of the processes of the continual recreation of organic material within that ecosystem.*

Unlike most, (perhaps all), animals, we are able to reflect upon our experiences which include both a consciousness of our own self and awareness of its interaction with the environment. Unlike other animals we are able to "rise above ourselves" and, upon reflection, recognize not only that the functioning of our bodies is part of our embodied selves but also that we are capable of being aware of this embodied self and its interaction as part of the cycles of nature. Such recognition may be practical as we pursue a variety of human purposes which affect or are affected by the environment. Such recognition may be theoretical as we reflect upon those purposes and the ways in which the interactions with nature operates to shape them. As both Aristotle and other ancients realized, a full understanding of the biology of man includes an understanding of the human purposes that such a human biology serves, and an understanding of the human persons is part of the awareness of a "self".

6. The Embodied Self

The notion of an embodied self, pursuing its purposes in interaction with the environment, has a rich history in the canon works. It begins with the ancient idea of "the soul". When we look at the modern history of the canon, we are confronted with multiple and sometimes competing views of "the soul", either as self and as mind — the latter being conceived in different ways as either a thinking substance, or an organized collection of cognitive faculties, or an intelligence, or a self-consciousness or a totality of mental processes. Given this variety of views of soul, mind and self in the rich history of the canon, the best I and my reader can do as we confront this complexity is to recognize the rich variety of views of the self. When confronted by the array of differing views of the self, I have been persuaded by Aristotle (and his modern interpreters) who set forth the notion of the individual *psyche* as simply the functioning of life through the organization and animation of the body and mind. In this view, the mind is simply an aspect of an organism's living; this aspect may be cautiously labeled one of its "faculties", i.e. powers whose activities, operate along with the other functions of the body, (such as the vegetative part which promotes growth and the sensitive part which enables sense and imagination, and the part which promotes locomotion). In viewing the *psyche* as simply the principle of organic life and the mind as simply the rational part of that life, Aristotle links our body and mind in one unity providing a basis by which we can approach the change of ourselves in aging. We can reach to comfortable conclusion that aging affects our "self", both body and mind, without separating ourselves into two different and irreconcilable worlds of mind and body within the self.

(Of course, long after Aristotle, Descartes maintained that the "soul" was simply a distinct mental substance separate from our body. After Descartes, the English philosopher, David Hume, reflected on the impressions and ideas of this mind, and was unable to find a principle of the mind's unity aside from the habit of linking these ideas and impressions. In response to Descartes and Hume, Kant labeled this mind "a transcendental ego". The internal unity of the self was "deduced" by Immanuel Kant in his "proof" of this transcendental apperception of the ego in which he found our the unified experience of impressions and ideas within our mind. Following Kant, the American philosopher and psychologist, William James, (as well as the novelist, James Joyce), viewed the mind as the given unity established by an empirical stream of consciousness rather than a transcendental unity. The empirical view of the mind was revolutionized by the discovery of the unconscious by Sigmund Freud. In his theory of the unconscious, Freud re-established the connection between mind and body by discovering the influences which the unconscious mind had upon bodily symptoms and the influence which the body itself had upon the unconscious mind. For Freud, mental functioning not only interacted with the environment through the ego, but also interacted with our body; the mind played a major role in the regulation of the body's internal functions as well as influencing its "external" interactions with the environment.

The Biology of Aging

This brief and admittedly oversimplified history of the biological functions of body and mind has implications for aging. If, as Descartes and his followers maintain, our conscious mind is distinct from our body and if our bodies age, *it may be suggested that our mind may still stay intact since it is distinct from the aging body.* Such a view of the separation of mind and body sometimes appears to be confirmed in old age when some of us elderly have an eerie feeling that our mind stays the same while our body is aging. But despite this momentary feeling of mental autonomy, we aging also often have a subtle recognition of "ourselves" losing a sense of vitality of both body and mind, a loss which is often a sign of biological decay. We can "feel" old. This recognition of our own biological decline extends beyond our awareness of our own body and mind and may be reflected in the way we interact with our community and its history in the pursuit of our human purposes.

Such awareness is marvelously captured in the famous novel by Guiseppe Lampedusa, *The Leopard. The Leopard* is the story of the life and death of Prince Fabrizio, a large land owner in Sicily. The Prince was a powerful man, personally and politically. Therefore, when his old age came upon him, his story became a story of the decline of a man with power. This loss of power is poignantly portrayed in a scene in which Fabrizio gives a grand ball. Despite the stature of Fabrizio as the host of the grand ball, he senses his aging; he is alienated from the guests and he experiences weakness when confronted with the expectation that he dance. Although meeting the challenge, he leaves the ball by himself withdrawing from the life of the ball, much as the aging often withdraw from everyday life. As he left, he caught a glimpse of the planet Venus, and wondered "When would she decide to give him an appointment, far from stumps and blood, in her own region of perennial certitude?" When that "appointment" at the end of his life arrived for Lampedusa, while completing his novel, he wrote the following words:

> "Don Fabrizio had always known that sensation. For a
> dozen years or so he had been feeling as if the vital fluid,

the faculty of existing, life itself in fact, and perhaps even the will to go on living was ebbing out of him slowly but steadily, as grains of sand cluster and then line up one by one, hurried, unceasing before the narrow neck of an hour glass. In some moments of intense activity or concentration, this sense of continual loss would vanish, to reappear impassively in brief instants of silence or introspection; just as a constant bussing in the ears or ticking of a pendulum superimpose themselves when all else is silent, assuring us of always being there, watchful, even we do not hear them."

The story of Don Fabrizio is not merely the history of an individual, his old age and death. Like the author of the *Leopard,* the Prince has lived through both the decline of his family's fortunes and the historical decline of Sicily, a nation which itself has grown old. During the course of his life as a proud and rich landowner in the Kingdom of Sicily, Fabbrizio experienced the gradual impoverishment of his family descendants and, at the same time, the eclipse of the Sicilian kingdom. Thus, the story of the aging of Fabrizio against the background of his family and the history of Sicily, helps us to understand that our aging body and mind are not merely biological matters; our identity's growth and decline may also be shaped through our habits, customs and education, in short, by human culture, in all of which we participate. If our culture is in decline, that decline may accompany and be part of our own personal decline. Thus, the biological component of our self which is shaped by biological instinctual needs and capacities in their interaction with the natural environment, also interacts with the cultural environment and, in so doing, may also thrive or fail within a historical culture of which it is a part.

Having recognized the interaction of our bodies, minds and cultural identities in the aging process, nevertheless, it remains the decline of the body and brain which remains the fundamental engine of general decay. This biological decline which is part of aging — the normal, inherent, progressive decay in the parts of the body, including the brain - is irreversible, although modern medicine may delay selected changes and replace some aging body parts. The decay in the parts of our body, such as the weakening of muscles, the changes in the brain's prefrontal cortex, the thickening of arteries, etc. interferes with the effective functioning of our physiological systems. The weakening of muscles affect our mobility, the changes in our cortex affect our planning and initiative, the thickening of the arteries interfere with the transport of nutrients as part of the nutritional system.

Although some of these changes can take place at an unconscious level and our mind may be unable to grasp all the changes taking place in our bodies or our brains, we elderly may be aware of many of the mental changes which take place. Forgetting, making mistakes, encountering difficulty in articulating our thoughts, losing the strength and energy to systematically pursue ideas and losing the capacity of hearing and seeing the facts necessary to support those ideas, are some of the most obvious signs of our decline. Our friends and family may be aware of our decline as well, but may enter into a conspiracy of silence regarding it. Insofar as our identity is made up of our own consciousness as well how others regard and treat us, this identity may well be affected by these changes due to aging.

The malfunctioning of our physiological systems and mental function disrupts the homeostasis or vital balance of our entire body and mind resulting in a variety of symptoms or "signatures" of aging. With the impairment of physiological systems and our vital balance, our relationship with the natural and cultural environment is impaired. Thus, our ability to pursue all of the natural and cultural goods we value may be affected.

Intellectual Consolations for Biological Aging

Even if we adopt an objective and scientific view of the physiology of aging, we do not fully achieve detachment from biological decline and its pain. In reviewing the canon works, I have found three philosophical approaches to biological decline. The first approach to our decline is the acceptance of the existential reality of our old age. The second approach adopts a humanistic perspective which universalizes our biological decline as part of the stages of human life. The third approach places our own human aging into a comprehensive vision of the world beyond ourselves dwarfing the importance of our life by making it a small part of a grand pattern of nature.

1. Existential Decline

The experience of old age decline is a unique experience for each of us. As we read about the last days of saints and philosophers, (except for suspicious hagiographic accounts), one is struck with the ordinariness of their old age decline and death when compared with the significance of their works which have lived after them. Jesus asked on the cross: "My father, why hast thou forsaken me?" In asking such a question, Jesus appears to have doubted the very beliefs he gave to the ages. Similarly, in approaching death, St. Thomas is reputed to have renounced his works as "so much straw". He appears to question the value of the magnificent intellectual edifice he had created which has shaped Catholic belief through the ages. But perhaps the moment of death is not the same as the experience of biological decline in old age. To take another example, St. Augustine is known to have gone on reading to the very end!

Turning to experiences in old age, the great German philosopher, Immanuel Kant, while not renouncing his philosophy in old age, seemed preoccupied with his physical comfort and terror of life after death. In his biography, one finds little evidence in his final years of the deep philosophical penetration into scientific knowledge and moral life which he demonstrated during his life. Such despair in old age is not universal. The English philosopher, David Hume seems to have lived in old age and died with grace and style. Perhaps his deep skepticism about the nature of knowledge limited his expectations when facing death. Montaigne's later essays share with us his own personal pain in late life but, like Hume, he seems to have borne them well. Like Montaigne, most of us aged have been sick and have already begun to experience the unique pains of old age — failure of strength and energy, muscular pains, increased frequency of disease. Given the peculiar quality of decline in old age with its consequent sorrows, we may have to abandon any notion that we can find meaning in the books and ideas which we so valued earlier in our life.

One account of a vivid personal experience of old age is set forth by the modern French existentialist, Jean Amery in his deeply pessimistic books, *On Aging* and *On Suicide*. Amery regards the experience of time as the core of being of the aged. His sense of old age decline is the growing awareness of his body as a stranger. If old age is a time of "toil and trouble", toil is the sense of the incurability of our maladies and trouble is the awareness that, after partial recovery of each malady we are not quite as healthy. In Amery's eloquent words, "pain and sickness are the festivals of decay the body organizes for us". Yet, Amery argues that, although perceived as old and declining by others, we revolt and deny our state, despite the secret knowledge that the revolt will not be successful. For Amery, no matter how hard we try, in old age, we will no longer understand the world because it is no longer our world of the past. We withdraw into a world of memory and live with dying by striking a compromise in which we recognize the proximity of death while denying its personal and irremediable reality. Thus, unlike Christ or St. Thomas, who appear to find a new reality in the time near death, or Augustine, who keeps on reading till death, Amery suggests that one simply denies the reality of old age and death.

The consolation which one takes from the variety of individual responses to old age and death is found in their variety. There is no royal road, master plan, or grand manner by which to grow old and die and that can be a relief. There is a comforting freedom in knowing that there are no duties nor expectations for us in our old age or, at least, given the variety of ways in which our canon authors encountered their old age and death, there should be no such expectations.

2. Humanistic Decline

A second way of understanding our human decline is to see it as part of being human. Our humanity is to be understood by the humanizing arts and sciences. Thus, Greek poetry and drama regard aging as simply the back end of the human life cycle, the unfortunate downward slide after the development of peak capacities and their crowning achievements. This view is captured well in the works of Aristotle and the Greek poets, who found solace in the honoring of development and exercise of the potentialities of humans in the earlier stages of life. While recognizing decline, Cicero's homage to old age finds ways in which his own declining human potentialities can continue to be exercised envisaging his limited participation in political life, and his reading and translating of the Greek classics for the Roman people.

In modern times, the humanistic view of aging is best articulated by the developmental psychologists who describe aging as simply one of the "universal" stages in an entire life — stages which Augustine, Freud, Jung, and Erikson described (albeit differently). They understand that the limited segment of time in which the individual grows old and declines is to be understood in light of earlier stages of life. Humanism allows us to view our own particular aging decline within a complete narrative of our own lives. The decline we experience is not part of a universal human biological decline but also partly the result of an individualized decline, partly of our own making, partly the consequence of history. Since our entire lifetime, including our old age, takes place within a given society with its past and present, our own decline is part of that history. Recognizing old age decline as part of "our own historicity" helps to shape and give meaning to our decline and may drop a comforting curtain of thought between us and the existential pains we face in old age.

This historical and biographical account of decline in aging and society's treatment of that decline leads some novelists to find the meaning of the aging and biological decline in a historical setting where a particular society itself is "aging". Miguel Cervantes places Don Quixote's aging life in the context of the history of a society which itself has "aged" leaving behind the past ideals and practices of chivalry which have now disappeared at the time of Quixote's life. In his old age, Quixote momentarily harbors the futile hope to restore that chivalric ideal, both in his own life and in the current life of his society, but his powers ebb and he finally fails in his quest. Similarly, Henry Adams, in *The Education of Henry Adams* views his own decline in light of what he takes to be the entropy of the modern industrial America of the 1800's, symbolized by "the dynamo". The old age decline of Don Quixote or Henry Adams, like Fabrizio in *The Leopard*, find meaning within the tragedy of the civilizational decline in which the lives of each takes place. The importance of their decline is magnified by being viewed as being a symbol of a changing history portrayed in literature, history and biography. To the extent that in our period of old age decline, we can experience that decline as part of the history of our own civilization and imagine our lives and that history to be intertwined, we can follow the models provided by Cervantes, Lampedusa, and Adams. We can place our own decline in a broader story to find consolation.

3. Decline Within Evolution and the Cycles of Life

Rather than view our biological decline with existential dread, or through the lens of psychology, biography, history and literature, we can turn to the biological and medical sciences and accomplish the same feat of detachment and find consolation by treating decline as reflecting the processes of nature. In modern times, three biological causes of aging have been suggested. One is that all creatures are preprogrammed in their cellular structure to age. A second explanation of aging is simply the process of wear and tear; life simply wears out the human body, perhaps with the help of free radicals bombarding us over time. One example of this view is William James, who, in his *Principles of Psychology*, explains our memory losses in old age as simply due to corresponding changes in the tissue of our brain. A third explanation is that, whether preprogrammed or the result of wear and tear, the aging and death of the organism is the consequence of selective competition in a more extensive evolutionary process.

This third explanation is set forth in the classic work — the *Duration of Life* by Alfred Weismann. Alfred Weismann was a German zoologist who taught and studied at the University of Freiburg in the late 19th and early 20th century. In his book on the duration of life, he sought to find the explanatory principles for the different life spans of plants and animals. Rejecting appeals to size or structure, he found the "wear and tear" of animals preprogrammed in the cellular structure of the organism. But, as a Darwinian, he found the preprogramming of aging to be explained by its utility in the continuation of the species. After reproduction and, in some organisms the care of the offspring, further life created competition with new organisms of the species. In Weismann's words:

> "...the duration of life is extremely variable and not only depends upon physiological considerations, but also upon the external conditions of life. With every change in the structure of a species and with the acquisition of new habits, the length of life may and in most cases must be altered...life is endowed with a fixed duration, not because it is contrary to nature to be unlimited, but because the unlimited existence of individuals would be a luxury without any corresponding advantage..."

Weismann anticipates and unifies the three explanations for the duration of life. These descriptions of the causes of aging help us to "objectively" regard our fate placing it within a more comprehensive history of evolution of life. Like Weismann, we can regard ourselves as part of an array of human and plant life, some of which lives nearly forever, some, like the mayflies, live for a brief moment. Like other life forms, our aging serves a larger biological purpose -the facilitation of the perpetuation of our species through reproduction. We are part of an evolutionary natural history, of ourselves and humans. This biological vision gives us a sense of detachment when we regard our aging as simply biological fate.

Perhaps an even deeper and more comprehensive natural treatment of our biological aging can be found in both ancient and modern physics. As we have seen above, modern physics can offer explanations as to how free radicals may damage the human cell resulting in "wear and tear". But perhaps a more compelling picture of our aging was provided by the ancient scientists and philosophers. The physical description of human decline was first vividly portrayed by the ancient Roman poet, Lucretius, drawing upon the works of the Greek philosopher, Democritus. Lucretius, in *On the Nature of Things*, describes the cycle of life in the seasons and in human life, both the product of a flux of atoms. At the end of his poem, he describes in brutal detail the dying of the Athenians in the plague as simply part of the broader cycles of nature. This description reflects the Stoic and Epicurean visions of the cycles of nature, into which our decline and death fits. These visions have been echoed in canon works throughout the ages. For example, such a vision of decline, disease, and aging is not unlike the modern ecological view of all life as part of the cycle of elements in the environment.

The view of biological aging as part of larger natural processes may be comforting, even if it fails to grasp the sense of individuality we experience in our decline and which is best expressed in existentialist writings. In contrast to these writings, the naturalistic view of decline supports an human effort to lose ourselves in a vision of something larger than ourselves, hence dwarfing the significance of our own decline. A unique comprehensive vision of nature which respects the individual, at least momentarily, in the course of natural processes may be found in the work of the modern philosopher, Alfred North Whitehead whose remarkable but difficult philosophy which will be discussed elsewhere in this book.

Conclusion

Old age is a stage of biological decline, in which our health, in the form of the integrity and equilibrium of our biological systems within themselves and the environment, is gradually lost. As the ancients recognized, this loss is a loss of more that biological competencies; it is the loss of former excellences based upon those competencies. The canon works of the medical and biological classics help us to understand this biological loss, the works of psychology and philosophy help us to understand how decline in our body may be part of an embodied self, the humanities help us to understand how this loss may be part of a broader history of cultural decline and finally, ancient and modern philosophies help us to see our decline as part of natural processes. Perhaps we cannot escape biological decline and its' consequent sorrows, but the canon may offer the means of detachment and consolation as we view such losses through the classics which explain our minds and bodies to us. The canon works help us to detach ourselves from being overwhelmed by the loss of old age decline either by helping us to face unblinkingly and objectively the reality of loss, placing it in a larger framework of the complete functioning of our bodies and minds and the story and history of the stages of our lives. We may also view this decline through a vision of the cycles of nature- in words of Lucretian Epicurean poetry – uncovering "the way things are".

The detachment gained from these works can be consoling. During our decline, some of the canon works, whether through literary accounts or medical reports, *familiarize* us with the realities of a progressing biological decline. Scientific accounts of the decline, philosophical meditations, and biographical meditations place the decline in a wider perspective helping to *minimize* the immediate losses from such decline. Some of us may even be *transformed* as we decline, learning that the capabilities and excellences we had possessed earlier in life were only part of our full life and its biological cycle. We *find substitutions* for the health and vitality we valued in early life as we recognize the new values in the experience of decline. In admitting the arrival and irrevocability of losses we dreaded earlier in our lives, we may paradoxically experience a sense of relief – an almost *cathartic experience*, now that they have arrived. The canon works can supply opportunities for all of these consolations of biological decline. As Boethius claimed, they are the "poultices of consolation" for the pain and sorrow of such a decline.

CHAPTER XIV

Retirement, Classical Leisure, and Solitude

I must go into exile. Does any man then hinder me from
going with smiles and cheerfulness and contentment?
—Epictetus

If possible, withdraw yourself from all . . . business . . .
tear yourself away . . . we have dissipated enough of our
time already. Let us in old age begin to pack up our
baggage.
—Seneca

*I began my retirement years almost sixteen years ago at the age of seventytwo.
I phased down my teaching over a period of two years. At 72, I "voluntarily"
retired with an emeritus status, which allowed me to tutor a few students
in the classics of jurisprudence, while continuing to write law journal
articles and edit books on jurisprudence. In short, I have had a relatively
pleasant slide into retirement. Yet, a certain persistent sadness arrived with
retirement. I have watched friends and colleagues, whom I used to see
regularly at work, slip away in retirement or death. I have sensed a growing
irrelevance - a lack of power and status - within my school as new deans,
faculty, and staff arrive. I sense the expectation from colleagues that my
principal role should be to cheer them on their way. Perhaps they are right! As
the bars of my iron cage of employment are removed, I found myself exposed*

to a world I was "protected from" while employed. The comforting routine of the work life was gone. This new world seemed foreign to me, and I sensed a diminished capacity to cope with it in my old age. But gradually, I began to embrace a new way of life. In my college years, I had been introduced to the Greek and Roman ideal of classical leisure – an ideal which I have found attractive throughout my life. Such leisure embraces activities which seem valuable in their own right – community activities, casual friendships and loving relationships, reading and writing, meditating, walking and gardening, listening to music, watching good movies. In my old age, I have discovered a rationale for this classical leisure in Aristotle's Nicomachean Ethics, *Seneca's essay,* On Tranquility, Sebastian de Grazia's Time, Work and Leisure and Michael Loughlin's Garden of Repose *As I sought to practice this leisure, I felt various pressures from friends and colleagues to abandon it and return to a life of "busyness", but I have discovered the deep satisfactions of solitude, which seems to protect my life of leisure. My love for a life of solitude has grown, leading me into a life of meditative reflection - reading, meditating and writing (for no one in particular)– engaging in what some authors have called "pastoral" or "literary leisure". Upon reflection, I realized that throughout my life, I have found and exploited opportunities for solitude—my childhood bedroom for reading, my college age summer work as a gardener alone all day in the gardens of the large estates, a guide in an unvisited museum of medieval armor, studying alone as student or teacher, running alone for many miles, (and many years!). I have always found niches in libraries, coffeehouses, nearby parks and forests, and secluded rooms in my home where I might "escape" to read and write and, yes, daydream. In old age, I have finally discovered the full meaning and value of the practices of solitude as part of a life of classical leisure and I have found the rationale for a literary solitude to be well stated in the works of Seneca, Petrarch and Montaigne. I now embrace the ideal and practice of solitary classical leisure as a fine substitute for the work I have left and write about it as one consolation for the losses of retirement. I feel "at home".*

Introduction

For those who enjoy their work and believe it to be valuable, retirement begins as kind of an exile. The Roman poet Ovid, at the peak of his career and fame, was exiled from Rome for the remainder of his life by the Roman emperor Augustus. He was banished for, among other things, his delightful lovemaking instruction manual, *The Art of Love*. In response to his exile, in what is now modern Romania, near the coast of the Black Sea. Ovid wrote *Tristia* (sadness). *Tristia* captures the feeling of exile and the sadness of old-age retirement. In Ovid's words, "I am an exile; solace, not fame has been my object"; these words might be the motto for this book! Just as Ovid was banished from his beloved Rome to reside in the cold and brutal ambience of Eastern Europe, modern retirees are banished from their former lives to the oft brutal regions of old age. Ovid might be speaking for the elderly when he wrote: "My wounds also, if I have committed no crime, may their maker, I pray, desire to heal and now at length satisfied with a portion of my suffering, may he draw off a little of the water from a brimming sea." In contrast to the happy talk about old age, by other ancient Greeks and Romans, such as Epictetus and Seneca, Ovid pours out his anguish in *Tristia* and, in doing so, introduces it with some of the sadness that I share as I write this book. In his words, but applicable to both our books:

> Little book, you will go without me—and I grudge it not—to the city, whither, alas, your master is not allowed to go! Go, but go unadorned, as becomes a book of an exile.

Although we aged may not have experienced all the torments of Ovid's exile, we are forced by old age to leave work and the "life world" it created for us, and we experience alienation - a certain loss of meaning, power and dignity in our lives, as well as a fading of the delight which the challenges of work had once offered us. Detaching ourselves to understand the loss resulting from retirement and its consequent pains requires careful reflection. Or so I have come to believe. Such reflection requires a reexamination of the nature of work we have left and leisure we may embrace to replace the work lost. Such a reexamination leads some of us to adopting a different, more ancient view of the nature of leisure, namely, classical leisure and for an even smaller number of us the discovery of the value of solitude as part of that leisure.

A useful start for this reexamination is an exploration of the definition of retirement and the architecture of ideas surrounding such a definition: such ideas as labor, leisure, rest and recreation. Retirement is our voluntary or involuntary change in status from compensated labor to uncompensated "free time"— time expected to be occupied by some form of rest and recreation. This change in status is ordinarily linked to the advent of old age carrying with it the societal assumption that old age experiences biological decline (as described in the last chapter) signaling a loss in the human capacity for labor. Unless the retiree finds other work (and many do find at least part-time work), the retiree must choose a new life, perhaps seeking the pleasures of recreation, spending free time with friends and family, indulging in prayer and related religious activities, engaging in community activities or taking care of his health. This choice of a new retired life is often the product of an unconscious choice – one in which is a product of tradition, custom and individual inertia. But whether a conscious choice or not, the retiree is entering a new way of life -determining who he is and will be for the remainder of his life.

Losses in Retirement

For many, such a retirement or rest and recreation is not a loss at all. For them, retirement is the abandonment of unpleasant routine work which characterizes much of modern labor or at least relief from a mere job one could take or leave. Assembly line work, whether in factories or at McDonald's, or in white-collar confinement within the bureaucracies of modern offices, often make work a painful experience or one simply to be tolerated; retirement becomes a welcome relief. Such a vision of work as painful is captured in the biblical story of Adam and Eve as their punishment for disobedience, they are expelled from the Garden of Eden. The view of work as a mildly disagreeable necessity is captured by Dickens' portrait of Bartleby, the Scrivener who sits alienated at his desk until "preferring not to do his work" and fading away. Many moderns share Bartleby's view of work and hence retirement to the golden years of rest and recreation, may be seen by them as letting them as welcome escape, returning to the garden of Eden at the end of their lives. The history of attitudes toward work and retirement is beyond the scope of this book, but the negative views of labor have been shared by many philosophers and poets ranging from the ancient Greeks to modern Marxists. It is little wonder that a recent history of old age, (Thane's *A History of Old Age*), contains many pictures of the elderly happily celebrating their freedom from work! (See for example, Nono's *The Golden Wedding* at 225.).

For many other retirees, retirement may be a different story. Retirement may mean the loss of the opportunity to participate in a work world which we enjoyed, indeed, valued. Retirement for us is a fundamental "social injury" which seems to express society's often unfair judgement that we are not able to work effectively any longer. Like the poet, Ovid, we regard retirement as an "exile," a painful exclusion from the workforce, preventing us, in the words of Thorstein Veblen, from exercising our "instinct of workmanship", removing the opportunity for us to exercise the capabilities we have developed over the years. Less recognized is the fact that retirement prevents us or at least makes it difficult for us to contribute to the public good though the practice of our occupation. Society's judgments about our inadequacy to contribute any longer to the general welfare may be the source of a secret shame we experience when we retire; such shame may make us choke on our reluctant admission to others that "we are retired". To be sure, we may volunteer for community activities upon retirement, but for most of us, such volunteering does not absorb the time and energy, nor, in our own minds, make the same level of contribution nor reach the same level of importance as our previous paid employment. In short, the current economic arrangements which create the societal demand or expectation for retirement challenge our lifelong pursuit of happiness through work.

Yet, for many of us, we must accept a fundamental truth: when we are subjected to "involuntary" retirement, whether through custom, employment rules, or law, society's rough judgment that, in "old age", either our mental or physical decline (or both!) are likely to take place and that, like it or not, such a decline may interfere with our work performance. (I have reviewed the experience of decline which accompanies old age in the preceding chapter and document its effects). Society's judgment may be justified as simply the reasonable statistically-based recognition of biological decline of the average elderly person, but, whether justified or not, it also may be an effort to accommodate the need to provide work opportunities for the younger workers who will replace us or the result of the blind workings of the market place when callous institutions seek to save money by retiring more highly paid older workers in favor of cheaper young ones. In our younger days, we may have benefitted from the very workings of such laws!

Of course, retirement in old age may be voluntary when the retiree silently makes his own admission of an incapacity to continue work, or simply seeks respite from a life of work, or (as I did) makes a conscious decision to take time to assess his entire life and, in the process define who he is, apart from his work role. *I have come to believe that the retiree, perhaps with a slight nudge, may make the decision that, in old age, time is needed to make sense of one's entire life or to pursue a different worthwhile use of one's time.* The recognition that such time is needed at the end of life may be animated by a realization that one's life is almost over, that old age is a stage of life without much future, and the time for reflecting on life's meaning has arrived. One philosopher, (David Norton, *Personal Destinies)* describes loss in old age loss as

> "...loss of a future, [and such] a loss of the future is the loss of self-actualized individuation ... this loss is the occasion of the rediscovery of the individual in his common humanity"

Whether voluntary or involuntary, for many of us, retirement signals a fundamental and transformative decision involving a significant loss of our previous work identity. Since a person is often identified with his job, or identifies herself with it, retirement strips her of that identity. The loss leaves us, in the title of one celebrated German novel, as "*The Man [or woman] Without Qualities*". In this novel, author Robert Musil's character, Ulrich, is without ambitions, apathetic, filled with the surfeit of unrealized ideas, bearing the symptoms of the nineteenth-century "fin di siècle" in Europe and carrying a nihilism which anticipates the subsequent devastating First World War, (perhaps the equivalent of the anticipation of death). Perhaps such a description fits the description of many retirees of the twenty-first century!

As I have suggested in earlier chapters, old age might be best understood in elegiac terms of loss, sadness, detachment and consolation. To cope with old age losses requires us to understand and assent to the losses and the emotions consequent to the losses, detach ourselves from the losses, and find consolation for them. To understand the loss resulting from retirement from paid labor requires an understanding of the nature of the paid labor we are leaving. If we are fortunate, labor, as a source of individual happiness in our past, supplied us the opportunity to exercise our capabilities called upon in our occupation and contribute through our work to others. The ancient Greek notion of *arete*—human excellence, (often translated as virtue), is often invoked when applied to the exercise of these capabilities, but, as applied to modern work, I shall turn to the terms of a more recent modern author, Thorstein Veblen, and his fine discussion of "an instinct of workmanship". Veblen claimed to discover that this instinct evolved before the advent of modern industrialism. In such work, one pursues "the interest with practical expedients, ways and means, devices and contrivances of efficiency and economy . . . [in] creative work and technological mastery *where there is work at hand*" (my italics added). Although the "discipline of the machine" for Veblen creates habits which can extinguish the instinct of workmanship, so, too, retirement can remove the "work at hand" by which such an instinct was once pursued.

To understand the significance of the absence of "work at hand", it is helpful to turn briefly to some of the classic economic works, such as those of Adam Smith, Karl Marx, Thorstein Veblen, John Maynard Keynes, R. H. Tawney, and John Kenneth Galbraith. These works have shaped, albeit indirectly, our understanding of our economy. All six authors were careful students of society's production of wealth, the division of labor in its economy, and the consumption of wealth. Adam Smith was one of the first to articulate an economic purpose for the state. Smith, in his *The Wealth of Nations*, views the state as designed to increase wealth through the promotion of a division of labor and the "invisible hand" of the marketplace. Exploring the distribution of that wealth, Marx, in *Das Kapital*, documents the history of a class-based society, in which the bourgeois owners of the means of production, exemplified by the industrialized factory system, exploit the surplus value created by labor and impoverish the worker, shortening his life and frequently making him "redundant." R. H. Tawney, in his *The Acquisitive Society*, echoes the theme of the detrimental pursuit of economic wealth alone, urging a society in which a new division of labor based upon the social functions. One of these social functions is the ensuring of social security for the retiree, as part of subjecting the uses of property to the comfort and health of the population. Influenced by the work of Max Weber, Galbraith, in *The Affluent Society* and *The New Industrial State*, sees our modern American economic world as a corporate industrial state, composed of large scale public-private bureaucratic corporations devoted to their own internal growth. The society which results is an "affluent society"—one in which private affluence is pursued and public needs are often left unmet. Veblen, in his *The Theory of the Leisure Class*, written before Galbraith's work, had already pointed out how private affluence is sought for "conspicuous consumption" and, echoing Adam Smith, finds a decline in the crafts and an "instinct of workmanship" on the part of the worker. Finally, John Maynard Keynes, writing during the twentieth-century world depression, proposed the need to promote employment through government spending when private saving failed to produce sufficient consumption. Keynes's work led to an expectation in modern times that, if necessary, the state would guarantee full employment.

Within these classic visions of our modern economic system, what is the position of the retired elderly person? For Adam Smith, the worker within the division of labor becomes "stupid and ignorant." In fact, Smith is surprisingly candid about the extensive harm which the division of labor wreaks upon the hapless worker. Although Smith suggests that government expenses should include some minimal public provision of early education, he believes such education should not interfere with the productivity of industry. Thus, despite tacitly recognizing the fact that workers are left with limited intellectual and physical capacities at the end of their working lives, Smith gives scant attention to the need for private or public support of such workers in their old age. Karl Marx, in *Das Kapital* and Friedrich Engels in *The Conditions of the English Working Class* also recognize the crippling effects of industrialization upon the worker. But, unlike Smith, they view the worker as the victim of class oppression, whose health is ruined by long working hours (which exclude any opportunity for leisure). These hours are due to the capitalist desire to maximize labor's surplus value, which the capitalist appropriates. Although Marx does not discuss the plight of the elderly, the implication of Marx's critique is simply that the worker is dumped from employment when he reaches old age after having supplied his surplus labor to his bourgeois owners. (The full Marxist documentation of the impacts of capitalism upon the elderly had to wait for another century when they were spelled out by Simone de Beauvoir in her classic *The Coming of Age*). As stated above, for Veblen, the retiree is the worker who is left by his lifetime participation in modern mass production without a desirable "instinct of workmanship" which might otherwise carry him through his retired years. For Keynes, the retiree's status is ignored as irrelevant to the principal purpose of government, which is to insure full employment for those who are employable. For Tawney, the retiree may be guaranteed comfort and health in a society reorganized according to a new division of labor based upon the social functions of property. For Galbraith, the retiree is the victim of the failure of the modern corporate state to supply public needs, including the pensions and other public services in an affluent society.

The deepest personal effect of retirement, however, was discerned by Emile Durkheim, who, in *The Division of Labor* and other works, such as *Suicide* grasped the essence of an *alienated retirement*. Durkheim viewed modern society as bound by an "organic solidarity"—the binding of society due to the interdependence resulting from the modern division of labor. Unlike the "mechanical solidarity" (the solidarity of custom) of the more primitive societies, which recognized an important role for the elderly outside of work, modern organic solidarity binds its participants in a shared commonality of the work world, all sharing in the recognized value of work. In a complex modern society, according to Durkheim, there is little societal role for family, religion, and the elderly. The exclusion of the unemployed, the disabled, and the elderly from the work world results in the "anomie" of these excluded individuals—a kind of alienation which, in Durkheim's view, leaves these groups more susceptible to suicide. For Durkheim, the retiree becomes an anomic individual, cut off from participation in the principal solidarity of society. Anomie characterizes those who are excluded from the work world and hence are no longer guided by the norms of life which the work world provides. Such anomie is part of a broader state of alienation which many elderly retirees experience. Such "alienation" carries many meanings bestowed by modern philosophers, psychologists, and sociologists and includes powerlessness, social isolation, meaninglessness, normlessness, even self-estrangement. Excluded from the work world through retirement, the elderly may face the reality of powerlessness, a sense of meaninglessness, the absence of norms to guide their lives and social withdrawal.

These classic economic views identified above, in one way or another, suggest rationales for the fundamental crisis faced by modern retirees, even those who once loved their work. For Smith, the division of labor leaves the retiree without the habits and skills necessary to function in their retirement. For Marx, the workers are simply are oppressed and impoverished. For Durkheim, they are alienated. For Veblen, they lack the wherewithal to secure status in life and lose the capacity for meaningful independent work. For Keynes, they are irrelevant in the eyes of a government which should be concerned with full employment. For Galbraith, "public needs" include support for the aged, and these needs are ignored in the corporate pursuit of economic growth.

These classics suggest that the treatment of the retiree in the modern economic system creates a fundamental problem: a societal failure to value the lives of the elderly retiree within the economic system and the reciprocal failure of the retiree to value his or her own retired status. The retiree is exiled from the framework of labor which in modern society had given meaning to his life and the emotions consequent to such retirement are similar to the sadness, "tristia", experienced by Ovid in his exile.

Detachment in Retirement

I have suggested above that one way to cope with the losses of old age is to detach oneself and reflectively meditate about them. In retirement, such detachment is aided by that fact that we are already socially detached; we are exiles from work. But something more than social detachment is required. Experiencing the exile of retirement requires us to redefine ourselves. In doing so, we face existential decisions as to who we are or who we will become for the remainder of our lives, *apart from work roles.* Once retired, whether voluntarily or not, we must freely choose a way of life which will define how we shall regard our former life and what we shall do in the last full stage of our lives. Such a decision, at the last stage before the end of life, calls for an authenticity which requires that we do not simply try to continue the work we have done in the past or fill our lives with the nostalgia of our past work. On the assumption that a life of work has not extinguished all capacity for living, we elderly must choose among the many such ways of life and identities which may be possible in old age.

Such a choice requires imaginative and intellectual detachment. I have suggested above that one can achieve that detachment by embracing other forms of detachment found in the imaginative and intellectual activity stimulated by participatory engagement with the classics. In painting and sculpture, music and dance, poetry and novels, old age and its sadness is a common theme. Similarly, the intellectual works of philosophy, history and the physical and social sciences help in the understanding of old age and retirement. (I have appended a list of such works to this book). As described above, I have suggested that poetic and prose elegies are especially central vehicles for understanding old age in general and the stages of loss in particular. To take two examples of imaginative works of the old age anticipation of death: Elinor Wylie's *Nadir*

> "Let us at least pretend- it may be true
> That we can close our lips on poisonous
> Dark wine diluted by the Stygean wave;
> And let me dream sublimity with you
> And courage, liberal for the two of us.
> Let us at least pretend that we can be brave.

And Dylan Thomas's well known: *Do Not Go Gentle into that Good Night:*

> Do not go gentle into that good night.
> Old age should burn and rave at close of day
> Rage, rage against the dying of the light. …

suggest two very different emotions from the old age anticipation of death allowing us to contemplate these or other suggested emotions found in elegiac works. Similarly, works of philosophy force us to stop and seek to understand our old age and retirement. Simone De Beauvoir suggests that

> "…old age may also bring liberation; it sets one free of
> false notions… the clarity of mind that comes with it is
> accompanied by an often bitter   disillusionment.
> But once illusions have been swept away, [age can bring

a questioning, challenging state of mind. Doing while at
the same time, "placing one's activity into a parenthesis"
means achieving authenticity… This sweeping away of
fetishes and illusions is the truest most worthwhile
of all the contributions brought by age…."

Such a quote suggests that freedom might accompany old age
retirement. Following the achievement of such detachment and its
freedom, or accompanying it, consolation for the loss of work may
arrive. Such a consolation may come through many avenues, but one
such avenue is the replacement of work with another way of life. That
way of life I call "classical leisure".

Classical leisure is a way of life, a state of being, a personal condition
in which one is free from paid labor, the ambitions of career, the pursuit
of fame, power or wealth, and a frantic search for pleasure. Possessing a
character with modest moral virtues and intellectual capabilities, shaped,
in part, by a liberal education, such leisure may embrace, among a large
range of possible activities, allowing for the selection of a few valued
and valuable activities undertaken for their own sake. The activities are
valued by the leisured practitioner as essential parts of the one's own
lifelong integrity, simply defined as a coherence of character. (To assure
that these activities are indeed part of one's lifelong integrity, the elderly
leisured practitioner may need to reflect upon his or her life, whether
through personal therapy, consultation with friends or participatory
engagement with the classics). These activities of leisure are valuable
because they are guided by central and universal values -beauty found
in art and craft, love in friendship and family, truth in intellectual
pursuits, sacredness in religious pursuits and good in continued moral
deliberation and action.

The ancient Greek, (Aristotle, Plato, Epicurus), and Roman
literati, such as (Seneca), and their Christian and Renaissance followers
throughout history embraced one or another version of classical leisure.
They supported a political and intellectual aristocracy, either social
or political, which possessed the leisure necessary to pursue civic

participation or intellectual activities, whether philosophy or poetry, friendship or prayer, enjoyment of nature or serious conversation.

Although ornamental accounts of such leisure are frequent through the ages, (Ovid, Horace, Virgil, and many others), it is Aristotle who in his *Ethics* set forth the intellectual premises of such leisure. For Aristotle, leisure is continuous activity which realizes the good sought in life, not momentary actions, resulting products of action nor pleasant rest. Aristotle recognized that the core of leisure is an activity pursued for its own sake; its purpose is immanent in the activity itself. It is "auto-telic", while at the same time, the actualization of a natural and developed human capacity. Since its purpose is implicit in the activity itself, it is completed at each moment of the activity, while, at the same time, paradoxically, it is often experienced as a feeling of flow, Thus, for Aristotle, leisure is a condition of life in which the person is free from necessity and can voluntarily choose to engage in activities valuable for their own sake. For Aristotle, these activities were civic activity, moral decision, serious friendship, and intellectual activity. In his *Politics,* Aristotle made clear that support of leisure was the to be the fundamental purpose of the best political community

It is remarkable how well Aristotle's ideal fits old age. The fortunate old person is a person of leisure. He sees his actions in the context of his entire life and evaluates them in light of that life. He realizes that his activities are the product of his character shaped over a lifetime. Since his time is limited, the classical notion that these activities are complete at each moment is a notion which seems admirably suited to his situation, since his life is likely to end in the near future. He can now reflect upon the activities in which he engages, not in terms of the consequences of those activities in the distant future, but in light of goods inherent in the activities in which he is engaged and to the extent to which they conform to a praiseworthy character. Each of these implicit goods are, in some sense, universal. Participation in the loves of friendship and family, the beauty of nature, the truth of contemplation, the goods realized in community participation, and, for some, the salvation of religious experience, although momentary in this life, are also eternal in the moment of realization.

The Decline of the Classical Leisure

Sebastian de Grazia, in his *Time Work and Leisure,* has documented the historical fact that two millennia have seen social, political, and intellectual developments which challenge this ancient ideal. Most modern societies are far from embracing any ideal of classical leisure for many reasons, including, especially, their unremitting pursuit of economic affluence and the importance of a political equality of happiness which seems inimical to many who may not be able to enjoy such leisure. Underlying the modern rejection of a leisured aristocracy and a liberal education lives a modern instrumental means-ends thinking, which Jacques Ellul, in his *The Technological Society,* called "technique," and which is the dominant form of thought in modern life. Such thought takes place when acts or thoughts are viewed as simply a means to some further distinct goal or purpose. This modern view rejects a fundamental assumption of classical leisure -that activities of classical leisure are those which realize their own goal *within* the activities as they proceed. Finally, the social and economic conditions of capitalism fail to support a social structure for classical leisure in modern societies. (I am aware of only one modern philosopher who, while accepting capitalism, nevertheless seeks to reconcile it with the values of classical leisure, but, Mortimer Adler, in his *The Capitalist Manifesto,* requires that capital ownership be radically equalized!)

Sebastian De Grazia documents how modern patterns of modern social life have eliminated much of "free time" expected with the arrival of economic growth and its reduction in work hours. Even when working hours are limited and free time remains, the resulting leisure is merely free time *from* work and is occupied by a concern for rest, recreation and consumption to prepare us to return to engage in work again. *Unfortunately, rest, recreation, and consumption, when undertaken by the elderly in old age, do not replace the values lost in the abandonment of work in retirement.*

Modern socialist and capitalist thought have reconceived the nature of work to be a vehicle for achieving national wealth and work; no matter how demeaning that work may seem, it is accorded both dignity and honor. Religious faith ratifies such an accord. At the same time, many of the intellectual activities, which ancients and their followers identified as "liberal" (free from necessity), are now undertaken as paid employment, especially the work of the professions. The Greek ideal of a leisured aristocracy has been replaced by the ideals of a capitalist democracy; hence, we moderns no longer view as legitimate an aristocratic class who practices the leisure pursuits in ancient or medieval times at the expense of slaves, serfs or paid industrial workers. At the same time, the modern form of education suited for leisure—traditional liberal education - which aims to prepare its recipients to engage in classical leisure activities, has declined in favor of more utilitarian aims of today's education.

With modern society's rejection of classical leisure, how can the modern aged restore the ideal and practices of classical leisure? There are some helpful trends which increasingly increase the possibility for the spread of classical leisure in retirement. The rise in the number of educated seniors, their affluence without working, the improvement in their health, the increase in cultural and educational opportunities available, the spread of an ethic of community participation may contribute to an increase in classical leisure activities among the elderly. However, all these activities are part of a public culture which remains dominated by the modern work ethic. Although there is an increase in many new opportunities for the elderly to pursue classical leisure, a work oriented public culture may continue to dominate the meaning of any effort to create a full sphere of classical leisure for the elderly.

Hence, there are tremendous obstacles to the realization of the ideal of classical leisure in old age. Perhaps the most significant obstacle is created by the affluent lives which many elderly in the western world have lived and continue to live. Ironically, although affluence might supply the conditions for making leisure possible, the process of achieving such affluence in a life-time often shapes a character ill-suited to classical leisure. Such a character finds its satisfaction in the endless variety of external goods and pleasures which modern life can supply, rather than the embrace of classical leisure. Nevertheless, insofar as the elderly are required by circumstance or elect to withdraw from the consumer culture, new opportunities to engage in the activities of classical leisure arise. Classical leisure becomes more possible with retirement in old age, since the retiree is separated from the culture of a work which supports and feeds the acquisitive instinct. For some aged, their "natural" withdrawal from social life helps to eliminate their need for conspicuous consumption. Similarly, in old age, the race for status in adult life may ease. In old age either one has proved one's success or accepted one's failures or one has come to realize the shallowness of such a quest for success. In addition, there may be one specific kind of classical leisure which may be pursued despite the public pressures against classical leisure: namely, literary and/or pastoral solitude.

Literary and/or Pastoral Solitude

I have pursued one kind of classical leisure – reflective meditation on classic works – which may be pursued in relative solitude – a solitude which requires both sustained disengagement from the presence of people, but permits periodic engagement with friends. Such a solitude cuts off the immediate influence of the public economic, social and intellectual pressures against classical leisure. Paradoxically, many of the losses experienced in old age may support a mindset suited to engagement in solitary leisure. Biological decline may stimulate withdrawal, (although it may also produce dependence upon others). The foreshortening of our futures may cut off the undertaking of many projects which would ordinarily keep us in contact with others. Loss of faith in the inevitability of progress may weaken our desire for pursuing a civic leisure in old age and lead us into a conservative retreat. The prospect of death may encourage a similar withdrawal.

Many philosophers and theologians who have advocated for classical leisure have proposed a following of the ideals of classical leisure by socially separating themselves from the dominant society. Whether through educational academies, (Plato and Aristotle), groups of friends, (Epicurus, Plotinus), or the monastery, (Ambrose and Jerome), many of the ancients supported their classic leisure through social separation of its practitioners from society. But even beyond such separation of groups of practitioners, there has been the extensive tradition of philosophers and scholars, poets and novelists, who have embraced solitude. This tradition of solitary leisure, as set forth in the writings of the Roman philosopher and dramatist, Seneca, recommended philosophy as a solitary pursuit. He complained bitterly about the intrusion of the city and public affairs into his desire and practice of a solitary tranquility. Despite writing a book on the solitary life, documenting its practice in the ages preceding his own, Petrarch made similar complaints but also confessed that his desires of fame often usurped his solitude. Recent biographies of Montaigne reveal that despite his retreat to his tower library, he still was tempted to participate in political affairs from time to time.

The importance of solitude to philosophy cannot be denied. The modern French philosopher, Pierre Hadot, in all his writings, but especially in *What is Ancient Philosophy?* rediscovered the tradition of philosophy as a "way of life" occupied by solitary "spiritual exercises" including reading, meditation, contemplating the whole world, becoming aware of one's being, and foreseeing death. Hadot traces this tradition of philosophy as a way of life of spiritual exercises from Plato to modern philosophy. Modern philosophers enjoyed solitude during periods of their lives. Descartes, Locke Pascal, Spinoza, Kant, Leibniz, Schopenhauer, Nietzsche, Kierkegaard, Wittgenstein, and Jung embraced solitude as part of their creative process at some time in their lives.

However, philosophy need not be the only occupation within solitude. Even before these authors approved, the ancient view of pastoral leisure seized the imagination of poets such as Theocritus and Horace and philosophers such as Epicurus and Lucretius. In the somewhat fulsome words of Horace:

> Me, the ivy, the reward of poets' brows, links with the
> gods above; me the cool grove and the lightly tripping
> bands of nymphs and satyrs withdraw from that vulgar
> throng, if only Euterpe withhold not the flute, no

Polyhymnia refuse to tune the Lesbian lyre. But if you rank me among the lyric bards, I shall touch the stars with my exalted head.

In the words of O'Loughlin's marvelous *Gardens of Repose*, a modern commentary on classical leisure, "the [Horace's] poem ends with the poet and reader at the center of the dance at the heart of the groves which secludes him from the world. It ends with the withdrawn contemplative man enjoying a triumph which towers over all these apotheoses sought by the activities of the uncontained".

A different kind of solitary leisure was described in the Middle Ages by advocates of the religious contemplative life such as St. Thomas Aquinas, and practiced by many monks of the age. Much western literature pertaining to solitude originated in this period of "monastic silence". In the early Renaissance, the life of a secular literary solitude was practiced by Petrarch, who wrote a treatise on the solitary life, (*De Vita Solitaria*). Montaigne (*Essays*) and Gibbon, (*Autobiography*), in the early modern age continued the accounts of solitary classical leisure.

In our contemporary world, there remain persuasive proponents of a solitary classical leisure, including such thoughtful philosophers as Sebastian de Grazia (*Of Time, Work, and Leisure*), Josef Pieper (*Leisure, the Basis of Culture*), the historian of ideas, Michael O'Loughlin (*The Garlands of Repose*) and Philip Koch (*Solitude)* And there are a variety of contemporary efforts to describe a life of solitude including the writings of May Sarton, Paul Auster, Edward Abbey, Anne Dillard, Sue Halpern, Rainer Marie Rilke, Thomas Merton and many others.

My ideal solitaries are Lucius Annaeus Seneca, Francis Petrarch and Michel de Montaigne. Seneca, despite living in the age of the Roman Emperors and working for Nero, was able to set forth in essays and letters, his belief in the value of a literary solitude. In the middle of the fourteenth century, Petrarch left the busy intellectual life of writing and rescuing the works of ancient thought in libraries throughout Europe and retreated to the small village of Vaucluse in France and the Eleni hills near Padova in Italy. It was in such refuges that he wrote his *The*

Life of Solitude which, in largely secular terms, sets forth the goals of solitude, while also describing those classical and religious figures practicing solitude throughout the preceding ages. (He also authored a separate work on religious solitude). Following Petrarch almost a century later, in 1571 at the age of thirty-eight, Michel de Montaigne, tired of his public duties, retired to his home and library, where he spent most of the remainder of his life reading and writing. Thus, unlike Petrarch, Montaigne devoted the final decades of his life to a literary solitude. This retirement of solitary leisure is captured in the words of his essay, *Solitude:*

> When, not long ago, I withdrew into my own house, determined, so far as it was in my power to take no thought of anything except to pass as I please and by myself a little life that remains for me . . . but I find "leisure breeds an inconstant mind," a hundred times more active . . . that, to consider their absurdity and strangeness, I have begun to put them on paper.

Montaigne confesses his purpose is "to live more at leisure and at ease." He found this ease, however, to be a difficult thing. We "carry our fetters with us," "our sickness of the soul", "so we must bring it home and withdraw into ourselves. That is true solitude. . . . [W]e must reserve for ourselves a private room, all our own, subject to no one, in which we may establish our true freedom and our principle retreat and solitude." Montaigne believes that solitude is most suited to old age retirement:

> "solitude seems to me to have most fitness and reasonableness for those who have given to the world their most active and vigorous years. . . . We have lived enough for others; let us live for ourselves at least this latter end of our life; let us bring our thoughts and our purposes home to ourselves and for our full content . . .

let us pack our trunks . . . our powers are failing; let us draw them in and concentrate them in ourselves."

In his last essay, Montaigne sums up:

"It is an absolute perfection and virtually divine to know how to enjoy our being rightfully. We seek other conditions because we do not understand the use of our own, and go outside of ourselves because we do not know what it is like inside. Yet there no use mounting on stilts, for on stilts, we must still walk on our own legs. And on the loftiest throne, we are still sitting only on our own rump. The most beautiful lives, to my mind, are those that conform to the common human pattern, with order, but without miracle and without eccentricity."

Literary (and religious) solitude are not the only kinds of solitude appropriate to old age. Authors such as Henry David Thoreau and John Muir have articulated lives of solitude attuned to nature although they are also intellectually reflective about such attunement in their writings.

Their works echo the ancient poets who celebrated the more retiring life of "pastoral leisure" which savors individual experiences of nature. (One tradition of such celebration is found in the works of the nature elegists extending from Theocritus to Milton as described by Ellen Lambert in her *Placing Sorrow* and continued in contemporary works such as *The Embers and the Stars*).

Found in both Petrarch's and Montaigne's account of solitude and in the poetry of solitude is the presence of silence. To be sure, the original ideal of classical leisure included civic activities and friendships, both of which appear to ignore the subtle values of silence. On the other hand, as early as St. Augustine, who admired the silent reading of Ambrose, the peculiar values of silence in reading, prayer, and meditation were recognized. These values of silence included the absence of the distractions of noise, but also a hoped-for awareness of

God's presence. So began the rich tradition of "the silent life" in the Christian monastery, a life so well lived and described by Thomas Merton in his *The Silent Life*.

The ideal of solitary leisure, whether accompanied by silence or not, and whether part of the broader concept of classical leisure or not, is not a mere historical artifact; it is also part of the larger American tradition of the "simple life" described and lived, albeit briefly by Thoreau and a myriad of other nature authors such as John Muir and Edward Abbey, poets such as Emily Dickinson, and more recent advocates of solitude, May Sarton and Alice Stoller. These authors find a certain healing not only in nature but also in other solitary activities, and they also embrace aspects of the ancient classical ideal of leisure which includes attunement to nature, friendship, moral action for its own sake, intellectual activity, prayer, and contemplation. It is this social detachment of solitude which is an important part of classical leisure in any age.

The Problem of Acedia

A serious threat to the pursuit of classical leisure is the enervating boredom and "acedia" which frequently accompanies the solitary pursuit of secular and religious leisure. From the time of Aristotle's recognition of the deleterious effects of black bile, to the religious recognition of the "noon day demon" of acedia in the monastery, to the "nameless woe" recognized by Petrarch to the arrival of ennui and alienation in modern literature and life, many have recognized internal threats to any embrace of leisure with dignity. Ironically, the very figure whom I cited as the exemplar of the solitary life – Francis Petrarch – recognized the threat of acedia in is own life. Before completing his work on the solitary life, Petrarch wrote his better-known work, *Secretum,* an imagined dialogue with Augustine. In the dialogue, Augustine accused Petrarch: "you are the victim of a terrible scourge of the soul, melancholy, which the moderns named "acedia" and ancients "aegritudo." Petrarch admits his susceptibility to many of the seven deadly sins, but trembles when faced with the seventh: acedia. He states: …"in this condition of

sorrow, all is bitter, lugubrious, and frightful; the road is always open
to despair..." Yet, at the end of the *Secretum*, Petrarch pledges to carry
on his humanistic endeavors and later, he leaves his acedia unmentioned
when he drew his portrait of the solitary life. Perhaps, as some have
suggested, his acedia was merely a passing phase.

Although Petrarch occupies a prominent place in those who write
the western history of the idea of acedia, just a century later, one finds
little mention of such a condition in another scholar who relished
solitude: Montaigne. Nevertheless, modern scholars of such a state have
found the experience of "the noonday demon" in many of the solitaries
throughout history and have arrived at its' definition as "the state of
emptiness that the soul feels when it is deprived of interest in action,
life, and the world (be it this world or another), a condition that is the
immediate consequence of the encounter with nothingness and has
as an immediate effect a disaffection with reality." A fair conclusion
might be that although such a bleak prospect faces some who embrace
the solitary life, *when there is societal support and acceptance for a freely
chosen solitude in old age, there will continue to be a significant number of
aged persons who happily find the freedom and silence granted in solitude
to enable reading, appreciation, and quiet reflection, attunement to nature,
appreciation of artistic or intellectual works and a degree of self-knowledge.*

Conclusion

In Chapter IV above, I identified the ways in which consolation in
old age might be attained. We may *familiarize* ourselves with the losses
in advance. The losses might be placed in perspective or a *substitute* for
the losses might be found. We may be *transformed*, in whole or in part,
and, in the process, no longer experience the loss of earlier aspects of our
lives. Whether through therapy, confession or the artistic experience, a
catharsis may take place and blunt its cruel edges of loss. And we may
find solace in continuing *to seek the truth*. These consolations may be
found in retirement. We may familiarize ourselves with its prospect in
advance. We may see retirement as merely part of the larger workings of

modern economy. Upon retirement, we may find ourselves transformed, no longer mentally shackled to our work and its ambitions, and, in the process, we may experience a sense of freedom and relief. And, if we embrace a classical leisure, we may find a substitute for the work world – one which, in one way or another, allows us to find new value in our concluding lives.

It is classical leisure which, I believe, offers dignity and honor to retirement. Although many have made fun of Cicero, he is correct in his appeal to "otio cum dignitate" – leisure with dignity. This dignity of classical leisure is not dependent upon the attitude of others, nor upon its contributions to the general welfare. In the work world, honor is largely attributed to power and accomplishments are based upon the standards of that world. When the retiree leaves the work world, he leaves these external standards behind. Instead, the dignity of leisure is based upon a unique self-esteem—not simply a psychological feeling of adequacy, but a fundamental respect for oneself and the activities one undertakes. This respect is based upon the belief that classical leisure activities realize permanent goods: the beauty of art, the good of civic or moral action, the importance of true friendships and the truths found in the classic works.

The Roman Stoic philosopher, Seneca, in his *Essays and Letters*, Petrarch in his book on solitude, and Montaigne in his *Essays* have drawn an attractive picture of the many deep delights of withdrawal and retirement into solitude, including the delights of the reading and appreciation of classic works. In this book, I suggest that it is the tradition of classic works which can help us understand the losses of old age as well as the emotions resulting from such losses. These classics can also help us to detach ourselves from these losses and provide consolation for them. In this chapter, we have seen how the economic classics can help us to understand the nature of work and loss in retirement. Emile Durkheim's sociological classic helps us to understand the dimensions of alienation which many of us experience at the time of retirement. Classics, such as Horace's *Odes* supplies an imaginative vision of the classical leisure which can replace work; the *Ethics* of Aristotle traces the intellectual outline of this classical leisured way of life; the works of Petrarch and Montaigne assist us in considering the worth of social detachment to support such classical leisure; the letters and essays of Seneca suggest the ways in which consolations can be found even in an exile which, in its own way, mirrors retirement.

Part of the tradition of classics is the heritage of works exploring the values of solitude. Philip Koch, in the exploration of this tradition, in *Solitude, A Philosophical Encounter,* finds an articulation of five "virtues": freedom, attunement to nature, attunement to self, self-reflection and creativity. These virtues of solitude are admirable suited to the stage of old age. These virtues of solitude help us to screen out the forces which seek to destroy the values of classical leisure. Asserting retirement to be a new freedom and building support for that freedom, forging connections of contemplation of nature, attending to oneself, with a vivid awareness of one's old age and its losses, reflections upon one's entire life and old age with the help of classic works, and undertaking those kinds of creativity suited to one's old age capabilities and interests permits successful escape from the world of work and provides consolation in retirement.

CHAPTER XV

Recovering and Recreating the Vanished Past

"But those who do not preserve or retrieve the past in memory, but allow it flow away under them, make themselves needy every day in actual fact, and empty and dependent on tomorrow..." Plutarch *On Tranquility*

My memories are of family, work and education. Since memories of family and education preface other chapters, my memories of past work serve to illustrate a past threatened with eclipse. In the 1960's, after law school graduation and a brief stint in private practice, I found work in New Haven, Connecticut's model urban renewal and anti-poverty program. With my previous experience as a welfare worker in Chicago and New Haven and having been a student Director of Legal Aid at Yale Law School, I was hired to draft proposals for the first neighborhood legal program for the poor. In my student days, I had met with clients coming to legal aid with problems of installment sales, eviction, and garnishment of wages. These problems stemmed from deeper economic, family, and psychological problems and I designed the new legal services program to address those problems. The program was not adopted, but replaced by a program designed to legally challenge the institutional obstacles to social mobility. Following my New Haven experience, I founded and directed the Thames Valley Council for Community Action, a regional anti-poverty program- which oversaw housing, job training, child development, family planning, legal services, and citizen participation programs. These anti-poverty programs were organized and directed to the neighborhoods of the central cities and rural towns where the poor were concentrated. They were part of President Johnson's "Great Society" legislation; their success or failure has been much debated since the 1970's. My interest in community based reforms in old industrial cities led me, in the late 1960's and early 1970's, to become a consultant to the Rouse Co., the developer of the New Town of Columbia, Maryland. Columbia was a unique laboratory for social planning of an urban community located in the sprawling suburbs between Washington, D.C. and Baltimore, Maryland. My task was to help with the formation of a council of the new institutions of the town and coordinate their activities. This effort was not successful. My major interest was Columbia's unique effort to plan and build "from scratch" an "urban community" — an effort which I later evaluated harshly in a book entitled New Towns and Communal Values. *Now, in my old age, I regard this decade as one of the most important parts of my life and often try to remember and recover its details. Forty years later, I remain unsure as to the lasting importance of the anti-poverty and new towns program for the nation. Despite these programs, the cities of New Haven and New London have suffered serious decline in their economies and social fabric. The New Haven legal services program continues, but in a form different than I envisaged. The regional anti-poverty program I founded continues, but few remember its past programs. The New Town program of the early 1970's has faded into history, and, although the New Town of Columbia has prospered, it has realized few of the ideals which animated its founding. Few of my current friends or colleagues know of my work during this decade of my life. This work has disappeared into the mists of history and memory. The second part of my career, which I discuss below,is in the field of environmental law – also fading rapidly into the past.*

Introduction

When, in old age, we begin to review our entire life, we realize that most of our life is now made up of the past – a past, much of which we do not remember. Aristotle noted that old men "live by memory rather than hope, for what is left to them of life is but little as compared with the long past…" Despite dim old age memories, many of us recount parts of our past lives (often to unwilling listeners), hence expressing our desire in old age, in the words of Proust, to "recapture past time" — a past which is largely completed — finished long ago, yet lingering, often hidden, in the depths of old age memory. Our elderly preoccupation with the past confirms the observation of the German philosopher, Heidegger, who suggests that temporality is at the core of our being; many old people would agree. The heightened consciousness of time, our limited future and, for Heidegger, our "being toward death" drives us to look to our past, as if by doing so, we could add on to the total years of our lives or at least fill in our very identity which seems hollowed out by time.

Shakespeare said it all:

> When I have seen by Time's fell hand defaced
> The rich-proud cost of outworn buried age;
> When sometime lofty towers I see down-razed,
> And brass eternal slave to mortal rage;
> When I have seen the hungry ocean gain,
> Advantage on the kingdom of the shore,
> And firm soil win of the watery main,
> Increasing store with loss and loss with store;
> When I have seen such interchange of state,
> Or state itself confounded to decay;
> Ruin hath taught me thus to ruminate
> That Time will come and take my love away,
>> This thought is as a death, which cannot choose
>> But weep to have that which it fears to lose."

To be sure, preoccupation with the past is not limited to poets and the elderly. Upon reflection I realize that concern for the past, in one way or another, has informed my entire life. Much of my liberal education was the docile study of past great works; my study of the law was, at least in part, the study of past laws and their precedents. At different times in my life, my work and scholarship led me to study the past history of urban communities and the trajectory of environmental protections. In old age, I find myself editing studies of ancient jurisprudence. But exposure to the past in my youthful liberal education and my middle age scholarly work were largely academic enterprises. In them, the past was an object of study — not the core of my being. Now, in old age, my study of the past has become the recovery of my forgotten self.

To be sure, the past is not simply an independent depository of the residues of the present. The French philosopher, Bergson, rather than adopting the notion of a mechanical succession of equal moments of scientific time, established an essential connection between the present and past, introducing the concept of "duration" which embraces the interconnection and flow of past, present and future time, reflected in the words of T.S. Eliot: "Time past and time future, what might have been and what has been point to one end, which is always the present". At any age, past time lurks in our present habits, capabilities and character, shapes the customs we follow and decorates the traditions we honor. The past tacitly inheres and is reflected in our present surroundings. As historical ecology has discovered, even nature has been shaped by the past, as attested to by the stone walls found in the second growth forests of Vermont and by the carbon accumulated over the years within the atmosphere to produce global warming of the present Thus, our past is presented to us within our present. For me, it is most vividly presented to me by the memory of my late wife of many years, my adult children and their children, my old home — all emerging out of my past and bursting into the present (and headed into a future beyond me!) Similarly, my educational past is reflected in the books I have saved in my library, the universities I fondly remember, and whatever academic capabilities and ideas I have retained. Most of the thoughts I entertain, I learned long ago. As the prologue suggests, I still reminisce with cautious pride about some of my past work related "accomplishments". Such a reminiscence suggests that the losses of the present old age assume that something which existed in the past and which is now lost were the goods of yesteryear.

With limited future and a leisured present, many of us aged are inevitably concerned if not preoccupied with the past. We find this past primarily through individual reminiscence — the proverbial old men chatting on a park bench. We regard this past not as if we were a scientist searching for causal connections, nor, for that matter, scientific historians. Nietzsche in his *The Use and Abuse of History* found such "objective history", if over indulged, would weaken the personality, and fail to "serve life". Recent research of aging memories vindicates Nietzsche's insights, demonstrating that, in the present, we unconsciously or consciously select among past events, forgetting some and misremembering others; in our current life, we weigh the value of the past events represented by those true and false memories.

We weave the past into our lives not only through personal reminiscence and public commemorations: birthdays, funerals, weddings, graduations of our children and grandchildren, but also through conscious efforts at recollection and, perhaps, invention. Communities perform similar acts of public remembrance and invention. In so doing, we may simply seek the pleasures of a reminiscence which sanitizes the pains of the past, or we seek to rebuild our entire lives by trying to construct a plausible and coherent story of them.

In this chapter, like the other chapters, with the help of the classic works, (many of which are themselves products of the past), I discuss the nature of the goods lost to the past in old age and some of the emotions such losses produce. Then I suggest ways in which detachment from such losses may be found. Finally, in addition to detachment, some form of consolation is to be found in remembrance and re- interpretation of our lives, (including therapy), including perhaps the creation of historical myths and criticisms of our past, and even, perhaps restructuring the nature of time itself. In all of these consolations, we can turn for help to the classics.

The Nature of Old Age Loss of the Past

Despite these efforts at remembrance, we elderly have lost much of the past in two very different ways. On the one hand, people, events, and our own activities which were important to our lives at the time are now gone – they are, well, past, lost to history. Such events, now in the repository of an "objective" past are over, closed off to change, (but, as we shall see below), still open to reinterpretation. On the other hand, there is another loss contained within the idea of temporality – i.e., our subjective sense of time. In old age, the memory of our past –our very past selves - has faded, despite our capacity for some vivid recovery of earlier episodes in our lives. As a consequence of this lost memory, our identity may be hollowed out. Thus, in old age, we encounter two different losses as the present fades into the historical past and a failing memory eclipses our "personal past".

Of course, everyone, at every age, has a past and forgets much of it. William James in his *Principles of Psychology* establishes that forgetfulness serves a positive function of freeing us to go about our lives in the present and pursue our projects for the future. But in old age, there is a special "tragedy of forgetfulness of the past". This tragedy lies in the fact that such forgetting interferes with attaining a final comprehension of the complete story of our lives. Such a comprehension is a fundamental task in old age. Instead of having a coherent comprehension of our lives, we elderly are customarily radically incomplete - stuck with a hodgepodge of ill-assorted reminiscences. We are like Eliot's hollow men, we "whisper together ...quiet and meaningless" on park benches. Many of us, even if we are not in dementia, are unconscious of our failing memories, and the loss of the past resulting from that failure. We are often only dimly aware of how that loss contributes to an incomplete vision of our entire lives.

As our brief present which quickly flows into the past and our memory fades, this double loss grows more important with each passing year, since the past is an increasingly part of what makes up who we are! The time of our past life increasingly composes most of the time of the biography of our lives and yet that time is diminishing! We have the uneasy sense that our past is an important part of our identity and its loss is a loss of our identity. But not only is this disappearing past an increasing part of our old age, but this past becomes the repository for all the losses in old age. Our youthful biology is lost to the past. In our retirement, we lose our work to the past. Our expansive future possibilities disappear into the past. The extensive future which offered the field of dreams we once had is now been eaten up by time; the possibilities we once entertained are now gone. In a later chapter, we shall see that, with age, we lose independence and self-sufficiency which we possessed at earlier stages of our lives. And, as history marches on, we elderly experience the disappointment of the ambitions we held for our community and for history more generally; these grand hopes we once held become dreams of the past.

These losses are not merely subjective losses – the product of old age pessimism. In old age, most of our lives are buried beneath history. The events of this history were peopled by many who witnessed or participated in them and are now gone. These actual events are now part of our past lives, lost, not only to fading memory but to history itself. The places where we lived often have been transformed. The nations we have visited are different now and we may only dimly recognize them when we return to visit in old age. Many of our old friends and classmates or co-workers from our past life have changed over time and, like Proust returning on a visit, we may not even recognize them. They also have dimmed and failing memories of us. Our lives will completely disappear into history, as part of a collective forgetfulness, both private and public, in a history which often buries the past or misremembers it.

Emotions from Our Waning Past

The novels of Virginia Woolf remind us of our losses of the past; they also inform our perception of moving time which, as it passes creates the past. Thus, Virginia Woolf's *To the Lighthouse* captures the poetry of the passage of time in one's life when, after her vivid description of a lively summer house vacation in the first part of her book, turns, in the second part of her novel, "Time Passes", to chronicle the emptying and decline of the summer house.

> "…The house was left; the house was deserted. It was left
> Like a shell on a sandhill to fill with dry salt grains now that life
> Had left it. The long night seemed to have set in; the trifling airs, nibbling, the clammy breaths, fumbling, seemed to have triumphed.
> The saucepan had rusted and the mat decayed. ..For now had come
> that moment, when dawn trembles and night pauses… One feather
> and the house, sinking, falling would have turned and pitched downwards to the depths of darkness…Then the roof would have fallen; briars and hemlocks would have blotted our path, step, and window; would have grown, unequally or lustily over the mound…the whole house would have plunged to the depths to lie upon the sands of oblivion….

Many of Virginia Woolf's novels can help us to understand loss through time. For example, she describes in *Jacob's Room* a loss which may be the disappearance of the loved one into the past. The reader comes to know Jacob, throughout the book. Only after indirectly learning that he went off to war and then disappeared — a casualty of the First World War, do we realize the significance of the war and his death, when his friends visit his absent room. We discover his absence not with accounts of his death in the war, but indirectly, in the last chapter of the novel, when his friends visit and plaintively call out his name in his room — an empty room except for those objects which offer reminders of his past life and the unseen war in which he died. In this chapter, death is the absence of a loved one from the past. Jacob is now the empty past or, to put it another way, the past is Jacob's empty room.

Similar emotions are provoked when our past lives are enveloped in a larger societal forgetfulness, which takes place in the course of history. Communities and nations forget their past and graveyards are abandoned. Huizinga's vivid history, *The Waning of the Middle Ages* illustrates the point. Out of a forgotten past, Huizinga recreates the cultural world of the late European middle ages complete with its way of life, its bells, processions and symbols as well as its unique institutions and ways of thinking. These "middle ages" lingered into the Renaissance, only to disappear before modern consciousness arrives. Huizinga's book is one of the major histories of western thought, which helps us to better "remember" a very different and forgotten historical past — the vivid portrait of a lost way of life. Like the novel *Jacobs' Room,* it reminds us of something we have lost in the past. Similarly, histories, such as Gibbon's *The Decline and Fall of the Roman Empire,* de Tocqueville's *Democracy in America,* or Adams' *The Education of Henry Adams* help us recover in our imaginations ancient Rome, early rural American life and the industrialization of America, all of which take place long before our own lives began but which continue to influence our lives. The Roman Empire, medieval life and the early America are in the past, gone, just as Virginia Woolf's Jacob is gone.

The disciplines of literature and history are not the only routes to a discovery of the losses of the past. Works of psychology offer another route. The works of Freud, Jung and Erikson outline the stages of life and provide therapies by which help us to uncover events in our personal and often repressed past stages. In the case of Jung, we even recover a past which extends far beyond ourselves, i.e. the collective unconscious of which we are a part. The combination of a narrative of life and a therapeutic technique for recovering the past within that narrative helps us to discover the losses of our past.

In Chapter II, I recounted the emotions of sadness and regret which accompany old age.

Sadness or sorrow comes from loss and, as St. Thomas Aquinas noted, the sadness of loss points to the past goods we once possessed. Similarly, regret is the emotion in response to the possibilities we have lost in the past. Both emotions are common in old age, but not unique.

More important, both sadness and regret do not focus upon the past, but on the losses which took place in the past. One emotion common to old age ordinarily focuses upon the past – nostalgia.

Nostalgia has been defined as the "bitter sweet longing for things" but, perhaps a more ironic definition based upon its roots – "nostro" – home and "algia" –yearning. Nostalgia is the longing for return to a home either in time or space which was never there or is there no longer. As such, nostalgia desires repetition of the unrepeatable, whether the repetition in individual lives or in the lives of communities. Like exiles who long for their original homeland, we elderly are susceptible to such longing for the past with a corresponding sentimentality which may result. Both exiles and the old may be outsiders – one outside his country, the other outside the life he once led. One author has described nostalgia as essentially history without guilt. Such nostalgia for the past may increase as the present loses significance and the future becomes limited by mortality.

As a feeling, nostalgia is described by the ancient heroic epic of Odysseus longing to return to his homeland, ("...this one alone, longing for his wife and his homecoming..."). The longing for a past may be the longing for a past home. Nostalgia is the longing described by the both pastoral and romantic poets and one can find a hints of nostalgia in the theories of a golden age, both ancient and modern. One can find nostalgia in Rousseau's *Confessions,* (but not those of Augustine), his political writings, even if it was yearning for a time he never experienced, and his old age reveries on the past. Such nostalgia is closely related to the feelings of elegies and many of the elegiac poets such as T.S. Eliot mix both nostalgia and regret in their poetry. Rather than the elegiac mourning of loss, nostalgia is an emotional response to the restoration of the loss. Restorative nostalgia seeks to restore the lost home and patch up the memories. It seems to say: "you can go home again".

Detachments from Loss of the Past

Just as it is possible to detach from other old age losses, it is possible to detach ourselves in old age from the losses experienced through the course of our entire lives as time moves on and we realize, in old age, that time *has* moved on. Similarly, we can detach ourselves from the eclipse of that past – our failure to remember it due an inevitable failure of old age memory. We can also regard at a distance, the emotions of sadness, regret and nostalgia which we encounter during old age. To find this detachment, we must turn to the tradition of those great works, which, ironically, emerge from the past themselves. Such works, with the help of a lifelong liberal education, may be recovered from the past and deposited in the present. The tradition of great works stimulates remembrance of our personal pasts as well as past communities of which we have been part and which have shaped our lives. Our delving into the works of this tradition help us to entertain universal ideas and principles by which to interpret our losses and the emotions these losses provoke. In this chapter above, we employed the works of Shakespeare, Woolf, James, Homer and Nietzsche to help us understand the past and its eclipse. Other religious and philosophic works, such as Augustine's *Confessions* and *The City of God* and Heidegger's *Being and Time,* address the nature of time and temporality, Hegel's *Philosophy of History* and Toynbee's *Study of History* suggest patterns of history in our past, present and future, and Proust's novels as well as other literary works provide materials by which we can understand in a detached manner our own lost past. Even natural histories such as Darwin's *Origin of the Species* suggest scientific principles within the history of our natural descent through evolution and we can place ourselves objectively within that history.

Just as these works help us to understand the past, there are works which help us to understand the nostalgia such a past produces. Scholars of nostalgia distinguish between restorative and reflective nostalgia. Restorative nostalgia assumes the truth and desirability of the past we long for and seeks to restore it intact. Reflective nostalgia recognizes the longing for the past, but also realizes that such a past might never have existed, is incapable of restoration or requires modification to be used in the present. Readers of this book, in which I draw upon the classic works to understand old age, may accuse me of a restorative nostalgia in which I seek to reestablish through liberal education and the classics an earlier period in my life and the life of liberal education - a period when reading the great books was a central activity in education. I would argue that my nostalgia is a reflective one in which I argue for old age meditation upon the great works – a testing of the works in light of old age experience - rather than simply accepting them back into our minds as we once remembered them to be.

The reading the classics in old age encourages not a blind but a reflective nostalgia. Take for example, Homer's *Odyssey.* As stated above, since arriving at Troy, Odysseus nostalgically longed to return home. But after his adventures and his arrival home, the past is not recaptured. When Odysseus returns, he initially is unrecognized by all but his faithful servant, and he is confronted by a host of suitors for his wife. Even after his wife finally recognizes him and he kills the suitors, he feels he cannot stay long but must go to the underworld to visit, among others, some of those fellow soldiers lost at Troy. Upon reading Homer, we not only feel his bitter sweet pangs of nostalgia, but also reflect upon the snares of a hoped-for return which does not pan out as expected.

Ancient satires are another vehicle for reflective nostalgia. Horace paints an idyllic picture of pastoral living free from the busyness of the city life, only then to reveal that it is the day dream of a moneylender who, upon facing again the pressures of his work, abandons the dream and returns to lending. We have often encountered those who seek in some way to replicate their past, only to become bitterly disappointed. Thus, we learn to discount the value of restorative nostalgia and, at most, become reflective "nostalgics".

If the plots of the Greek and Roman classics provoke a reflective nostalgia in the reader, more modern authors also may explicitly suggest a more reflective nostalgia. Thus, in Edmund Burke's *Reflections on the Revolution in France,* he offers continued appeals to the revolutions' ignoring of the beneficial social and political institutions of the past; Burke contrasts the French revolution with the English reverence of tradition. ""...the gifts of providence are handed down to us...our political system is placed in a just correspondence with the order of the world..." But Burke does not endorse blind nostalgia; he recognized the need for change, but in accordance with the political principles inherent in past institutions. His approach is similar to Blackstone's extolling of the common law which looks to past precedent but reasons to principles which extend beyond that precedent. In another example of reflective nostalgia, James Joyce, in the *Portrait of an Artist as a Young Man* offers a story of his native Catholic Ireland – a story which is partly nostalgic, but also partly deeply critical of the home he is leaving. Thus, whether in poems, novels, political tracts, a reflective nostalgia can be found which in many different ways is able to detach itself from a blind longing of the past.

However, it is history which best provides detached attention to the past. The canon historical works, such as those mentioned above, as well as ancient histories, (Thucydides, *The Peloponnesian War;* Tacitus, *Histories)* begin the building of a historical discipline which seeks objectivity in historical accounts. de Tocqueville's *Democracy in America,* although a contemporaneous account of American life in the early 1800's, may be read in a nostalgic manner as an account of America's historical march toward "an equality of condition". But the author encourages a reflective nostalgia since he is also critical of various traits in American life and projected the possibility of the centralization of government power in the future. A more recent history, Henry Adams' *Chartres and Mont St.Michel* expresses great nostalgia for the medieval culture which animates this and other great gothic cathedrals, at the same time, recognizing that the course of history has moved on, in the words of Adams, to "the dynamo".

The mixture of memory and history is well explored in Nietzsche's little tract, *The Use and Abuse of History.* Nietzsche was anxious to attack the "historical men" of his age who sought a mere objective history, in favor of a history to serve life. For Nietzsche, such a "history for life" would not totally reject an antiquarian history which seeks to preserve and reverence the past, nor a monumental history which seeks to understand and appreciate the monuments of the past, nor a critical history which focuses upon the shortcomings of the past. But Nietzsche nicely summarizes the limits of such histories and suggests that only a history which is written by a man of character and experience who has lived through something nobler and greater than others will be able "... to explain the great and noble of the past..." Similarly, someone who has experienced the losses of old age and has read and appreciated the great works of the past and present can regard the past with proper detachment.

Recovery, Assessment and Reweaving the Past

The reading and meditation upon great works can help us to understand our old age losses due to the passage of time, reflectively recognize the dangers of nostalgia and secure a certain detachment from our past. *These works can also offer consolation, helping us to recover through remembrance and therapy, assess through therapy and historical critique, and re-weave though interpretation and creation the meaning of past time in our lives.* It is the old age meditation on the canon works which yields meaning in time, history and life. To be sure, such works may not supply all of the missing moments in our own personal past. But based partly upon what we can remember and partly upon what we can research, these works can demonstrate through historical narrative, poetic form, literary plots, and philosophic argument that the events in our lives are parts of larger patterns which can shape the meaning of life. A more detailed examination is needed to describe how that recovery, assessment and re-weaving takes place.

1. Restoring the "Real Past".

The starting point for consolation in old age is the restoration of the "real past" through memory and history. There is another past — a past which is "real", independent of our own lives, and beyond mere personal remembrance. When we try to recover the past in old age, it quickly becomes evident that such a "real" historical past extends beyond it, both in time and space. To recover this real history, one must turn to the historical discipline mentioned above. For example, Gibbon, in his *Decline and Fall of Ancient Rome,* recovers a distant age for his and our contemplation. In his autobiography, Gibbon tells the story of the origin of his magnum opus when, in his youth, he sat among and contemplated the ruins of Rome and resolved to write its history. He sought to carefully document the decline of ancient Rome, beginning with the Empire at its glorious beginnings and ended his first volume with the sack of Rome. He offers a political history with vivid portraits of the Roman Emperors, the rise of Christianity, the eventual shutting down of the Hellenic schools of philosophy, and the formulation of the Roman system of government and law. His compelling story documents the civil wars within the Empire, the split of the empire into its Roman and Eastern branches, the adoption of the Christian faith as the official religion and the eventual persecution the old civil religion. After reporting on the invasion of Rome and its collapse, in his second volume, he offers an account of the long history of the Byzantine Empire, the threat (and contributions) of Islam, the invasions from the East, and the Crusades. He concludes his final volume by surveying the complete decline of Rome as the result of natural disasters, hostile attacks of both barbarians and Christians, domestic quarrels, and "the use and abuse" of its economic and cultural resources.

Gibbon's multi-volume study with its myriad of facts makes the ancient Roman civilization come alive again before our eyes. *It reminds us that there is a past beyond our own memory, recoverable by the craft of history and as we read Gibbon, we come to realize that the past affects us, even if we did not know it before we read about it.* For example, when we read about the Justinian Codes of Law, we can see that such Codes of Law are early prototypes for the modern Codes of Law adopted by Napoleon and that since Napoleon's time, these Codes have shaped modern law in a variety of modern European and other nations. To read Gibbons' history of Roman law gives us as sense of the origins of part of our modern legal history and helps us to understand that history *of which we are a part.*

Gibbon's history of Rome is something more than simply selected examples of ancient institutions which are perpetuated into the present. The history of Rome is the story of decline and eclipse of the power and glory of a great Empire. It reminds us that even the most extensive and long lived empires can decline and fall. Identifying the causes of the decline, Gibbon gives a cautionary lesson to those with present ambitions for modern empires. In this sense, the past of Rome is a humbling story and, as we become study that past, we also may be humbled. "Sic transit gloria mundi" is not merely a cliche — it is a sobering truth from the past. Drawing a parallel between Rome and modern empires, suggests that our history may also be part of cycles of civilization destined to rise and fall. (Nietzsche would question our reliance upon Gibbon's history as an example of relying upon monumental history. Such reliance, he suggests, poses the danger of viewing the Roman age through false historical analogies to our present age. But he does not abandon monumental history, but urges reflection in light our present experience. Hence, we must carefully assess whether the causes of Roman decline accounted for by Gibbon, are present in our current civilization).

2. Weighing the Past: Forgetting, Regretting, Rejecting, Commemorating

I do not claim that we elderly must remember all of the past. After recovering what we can, whether through memory or history, we must weigh what past we have, rejecting some and commemorating some. There is some past which is not worth remembering or which so threatens us that we should bury it. Forgetting is useful. Nietzsche believed that the Germany of his age was overwhelmed with history and might better forget much of it. Such personal or societal forgetfulness need not require an act of suppression. William James addresses memory in his magisterial *Principles of Psychology*. Memory for James is only one part of our past - a past seen in habit, stream of consciousness, personal identity, associations, perception of time and things, imagination, emotions and necessary pre-existing truths. For James, forgetfulness may, of course, be the product of organic damage to memory — a damage resulting from aging, injury or birth defects. But forgetting is also necessary and normal at any stage of life. Through forgetting, we winnow the welter of the past in order to remember selected events. Recognizing the value of selective memory frees us in old age from seeking to recover our complete past rather than to concentrate upon such events.

Some of the canon texts suggest deeper reasons for forgetting of the past. These deny the importance of the past, regarding it as the enemy of freedom. Nietzsche seeks to escape his Christian past, finding it symptomatic of "decadence". Foucault creates 'counter histories' in a heroic effort to assert the exercise of free will and creativity to shape the future against the past. James Joyce's *Portrait of an Artist as a Young Man* finds much fault in his Catholic upbringing, his education and the Irish society of his time and seeks to escape it. At the end of his novel, he finds his freedom to create and bids goodbye to Ireland, (but later novels that he did not completely escape). A forgetful disposal of one's past in old age, with a resulting sense of freedom may be a boon, especially to those who are feel imprisoned by physical decline and the imminence of death and simply seek to escape to another world.

Of course, forgetting may not be all good. The past may have shaped and continues to shape our old age character and our community. Unfortunately, the past's influence may be hidden — the result of active forces blocking memories within ourselves or within our society, affecting at an unconscious level how we think and act in the present, it may be necessary to cope with those forces. Freud, in his *General Introduction to Psychoanalysis* has shown us how individual forgetting may be the product of repression. The mistakes of everyday life, the dreams we have, and the neuroses we encounter as well as their manifest and latent meanings reveal the role of the past within the unconscious, signaling a resistance and repression of past thoughts and events. Although Freud seeks to interpret present associations and actions of his patients and, by doing so, cure their present mental illnesses, he traces these actions and illnesses to events rooted in the past. Past intentions interfere with present speech to create mistakes in speech. Past "archaic" and infantile features are found in dreams. Neurotic symptoms are the consequence of past events and sexual behavior is shaped by the development of sexuality in our past life. The role of analytic therapy is to wrestle with these demons of the past. Freud says it best when he describes the fixations due to past trauma:

> "...the patients...are fixed to a particular point in their past... marooned in their illness...just as in former times people used to withdraw to the cloister to live out their unhappy fate there. .."

If Freud is correct, just as current habits, character, and skills may embody a story of our past, our current emotional states and actions are influenced by our past lives, even though we may not be aware of the influence. Through self-awareness, whether or not enhanced by reading Freud or engaging as patients in psychotherapy, we may recover a piece of the past finding out who we were and now are. Therapy is an important and insufficiently used treatment by which the aged can recover their past or consciously choose to honor or ignore it.

Perhaps Jung has an even deeper or broader grasp of the historic past than Freud. He views that past as resting at the core of the personality in the form of the collective unconscious. This collective unconscious contains contents of the mind peculiar to mankind as a whole. It is organized according to mythological patterns called "archetypes". These archetypes can be found throughout all cultures and, in psychoanalysis, the workings of the archetypes are uncovered within the patient. Thus, through the collective unconscious, each of us is linked to universal patterns in history. In old age, Jung envisages us to return to the collective unconscious.

Freud and Jung have also revealed how societies and their history may "repress" the memory of events, reshaping their meaning. In the twentieth century, I have witnessed the effort of the Soviet Union to remake its history by denying the early decades of communist cruelty. Such historical denials are satirized by George Orwell, in his classic, *Animal Farm,* when he recounts this story of how the animals led by the pigs on a farm, made a revolution in the name of equality kicking the humans out. The pigs gradually forgot their revolutionary ideals until they revised the principles of revolution to permit inequality once again. But the Soviets and Orwell's pigs were not alone. We Americans were not exempt from rewriting history. In the American war documentaries which I watched as a boy in the 1940's, the USSR was heralded as our great ally in the Second World War. This view was "repressed" during the cold war era which followed the war; the Soviet contribution to the Allied victory was forgotten in the era of communist witch hunts and other anti-Soviet propaganda.

The revealing of a repressed past is a way to critique it. If the past is not important, once revealed, if freedom from it is secured, there is no harm, no foul, in forgetting it. Two of the most vehement critics of the past are Hegel and Marx. Their histories regard the past as in some way inadequate, falling short of achieving the full freedom of the present or the future, whether because of inadequate patterns of historical rule or class oppression. For both philosophers, the past may be important to understand the present, but it need not be a past to be recovered and restored, but a past to be avoided. Like Hegel and Marx, contemporary adherents to philosophies of self-development and societal progress may tacitly assume the past is somehow deficient and should be ignored. As I shall discuss in another chapter below, old age recognizes the limits of philosophies of self-development and societal progress, and, in so doing, no longer escapes the past by simply critiquing it.

3. Re-weaving the Past

St. Augustine's writings exemplify the effort to recapture the private and public history of his life, criticizing some of his past as sinful, yet recognizing its importance as an avenue to the revelations of Christianity, a new life of faith on this earth and an eternal future life. St. Augustine was born in Africa in the fourth century A.D. and returned there after his conversion where he remained a Catholic bishop. He wrote a myriad of works which were to help shape the early Catholic tradition. Augustine wrote his best-known work, *The Confessions* in mid-life after his conversion. *The Confessions* offers a model of someone who seeks to remember, recount *and reinterpret* his past, placing that past in the pattern of a narrative embracing an entire life and afterlife. Through *The Confessions*, he is able to look back and place his own past within a meaningful pattern of his own life and, in his *City of God,* the patterns of the history of Rome and Christianity.

He wrote *The City of God*, at the end of his life at a time when the Roman Empire was collapsing. Just as Augustine's *Confessions* dealt with his own personal history and salvation, the *City of God* discusses the history of Rome and Christianity and the possible salvation of believers. Augustine's history stretches from the Creation, the separation of the good and evil angels, the ejection of Adam from the Garden of Eve, Abel and Cain, Abraham and other Old Testament figures, the birth and death of Christ and the coming of the Judgment Day. He also describes the history of Rome, with all of its savagery and lust for dominion; he finds its rise to empire not in the old Roman virtues but in God's providence. And he finds its demise, not caused by the Christians, but by the Roman lust for power. Thus, he offers two stories: the story of a "Earthly City", created by God but subject to the free will of man and the influence of man's evil choices. The second story is a story of the triumph of the City of God.

Augustine's works illustrate how, with attention to the tradition of central texts, we might weave our own personal and historical pasts into the distinctive pattern of our entire life in the world. Augustine recounts his past sins and erroneous education seeking forgiveness and how guidance from his mother helped to lead him to his faith. Just as I turn to the canon works of western civilization, Augustine began with his past reading of the Greek and Roman classics, first the rhetorical works of Cicero, then the works of Plato and the neo-Platonic philosophers. Later, his reading of the Bible led his conversion. After his conversion, the systematic reading and interpretation of the Bible, following the method set forth in his *On Christian Doctrine* clarified his beliefs and helped him to refute the beliefs of his enemies. Throughout the *Confessions, The City of God,* and *On Christian Doctrine,* Augustine cites books as part of his past search for truth in his life. He often cites the works of Plato, Cicero, Boethius, and others which played an important role in his early rhetorical and philosophic life as well as the works of

Plotinus and Porphyry, who were transitional figures for Augustine; their works gradually lead to his return to the Bible.

Augustine introduces us to the important interpretive skills by which we may reweave our own pasts into a narrative our lives. His interpretive approach to reading is outlined in *On Christian Doctrine.* It begins with faith and ends with recovering the ancient liberal arts which help him to interpret the Bible. As applied to his own life, Augustine finds the origins of his belief in God in his memory of his past. He comes to understand the past as both a remembered and historical past leading to a present containing an anticipated future; the past, present, and future are parts of his life viewed as a whole. Augustine's history of mankind in *The City of God* reveals a story with a pattern similar to his own life. It starts with the Roman preoccupation with secular glory and power. (Augustine was also tempted by such power and glory in his youth). He recounts the bloody history of the earthly city of Rome, thus destroying any veneration for its statesmen. But included in his history of Rome is an account of the works of the pagan philosophers, some of whom he followed in his early days. Augustine treats this Roman intellectual tradition to be important enough to dispute and then reject. In rejecting Roman secular history, he turns to another history which moves towards the Day of Judgment, when the damned are consigned to hell and the blessed to an eternal life of bliss. Thus, both the pattern of the history of Augustine's life as well as the life of the earthly and heavenly cities is a Christian tale of sin and redemption. *Such an account of his life as well as his history of Rome and Christianity, suggest how we might also weave our pasts into an ordered narrative of our whole lives, understanding that past as part of the arc of our lives and the history of the society of which we are a part.*

Augustine's account of his early sins offers an example of the important role which guilt and regret can play in the re-weaving of our past into a view of our entire life. Just as Augustine's confessions recounts his early childhood sins, which he regretted, many modern works of literature deal with regret arising out of the past— the romantic regret of *Great Expectations,* the comic regret of *The Ambassadors,* the tragic regret of *Notes from the Underground,* the ironic regret of *Mrs. Dalloway.*

One modern home of the feeling of regret is the poetry of T.S. Eliot's *Burnt Norton*, which "mix[es] memory and desire" in a detached ironic mode of regret. The poem continues: "footfalls echo in the memory, down the passage we did not take, towards the door we never opened, into the rose garden." To pick another example, In Eliot's *La Figlia Che Piange*, he bids a lost love to "stand on the highest pavement of the stair — lean on the garden urn, — weave, weave the sunlight in your hair..." He muses, " so I would have him leave... She turned away, but with the autumn weather, compelled my imagination many days..." In another poem, Eliot suggests that "old men ought to be explorers, here and there does not matter..." suggesting that we pursue our regrets, at least in memory.

4. *Changing the Patterns of Time*

Rather than simply restore the past, critique it away, or interpret it as part of the narrative our lives, we may seek to reconceive historical or natural time in order to preserve the past. There is among the central texts, a kind of history which recaptures the past as part of the eternal recurrence. This may be the philosophic history of Plato's *Timaeus* or Nietzsche's myth of eternal return, or the natural history of Lucretius's *The Nature of Things,* or the social history of Toynbee. All of these histories, in one way or another, save the past by recycling it. Although such histories are out of fashion, Mircea Eliade, in his *The Myth of Eternal Return,* suggests that such a belief may be hidden among the lower strata and returning in some modern works.

There is also a kind of philosophy which recognizes a time which can be present, yet in some sense, eternal, embracing past, present and future: an "eternal now". As mentioned above, (Chapter X), this kind of time is suggested by the classical view of leisured practice of the liberal arts in which activities such as speculation and contemplation, aesthetic appreciation, and noble acts carry a timeless aspect to them. Another version may be Bergson's duration, which not only embraces the past, present and future, but also, in Bergson's words:

"Time is not the interior to us, but just the opposite, the interiority in which we are, in which we move, live and change…it is Proust who says that time is not internal to us, but we are internal to time, which divides itself in two, which loses itself and discovers itself in itself, which makes the present pass *and the past be preserved.…*"

Throughout this book, I have suggested a way of "recapturing the past" is through the entertainment of timeless ideas and principles. These ideas come from a tradition of great works (either presented by the texts or abstracted from them). I have described this tradition in Chapter IX above. Since these ideas are timeless, they are unaffected by the lost past of the aged who entertain them. Like Bergson's description of time, these ideas are not our subjective ideas, but we share in them and subordinate ourselves to their inclusivity. As Plato pointed out so eloquently in the *Republic* and *Phaedo*, we approach these ideas through our education and experience or, as all of the other Platonic works point out, through a dialogue which engages both heart and mind.

Conclusion

Behind the ideas of history and memory discussed above lurks the idea of time. The passage of time is implicit in this account of the losses of old age and their consolation. As Jean Amery has noted that the aged are time, that, "as aging persons, they are still only time which they are completely, as persons who are time, possess time and know time."

The canon works have offered up a variety of notions of time – eternal time or timelessness, scientific time, temporality, (the sensed passage of time), duration, (an extended present embracing the force of the past and the pull of the future). All of these ideas of time touch upon our aged lives and their losses. It is no accident that gold watches were presented at retirement celebrations, since work schedules are no longer available to help the retiree keep track of the time. Without family and work responsibilities, some aged succumb to boredom with its exaggerated consciousness of the passage of time. The scientific time measures our biological decline and guides scientists who seek to retard or mend that decline. The eclipse of time though the passage of history or fading memory means time lost from a life. If losing our past is not enough, the future time of our aged lives shrinks. The promise of time may wither in old age as we abandon plans and projects and lose our commitment to self-improvement and historical progress. Our sense of time in old age may be most poignant in the waiting for death.

And yet, I have suggested that past time may be recovered in old age reminiscence and with the help of the discipline of history. When the past is uncovered, some parts of that past time may be devalued; through therapy, we may gain freedom from the past. Other pasts may be valued, indeed commemorated and, in old age, we may be able to weave our past time into a unified narrative of a life which gives duration to our present time. Finally, with the help of the classics, we may participate in a tradition which is the source of timeless ideas. Interestingly, time itself, even the idea of temporality and the passage of time, is a timeless idea. Shakespeare, afraid that time will decay beauty suggests that "…that in black ink my love shall still shine bright."

CHAPTER XVI

Diminished Future: The Autumn of Possibility

"Now I shall make my soul,
Compelling it to study
In a learned school
Till the wreck of the body...." Yeats

As a Catholic child, I was deeply concerned about the immortality of my soul. At church, as the host was lifted during consecration, I would follow the instructions of my missal and, hitting my chest three times, I said "my Lord and my God". The missal assured me that if I said this with true faith, it would take seven years off my time in Purgatory. That prayer seemed to be the storing of a good legacy for my afterlife. In my first law practice job, we drafted wills for our rich clients to enable them to control the future after their death. The associates gathered at the will signing to witness the will and sip sherry with the client. The ceremony offered a touch of elegance to our practice and, no doubt, softened the pain of the subsequent bill we sent to them. With the birth of my children came another intimation of an effort to reach out into the future - the prospect of extending one's life to another generation through one's children. Recently, I have keenly felt the importance of this legacy as I hold daily conversations with them.

In old age, I have become aware of a rapidly shrinking future, which leaves little time to realize former grand plans and ambitions. Without a sense of urgency, I have begun to turn serious attention to the limited time left in life. My late wife and I slowly and reluctantly sought to extend our lives through legacies – purchasing a plot at the Hillside Cemetery in Norwich- arranging to leave our body parts to others or to science, while asking our heirs to scatter most of the remains to the winds - revising our wills. I now worry about finding the proper beneficiaries of my many books. Before she died, Mollie worried about who will take care of the cat. We talked about what the other might do, and where the survivor might live after one of us dies. This attention to the future after our death may be regarded as an effort to extend our influence beyond our lives – thus extending "our" rapidly diminishing future. My wife once suggested that her legacy rested in the minds and hearts of the patients who outlive her. I harbor hope that the students I have taught, and the organizations I started are part of my legacy.

But neither of us were naive. Our contributions have been modest compared to more historic accomplishments of others; we recognized that the memory of us is doomed to oblivion as descendants die and memories fade. (There is nothing more sobering for an academic than finding one's writings in the remainder bin of a second hand bookstore or the storage warehouse of a library!) With our limited accomplishments, our lack of religious hope in immortality and our realistic appraisal of future oblivion, I ask myself whether legacy in old age has much meaning. If so, what might that meaning be?

Introduction: The Old Age Loss of a Future

In past chapters, I discuss the present time of old age, i.e., how to cope with retirement, our physical and mental decline, and the eclipse of our past. But old age can concern itself about the future as well, specifically, the rapidly contracting future in our old age lives. That contracting future is displayed in tables of life expectancy which document the remorseless decline in the years of life expectancy as one gets older. The shrinkage of future years is often viewed as the loss of possibilities – the diminishment of opportunities to realize one's dreams and desires. This is the lesson of Kelly Cherry's *Lines Written on the Eve of a Birthday:*

"It is the loss of possibility which claims you bit by bit...."

And this is why Samuel Johnson penned the request:

"Enlarge my life with multitude of days In health and sickness, thus the suppliant prays...."

If life is subdivided into continuous uniform moments with their corresponding equal number of possibilities, then, indeed, as old age arrives, most of life's possibilities have disappeared and the futile hope of "enlarging our multitude of days" follows, along, perhaps with regret and despair.

But more analysis is required. What may be lost is not some form of statistical possibility, but the loss of personal potentialities – capacities which lay underdeveloped or unused (and are now incapable of use) or have withered in the course of our lives. The underlying assumption is that our life-time potentialities are the result of our biological capacities in early life and since, as a previous chapter pointed out, some of these biological capacities wither in old age, it is the corresponding potentialities that are lost. For example, the lost ability to reproduce in old age. The assumption, shared by many ancient Greek authors, is that our potentialities are present in our youth and early adulthood, developed, perfected and exercised during the middle years and diminished thereafter. Old age despair, regret, and nostalgia are then the result of the realization of such losses in old age.

One curious fact seems to refute this view. Many elderly are curiously optimistic. We do not obsess about the shrinkage of the future, the loss of possibilities, and our failure to realize the host of potentialities we are alleged to have when young. To be sure, as we have seen in the previous chapters, some elderly seek to extend their lives with the help of religious beliefs or medical technology, and perhaps such efforts mask an awareness of the running out of the future in old age. More often, many in old age do not mope about the waning of their golden years, but seek to metaphorically extend their lives by creating legacies of those lives: having children, doing good works which perpetuate honor and reputation or at least extend in some way the benefits of one's good works beyond old age. "Old men plant trees". More prosaically, the writing of wills or disposing of property to the next generation is another effort to extend such influence beyond one's lifetime.

There is however a "legacy" which can serve to bridge our lives and beyond. That legacy is the achieved by participation in the tradition of classics. In reading and appreciating those classics during the ever-shrinking future of our old age, we participate in a tradition which extends back in time before our own life and will continue after our lives are completed. By participating in this continuous tradition, we transcend the limited future we have in old age.

Metaphorically, we expand our old age future.

The Differing Kinds of Legacies

1. The Biological Legacy

For many of us, our legacy is biological — the heritage of our children. Aristotle believed that the urge for reproduction was based upon the desire for immortality. That notion of immortality is given a biological basis in modern genetics, the origin of which is found in the work of Gregor Mendel, in his hybridization of peas experiments in 1865. After securing a pool of pea plants with constantly occurring differences in color of seed, seed coat or unripe pods and differences in the position of the flowers, the length of the stem, and the form of the ripe seeds, Mendel cross pollinated these seeds in a series of separate fertilizations. He sought to control the effects of foreign pollen. He found that three of the immediate offspring shared the characteristic of one of the parents, (which was called a dominant characteristic) while another characteristic of the parent was observable only in one plant and hence was called a recessive characteristic. In the next generation of the plants with a recessive characteristic delivered a constant group of plants with recessive characteristic, while out of those with a dominant characteristic, two thirds showed the same ratio of the dominant characteristics while one third showed a constant dominant characteristic. Mendel then traced the characteristic through several generations and similarly traced them in tandem with other characteristics which would change through hybridization. He was able to take the egg cells and pollen from plants with different characteristics to show similar patterns of hybridization.

Such genetic analysis, when rooted in more recent knowledge of DNA, carries a double lesson. On the one hand, we can claim that our genes are carried forth to provide certain characteristics to future generations, but these characteristics are not our entire physical (or mental) make up. Moreover, as Mendel pointed out, some of our genes are recessive and hence not observable in some generations, (although they represent "potentials" for the future). In any case, our unique genes for a biological characteristic are quickly mixed into a pool of genes generating many characteristics and our contributions to this unique mix of genetic contributions is small indeed. Thus, our genetic link is diffused through time. We cannot rely upon biology to deliver a unique personal immortality. Such a diffusion is not unlike the diffusion of the atoms of the body which the ancient poet-philosopher, Lucretius, in his *De Rerum Naturm,* described as returning to the flux of the atoms in the universe.

2. *The Legal Legacy*

Perhaps the uncertainty of any strong link between our own unique genetic makeup and the succeeding generations spurs us to adopt more artificial ways of insuring our unique legacy, namely leaving our property. The notion of legacy is often associated with the leaving of property, especially by last will and testament. Rather than relying upon genetic inheritance, or the abstract permanence of scientific entities such as atoms to insure our individual immortality, a more down to earth approach may be taken: the making of a will and testament, in which property owned by the old is transferred to the young. To be sure, a legacy can be a simple gift — an act of altruistic love which can take place at any time in life. But the making of a will may be viewed as a unique effort to have some effect upon the future beyond one's death through the operation of "the dead hand" of a last will and testament. The classic legal statement of a such a will is set forth for ancient Roman law in Justinian's *Institutes*, Blackstone's *Commentaries on the Common Law,* and the *Napoleonic Code* in the 18th and early 19th centuries. I will concentrate upon Blackstone, who through his legal classic, borrowed from Roman law, and helped to shape both English and American common law and our modern Anglo American law of inheritance.

Blackstone founded an absolute individual right to property; such "property" was taken out of an original common property make private by our own individual possession. The property, if owned in "freehold", would pass automatically to the first-born male. Blackstone rationalized the right of male primogeniture by appealing to the need to keep property intact through succession, in a sense supporting the continuity of both capital and the family. Over time, the law of succession began to permit the disposal of property by testamentary devise, to pass by written will according to the intent of the owner. Such a bequest often continued to honor primogeniture, but flexibility was permitted the owner who could prepare a will and disinherit someone. Such bequests may have good or horrible consequences both upon those who are offering such bequests as well as those who anticipate and those who receive such bequests. Legacies are the gift of external goods. As Aristotle recognized, such goods have limited effect upon our character and destiny.

Shakespeare's *King Lear* is the *locus classicus.* Lear mistakenly leaves his kingdom to his two evil daughters who sucked up to him in his old age need for love. Ophelia rightly rejects his demands for love in return for her share of the kingdom. The evil twins turn upon their father, limiting his retinue and his visitation rights. The two evil daughters and their spouses battle over the kingdom and, to make a long story short, all of his children and he are killed obliterating those who might carry his inheritance.

The English, German and French novels of the 19th century and especially the novels of Dickens and Jane Austin abound with wills and their dubious consequences. The 19th century English novels revolved around inheritances which helped to shape the lives of those who inherited or failed to inherit wealth: Thackery's *Vanity Fair*, Eliot's *Middlemarch*, the Jane Austin's novels, Evelyn Waugh's *Brideshead Revisited*, E.M. Forester's *Howard's End*, Bronte's *Jane Eyre* and many more. The stories of the wills found in these books are, in part, stories of the testators' benevolence or evil effort to control the future, and the corresponding hopes and moral claims of future generations. In many of these novels, however, the will is incidental, often operating as a "Deus ex machina" to resolve a problem with the plot.

One example of last wills and testaments which best captures the importance of the will and testament, as well as its problems, is Dickens' *Bleak House*. For Dickens, inheritance was important, since such an inheritance in his own life aided him with his albeit brief education. Bleak House was all about an inheritance, beginning with a damning portrait of the Chancery Court which administered inheritance in the infamous case of *Jarndyce v. Jarndyce* in an incompetent manner. The message of Dickens' *Bleak House* was cautionary lesson for those who depend upon legacies to insure their wishes for the future. In *Bleak House,* it was Richard's expectation of a legacy which motivated him to abandon his career in a futile quest for an inheritance. The not too subtle lesson of the novel is found in the good deeds of Esther, who, abandoned by her mother (and hence lacking a legacy), was able to find happiness in life though her virtues and charity.

3 The Religious Legacy

Aside from wills, the other conventional "legacy" is bestowed by religious faith. Many religious faiths hold onto a set of beliefs in the afterlife, whether in the form of the ancient Greek Hades, the Christian heaven and hell, or the Eastern transmigration of souls In short these religions promise immortality which, as we shall see, may be the hidden premise of any concern for a legacy. As my readers now know, I do not turn to religious beliefs to insure my future. Nevertheless, I am imbued with the religious works of the canon — the theological works of Augustine, Aquinas, reformation thinkers as well as the poetic works of Dante and Milton. All offer a rich portrait of what afterlife might be like.

If these classic works are built upon a religious faith which I no longer embrace, what possible reason can there be for reading them? Dante's *Divine Comedy* supplies an answer.

The *Divine Comedy* paints the most vivid picture of a Christian legacy after death — with the help of Virgil, his guide, Dante visits Inferno, Purgatory, and Paradise. The Inferno of Dante was a place of punishment exquisitely designed to fit precisely the mortal sins of the unrepentant. For example, the evil counselors who stole the virtues God bestowed upon them, using them for evil purposes working in hidden ways on earth, are hidden by Dante in the flames of hell. To give another example, Dante's Purgatory is a place where its repentant sufferers, anticipating an eventual entrance into paradise, voluntarily seek purification through painful effort designed to pay for unpaid sins when alive. Those who delayed in repenting during their life, have to sit and wait before entering Purgatory. Approaching paradise, Dante replaces the guiding reason of Virgil with the faith of his love Beatrice. Thus love replaces reason. As he ascends, he meets the souls in heaven, the great warriors, law givers, just rulers, saints, contemplatives; in each step, he moves in love closer to God.

Modern secularists, I included, have rejected the legacy of an afterlife of Aquinas, Dante, and the fantasies of the modern Catholic Church. In doing so, we have abandoned the theological hope for divine happiness. But the literal belief in an afterlife, is less important than the symbolic meaning of such a life. The legacy of Christian afterlife symbolizes justice, purification, and love which is not fully realizable during our human lives. Human justice is not complete on this earth, and hence must be doled out in the afterlife. We cannot achieve intellectual or moral perfection in this world; hence a stay in

Purgatory is recommended. Our love in this life is, at most, the "lesser" love of our spouses, family members and friends — not the full bliss of the love of God which we can only reach in heaven.

Thus, religion and the classics which describe an afterlife offer irrefutable lessons about our limits on this earth, *whether or not one is a believer. It is in old age that we most vividly become* aware *of these limits — that justice will not be achieved, that perfection will not be achieved, that our loves are limited human loves. The religious canon contributes* a certain clarity of vision in a secular old age, perhaps along with a certain sadness. Just as those who look to biological inheritance to perpetuate themselves, only to find their biological inheritance scattered and diffused and just as those who depend upon the leaving of property as a legacy must recognize the limited and unpredictable nature of such external goods, secular non-believers must find and accept a limited justice, finite perfection, and human love in their own lives and abandon the hope that descendants will find something more.

4. *Legacies of Honor – "The Frenzy of Renown"*

Even if we do not believe that our biological genes, our wealth, or our personal souls live on after our death, we may harbor the hope that the recognition of our deeds or works might live on in some fashion — imperishable, continuous, eternal. Like ancient Greek heroes, memorialized with plaques and statutes, we might hope for a personal legacy of memory and honor built which extends our individual lives through time, not through the immortality of the soul, but through public memory or fame or glory. Many of us hope that our individual fame and honor will remain beyond death — the product of praiseworthy acts, heroic deeds or great works. Seeking such fame is not the business of the elderly, but old age may be a time in which one can coldly assess the success of the ambitions of one's life and whether memory of one's success will last beyond death. Accounts of ambitions for honor are the stuff of the biographies of great men and novels which tell the story of the hero who succeeded or failed. The canon is replete with works dealing with the individual and community pursuit of honor.

Perhaps one of the most vivid novels of ambition is Stendhal's *The Red and the Black* in which the protagonist, Julian Sorel, pursues his ambitions in both the clerical and political life, only to be frustrated in his ambitions by both by his low social origins and his illicit love affairs. At the end of a turbulent life of ambition pursued in both the church and politics, he is frustrated by the revelation of his early misdeeds. After shooting (but not killing) his first lover, he finds peace in jail before his death — a peace in which he finally found himself independent of the need for praise from the outside world.

Insofar as such honor and fame rests upon the opinion of others through the ages, its' story may be best captured by epic accounts which look back to the deeds of past heroes. Thus, Homer's *Iliad* and *Odyssey* as well as Virgil's *Aeneid* offer such an account of Greek pride and the origins of Roman pride. The Greeks recognized the importance of honoring great deeds for posterity, but they also held to the notion that the deeds were to be undertaken for their own sake; such a pursuit of honor found its value because such deeds exhibited one or another virtue. Aristotle, who recognized that honor was a fragile "external good" subject to the uncertainties of history. If true, the pursuit of honor in order to find a place in history would not be a good bet!

History, such as that set forth in Thucydides' *History of the Peloponnesian War* or Gibbons' *The Decline and Fall of the Roman Empire*, may ironically nullify epic accounts of heroes and their fame as guarantors of immortality. Thucydides' account of the Athenian pursuit of honor and glory laid bare her rationalizations for her failed efforts at dominance of her allies and enemies, only to ultimately lose the war with Sparta. Gibbons documented the decline of Rome's effort to find honor through an empire which she could neither manage or protect. Both authors document the decline of the very communities which had honored heroes and their deeds in the past. Hence, even if the political community chooses to honor one after his or her death, such honor is not permanent since the political community is itself not permanent. We learn from these histories that few of us can be immortal heroes and fewer still can find an immortal community to honor our heroic deeds through the ages.

Just as political leaders and generals seek honor, authors, sculptors, painters, composers frequently seek an reputation for works which meet "the test of time". Perhaps the character of Casaubon in George Eliot's *Middlemarch* is an object lesson for those of us who seek immortality through written works. Casaubon, an old professor, is seeking to undertake a grand work — a *Syntopicon,* which will hold the key to all the myths of the world; he is unable to complete his ambitious project before dying. In his desire to aggrandize his own reputation, he futilely seeks to enlist her help in completing his magnum opus after his death and he is soon forgotten as life moves on.

Perhaps because philosophers frequently seek honor beyond their death, they often reflect upon the permanence or impermanence of honor and whether it constitutes part of a good life. Honor as fame and reputation depends upon others' often fluctuating opinions; Aristotle recognizes that such recognition, like other external goods, is not at the heart of virtue. Rather, he recognizes an honor which is deserved for the practice of virtue or the performance of great deeds, although even then, such an honor must be granted by the right persons for the right deeds and should be proportional to the virtue or accomplishments. Such a philosophy, as well as many of the histories and novels of the canon suggest that it is a mistake to seek honor since such ambition may demand a character and deeds which, paradoxically, are not honorable. In short, relying upon honor or fame is probably an unwise strategy for leaving a legacy.

Communal Legacies

The legal legacies described above may be part of "succession" — an instrument of continuation of a family's patrimony. From this point of view, one leaves one's property to insure the continuation of the family (and its property) through the ages; both the testator and the recipient are part of that succession. Some of the English novels seek to portray the merits and perils of such family successions. The novels of Anthony Trollope, Evelyn Waugh, or Thomas Mann illustrate the efforts of their protagonists to sustain the succession of the family. The continuity of family is closely linked to the notion of securing immortality through the generation of offspring. Thomas Mann's portrait of the decline of a family in *Buddenbrooks* reveals its continuity through its ownership in the grain business, as well as such instruments as a family home, a multi-generational diary, a family bible, and family documents shared through the generations. But the family and its business do not last as its descendants marry fools, or persons with bad character, or those with fatal weaknesses of energy. Even chance in the form of an unanticipated failure of the crops helps to bring down the family business. At the end of four generations of the Buddenbrooks family, with the business failed and the grand home sold, the most that can be hoped for is that the final descendant would be met in heaven!

The notion of participation within succession is not limited to being part of family succession. It also extends to belonging to the nation sharing its history and heroes through time. Some "heroes" play a major role in the life of the community, and their speeches, laws, and heroic actions may live on as part of the community, but slaves, the poor, the ordinary are also and part of the history of that community and hence we share in the lives of both groups. With regard to heroes, the lives described by Plutarch may serve as examples. For our modern nation, the Declaration of Independence, the Constitution, and the lives of Jefferson or Lincoln are part of such a legacy. Lincoln's address at Gettysburg recognized the legacy established by those troops who fell in the battle of Gettysburg in order to preserve the federal union. Similarly the legacy of our history is codified in our Constitution which, in its oft ignored Preamble, secures "the blessings of liberty and justice for ourselves and posterity", thus committing our political community through its Constitution to a shared pursuit throughout ages before and after our lives. (The Greeks believed that citizens shared in the constitution of their community, although the harbored different notions of what citizenship and constitutionality was all about!)

Edmund Burke's *Reflections on the French Revolution* is the paradigm statement of the notion of a nation as a succession of generations and a partnership between them; hence the importance of preserving one's a political legacy. In Burke's eyes, the political leaders of the French Revolution, animated by ambition and ideology, forgot the importance of such a succession, as embodied in the institutions of the French state — the royalty, private property, the Church. For Burke, the individual participates in these institutions and hence is part of the succession through time. For Americans, this sense of historical continuity is captured in the history we learn as children.

Burke's conservative view of succession looks backward — the partnership between the past and present. More recently, legacy has acquired a meaning of succession between the present and the future. Many of the political utopias assume legacies of obligation toward the future — "pyramids of sacrifice" of the present on behalf the future. In the past century Communism demanded such sacrifices and Marx offered a rationale for such a sacrifice. Modern environmentalists want similar sacrifices of present economic activities to preserve nature's capital for future generations - a legacy of sustainability.

All of the above efforts to secure a secular legacy aim to insure some form of immortality extending beyond our deaths thus extending the diminished future of old age. Preparing gifts to our descendants, drafting our last wills and testaments to insure memory of ourselves, fulfilling the ambition of individual renown and honor, and participating in the continuation of family or community succession are dubious ways for seeking immortality. There is, however, another way which does not require us to extend our influences through the ages relying upon fragile human memory or long lived but fallible institutions to preserve the echo of our presence.

Instead, we may participate *now* in eternal ideas, or principles which are set forth in the canonic classical tradition described above. This tradition began before our life began and promises to extend beyond our life. Participating in this tradition enables us to ignore the shrinking of our future in old age because the immutable ideas, principles and truths are not subject to the vicissitudes of time. We can participate in this tradition through the reading and works of this tradition along with the realization of the place of those works in the tradition. A fortunate few can also contribute to this tradition with their own works, which embody, to a greater or lesser degree, a response to that tradition.

How does participation through reading, appreciation or creation extend the time of our lives or, at least, permit us to ignore the shrinking of the ordinary time of our lives? The works of the tradition deal with subject matters such as the processes of nature and the workings of culture through history — subjects which themselves are perennial. In reading and apprehending these works, one encounters immutable ideas, principles and truths. For example, within the study of nature, ideas such as nature itself and its elements, genes, and processes of change and evolution emerge. Lucretius, the ancient poet-philosopher, the author of *The Nature of Things,* believed in the permanent atoms of the soul — atoms which extend their cyclical life beyond our deaths. The Enlightenment philosopher, Spinoza believed that man and nature were "modes of God", the scientist, Mendel, and his successors laid the basis for the genetic theory, revealing how genes might extend before and after our own lives. Darwin documented the processes of evolution in nature. The modern philosopher and mathematician, Whitehead, suggested how "eternal objects" may enter the ongoing processes of nature. These philosophers, biologists, and mathematicians believed that eternal elements and processes of nature are part of us and we are part of the eternal elements and processes of nature.

If we are part of nature, we are also part of history and its patterns. Within the works of culture, one discovers the ideas of the soul, man, progress, justice, beauty and happiness. For example, the German philosopher, Hegel, believed that we participate in a pattern of history infused with the universal principle of freedom, which is immanent within history. This idea of freedom gives meaning to history which extends both before and after our individual lives and the lives of our own political communities. Other theorists, such as Adam Smith finds the march of history in the growing wealth of nations. The Frenchman, de Tocqueville, who visited the United States in the early 19th century, finds the march of progress in the gradual realization of idea of equality of condition in the history of the United States. Marx finds it in the stages of class warfare with its final resolution in revolution. Toynbee finds principles of history, at least in part, in the cycles of civilization. The fact that different historians find different ideas immanent in history, means that several patterns may be found within history and may contest with each other as the true interpretation of history. In short, our historical legacy may be a contested legacy. This contest is laid out within the works of the canon. But whether true or not, these *ideas are permanent universals extending beyond* the *life of any one person.* They live in the natural and political histories; our lives, as part of those natural and political histories embody these ideas. We are part of evolution and the cycles of history.

In our old age, in so far as we participate in the reading and apprehension about the ideas within the canon, we can participate *now* in the eternal ideas found within the major works of our civilization. The notion of a canon of eternal ideas was best set forth by Plato — in all of his dialogues. In the *Phaedo*, Plato is in jail and awaiting death. In response to questions about death, he suggests that he is not concerned since he knows he will go to another place. The presence of another place is revealed by the presence of ideas remembered from another time before birth and which are found to be eternal since they logically exclude their opposites. These "quaint" notions of Plato, comprehensible only within the context of his dialogues are echoed by the modern mathematician-philosopher, Alfred North Whitehead who, as mentioned above, argued that ideas are universals, i.e., "eternal objects" which enter into a process of "actual occasions". One such occasion is the individual life into which such eternal objects "ingress". In doing so, these eternal objects are part of our lives and, according to Whitehead, we become conscious of them through education – "an adventure in ideas". Thus, we participate in the forms or formula of natural change, the patterns and meanings of history, and the principles and ideas within the canon works. We participate intellectually in these forms, patterns and ideas as a consequence of an education - a development of the self, which morally, emotionally and intellectually enables us to grasp them. We hold onto them with the help of our instinct, our knowledge, as well as our feelings and character. In the words of Whitehead, *"the entertainment of ideas is associated with an inward ferment, an activity of subjective feeling which is at once immediate enjoyment and also an appetition which melts into action".*

Whitehead emphasized that our participation in nature, history and the perennial ideas found within them, is not merely an exercise of reason, but a participation which involves our whole self - our physical, social, and intellectual self. This participation is animated by love - a basic tendency, which, in the case of humans is informed by judgment. *When some form of legacy is sought, whether personal or impersonal, it is love which fuels the seeking of immortality.* When wills are drawn and bequests made, the recipients are customarily loved ones living beyond our own lives. Belonging to the succession of a family or a political community is a kind of love for that family or community. Even if a legacy is animated by personal efforts to control the future of recipients or aggrandize personal honor in memory, such a legacy expresses an acquisitive self-love which seeks to extend its power beyond the life of the self. A personal or impersonal legacy is participation within the processes of nature, history or the realm of ideas; love animates that participation. We are all, as Whitehead and others have recognized, attached to nature, history and its ideas and principles. The canon offers us remarkable portraits of that attachment - love, from the intense and searing passions of Paris in the *Iliad*, the extension beyond those passions to the love of our neighbor set forth in the story of Jesus in the *Bible*, the ascension within the intellectual love described in Plato's dialogue, *The Symposium*, (or in Plotinus's *Enneads*).

Conclusion

Thus, I arrive at the conclusion that the desire for a legacy in response to the shrinking future of old age stems from the desire to expand the shrinking future of old age. A kind of immortality or at least an expanded life can be sought in children and their children, wills and testaments, the traditions of one's family or political community or even honor or glory within that community. However, I find more appealing the attempt to embrace an expanded future through consciously sharing in the immutable ideas and principles of the great works of the classical tradition, thus finding an "eternal present" to counter the shrinking future of old age.

CHAPTER XVII

Dependency and Dignity

"And I will gladly share with you your pain,
If it turn out I can no comfort bring;
For 'tis a friend's right, please let me explain,
To share in woful as in joyful things."
                    Chaucer, *Trolious and Cresida* I, 85

When I was a graduate student at the University of Chicago and later, a law student at Yale, I also worked as a welfare worker for the cities of Chicago and New Haven. I was an "intake worker" visiting single parent families to determine their eligibility for "ADC" – aid to dependent children. Among other tasks, I would carefully tote up any income the family might have and determine the families "need", based upon a detailed schedule of needs for each family member. I was young and not very sensitive, but I was an agent of the state reluctantly distributing public funds for people who had very real needs and little resources to meet them.

Now I am the dependent – at least in part. My medical needs are met with Medicare and some other needs are met with Social Security payments. Fortunately, there is not the same demeaning process of determining eligibility as there is for receiving ordinary welfare. Either a card is flashed to secure medical services or regular monthly payments of social security are made to our bank accounts.

In old age, I have experienced other needs not met through pensions and health programs. I need comfort (at an uncomfortable age), recognition (when there are few who acknowledge my existence), energy to initiate actions (when energy runs low), renewed passion, (when old age passions wane), and meaning of my life (when meanings come into question). These needs depend, at least in part upon others.

We elderly feel a more intense and immediate form of dependency as our medical condition worsens and our ambitions fade. We gain an intimate awareness – not only the medical measurement – of our needs. Both my late wife and I turned to each other for help, in moments of imbalance, forgetfulness, and pain to perform the everyday tasks of living and hold onto fading dreams (or generating new ones) – all the results of growing old. We were both co-dependents, learning how to help each other as best we can.

Introduction

In a previous chapter, we saw Oedipus, before his death, dignity intact, yet dependent upon his daughter, Antigone to minister his needs in his old age, and upon the good will of Theseus of Athens to protect him. Dependency – the reliance upon others to meet our needs is the frequent lot of old age. The classics document these needs in painful detail and often the story is not pretty. Unlike *Oedipus at Colonus*, Shakespeare's *King Lear* tells the story of Lear's mistaken dependence upon two of his daughters. In Eliot's *Middlemarch*, Casaubon's relies upon his wife, Dorothea, to continue his great Syntopicon after he dies, but is frustrated by her disinterest in his great project.

Perhaps the most moving of portraits of dependency is grandfather's dependence upon Nell in Dickens' *The Old Curiosity Shop*. The grandfather's recognition of Nell's dependency upon him leads him to unwise gambling, wasting away any wealth he might have had to support Nell after he died. Upon the loss of his wealth, he becomes dependent upon Nell who helps lead him out of London and supports him in illness and old age. She ultimately dies in these efforts to support him, and he dies shortly thereafter. This Dickensian story is a moving portrait of the vulnerability of the aged and the high personal cost of such mutual dependency which results in the brutal conditions of poverty in nineteen[th] century London. Karl Marx, in his *Capital* and Simone de Beauvoir, in her *Coming of Age* describe the condition of the aging workers in the nineteenth century factory and their poverty upon retirement. (Of course the poverty of the Nell and her grandfather was a personally caused since their dependency resulted not as much from direct class oppression, as from their personal vices and failings as they tried to survive in the 19th century urban life).

Some of the most moving portraits of old age dependency are found in modern stories of dependency, such as John Bayley's *Iris*, a moving account of the slow decline of his wife, the philosopher, Iris Murdoch, and his loving care for her during her Alzheimer's. Many of us find such dependency painful to behold and even more painful to experience. As dependents, we view it as threatening to our autonomy and dignity; we even find it humiliating. As helpers to others in old age, we sometimes regard dependency as burdensome and confining, a prison of obligations. But when such dependency is visited upon an outstanding philosopher and novelist, it poses a special problem for one who argues that the classic works are the means of consoling the losses of old age.

Old Age Needs and Wants

"Dependency" is based, at least in part, upon the reality of basic biological human needs, - the result of our animal nature and its' growing dependence upon human relationships over the years. Old age dependency is the immediate consequence of our biological decline in old age, a decline which creates new needs while weakening the capacity of self-reliance to meet those needs. Three kinds of needs may be identified within the canon works: biological needs, the need for social goods, such as friendships, respect and self-esteem as well as the need for meaning in our own lives and in life in general. All three kinds of "needs" can increase in old age. The old age biological needs include food, shelter, and medical care; these needs often arrive in old age when resources may become more limited. The decline of resources as well as the mental and physical capacities to use those resources in old age limits freedom for the aged to pursue the life to which they were accustomed in their earlier years. Often, the loss of capabilities eliminates work relationships, reduces the social life of the aged with friends and family, and encourages withdrawal. Confronting a shrinking future and imminent death, the elderly, if not in denial, seek to find meaning in their lives and in the death which confronts them.

These old age needs can be thought of in two ways – as "wants/ desires" or as required essential goods. The notion of "want" suggests that something which is desired is missing. One example of a want as "something missing" comes from Plato's *Symposium* in which Aristophanes offers an account of love as the desire and search for one's missing half after the gods had split rounded persons in two. I prefer to follow the lead of Aristotle and view needs as the desire for goods necessary to support and facilitate human functioning. Aristotle identified needs as such necessary goods to enable the natural functioning of life. These goods and their respective activities include life itself, health, (including food, shelter, and medical care), bodily integrity, exercise of our senses, imagination and thought, emotional health, family and friendships, pleasures, a variety of intellectual and moral excellences developed over time, autonomy, and a modicum of external goods to facilitate all of these. This list of needs includes not only biological needs and the need for freedom to realize them, but also the need for meaning.

Needs, whether biological, ethical, or spiritual, emerge out of nature, habit, or education and assume their shape within our lives As we age, our minds and bodies decline and our social situation changes, our needs change as well. When we look at the list of goods which Aristotle thought to make up the good life, we can see that old age may remove the need for such "basic" goods as the pleasures of sexual activity, the thrill of vigorous sports, or to impetus to improve one's moral and intellectual virtues. At the same time, there may be heightened needs for medical care to maintain health or the need for family or friends to provide support of all sorts. If freedom is one of the goods of life, (and it is), we realize in old age that the easy exercise of will power to carry out our plans in our youth was based upon physical and mental capacities that we took for granted. With old age, we may no longer possess those capacities, *and hence, we may need help to carry out the full freedom of agency.*

Perhaps the most important need in old age is "spiritual", that is, the securing of a sense of meaning in our lives. In old age, time has removed some of the ordinary props for our sense of importance as we have had to abandon work activities and family responsibilities which may have given our former life a sense of vital importance and meaning. As a consequence, we need to find other avenues for finding significance in our lives. Cervantes in *Don Quixote*, Goethe in *Faust*, and Shakespeare in *King Lear*, portray the protagonist's urgent need to find meaning in their lives – need which emerges in their old age as circumstances changed. In Don Quixote's old age, he recreated the world of chivalry and all it implies. King Lear envisaged an old age retirement with loving respect from his daughters. Goethe's story of Faust is particularly compelling. Goethe himself, as the prologue to *Faust* suggests, was acutely aware of the challenges of old age. His "hero" Faust is an aged scholar, having mastered philosophy, law, theology and medicine. He finds his learning gives little satisfaction in his old age. In his words:

> "…philosophy have I digested,
> The whole of law and medicine,
> From each its secrets I have wrested,
> Theology, alas, thrown in.
> Poor fool, with all this sweated lore,
> I stand no wiser than I was before…."

Thus, like many scholars in old age, Faust finds himself abandoning his old scholarship to look for meanings in life elsewhere. (Of course, there is an irony here. Goethe, in telling the story of Faust, does not abandon his own scholarship, since his poem is replete with references to the canon works of all ages preceding Goethe!).

The unmet needs of any age, especially the loss of meaning in old age leads to a certain sadness. Faust, at least at the beginning of Goethe's work, is deeply melancholic. He finds no satisfactions in the ordinary pleasures of life – even when his townspeople extend honor to him for the medical works he and his father performed earlier in his life, he remains unsatisfied. His mood is one of the "acedia", the medieval vice of alienation from God and his creations. (This deep feeling of melancholy and boredom can also be found in the old age of Don Quixote before he undertook his knight errantry.) At the beginning of his old age quest, Faust still finds two souls housed within his breast –"the passions' craving crude for love and hugs a world where sweet the senses rage", the other "longs for pastures fair above, leaving the murk for loft heritage". These are needs of meaning - love and transcendence which range beyond the ordinary biological needs of the elderly or even the need for freedom.

Minimizing Our Needs

The ancient Hellenic and Hellenistic philosophers allegedly escape the problems created by needs by finding ways in which the individual or society might limit or eliminate those needs. Helen North, in her remarkable book, *Sophrosyne* traces the history of the ancient Greek, Roman and Christian ideal of temperance or limiting one's desires. For Aristotle, needs were limited by the development of character through habit and education in which excess is not pursued nor "grasped" and taken from others. Virtues ensure limits in the pursuit of good, and a society whose members shared a commitment to virtue limits its own pursuit of wealth, population growth or innovation. The "wealth of nations" is not the purpose of the political community for the Greeks.

Hellenistic philosophers, whether Stoic or Epicurean found more drastic means for limiting needs. For the Epicurean, needs are limited by an awareness that absence of pain – comfort – is the pleasure sought. This comfort is a pleasure unmixed by any pain which might result from the pursuit or realization of more intense pleasures. Thus, wisdom is the pursuit of limited pleasure – not a bad recommendation of the elderly! As Epicurus stated: "Nothing satisfies the man who is not satisfied with a little." For the Stoics, the exercise of will permits a person's taking distance from her appetites through the exercise of reason. It is Epictetus, who has lessons for greedy booklovers with this paragraph from his *Discourses*:

> "Remember that it is not only desire of office and of wealth that makes men abject and subservient to others, but also desire for peace and leisure, travel and learning. Regard for any external thing, whatever it be, make you subservient to another.... For books, like salutations and office, belong to the outer world which is beyond your own control.... Books are, no doubt a preparation for life, but life itself is made up of things different from books ... we should cease to calculate ... today I read so many lines, wrote so many, and should reckon, thus, "Today I governed my impulse by the precepts of the philosophers, I did not entertain desire, I avoided only things within the compass of my will ... there is but one way to peace of mind... -- to give up what is beyond your control....

For the Stoics, acceptance of the limits on needs provides a freedom even if one's circumstances are constraining. Thus, Epictetus, the slave, states that "we must make the best of those things which are in our power." It is the willing acceptance of limits which constitute freedom for the Stoics. Thus, the external constraints placed upon us in old age need not interfere with our Stoic freedom. Most of us, especially if born and raised in affluent pleasure- loving modern democratic societies, are not able to easily accept these arguments from ancient thought. Freedom is a personal freedom of circumstances or a political freedom in which we participate in self-rule, seems essential to us, even in old age. But in light of the Hellenistic philosophers, we elderly may wish to reconsider our beliefs about freedom, since, in old age, our freedom may be more or less constrained by the realities of old age.

Some of the Hellenistic philosophers not only question the desirability of riches and the need for freedom, but also the need for meaning. In their study of mathematics and philosophy, the Hellenistic Skeptics discovered unresolvable contests over meaning – arguments pro and con which rage on without resolution. They suggested that the most that can be hoped for is some kind of gentle tranquility which comes from recognizing the balance between contending and incommensurable arguments. Such a view might be undertaken in old age since it relaxes the urgent search for truth leaving us with a skeptical peace.

Many of the Stoics, Skeptics and Epicureans, adopted a simple life. Like these ancient Hellenistic thinkers, the search for simplicity may be found throughout the tradition of America thought. The illustrative American text is Thoreau's *Walden*, which offers an account of Thoreau's life of solitude and simplicity at Walden Pond. In his meticulous essay on economy, Thoreau concludes that "most of the luxuries and many of the so-called comforts of life, are not only not indispensable, but positive hindrances to the elevation of mankind." Despite *Walden*, Thoreau's experiences, and various groups and thinkers urging the pursuit of simplicity throughout American history, these cultural attitudes toward the "simple life" and "self-sufficiency" in the United States are clearly a minority sentiment. Most of us flee from self-sufficient simplicity to embrace the privatized happiness based upon the purchase of commodities produced in our "affluent society." We elderly are no exception.

What I am suggesting is that we elderly, with reduced income, fading ambitions at the end of life, and experiencing a variety of mental and physical conditions which limit our freedom, have some good reasons to limit our needs and desires in our old age. Unfortunately, in our earlier lives, many of us developed characters with needs and desires of the affluent– desires which plague us in old age and which accentuate our dependency at the very time we lose the capacity to realize those desires.

Dependency in Old Age

Even if we minimize our wants, we elders still have real needs remaining, and we may be less able to secure such necessary goods on our own – our health fails, income lessens, our senses dull, emotions wither, friends die, and previous excellences are dimmed. We become more dependent upon others to enable us to continue functioning as human beings and citizens. *Dependency in one form or another is a central experience in most of the lives of the elderly.* We elderly may need assistance to meet our basic human needs, our desire for freedom, or our search for meaning, We may become sick, needing medicines and medical care or simply the assistance of a family member to maintain our health or carry on the routine of our very lives. Even with more subtle declines of mind and imagination, we become less able to control and manage the quality of our lives. With the infirmities of age, we may require assistance in the performance of everyday activities. And since we oldsters are less able to avoid the risks of everyday life, we may need increased protection from harms created by others.

This help and protection to the aged is not limited to the basic biological needs, but also to the needs for freedom and meaning. Even if we are compos mentis and can deliberate prudently and make sound judgments, we still may need assistance to carry out decisions in old age, i.e., to be free. . *Don Quixote needed Sancho Panza; Faust required the help of Mephistopheles; King Lear needed the help of his daughters.* In addition, to achieve meaning in our lives, we may need the help of others. If we do, there are many sources of help; we may turn to our family and friends, the church, the market place, and the state.

1. The Family and Friends

The family as the refuge for meeting the needs of the elderly has never been a satisfactory solution. To be sure, in some societies, the ancient family might have been the center of economic production, enabling it to absorb dependents. But since the rise of wage labor and, more recently the fragmentation of the family itself, many families can no longer meet the needs of "their" own elderly. Dickens' story of Nell and her grandfather, a story which takes place in an urbanizing London, illustrates the problems of dependency within the family in our modern age.

Friendship is a similarly ineffective modern remedy. The classic works suggest high expectations of friendship. Aristotle, Cicero, Aquinas, Montaigne, and Tolstoy sing the praises of friendship. Certainly, the Greek academy, the medieval monastery and teaching orders, as well as the modern communes offered a social basis for the construction of friendship. But for most of us, modern realities of individualism and mobility create a situation of limited commitments from and to friends during our lives. More important, in old age, we lose many of our friends. Few are fortunate enough to have a friend like Montaigne or his friend, Etienne de la Boetie, whom he nursed at his side at his death bed. As a consequence, Montaigne had a very high standard of friendship:

> "Our friendship has no other model than itself, and can be compared only with itself. ...I know not what quintessence of all this mixture, which having seized my whole will, led it to plunge and lost itself in his; which having seized his whole will, led it to plunge and lose itself in mine, with equal hunger...."

By his own admission, such friendships were rare and Montaigne was unable to duplicate it during his own life. Most moderns cannot hope to look to friends for significant help in old age dependency.

2. The Church

The churches have been and continue to be sources of support for some of the poor elderly. They offer this support in the context of beliefs which help to meet the needs for spiritual meaning in old age. For many of us who were nurtured and educated in a Judeo-Christian world, the Good Samaritan story of the New Testament lives in our collective unconscious. The story begins with Christ stating that we should love our neighbor. A lawyer asks Christ who is his neighbor. Christ tells the parable of a man injured by thieves on the side of the road. A Good Samaritan stops, dresses his wounds and takes him to an Inn to heal. This story seeks to epitomize the value of recognizing needs and helping the needy.

Charity touches deep chords within our heritage and this recognition finds its expression in the western canon works which spring from our Judea-Christian heritage. Augustine's *Confessions*, Aquinas's *Summa Theologica*, Dante's *The Divine Comedy*, Milton's *Paradise Lost* to name but a few. Unlike the Greek philosophers' notion of needs as the natural seeking of essential goods, the Christian tradition views needs as fundamental lacks indicating man's necessary finiteness and imperfection to be rectified by human and God's love. Perhaps the most eloquent of the canonic works recognizing human finiteness, imperfection and consequent dependency is Pascal's *Pensees* – one of which recognizes a cosmic dependency based upon Pascal's unique scientific and Christian perspective.

> "Let us, then take our compass; we are something, and we are not everything. The nature of our existence hides from us the knowledge of first beginnings which are born of Nothing; and the littleness of our being conceals from us the sight of the Infinite…. Limited as we are in every way, this state which holds the mean between two extremes is present in all our impotence… Man, for instance is related to all he knows … in short, he is in a dependent alliance with everything…."

One form of recognition of this dependent alliance is compassion, the empathetic recognition of vulnerability of the aged combined with a sense that their vulnerability is not the product of their fault and in fact, that we too are subject to such vulnerability. Such compassion is sketched eloquently in Rousseau's *Emile:*

"...It is man's weakness which makes him sociable; it is our common miseries which turn our hearts to humanity; we would owe humanity nothing if we were not men. Every attachment is a sign of insufficiency. If each of us had no need of others, we would hardly think of uniting himself with them. Thus from our very infirmity is born out frail happiness...I do not conceive how someone who needs nothing can love anything, I do not conceive how someone who loves nothing can be happy...."

Although charity and compassion are customarily viewed as forms of altruistic love, they may also be viewed as aspects of the reciprocity of the marketplace and the principle of government action.

3. The Market Place

One way of seeking to meet our old age needs is to turn to the market place to purchase the goods and services we need. Adam Smith, (like his ancient predecessors), in his *Wealth of Nations*, recognized that a natural division of labor emerges in society, growing out of differential talents and experience and leading to "truck and barter." On the assumption that elderly have financial resources, they can purchase in the market place many of the things they need, including some goods and services to facilitate their freedom. It is the lack of resources of many of the elderly – a fact noted by Marx and Simone de Beauvoir, which limits their access to a market which can supply at least some of their needs. In *Das Capital*, Marx documents the needs of the laboring classes. In *Coming of Age*, de Beauvoir documents the fact that many elderly, both in America and in the world, lack the resources to meet their basic biological needs, to support their freedom and even to permit them to engage in the search for meaning in life. And, of course, the meaning of life may not be fully attained through the marketplace.

4. The Welfare State

The Christian acceptance in humility of our limitations and a corresponding compassion has found a secular home in the modern welfare state which affirms the role of government to assist those who lack the means for meeting their basic needs. This modern welfare state results from a curious combination of the widespread modern market, its various failures in the modern age of industrialization and urbanization, (as documented by Marx and others), the spread of sympathy for its victims and the acceptance of the consequent need for government aid for these victims. However, this recognition of the role of the political community in meeting human needs was not limited to moderns. Plato and Aristotle, in their writings on ethics, politics and economics recognized that needs are to be met not only through a family's economic production and the marketplace, but also with the help of friendships and the political community. This view was echoed by the German philosopher, Hegel, who believed that the securing of necessary goods at any stage of life helps to perpetuate freedom. As Hegel viewed matters, the history of our world is both the history of the formation of the modern state *and* the expansion of freedom. For Hegel, it was the full flowering of a political community which makes individual freedom possible since it both provides protections for individuals and supplies goods to them. Since old age may diminish the individual capacity for freedom as agency – the capacity for decisions and actions on one's own, the attaining of full freedom in old age may not be possible without the support of the political community both to protect and enable us to survive and flourish, at least according to Hegel.

But it was the doctrines of the English utilitarians of the 19th century, who advocated the maximization of utility and the greatest good for the greatest number which led more immediately to the modern welfare state. Over a period of two centuries, David Hume, John Stuart Mill, Adam Smith, Maynard Keynes, William Beveridge and John Rawls recognized, either explicitly or by inference, the desirability of a basic sympathy among and between all citizens. They also recommended the steps needed to facilitate a welfare state to express that sympathy. Mill helped to extend political suffrage, Adam Smith offered ways by which the nation could grow the wealth needed to support welfare. Keynes suggested economic policies to promote full employment, Beveridge outlined the need for social insurance and John Rawls supplied the modern rationale for the justice of the welfare state. In my lifetime, I have witnessed the growth of the welfare state in the United States and other western industrialized countries, which is based upon a feeling of sympathy for all citizens. It is this welfare state which guarantees many but not all of the needs of the elderly. A state is required in order to insure sufficient production of wealth and its proper distribution.

The Limits of Government Welfare

Although the welfare state does provide basic goods for the elderly poor and many others, that state has grown in modern times into a powerful centralized bureaucracy. The phenomenon of bureaucracy was first recognized and described by the German sociologist, Max Weber in his famed book on *Economy and Society*. Weber's classic description finds bureaucracy to be a rule governed organization, with specialized offices, occupied by trained staff, conducting public functions separated from their private lives. For the elderly, such a bureaucracy delivers aid to them in an impersonal manner according to detailed rules. In doing so, such impersonal assistance may efficiently distribute money and goods, such as social security checks, but may fail to meet the recipient's other important needs of full freedom of agency and a meaning in life. A freedom of agency may require assistance flexibly fitting the specific situations – situations which are not recognized by rule-based organizations. The need for the elderly to pursue meaning in their lives may not be found in the services provided by impersonal bureaucrats.

The modern consequences of the bureaucratic supply of government assistance have other impacts as well. Reliance upon government welfare brands the recipient as "dependent". Some citizens, especially in the United States, regard elderly dependents as not worthy of assistance.

They ask: "To what extent is the elderly person who blithely fails to save for her old age and turns for help to the government "worthy" of financial assistance?" Even if the government aid is "earned" through social security, many fear that such assistance to elderly dependents may turn them into "passive recipients", i.e., dependents. This passivity may be accentuated by institutionalization of the elderly in continuing care and nursing homes. They ask: "If we choose to meet the needs of the elderly, or society chooses to meet our needs, we may be diving into a bottomless pit of need which requires immense resources? Should welfare assistance for the elderly include money for cigarettes and pipe tobacco? How about family assistance to support the upkeep of the oldster's favorite Ferrari? Finally, some fear that attempts to meet the needs of the elderly constitute or may lead to "paternalism" or, at least, "officious intermeddling", (like the protagonist of Voltaire's *Candide*, who, in his ignorant efforts to help the fair maidens being chased by apes, merely made the situation worse by killing the apes who turned out to be their lovers. Perhaps Candide's help is like some modern government welfare assistance which may encourage the breaking up and dependence of certain welfare families).

Autonomy and Dignity

The encouragement of dependency through welfare paternalism may lead to a societal failure to recognize the autonomy of the elderly and treat them with a dignity and respect which contributes to their sense of self-esteem. Even if one's dependence upon others for basic needs is recognized by government without the recognition of fault or blame, the dependent often feels a sense of shame or worthlessness. This shame may come from a sense of a loss of autonomy – loss of the control over one's decisions and the loss of dignity. Thus, *one central issue which arises with the recognition of our old age dependency is the apparent conflict between the very real growing dependency of old age and the self-esteem of the aged, based upon respect for their autonomy and dignity.*

To understand and reconcile dependency with autonomy and dignity, it is necessary once again to turn to the canon works. The notions of dignity and respect are often identified with honor – a staple of ancient Greek thought. "Honor" refers to either to the esteem granted to one by the community or oneself. Or it may connote the additional notion that the honored person is worthy of the honor. Such persons might be said to have dignity. Dignity and honor were hence closely linked, although it often was not clear whether the individual possessed dignity because he was honored or was honored because he had dignity.

New formulations of the ideal of dignity began with the recognition of autonomy and self-determination. Both ideas of autonomy and self-determination began with the Greeks; autonomy came from the Stoics who believed in the complete freedom of the will, independent of any outside influences. Self-determination was advanced by Aristotle who, while recognizing the influences of nature and habit, still believed it was possible of a person to deliberate and choose among alternative courses of action. Insofar as these freely chosen course of action were morally right, the person deliberating and action them was worthy of honor.

It was the modern Enlightenment philosophers, especially Immanuel Kant, who articulated the dimensions of autonomy. He argued that the capacity of individual to will actions which might be universalized for all and which treated persons as ends, not means. According to Kant, such universalization enabled the individual to escape from the necessity of physical laws which determined his natural desires and needs. Since Kant's time, autonomy has been defined more broadly as the individual's independent ability to make informed free choices about what should be done, freely consent to the choice made and freely determine consequent actions. Such a person was said to have dignity and deserve respect.

Obviously, our old age natural biological decline and our lessened capacity to deliberate, choose, and carry out that choice can erode our autonomy and self-determination as well. In addition, any help to the competent elderly persons, (if such help is not consented to), interferes with their informed choice about what should be done and how to do. As a consequence, it also takes away autonomy or at least some amount of self-determination. On the assumption that dignity is based upon a self-respect, which is in turn dependent upon self-determination or autonomy, any removal of these takes away the basis of self-respect and dignity.

Thus, we see that the ideal of dignity is apparently closely related to autonomy and self-respect. At the end of the last chapter and the beginning of this chapter, we saw that Oedipus had a dignity despite his dependence both upon his daughter and Theseus. The canon work which first explicitly laid out a view of dignity was Pico della Mirandola's early renaissance work *Oration on the Dignity of Man* in which he argues that God created man after all other things and, since there was no niche in which to fit him, God endowed him with the freedom to define his own identity. "Thou… shalt ordain for thyself the limits of thy nature". Hence Pico's view supplies a new dimension to the notion of dignity. Combining (with some unease) Aristotle, Kant and Pico, dignity finds its value in a uniqueness of each individual as determined by his free choices which are shaped at least in part by the satisfactory universalization of his desires. Old age and its disabilities may inhibit the continued self-sufficient realization of that uniqueness.

Love and Reciprocity

Biological decline and dependency on others may block the effort to express one's identity in old age, but a new identify which accepts decline and dependency may arise and the love and reciprocal support of others may support the expression of such an identity and a new identity may be forged. Dependency is not unique to old age. Many needs may emerge in earlier stages of life. During all the stages of our lives, we encounter serious losses; we get sick, lose friends and loved ones and leave jobs. Even without life's crises, all of us are dependent upon others at various stages of our lives. As children, we are dependent upon our parents. As students, we may depend upon teachers. As young workers, we may depend upon our colleagues and co-workers. All of these dependencies are conditioned by either love, as in the case of parental love, or reciprocity as in the case of student-teacher relationships. To be sure, these early life dependencies are transitional stages of life; childhood (hopefully) leads to adult autonomy or self-determination, students graduate with independent skills, young workers gain the needed skills and knowledge to perform on their own. As we experience these stages, many of us are not aware of our dependency in our earlier lives because it is temporary and transitional.

Recognition of dependency relationships which are part of the bonds of society are often not recognized because such dependency as such is not always valued by our culture. In the United States, with its traditions of self-reliance and individualism, we may not be conscious of how dependent we have been on others throughout our lives. Part of our dependence is also hidden within the division of labor and the market-place. Adam Smith, in his *Wealth of Nations*, recognized that the production of wealth *depends* upon the division of labor which enables us to purchase services we cannot produce ourselves. We do not view such purchases as "dependence", since our purchase such goods and services are part of reciprocal exchanges. In fact, the division of labor makes us more dependent upon others since, as we become specialized in our own labor, we may lose the capacity to produce the other goods and services we require.

Nevertheless, these dependencies of childhood, youth and early adulthood are different from the needs of old age in several ways. Old age dependencies are likely to be more permanent – lasting until death. As a consequence, dependency has a different meaning as part of the decline of age – it is tinged with a touch of loss, hopelessness and vulnerability. It is this permanent decline in the capacity of self-help which leaves us vulnerable; we are unable to rely upon ourselves to meet or eliminate the needs; we are dependent upon others. Nevertheless, despite such dependency, many of us elderly seek to hold onto our autonomy and dignity as long as possible. We may be able to retain our decision making capacity until our last days and hence we can retain the basic requirements of dignity – the exercise of choice through reason and the capacity to express and follow that choice. As long as we retain that reason and the capacity of choice, we can accept our necessary dependence in dignity.

Unfortunately old age decline, especially mental decline, may even remove the capacity to reason and express one's choice and hence seriously eroding our dignity. The canon authors have faced up to this dilemma in two ways. One way is to modify the very notion of the charity given to the dependent elderly; the other is to modify the notion of dignity itself. The canon makes quite clear in such works as those of St. Thomas Aquinas (and others) that charity is a form of love. The analysis of love in the canon (Robert Hazo, *The Idea of Love*), reveals that a least one notion found in the literature is that love (or charity) may be regarded as simply a benevolent self-interested tendency (desire) towards another without making any judgment about the value or worth of the loved one. Without the need for judgment, the act of charity does not require the recipient to meet any standards of capability. Similarly, the notion of dignity has been modified, (Kateb, *Human Dignity*), to apply not only to the characteristics of humanity, (such as the exercise of reason), but also the "existential" aspects of an individual, i.e. their individual identity as expressed in all aspects of their lives. This "existential" dignity seems most appropriate to the aged who have forged their identity throughout their lives. Erich Fromm, in his *Art of Loving*, has grasped both notions of love as a tendency without judgment and existential dignity. As he suggests: "...the desire for interpersonal fusion is the most powerful striving in man...[we call] love ...the mature answer to the problem of existence...mature love is union under the condition of preserving one's integrity, one's individuality."

Taking language from Robert Hazo's *The Idea of Love*, I have labeled such charity towards the dependent aged "self-interested" only in the sense that, at the same time that it seeks to benefit the recipient, it provides a mutual benefit, since both the giver and the recipient are joined in the mutual fate, and either sooner or later, both will encounter decline and dependency in old age. A recent description of such a loss is John Bayley's *Elegy for Iris*, the loving story of his beloved wife, Iris Murdock, the modern English philosopher, who contracted

Alzheimer's disease and was gradually reduced to the stage of watching "telly tubby" – a children's cartoon show on TV. During her decline, her changed condition did not remove Bayley's love for her. In her final stages, his love for the residue of her aged self was the last noble response to her dependency. At such a time, the dependent aged receives dignity as a gift - given by others.

Conclusion: Dependency on the Classics

There is one kind of continual dependency which I am recommending in this book – the dependency upon the canon and the heritage of thought it embodies. It is this canon which can yield the "transcendence" which Faust sought in his bargain with Mephistopheles. Such a dependency rests upon reading and reflection about great works – an activity in which some elderly, especially those who are at advanced age, cannot or will not engage. Most of us, unlike Augustine who read upon his death bed, will probably not be able to pursue reading to the very end. But at least some of the arguments and ideas of great works can remain with us during most of our old age. And hopefully we can meditate upon these. In Montaigne's words:

> "...Meditation is a powerful and full study for anyone who knows how to examine and exercise himself vigorously... Nature has favored it with this privilege, that there is nothing we can do so long, and no action to which we can devote ourselves more commonly and easily. It is the occupation of the gods, says Aristotle, from which springs their happiness and ours."

Reading and meditation will not meet our basic needs and may, at best, have only an indirect effect upon our free agency, but they may help to provide meaning for our lives, indeed, perhaps even alternative meanings for our lives in our old age at least until we can no longer engage in them. It is the final dependency with dignity.

CHAPTER XVIII

The Abandonment of Faith in Progress

"…nature has set no term to the perfection of human faculties; the perfectibility of man is truly indefinite…" Condorcet -*The Progress of the Human Mind*

"…'That is well said' replied Candide, 'but we must cultivate our garden.'" Voltaire - *Candide*

I reached adulthood in the 1950's when American economic and political power was at peak. The Midwest of the United State, where I spent my youth, reveled in the growth of national prosperity. The slaughter of the first and second world wars was quickly being forgotten and even the experience of the brutal Korean War did not cast a shadow on the optimism of our nation. With parents who had worked their way up to achieve professional status and modest comfort, I, like my brothers and sisters, was expected to attend college and "succeed" so I attended college and law school, married, had children and proceeded to live the American dream. As prior chapters in this book indicate, I committed myself to urban development, anti-poverty, environmental and liberal education causes, (without unduly sacrificing my own and my family's prosperity). In my life, I had every reason to believe in the smooth inevitability of progress. But, towards the end of the twentieth century, I began to doubt the reality of both historical progress and my own smug efforts at moral improvement.

In the   late twentieth and early twenty-first century, our nation appeared to triumph over the USSR in the cold war, but this victory left a bitter taste as new world enemies arose. Despite the growth in world income in the latter half of the twentieth century, billions of people remained in poverty. The scourge of AID's spread in Africa and Asia. At home, despite rising affluence, economic inequality has deepened. Despite a myriad of education programs, there remain deep questions about the quality and justice of that education. In my old age, a mild pessimism has taken hold of me. Reviewing the reform ventures I had undertaken, I find that the modern city remains broken, poverty and discrimination linger, and, despite some new controls of pollution, the environment faces not only the continuation of past pollution, but the environmental harms of unrestricted growth and the threat of a new environmental catastrophe, global warming. In short, the recent events of the world and America offer weak evidence for belief in historical progress. Along with newly acquired historical pessimism, I have grown increasingly pessimistic about my own moral and intellectual "progress" during my life and into old age. My past belief in the possibility of "improvement" had depended largely upon a faith in education and participation in a variety of efforts to "do good". In my old age, I have begun to take a more jaundiced view both of my education and the projects I have promoted. To be sure, I am blessed with a marvelous wife and successful children and grandchildren, and I continue to reside in the United States- a world of modern affluence, and perhaps that is enough. But such blessings hardly constitute the personal and historical progress I once hoped for many years ago, I now find myself embracing a conservatism which focuses upon cherishing and protecting the present goods found in our lives.

Introduction

Among the many losses in our old age, a less recognized loss is the abandonment of a belief in progress in history and the ideal of the unlimited individual development of human capacities. Such an abandonment flies in the face of our faith in progress inherited from the 18th century

Enlightenment. That faith has been boldly articulated by the 18th century French "philosophe", Nicolas de Condorcet, who like many of the Enlightenment thinkers, was an enthusiast for progress. His *Sketch for the Historical Picture of the Progress of the Human Mind,* which marked the culmination of the Enlightenment period, described the inevitable betterment of society and human nature, fueled by science and education. The optimistic belief in individual moral and intellectual improvement accompanied the Enlightenment belief in historical progress. Faith in one's own personal progress – specifically one's continuous intellectual and moral improvement over a lifetime – although articulated in the Enlightenment era in the works of Diderot and Condorcet - has the more venerable heritage originating with ancient Greece. The belief in moral improvement was best captured at an earlier stage of human history – with the ancient Greek ideal of "paideia" which viewed education as guided by the molding of a human character and the development of intellectual capacities in accordance with ideals of virtue and rationality.

In an ultimate irony, Condorcet was almost jailed by his comrades, the French revolutionaries for whom he spoke and apparently died from his hiding in anticipation of the guillotine). Despite Condorcet's fate, his halcyon period of intellectual history in the 18th century, helped to shape the culture of modernity and the 20th century world of America. In regard to the aging, Condorcet envisaged the future welfare state when he predicted a future in which old age misery, "can, in great part be eradicated by guaranteeing people in old age a means of livelihood produced partly by their own savings, and partly by the savings of others who make the same outlay but who die before they need to reap the reward". Social security!

The Elderly Loss of Faith in Progress

Despite this strong cultural commitment to progress inherited from Condorcet and others, we elderly find the abandonment of belief in history's necessary march of human improvement to be quite natural.

As we reflect upon the history of the past century with its trail of wars, genocides and natural disasters, and we think our own past failed projects and disappointed hopes for our community and nation, we cannot help feeling at least some disappointment or even a deep pessimism about our future prospects. We may reject not only the perhaps naïve belief in the necessity of progress, but also the more reasonable belief that, if people desire it, they can reshape history, whether through political revolution, technological breakthroughs or mass education.

Our old age pessimism is not merely a symptom of our failing state; it has deep historical roots. The ancients would agree with such pessimism. The Greek, Roman and early Christian philosophers, poets and historians all proposed a different picture of history – one which, at best, exhibited a cycle of progress and regress, at worst, simply a tragic regression from a golden age. Thus, some interpreters of Thucydides' *History of the Peloponnesian War* found it to be a tragic account of Athenian hubris and nemesis. A later poem by the Epicurean poet, Lucretius, *The Nature of Things,* begins and ends with the Athenian plague! Even Augustine, who envisaged salvation in another world, witnessed and documented the cruelties of early Rome and its later collapse, refusing to let the Christians take the blame for the ensuing chaos. These ancients, whether Greek or Roman, had seen enough historical disasters to avoid being unduly optimistic about the course of history.

As for individual improvement as opposed to historical progress, Werner Jaeger, in his classic three volume work, *Paideia, the development of individual excellence* sketched how paideia was expressed in the art, poetry, drama and philosophy of ancient Greece. Perhaps the best known example of such paideia is Plato's account of the education of the guardians in the *Republic.* But other forms of paideia were articulated by the philosopher Aristotle and the rhetorician, Isocrates, and Jaeger included the Greek poets, such as Hesiod and the playwrights, such as Sophocles and Euripides as part of the formidable force for the education of the Greeks. If Jaeger had continued his study to embrace Rome, he might have included the works of the Roman orators, Cicero and Quintilian. In short, the commitment to individual moral and intellectual improvement was a central preoccupation for the ancients.

(Not all the Greeks were entranced by the possibilities of paideia. One of the most delightful plays of the age, *The Clouds,* was penned by the comic playwright, Aristophanes, who made fun of the academy which he labeled Socrates' "Thoughtery" in which its pupils escaped from doing useful work, learning how to make the worse argument the better. The upshot of the play is that after the failure of the elderly father as a student, the son enrolls, turns into a pale intellectual, and then defeats and beats his old father and threatens to beat his mother as well!)

Even when the Greeks praised paideia, they did not seriously contemplate the implications of such an ideal for elders, perhaps because, at that time, old age was so rare or perhaps because they recognized that old age marked a decline from the realization of such an ideal. As a consequence, many of the ancient Greek works did not respect the elderly. For example, the early Greek poet, Hesiod, when he proposed three great ages of mankind, identified the old people with the lowest level Iron Age since the color of their hair matched the metal! In other works he documented their vulnerability and ill-treatment. Thus, if the Greeks embraced paideia, they also questioned whether paideia or human improvement would extend over an entire lifetime.

Aristophanes' skepticism of the value of education is echoed through the centuries. Francois Rabelais in his *Gargantua and Pantagruel,* made fun of the students from the country who learned pretentious Latinized words at their Paris school. Rousseau predictably concluded that "… in the midst of philosophy, and civilization…we have nothing to show for ourselves….Montaigne wrote essays on pedantry and concludes in his long essay, *Apology for Raymond Sebond* that "man's knowledge cannot make him happy". For the aged, perhaps the best example is Goethe's *Faust,* in his library, finding no satisfaction with all his scholarly knowledge which simply smothers the springs of life and yields neither wisdom nor honor. To be sure, none of these nor many other authors disparage all kinds and amounts of learning, and few, except perhaps Erasmus's ambiguous *In Praise of Folly,* actually praise ignorance and vice for their own sake. But the many works making fun of education suggest that the abuses of learning and its detrimental consequences were common through the ages and these descriptions of the abuses tarnish the shining image of paideia.

Despite the rich history of disparagement of education, we moderns shared with the enlightenment philosophes, a faith in the benefits of education. Until recently, we also shared with the Greeks and others the notion that education is not a venture for the aged. Therefore, it is little wonder that the aged themselves do not envisage their own "improvement" as a necessary project for old age. Although they may enjoy cultural events or sporadic educational ventures, until recently, they have doubted the project of human improvement for the aged. The experiences of biological decline, the sense of a shrinking future, the growing dependence upon others and proximity of death, cement a pessimism regarding projects of personal improvement. This pessimism is based upon the unspoken assumption that personal improvement is a young person's game.

For similar reasons, since the time of the Greeks, little if any mention is made of the moral development or educational improvement of the aged in the ethical writings in western thought. Those theorists like Aristotle who believed in the acquisition of virtue through the development of thoughtful habits, the character was formed by the arrival of adulthood, and old age was an afterthought. For ethical theorists like Immanuel Kant, the pure will which animates the "ethical categorical imperative" to guide our actions could operate at any age and was independent of age related circumstances. The utilitarian ethic introduced by John Stuart Mill, (and his father), viewed our actions as informed by pleasure and pains- a calculus of which might be made by any person of adult age. For these theorists, attention to old age as such is not a central concern for pursuing the good life. In short, we can begin with the sobering conclusion that, whether ignored or denigrated by education and moral theory, we in old age can abandon these disciplines which have little use for us. More important, we can abandon the underlying faith in progress and individual development which these disciplines are based upon.

If one assumes that in old age, the faith in historical progress and paideia wanes, what is lost? Perhaps a definition of progress will help us identify the loss. "Progress" is the gradual but steady march towards perfection, whether in morals, knowledge, or simply the circumstances for living a good life. We who live in communities and nations devoted to progress participate in their hopes and efforts generated by devotion to such progress. Even if we do not believe such progress to be inevitable, we still feel optimistic that our free choices will make things better over time. We may share with others some common destination to which we are headed. And we may welcome the passage of time as it measures the march toward that destination; time which passes as part of progress is hardly time lost; it is time well spent!

These characteristics of progress are illustrated well in the American Creed. America is a nation founded on a commitment to progress, as the Preamble of our Constitution confirms. This nation bears a history animated by a sense of manifest destiny. The French visitor to America in 1831-32, Alexis de Tocqueville, reported his observations on American progress in *Democracy in America,* written a half century after his countryman, Condorcet had sketched the pattern of human progress for all mankind. According to de Tocqueville, United States inherited Enlightenment values in the form of the settlers' deep belief in America's destiny as God's "city on the hill"; its' colonists quickly embraced belief in the inevitable movement towards the growth and equalization of "economic condition" and democracy. (In an irony of history, many years later, de Tocqueville found that his earlier worry that American might succumb to a centralization of political and economic power was echoed in France, where a centralization of power in France continued despite the revolution). America's continued commitment to economic growth, along with a perhaps naïve belief in the perfection of democracy continues to animate the American public. This commitment is accompanied by a deep belief in education as the vehicle to individual improvement has accompanied America's belief in general progress throughout her history. This belief was simply the latest version of paideia in western thought.

Given the definition of progress and its objects, as illustrated by the American ideal of progress, we can now see how serious the old age abandonment of belief in progress might be.

Lost is the sharing of a community's hope, optimism, destiny and simply the sense that "time is on our side". Insofar as we seniors are American and have, in our past lives, shared in the peculiar brand of American optimism, if we abandon belief in progress in our hour of need, we may abandon hope for America's presumed march toward equality and democracy. And, if we abandon paideia, we abandon the hope for individual moral improvement along with the hope for historical progress. Such pessimism is a serious business!

The Emotional Consequences of Losing the Ideals of Progress and Paideia

The rejection of the ideals of progress and educational advancement is linked to old age. In our youth we are optimistic participants in our society's pursuit of shared ideals. Middle age is often a time of waning ideals. In old age, if we abandon belief in progress and paideia, in doing so, we alienate ourselves not only from our fellow citizens who are in different stages of their lives, but also from our younger selves. Since, in the past, these optimistic beliefs gave meaning to our lives, our abandonment of them in old age and the consequent alienation threatens us with a deep sense of meaninglessness and normlessness, that is, a lack of structured beliefs to guide our actions. To be sure, some elderly, whether out of habit or conscious commitment, refuse to give up their belief in progress even in the face of the lessons they have received from the aging process. They will reassert their optimism and extend it, by defining the aged as lucky recipients of the benefits of modern technological medicine or as beneficiaries of a new period of old age delight. I have argued against these views in earlier chapters. Many aged may continue to vote (to protect interests and reaffirm earlier beliefs), but, at the same time, they begin a quiet withdrawal from active participation in projects of community and self- improvement.

The feeling of old age alienation is compounded by a sadness arising from beholding a disappointing history which lies at the heart of an abandonment of belief in progress - a different history from de Tocqueville's sunny perspective. This "other history" was advanced by other classics with a much more sobering view. For example, the German philosopher, Georg Hegel, (while still retaining his own brand of optimism), wrote in his *Philosophy of History*:

> "…when we look at this display of passions [in history] and the consequences of their violence; the unreason which is associated not only with them, but even…with good designs and righteous aims; when we see the evil, the vice, the ruin that has befallen the most flourishing kingdoms which the mind of man of man ever created; we can scarce avoid being filled with sorrow…. the miseries that have overwhelmed the noblest of nations and politics and the finest exemplars of private virtue, - form a picture of most fearful aspect and excites emotions of the profoundest and most hopeless sadness, counterbalanced by no consolatory result.

The industrial revolution following on the heels of Hegel's reflections, as described by Marx in *Das Capital,* ripped away any optimistic illusions and replace them with a vivid portrait of the miserable lives of the mass of workers. Since Marx, modern authors, such as Simone de Beauvoir have documented the impact of industrialization on the very lives of the aged. The easy optimism of the 18th century Enlightenment was further obliterated by two world wars and other disasters of the 20th century. Jonathan Glover, in his devastating *Humanity* documents these disasters, including the Holocaust, Hiroshima, the Gulag, Cambodia, Yugoslavia, Rwanda and others. For those who retain faith, at least in the progress of technology, it is worth noting that some of these disasters, such as the Holocaust and Hiroshima, were aided by the applications of modern industrial methods and perverse applications of scientific technology. These events called into question the faith in progress by means of the march of science and technology. It was the work of twentieth century philosopher, Jacques Ellul, in *The Technological Society* and succeeding works which has described a world increasingly dominated not only by technology but also by technological thought and its products.

If Enlightenment optimism was lost in the history of the industrial and technological revolutions of the 19th and 20th centuries, as well as the wars and genocide in the 20th century, to be replaced by a profound sadness, such sadness is reinforced in the pages of twentieth century poetry and novels, especially in the era during and following the First World War. Any optimism disappeared, along with Hans Castorp, who vanished into the First World War at the end of Thomas Mann's novel, *The Magic Mountain*. Most of the novels and poems of this era carry an ambience of gloom. The poetry of Rupert Brook, Wilfred Owen and Siegfried Sassoon capture the brutal realities of the trenches and respond to these realities sometimes with a comic irony, The English poet, Wilfred Owen reminded his readers what the front line was like in *Arms and the Boy:*

> "If you could hear at every jolt, the blood
> Come gargling from the froth-corrupted lungs,
> Obscene as cancer, bitter as the cud
> Of Vile, incurable sores on innocent tongues."

Other novels of the times carried similar messages, but often from the perspective of the home front. Thus, Virginia Woolf, in *Mrs. Dalloway* describes how a soldier's suicide pierces the civilian indifference symbolized by Mrs. Dalloway's party; in *Jacob's Room*, Jacobs' absence from his room is sufficient to reveal not only his death in the war but the continuing presence of the war. More brutal descriptions can be found

If descriptions of the pain and suffering of war can destroy the reader's faith in historical progress, comparable accounts can be found of the failure of moral improvement in the modern novels. One of many examples is James Joyce's *Portrait of an Artist as a Young Man* – the semi-autobiographical story of Stephen Dedalus, an Irish child and boy, growing up in Dublin. His country, his school, and his Church all sought to "contribute" to his moral development and he offers a devasting critique of all three. In the end, he declares his independence, leaving his family and church, refusing more schooling, to migrate abroad with the famous concluding words of the novel, "Welcome, o Life! I go to encounter for the millionth time the reality of experience and to forge in the smithy of my soul the uncreated conscience of my race." Joyce chooses the individual freedom of artistic pursuit rather than moral development as his goal.

Whether it be the story of James Joyce's alter-ego, Stephen Dedalus, who rejected the moral upbringing of his family, church and school, or Proust's *Swann In Love*, who, at the end of his love, exclaimed 'with the old intermittent caddishness which reappeared in him when he was no longer unhappy and his moral standards dropped accordingly: "To think that I've wasted years of my life, that I've longed to die, that I've experienced my greatest love of a woman who didn't appeal to me, who wasn't even my type!"' or Fitzgerald's Gatsby, whom the narrator, Nick Caraway, after complimenting Gatsby as "worth the whole damn bunch put together" (referring to Gatsby's rich acquaintances), reflectively added: "It was the only compliment I ever gave him, because I disapproved of him from beginning to end..." Nick then remembered Gatsby at first meeting when "the lawn and drive had been crowded with the faces of those who guessed at his corruption – and he had stood on those steps, concealing his incorruptible dream, as he waved them good-by." These stories of the rejection of a conventional morality in favor of artistic freedom, the fading capacity to love an unappealing woman, and the incorruptible dream of a corruptible man are hardly novels praising "moral development", in part, perhaps because their authors had learned that the ideal of moral development is indeed most complicated in our modern age.)

If alienation and sadness follow the abandonment of progress, the core disposition is a profound pessimism, the feeling that not only will the processes of history and paideia fail to produce perfectibility in society and individuals, but, instead, will deliver misfortune and misery. This feeling of pessimism found expression in many works of the classics – Blaise Pascal's *Pensées*, Voltaire's *Candide*, Albert Camus's *The Myth of Sisyphus* and George Santayana's *Domination and Powers*. These philosophers suggest that pessimism is not a disembodied and vague feeling but is based upon the practical recognition of the contingencies of life as well as the necessities of nature, the evils which they create and the tragic lack of political, economic, and personal resources to control these evils.

These evils may be diffuse, such as disease, poverty, pollution, ugliness, hate, ignorance as well as the losses encountered in old age. In the previous chapters of this book, where we have documented other old age losses. These diffuse harms are less visible than the intense often uncontrollable natural catastrophes and large-scale human cruelty highlighted in written histories. The canon has offered major works dealing with each of these latter harms. To take but one example, when the earthquake in Lisbon took place in the 18th century, Voltaire penned his *Candide*, the story of an optimist who, after encountering both natural disasters and human cruelty concluded that withdrawal to cultivate his garden was the proper solution.

Pessimism may not rest upon an observation of events in history. The 19th century German philosopher, Schopenhauer, who has been the preeminent spokesperson for pessimism, both in his *The World as Will and Idea* and in his entertaining essays, argues that we are all touched by a human condition which warrants pessimism. For this philosopher, pessimism is a fundamental condition of humanity; humans, by their very nature, pursue unsatisfiable desires often at the expense of others leading to their harm. This basic conditions is confirmed by the conflict and suffering found everywhere in a world. Schopenhauer counsels his reader to accustom himself *to* a life filled with misery and regulate limit his expectations accordingly. For this German philosopher, the only solution for living with such pessimism is either to enter the world of art or undertake the life of an ascetic which promises the control of human desire. These harms are evils often not subject to human control in part because they may be the result of uncontrollable human desire. The illusory progress of history and the education of individuals will not guarantee their control and hence it is appropriate that everyone, not only elders, lower their expectations and abandon faith in progress and paideia. Based upon this account, it is especially appropriate to be pessimistic in old age since the aged are especially vulnerable.

Detaching from Beliefs in Progress and Paideia

In Chapter III, I have suggested three approaches to detachment in old age – a social, imaginative and intellectual detachment. Social detachment involves the social withdrawal of the elderly from society. Hence, one means of detachment in the face of abandoned hopes for historical progress and moral improvement is a social withdrawal from participation in projects which find their justification in the promotion of progress and personal improvement. Old age projects are to be undertaken, if at all, only with the understanding that progress is not likely to occur from them. Perhaps, as Voltaire had maintained in *Candide*, gardening is such a project, since it is often pursued for its own sake! (I have suggested other "auto-telic" projects in my discussion of retirement above.) Similarly the aged might properly withdraw from projects for "self-improvement".

The withdrawal from such projects is the tacit acknowledgement that any expectation of such progress or improvement is mistaken. Such withdrawal might seem outrageous to many. Thus, even the ancient biographer, Plutarch wrote an essay entitled: *Whether an Old Man Should Engage in Public Affairs* answering that they should!) However, resisting such withdrawal from such projects is based upon a confusion between expectations and hopes. The abandonment of expectations of projects promising progress and self-improvement is based upon the *realistic expectations* regarding such projects; such withdrawal need not eliminate the hopes for such progress for one's community and loved ones. It is this difficult combination of lowered expectation, while continuing to retain hope which lies at the heart of social detachment.

The second kind of withdrawal from the loss of the ideals of progress lies in the imaginative recreation of alternative patterns of history and individual ways of life. The historical works of classics reveal a portrayal of vastly differing patterns of history. Some authors suggest that history betrays a regressive pattern. The ancient poet, Hesiod, in his famed *Works and Days,* sets forth an account of the ages of man which begins with a golden age and ends with an iron one, filled with discord and injustice. As mentioned above, one of the most remarkable historians to see history as a tragedy was the Greek historian, Thucydides. Writing a contemporaneous history of the Peloponnesian war, between Athens and Sparta, (and her allies), the old Thucydides, (who had been a general in the war and had been fired), wrote the detailed story of the rise of the Athenian Empire, its desire to dominate its neighbors in order to impose its remarkable culture, followed by a series of war time losses, the plague, internal dissensions, and foolish expeditions. Athens was ultimately defeated and soon thereafter occupied by her old enemy, Persia. It was only in his old age that Thucydides was able to view and write about the tragic denouement of Athenian power. More than two thousand years later, the regressive direction of history is once again embraced by the Enlightenment philosophe, Voltaire, who, as we recounted above, tells the story of Candide, an optimist naïf, who, following Leibniz's philosophy, initially believed that this was the best of all possible worlds. In his adventures, he encountered only disaster and evil, which eventually forced him to retreat and "cultivate his garden". This story, told in the shadow of the Lisbon earthquake, was hardly a story on behalf of historical progress. In short, although there was a strong tradition of belief in historical progress stemming from the 18th century, there were already signs from its most prominent philosophers and historians that historical progress may have its limits. In the same century as Voltaire,,Edward Gibbon would document the decline of the Roman Empire. More recent philosophers, scientists, and historians project a similar regression. Bertrand Russell, (philosopher), James Jeans,(scientist) and Henry Adams, (historian) project a gloomy future based upon the workings of nature. In Russell's words:

> "...the whole temple of Mans' achievement must inevitably be
> Buried beneath the debris of the universe in ruins...."

Another pattern of history is cyclical. Many of the ancients embraced a notion of cosmogenic cycles of history in which human history mirrors the cycles of the universe. In the words of Porphyry:

> "...the soul is immortal; next, that it changes into other kinds
> Of living things; also, that events recur in certain cycles, and
> That nothing is ever really new...."

Belief in such cosmic cycles is not unique to the ancients. Nietzsche, in upholding eternal recurrence has Zarthustra say:

> "Now do I die and disappear... I will come again with this sun, with this eagle, with this serpent, not to a new life, or a better life... to this identical and self-same life...."

Even if moderns are not able to embrace cosmic cycles, (since we moderns do not believe the physical workings of the cosmos are tied to particular workings of human history), a persuasive modern argument has been made for anthropogenic cycles in which the human history of civilizations betray cyclical patterns. Arnold Toynbee, the great historian of the 20th century, has documented the cyclical pattern of twenty-five such civilizations in human history in his *The Study of History.* From this point of view, the apparent progress or regress of specific times in history is subsumed in a broader cycle of the rise and fall of civilizations. Entertaining such an alternative view of history, whether appealing to the changes in the cosmos or not, can certainly produce a detachment from the blind commitment to progress in history.

A third approach to detaching oneself from the losses implicit in the abandonment of history's progress and human paideia is through intellectual analysis and abstraction. Fortunately, the classics helps with such intellectual detachment by suggesting that the original notion of a pattern of historical and moral development is illusory and hence nothing is lost in old age but illusion. As we have seen above, many of the canon's writings succeed in raising questions about the truth of any naive faith in society's historical progress and individual moral development and raise profound questions about the very possibility of a historical knowledge which assumes patterns of order in history. Thus, Karl Popper, in his *Poverty of Historicism,* argues that we cannot predict the course of history by rational or scientific method. Some classic works go further to suggest that there is, in reality, no pattern in history. The epochs of history are so radically different that they are not comparable. Furthermore, they suggest that any effort to find such a pattern is merely the assertion of subjective preferences. Thus, the German historian, Jacob Burckhardt, writing the mid-1800's, argues that progress "is an optical illusion" and "our assumption that we live in the age of moral progress is supremely ridiculous."

Just as there are doubts about historical progress through the ages, there are doubts about the possibility of the moral improvement of man. The ancient Greek Pyrrhonian skeptics, by means of arguments on both sides of any question, sought to produce suspended judgments, and thus refused to promote any moral theories. "Progress" for them, was the internal quietude which would result from such a suspension of opinion. An even more radical approach was taken by the ancient Cynics who sought, without a system of thought or particular goal, simply to "deface" the conventional moral and intellectual beliefs of society. These doubts of the skeptic and cynic regarding the possibility of individual moral improvement, can also be found in less extreme form in both Plato and Aristotle's accounts of the good life. Both philosophers accept, (for different reasons), the permanent reality of moral vice and incontinence, at least for some. A similar pessimistic assessment of the possibility of moral progress for everyone can be drawn from Christian views of original sin. During the Enlightenment, in the midst of the era of optimism, the French encyclopedist Diderot penned in his classic, *Rameau's Nephew* a marvelous portrait of a happy conniving psychopath, who rejected the usual progressive virtues. The modern age brought in its wake, Friedrich Nietzsche's "death of god", Freud's unconscious death instinct, and the "absurdity" of life allegedly discovered by modern existentialism, all of which do not offer grounds for optimism about the prospects of individual moral improvement. Now, in the early 21ˢᵗ century, we are offered dismal visions of a post-industrial, post-modern society which do not even pretend to describe "progress".

The detached recognition of the illusion of historical progress and the limited prospects of one's moral development – is deepened by the experience of old age. Today, many elderly are no longer committed belief in the triumph of historical progress nor do they readily accept "paideia" projects to crown their old age lives nor do they anticipate further moral or intellectual improvement in old age. Popular lore often accords wisdom to the aged, (but such a wisdom, if it really exists, results from the experience of living, not from a systematic effort at self-improvement in old age). Aside from such "natural wisdom", old age is deemed to be a time not only when historical optimism wanes but when the possibility of moral improvement fades.

There are some obvious reasons why old age brings a loss of faith in historical progress and moral improvements. In old age, one can reflect upon one's successes and failures against a wider historical canvass. That canvass is bound to reveal, at best, a checkered history of sporadic triumphs and defeats. A similar sense of loss can be found when one reviews one's own life and the lives of many others. The effects of withdrawal from colleagues in retirement, the physical decline which takes place, the eclipse of the past, the contraction of future time, the growth of dependence upon others all contribute to the difficulty of leading a life of moral self-improvement. The canon supplies many examples of old philosophers, historians, and statesmen taking stock of their lives – Augustine, in his *Confessions* and later *Retractions;* Cicero, in his essays *On Old Age* and Friendship; Seneca, in his *Moral Essays* and letters; Montaigne, in his later *Essays,* Edward Gibbon's *Autobiography,* Rousseau's *Confessions* and *Reveries,* Jefferson's *Autobiography,* and Henry Adams' *The Education of Henry Adams,* to name but a few. Few of these authors boast about their moral development in old age. The are more like the ancient Roman Stoic and politician, Seneca, who admits: "I am not wise nor…shall I ever be. Require me not to be equal to the best, but better than the worst. I am satisfied if every day, I reduce my vices and reprove my errors…" After other observations about the need to "harmonize talk with life", he ruefully admits that only the wise man can play the role of the man; the rest of us slip from one character to another". Ultimately, Seneca's boss, the Roman Emperor Nero, turned on him, (as well as the other philosophers in Rome), and Seneca and his wife killed themselves to avoid suffering a worse fate.

In short, the classic works help us to detach ourselves in old age from our faith in progress and old age cements the detachment. These works, by questioning the validity of historical progress and individual moral improvement, free us from a naïve commitment to such beliefs in progress and improvement. In so doing, such works offer the means for detaching ourselves from the abyss of historical pessimism and moral nihilism. Once one finds that a naïve faith in historical progress and individual development is not justified, the old age experience of feeling a loss of belief in such tenets is no longer an occasion of melancholy.

This abandonment need not destroy the understanding of history. Charles Van Doren's *Annals of America* offers another view of history which is appealing to me and offers a substitute approach to the problem of abandonment of faith in historical progress. His *Annals* set forth the printed raw materials of the chronicles of American history along with a narrative. But more important, the *Annals* offer a conspectus which identifies twenty-five themes, ideas, or issue which are relevant to that chronicle and an outline of the architecture of those ideas. Then, references to the historical materials are organized in terms of these ideas and their outlines. Thus, in Whitehead's words, one can see the ideas "ingressing" into history. One of those themes is a version of belief in progress in American terms: "national destiny". The Conspectus offers a brief overview essay and a detailed outline of "manifest destiny" with appended references to the historical materials. But the important conclusion is that this notion of progress is only one of twenty-five themes and hence one can gain a perspective on the relative significance of belief in progress in light of the other themes and their history. *In short, progress does not form the pattern of history but is only one idea among many which make up that history. Hence, the loss of the belief in progress is the loss of only one small part of the architecture of ideas which form our history.*

Consolation

The classic works not only help us detach from the sadness and alienation experience as we give up our faith in progress. These works also suggest other consolations which can be taken for the old age loss of faith in historical progress. One kind of consolation described above is the placing of loss in a broader context. For example, as we have seen above, selected classic works place the abandonment of progress into the broader perspective of history as cyclical. From the view of history as cyclical, one can view the momentary moments of history, whether progress, regress or neither as part of the cycles of history. Such cyclical histories may be peculiarly consoling since even if one is witnessing decline during one's life time, the cycles promise an upswing at a later date. In this regard, cycles operate like a religious afterlife, soothing the pains of the present life through hopes for the future.

The classics also helps us to find substitutes for the old age loss of hope for the future, whether in history or one's personal life. These substitutes are found in values which can be realized in the present and are not dependent upon further historical progress or personal improvement. From this point of view, each of the values to which historians of progress and educational advancement claim will advance in the future, may be enjoyed, indeed cherished, in the present activities of life. Rather than spinning one's wheels promoting increase in further wealth, the elderly might well enjoy the wealth he or she has. Rather than promoting schemes for the further improvement of education, the senior might simply read a good book, listen to music, or write a poem. Rather than promoting reforms of our government, elders might simply celebrate the government which protects and supports them. Such a viewpoint is profoundly conservative. It betrays a skepticism towards current reforms, honors existing traditions, savors friendships and family loves, and retains a quiet pessimism about the possibility of improvement in our lives. Such a conservative viewpoint is a good substitute for the abandoned belief in historical progress.

CHAPTER XIX

Death in Old Age

We perceive duration as a stream against which we cannot go. It is the foundation of our being and as we feel, the very substance of the world in which we live – Henri Bergson

All the metaphysical problems of form and substance, matter and the soul, of continuity and discontinuity of nature, which appear in the analysis of life, become more intense in the understanding of death. – M. Adler

Now that I am eighty-eight years old, I face the proximity of death. I have completed a living will with "no resuscitation orders", leaving my body to be cremated. I am revising my will and beginning to think about a cemetery stone. Neither I nor my late wife gave much practical thought to dying, (at least until I began to write this chapter — the one chapter that I sought to delay as long as possible!). Our parents, most of our brothers and sister, and some of our friends have died. I surreptitiously scan the obituaries each day. When I find someone I know, I secretly say to myself quietly: "well, I outlived him!" As the Stoics would add, "you're next".

My late wife and I differed about death, and sometimes I wonder whether this difference masked a deep difference about life as well. I read about death, think about it, and regard it to be an important event in one's

life, although I'm not quite sure why it is important. In old age, each twinge or pain suggests to me the possible onset of death, although I do not indulge unduly in old age talk about this or that pain or illness. My wife was not concerned with death, perhaps because she was more involved in life than I am. Perhaps she approached death through living her life fully, while I contemplate future non-being.

Since the pains of dying are difficult to imagine, the loss of consciousness seems banal, the end of one's life seems to be simply an end of life. The notion of one's non-being is difficult to understand. Perhaps, as I have learned from the recent death of my wife and my best friend, personal grief for others is deeply painful but perhaps temporary. Consequently, it is difficult for me to say anything meaningful about death. Yet, my beloved canon of classical works is filled with scenes and thoughts of death — Picasso's painting of Guernica, Michelangelo's statute of the Pieta, my favorite Faure requiem, Thomas Mann's Death in Venice, Beckett's Waiting for Godot *and many others. Philosophers especially seem to relish arcane discussions of the topic and recently, doctors and biologists are getting into the act. Perhaps, with their help, I can find permanent truths about death. Or not.*

Introduction.

The nearness of death in old age makes it a suitable topic for old age meditation. Death is the ultimate loss establishing the end of old age, but it is also present during old age. During old age, many friends, relatives and loved ones die. Well-known historical figures who are our contemporaries die. The presence of death lies behind (or in front of!) many of the losses we experience in old age. Biological decline leads to death, dependency in old age signals the approach of death, and limits on our old age future are set by death. Death also has more practical implications for old age, since it is a time that we begin to make arrangements for legacies and cemetery space. These arrangement may include serious considerations of suicide or euthanasia. In addition, many believe that death is not simply part of another world, but it enters our own living world, whether through a "death instinct", decadence, or the simply the implication of life itself. The German sociologist and philosopher, Georg Simmel and Sigmund Freud posit a presence of death throughout life. In the German philosopher Heidegger's words, we are "beings-towards-death".

Many of the assumptions in this book harbor a tacit recognition of death. For example, my notion of old age as a unique stage of life in which one may look *back* at one's life assumes one's life is soon coming to an end. The elegy, which I have adopted in this book to understand old age, originated in recognition of the death of a loved one. To my mind, the "enemies of elegy" – religious beliefs, life extension, old age delight, and pragmatic busyness hide an unspoken fear and denial of death. Accepting death is part of the obligations of old age. In short, death has been our silent companion in this book on old age.

Death is very important to any understanding of old age. Even if death is merely the ultimate end or limit to life, it forces us to frame the picture of our life. If death leads some to a different world from our living one, it invites some while still in this world to speculate about that different world – a world peopled with gods, angels, great ideas, myths, and divine justice. Even if we do not believe that death is the door to personal immortality, some of us pursue the ideal of a "good death" at the end of life which means a death which properly tops off a good life.

Most of us agree on the phenomenon of death, but not regarding the meaning of those facts. There is a perennial idea of death – one in which we participate, at least while we are living. But the specifics of that idea are much controverted in the course of the history of western thought. Jacquie Choron in his *Death and Western Thought* reviews the many philosophic meanings of death, tracing those from antiquity, such as Plato Aristotle and Epicurus; the Christian views of the Old and New Testaments; the Renaissance views of Montaigne and Bruno; the modern ideas of death of Descartes, Spinoza, Kant, Hegel Schopenhauer and Nietzsche; and contemporary views of Whitehead and the existentialists. Not only do we "participate" in death in the facts of our own mortality, but we also participate in the ideas of death as we participate in western culture. Two ways in which some of us share in contemporary ideas of death are our existentialist acceptance of the fact that death results in our non-existence and the Whiteheadian perennial idea of death which courses though western history.

Once awareness of our own death enters into our old age consciousness and we face the menu of different conceptions of death, we have several choices, although we may not wish to recognize that freedom. We may simply deny or make light of our demise, reaffirm life, or glorify death. Taking the first option, old Cicero, in his essay on old age, answered those who found old age to be a time of anxiety with the near approach of death:

> On the contrary, it [death] is an event utterly to be disregarded if it extinguish the soul's existence, or much to be wished, if it convey her to some region where she shall continue to exist forever.

Instead of denying death, many, such as French philosopher, Henri Bergson, reaffirms our awareness of the life forces within us when we experience the continuous duration of time. Awareness of these forces make the facing of death anything but easy; as Dylan Thomas's poem, *Do Not Go Gentle in That Good Night* advises: "Rage, rage against the dying of the light." Following a third approach, others seek to glorify death, finding within it some special value, such as freedom from one's bodily prison, (Plato), entry into heaven, hell or purgatory, (Aquinas), improvement of the species (Darwin), or finding union with the world spirit (Hegel) to name but a few such glorifications.

All of these options – denial of death, reaffirmation of life, and glorification of death itself - are inauthentic since they, like the enemies of elegy described above, fail to accept death for what it is: namely, the fundamental cessation of an individual's life, whether our own, a loved one or the death of anyone at all. *It is this acceptance of death which must be fashioned in old age through both an understanding of one's past life and impending non-existence which frames the narrative of that life.* Such acceptance requires that we must find a proper detachment without denial of death, and secure consolation from the prospect of death. Before discussing acceptance of death, I wish to explore the other alternatives identified above when facing death.

The Unacceptable Options for Facing Death

1. The Denial of Death

One way of denying death is to maintain that death is not important. Early in his life, Montaigne believed that one might prepare for death by emphasizing its' unimportance. In an early essay, he urged "that to think like a philosopher is to learn to die". Relying upon the early work of the Stoic essayist, Seneca, Montaigne filled this essay with their sayings to prepare us for death: "Think of each day that shines upon you as your last; the unhoped for hours will be welcome when they come;" or "alas, how small a portion of life remains for the old" or "let us become familiar with death" or "the first hour of our life shortened our life". These sayings were to encourage detachment by viewing one's life and death as part of an inevitable necessary cycle of nature, becoming acutely aware of the fate of death for everyone - those who have already died, those who die when we do, and those who will follow us in death. According to the young Montaigne, these observations prepare us for death by consoling us with its necessity and inevitability.

Seneca and the young Montaigne were not the only ones to deny the importance of death. Many canon works offer the cold comfort of a "scientific understanding of death", when they describes the underlying chemistry and physics of the dissolution of our bodies. A materialistic and mechanical view of death is very influential in the modern world. In this view, the importance of the death of an individual is denied by ignoring "superficial symptoms" and looking to the underlying transient physical substrate of death - the persistence of the natural elements, most of which will outlive us to be recycled in the environment. Thus, our lives participate briefly in the dance of the elements cycling both through life and death. In ancient times, there were even cosmic dances which sought to imitate or resonate with such cycles of the universe.

The ancient Roman poet, Lucretius captured the ways in which we and our lives and deaths, our births and old age fit within this natural world. Lucretius was writing at the period of decline of the Roman republic- a violent and pessimistic age. His poem, *De Rerum Natura*, (*The Nature of Things*, sometimes translated as *The Way Things Are*), claims to capture in verse the atomic philosophies of Democritus and Epicurus, Hellenistic Greek philosophers. Lucretius offers us in poetic form their objective vision of the universe, the earth and its changes, as well as biological life including mankind and its history, adopting an "insight into nature and a scheme of systematic contemplation" out of a " true devotion [in which] lies the power to look at all things with a peaceful mind," Lucretius sees our world and ourselves as part of an endless cycle of moving particles — "the ages past... recall the human generations taken away — "by-products"— " ... actions ... are byproducts, both of matter and of space". It is "everlasting motion" and different kinds of particles which account for "this arrangement [of the world] is kept through cosmic cycles", "each in its proper season".

Old age is similarly explained:

"But for a while our gain exceeds our loss
Until we reach that highest point of ripeness.
From there, we go, a little at a time downhill;
Age breaks our oak, dissolves our strength to watery feebleness.
...Nature can give no more...so things wither, die,
Made mean by loss, by blows within, without.
Assailed, besieged, betrayed, till at long last,
Food fails, and the great walls are battered in.

And death follows as part of the cycle:

"We often see men die by inches, toes and nails succumb
To lividness, next feet and legs, till soon
The other limbs feel the chill tread of death

And since the same thing happens to the spirit
Which never seems to issue all at once,
Out of the body, it also is mortal.

For Lucretius, the universe will also die, but "atoms [continue to] move in many ways, since infinite time began. Are driven by collisions, are borne on by their own weight, in every kind of way meet or combine, try every possible, every conceivable pattern. So no wonder they fell into arrangements into modes like those whereby the sum of things preserves its system by renewal." Similarly the motions of human history proceed from anarchy to law, then to the flourishing of nations, and then decline. In his infamous last book of the poem, Lucretius sketches the end of Athens. "Through noxious particles", such plague once visited Athens" and

> "Death piled them high in crowded stacks.
> Beside the aqueducts lay many who had crawled
> Or rolled close to the sweet water as their failing breath
> Would let them manage. All along the streets,
> In all the squares, you'd find bodies, caked with their
> own filth
> Rag covered or with skin the only drapery across their
> bones
> And almost invisible under the crust of sores and ulcers."

This Lucretian view of death is no different from the dominant view of much modern philosophy and science. Modern philosophy began the search for truth by breaking down through analysis and experimentation the world into "elements" — Descartes' clear and distinct ideas, Leibniz's "monads", Hume's impressions and ideas. The breakdown of the world into elements, whether in the world of words, the impressions of the mind, discrete actions or individual things has been a common method in all fields of thought. In the natural sciences, the study of cells, genes, molecules, atoms, sub-atomic particles all reflect this desire to find the common elemental simple constituents of nature. These simple elements are then to be combined in various ways to yield our world as we know it.

Modern science both followed and inspired modern philosophy. Lavoisier's *Elements of Chemistry* sought simple material elements in light and materials. Lavoisier, often regarded "the father of chemistry," held that "the principal object of chemical experiments is to decompose natural bodies, so as separately to examine the different substances which enter into their composition." In his first experiment, he was able to demonstrate that elements could take either gas, liquid or solid forms, hence leading to his formulation of the law of conservation of matter, modifying our common sense belief in elements as simply "solid" particles. After his experiments of combustion and fermentation, in which he sought to explore which chemical would join with another, Lavoisier sought to set forth tables of multiple "simple substances of common elements, metals, acids, and "combustible substances". Lavoisier's Tables were the beginning organization of the elements of matter, supplying a program for future research to discover more such elements. It was the discovery of these elements which led eventually to the Periodic Table of Chemical Elements which orders chemical elements according to their atomic weight. The contribution of modern chemistry based upon this table allows us to understand the process of dissolution of our bodies before and after death. The process of alkaline hydrolysis, the decomposition of compounds by water is only explicable in terms of the chemical processes and resulting elements which Lavoisier and his successors uncovered.

The scientific method adopted by Lavoisier and his successors not only led to discovery of the basic building blocks of our natural world and our bodies, but also shed light upon the aging process and dying and death itself. As Joseph Esposito has described in is modern old age classic, *The Obsolete Self,* modern biology has documented the inherence, irreversibility, progressiveness and deterioration of the body in the aging process. Not only in aging, but after death, there is little doubt that the human body undergoes a chemical decay in liquid, gaseous and solid forms, echoing the conclusions of the first experiment of Lavoisier and illustrating his law of the conservation of matter. The phases of chemical decay after death continue to be catalogued in some detail by the modern science of ecology which has traced how these elements are returned back into the environment. These modern findings appear to echo Lucretius's serene contemplation of the cycling of particles in the universe. And such contemplation appears to echo and buttress Lucretius' notion that the death of an organism is an insignificant phase in the general movements in nature. *In a sense, these findings conclude that there is no loss in death, only a benign rearrangement of the particles of the universe.*

2. *The Reassertion of Life*

In his last years, Montaigne changed his mind about the need to prepare for death in order to render it insignificant. In his last essays, *Physiognomy* and *Experience,* Montaigne finds death to be simply a natural event at the end of life. In these essays, Montaigne reveals that during his life he experienced death around him, in part from the religious wars, in part from his experiences with the plague, from which he and his family escaped for six months after witnessing much death from it. In "Physiognomy", he praises the natural experience of simple people and their direct and simple confrontation with death without the necessity for any "preparation".

Montaigne's most extended treatment of old age and death is his final essay, "Experience", in which he offers a somewhat different rationale for abjuring preparation for death. The title of the essay, "Experience" is central to his final old age approach to death. In this essay he turns to his own old age experience and finds that life slowly ebbs from him making the prospect of death easier. Recognizing this "natural process", he adds to his former essay, by urging the preservation and enjoyment of life in old age, despite the fact that such a life is limited and beset by old age illness. Ironically, he concludes with a quote from Horace's *Odes:*

> "Grant, I pray, son of Latona, that I
> Enjoy in full health and with mind unimpared
> The goods that have been prepared for me

And that my old age (not?) be unhonored,
Nor lack the lyre"

Thus, at the end of his own life, Montaigne endorses a commonly held notion that a focus upon death, even in old age, prevents the enjoyment of the last years or days of one's life and that it is better simply to enjoy life as long as possible. *The loss involved in contemplating death in old age is the loss of the final enjoyments of life!* Other classics have agreed with Montaigne and suggest that a romantic escape may be the answer to the prospect of death. Boccaccio's *Decameron* illustrates this approach. In the *Decameron*, the presence of death is denied. A group of young ladies and men, caught in 14th century Florence during the plague, (described in grisly detail at the beginning of the book), agree to leave Rome together — and to tell stories to one another. The stories are not religious stories, (except, from time to time to make fun of the Church). They are stories of life — dalliances, infidelities, the pursuit of wealth and so forth. They are a celebration of life and the deliberate ignoring of death from the plague. Even when the group returns to Florence, no mention is made of the plague, and a religious concern about death and salvation is not mentioned.

One more philosophical reaffirmation of the principle of life in the face of death was provided by the 18th /19th century philosopher, Arthur Schopenhauer who responded to Immanuel Kant's failure to establish how we might have knowledge of reality,- the "thing-in-itself". Kant maintained that our knowledge was by means of our own organized concepts through which phenomena are received. Schopenhauer found knowledge of a thing-in-itself or reality in our reflective awareness of the will to live. The will to live was not merely an individual possession, but part of the drive of nature itself. Hence, perhaps with the help of Darwin, the recognition of life-forces became the central tenet of not only his philosophy but Nietzsche as well Other "romantic" philosophers of the time, including Schelling and, more recently, Henri Bergson and Schweitzer, celebrated life along with the Romantic poets, such did Byron and Shelly. Given their embrace of the pre-eminent value of life itself, these authors struggled in different ways to reconcile the reality of death. Shelley's remarkable poem, *The Triumph of Life,* described life:

> And life, where long that flower of Heaven grew not
> Conquered the heart by love which gold or pain
> Or age or sloth or slavery could subdue not –

but recognized old age and death in the wake of the chariot of life:

> ... Behind,
> Old men and women foully disarrayed
> Shake their grey hair in the insulting wind,
>
> Limp in the dance and strain with limbs decayed
> To reach the car of light which leaves them still
> Farther behind and deeper in the shade.

3. *The Glorification of Death*

The glorification of death does not appear to deny nor turn away from it nor invent worlds of afterlife; rather it focuses upon death and finds some ultimate value in it – freedom, direct access to universal ideas, or participation in something more comprehensive or eternal. Such glorification is often, (but not always) found in rationales for suicide and assisted suicide. Customarily, euthanasia or assisted suicide is justified by nothing more than a welcome escape from the pains and indignities of dying, but the rationales for suicide are somewhat different and the history of the practices and philosophies of suicide are revealing. One such glorification can be found in the French existentialist philosopher's finding of freedom before death in *the Republic of Silence.*

> *Exile, captivity and especially death ... were the profound source of our reality as men... The basic question of liberty was posed and we were brought to the deepest knowledge that man can have of himself...the secret of man is the*

limit of his own liberty, his capacity for resisting torture and death.

The Acceptance of Death

Rather than adopt a strategy of denial, reassertion of life, or glorification of death, I contend that one must recognize and accept death. Such acceptance is illustrated by another approach which Montaigne takes towards death. Montaigne discusses the death of his dear friend, Etienne de la Boetie in his essay on friendship, death assumes a deep and personal significance for Montaigne who clearly loved his friend. Montaigne contemplates his own death through the imagined reciprocal feelings of his lover!

> There is no act or thought of mine in which I do not
> miss him even as it would have been with him for me;

It is in this essay on friendship where Montaigne appears to accept both his friends and his own death as "missing" i.e., non-being.

One way in which death may be accepted is by recognizing that since death ends the valued components of life in general and a specific life as well,, it cannot be unimportant. Consequently, death is one of the important losses encountered in the old age – an old age which is part of our entire life. Thus, despite Montaigne's final rejection of the need for an early preparation for death, or the Lucretian and modern scientific vision of the cycling of elements in the universe, both making death seem insignificant, human common sense concludes that death is important. In old age, the anticipation of death in the near future, the constant presence of death of others, and other death related losses encountered in old age, suggest that death is indeed important and must be "accepted" on its own terms, not denied or glorified.

There is a deeper refutation to those who seek to deny, turn away from or glorify death and that refutation is simple. *Common sense concludes that death is important because it is the cessation of life and life itself is valuable.* Consequently, through death, we all lose something valuable – a loss that cannot be denied through the Stoic preparations of the young Montaigne, the revels of the ladies in the *Decameron*, the Lucretian vision of the interminable cycling of the particles of body and soul or the grand Hegelian views of death as part of the spirit of history.

Life is what is lost, and so it is necessary to determine what life is so that we can determine what we "accept" when we die.

By "life" is meant an organism's biological functioning, as well as for some animals and humans, the consciousness, sensations, and other imaginative and intellectual activities; life also includes, especially for humans, a continuation of a "biographical life", and the self-awareness of the presence of one's own existence, in Bergson's words, as part of" the stream of duration". In the words of the modern philosopher of life, Hans Jonas in his *The Phenomenon of Life:*

> Independently of the story of its genesis, the manifold of existing life presents itself as an ascending scale in which are placed the sophistication of form, the lure of sense and the spur of desire, the command of limb and powers to act, the reflection of consciousness and the reach for truth.

All of these dimensions of life are valuable. There is a satisfaction which rests in the healthful functioning of our metabolism. There is delight in locomotion and sensation. The activities of the imagination and intellect seem intrinsically good. We revel in our capabilities to decide and act. We embrace the importance of the continuation of a life until its completion. As human beings, in old age, if we are fortunate, we are able to reflect upon our entire life and this final identity is what we possess at the end of life. The very being of all these dimensions of a living person as well as her identity seem important to us.

A definition of death is implied in this definition of life. Death is the gradual or sudden transition of an organism from life to non-life, from being to non-being - a change which ends those attributes of biological functioning, such as growth, self-replication, metabolic functioning and movement. In the transition, death shuts down individual consciousness and its consequent sensing and knowledge (if such consciousness, sensing and knowledge are present), and stops any capability of action towards the organism's goals. For humans, death is also the end of the completion of a biographical life and the formation of an identity. At the most fundamental level, death eliminates the individual's very being. Thus, the definitions of life and death call attention to the range and number of ideas — the biological functions of life, the entire biography of a person, the consciousness and knowledge of the mind, the identity of the person the being and non-being of the person, and the legacy of a life after death. The qualities of life make up the losses in death; we lose these qualities as the stages of death proceed.

The Stages and Aspects of Death

Different authors focus upon different stages and aspects of death and treat these aspects in different ways: These stages and aspects of the dying process include anticipation of death, the decline and end of biological functioning, the end of consciousness, recognition of the completion of a life, the state of non-being, and the individual's and society's response to these each of these stages and aspects of death. The first stage, the anticipation of death, is discussed in very different ways by Montaigne, as discussed above, and the playwright Samuel Beckett. Beckett, in such plays as *Waiting for Godot,* portrays its characters suffering the interminable boredom of waiting for death in a meaningless world. For both Montaigne, and Beckett, the anticipation of death produces a sense of absence of the full enjoyment of life itself, but the source of the sadness is very different for each author. While Montaigne finds meaning in the death of his friend in a reciprocity of love, Beckett finds that the end of life is merely a waiting for a meaningless death. For Beckett, what is lost in death has already been lost in life. In old age, there is, from time to time a sense of waiting for death; perhaps this is why a certain sadness hovers over old age. As described above, an elegiac sadness hovers over its anticipation.

The second stage, the process of dying is described in Tolstoy's *The Death of Ivan Ilyich,* and Elizabeth Kubler-Ross's *On Death and Dying.* Tolstoy gives the vivid account of an ambitious government judge who is diagnosed as terminally ill, initially denying the reality of his condition, feeling angry at the living, withdrawing from their world in the misunderstood solitude of the dying, finally accepting his fate and experiencing a transformation to experience love for his family. Upon an initial reading, one cannot help from thinking that Tolstoy's account is more the expression of the hopes and beliefs of an author who seeks to impose his own late age philosophy of love onto a literary account of a death! But Tolstoy's account of the stages of death is somewhat mirrored in more recent "scientific" accounts of the emotions of persons facing dying. Kubler-Ross's bases her study upon observations of the treatment of many elderly at the end of life and purports to find five stages of dying, including denial and isolation, anger, bargaining, depression and acceptance. There is a certain comfort in Kubler-Ross's account, since she suggests that therapy and other forms of appropriate care at the time of death may help the dying person cope with these common reactions to the prospect of death and accept the impending reality of her death, while holding onto hope. In the Kubler-Ross account, acceptance of one's death by the dying and her loved ones replaces Tolstoy's final stage of love.

In the third stage, the great biologist/physicians such as Galen and Harvey see death as simply the end of biological functioning. Specifically, Harvey traces the importance of the heart's pumping of the blood to produce heat, and, with cessation of that pumping, death ensues. Sherwin Nuland brings this biological description up to date in his remarkable book, *The Way We Die.* While providing a detailed physiological account of death by stroke, cancer, heart attack, Alzheimer's disease, suicide and accident, AID's and murder, this wise surgeon also argues for the acceptance of death in old age as the natural process of a wearing out of the human body, a "wearing out" in which several factors of death may be present at the time of old age death. What is lost are the normality of basic organs and their biological functions and capacities, but the specific nature of the loss often determines, at least in part, the consequent emotions of the dying, ranging from the depression of the suicide victim, the stupor of the Alzheimer's victim, the anguish of the AID's patient, the false hopes and anger of the dying person with cancer.

The stage of termination of biological functioning may also be viewed as a different aspect of death, viz., the end of a biographical life. Although Aristotle views death in a more comprehensive way, exploring its meaning in light of the various disciplines such as biology, psychology and "poetics", he also views death as the end of an entire life as described in his *Nicomachean Ethics*. Expanding Aristotle's generic account of death as the completion of life, more specific accounts of entire lives and deaths are found in many biographies such as Plutarch's *Lives*, and Boswell's *Samuel Johnson* as well as novels, such as Cervantes' *Don Quixote*, Flaubert's *Madame Bovary* and Hardy's *Jude the Obscure*. For example, Plutarch describes in great detail the death of Cicero by assassination, a fitting death since Cicero played hard in the game of Roman politics at the end of the Republican period and so became the victim of political revenge. Samuel Johnson, according to Boswell's biography experienced religious fear at the end of his life, a somewhat odd and ill-fitting conclusion to the life of a man who seemed courageous in every other way. On the other hand, Cervantes's description of Quixote's peaceful death somehow seems to be appropriate for the old man to find rest after his vigorous old age efforts to restore chivalry to Spain and even the death of Madame Bovary appears to be a "fitting" punishment to her wanton life. The death of Jude in Hardy's *Jude the Obscure* captures reflects Jude's principal failure to realize his dream of attending Christminster and he could hear the music of the college's "Remembrance Day" as he died. As Jude's death illustrates, each death can only be arrived at in light of the entire life each character and the surrounding circumstances of the death.

One way of setting the time of completion of one's life and controlling the means of death is suicide or euthanasia. The meaning of suicide or euthanasia differ in different historical eras. Thus, ancient suicide, however motivated, may, like the Stoics' suicides seek maximum control over one's life; yet the lesson of Seneca's botched suicide, as recounted by Plutarch, suggests that it is not a foolproof nor an "easy" method of death. A modern suicide may reflect an era when pleasure is important and the pains of old age or dying invite leaving this world. Of course, even if the meaning of suicide reflects the spirit of medieval, renaissance, enlightenment or modern ages, there may be more immediate determinates such as the character, values, and life of the person choosing suicide and the circumstances she faces at the time of death. Thus, Ernest Hemingway's death by means of a self-inflicted shotgun blast at a time when he could no longer act out his macho ethic in life. Similarly, the account of suicide in the French existentialist, Jean Amery's *Suicide,* was followed by his own suicide; Amery justified it by the claim that in voluntary death he found the freedom from the contradictions of life entering into "the breath-giving road to the open." Those "contradictions of life" might be found in Amery's experience of the concentration camps during the Second World War.

Another aspect of death involves the notion of death as the extinction of consciousness. Some, such as Shakespeare's *Hamlet*, compared death to sleep, although he quickly qualified it by noting that such sleep might result in unwelcome dreams. Some philosophers have suggested that the unconsciousness of death is simply like one's state before birth, but others suggesting that whatever death's state might be, non-consciousness before birth seems different from lack of consciousness after life has been experienced. The psychologist, William James, in his *The Principles of Psychology* describes personal consciousness in which the self is not a soul but merely a stream of subjective thought united by an ego - a stream which is "interrupted" presumably ending at death. A similar view is implicit in Hemingway's *The Short Happy Life of Francis Macomber* in which the death of Macomber when hunting a buffalo is described as follows:

"he could see the little wicked eyes and the head [of the buffalo] starting to lower and he felt a sudden white-hot, blinding flash explode inside his head and that was all he ever felt."

However, unlike a psychologist's account, the meaning of Macomber's death is given not in the end of Macomber's consciousness. The meaning is to be found in the story of Macomber's foolish but courageous act of standing up to the buffalo as an effort to impress his wife; in fact, the death is fraught with irony since the blinding flash he experienced may have been caused by a bullet his wife shot. In another account of death as the loss of consciousness, we have Thomas Mann's *Death in Venice,* in which the old professor, after following the beautiful boy to the beach and watching him play, is suddenly seen by a third person to simply slump over in death. It is not uncommon for accounts of death to switch discretely from the first person to the third person as if to admit what is true, namely that we do not know what the experience of lost consciousness at death is like. Nevertheless, what these works and other works like them suggest is that the loss of consciousness is in fact a loss of awareness of the continuity of life; death constitutes an irremediable interruption in the stream of consciousness. Some philosophers, along with Shakespeare's Hamlet, compare it to sleep; other find analogies to our state of non-existence before we were born.

The notion of death as a loss of consciousness seems different from the notion of non-being. Along with other existentialists, the modern German philosopher Heidegger captures the notion of our movement towards non-being in death in his notions of "being-toward- death" in *Being and Time.* The notion of non-being may imply the notion of nothingness as well as discussed in Heidegger's *The Introduction to Metaphysics.* For Heidegger death is found as part of one's very existence, which he calls "Dasein" i.e.," being there". Death is not viewed in the context of life, but in the context of being itself and Heidegger describes the paradoxical impossibility of conceiving of complete non-being despite our movement toward death. For Heidegger, our death is private, unrelated to others, and, in Heidegger's words, contains an unsurpassable possibility – "the possibility of the absolute impossibility of Dasein", that is, one's own being.

In a more accessible description, death is a particular sense of the person's absence as part of the core of grief, described by Virginia Woolf in *Jacob's Room*. Returning to Jacob's room after his disappearance in the First World War, his friends exclaim:

> Jacob! Jacob! Cried Bonamy, standing by the window.
> The leaves sank down again.
> "Such confusion everywhere!" exclaimed Betsy Flanders,
> bursting open the bedroom door.
> "What am I to do with these, Mr. Bonamy?'
> She held out a pair of Jacob's shoes.

The vacant room and the empty shoes once used by Jacob hint at the death of Jacob. But, more important, his very absence and non-being. Grief is the recognition of a loved one's non-being.

The above discussion assumes that death is defined by either the individual facing death or the scientist or philosopher describing the death. But the manner of anticipation of death, the dying process itself, and the treatment of the dead after their death obviously involve "bystanders" or loved ones, who along with the dying person himself adhere to customary practices. In this regard, others, including society at large may define the meaning of death in old age by means of the customs and laws which carry with them society's ascribed meanings of death. These social meaning may influence those who are anticipating their own death as well as those who are mourning the death of others. One example of dying as defined by society's reaction to death is documented by Huizinga, an historian who describes the medieval mind's view of death in the *Waning of the Middle Ages* while Philip Aries, in the *Hour of Our Death,* traces the ceremonial treatment of the dying and dead through the ages finding different "models of death" through the ages. Thus, although the dying, through anticipatory management of their own dying and after-death ceremonies, may exert some control over the meaning of their lives in accordance with their vision of their lives, they do not have full control over the societal treatments of their dying nor death which are frozen in custom and culture and which the survivors may adopt to give their own meaning to a death.

The Emotions Involved in Death and Dying

The discussion of the options in facing death reveals the losses and the emotions we may experience when we encounter death. If we ask what is lost in death, the first response is, of course, life. But after we identify the different aspects of death, each aspect involves a different loss! The anticipation of death for the elder Montaigne means the blocking out or at least the diminution of the enjoyment of life which produces sadness. For Beckett, death means waiting to die, the loss of the excitement of life and a period of paralyzing boredom. In the process of dying both Tolstoy and Kubler-Ross find, among other losses, a phase of isolation and loneliness, a loss of connection with the living, and anger. For those scientists and medical doctors, such as Galen or Nuland, who describe the changes in our bodies as we grow old and die, they find that in our death we simply lose the normal functioning of our organs. With Aristotle or Plutarch, a death is what finishes and completes our biographical life. Such a death may express who we were, but we lose any further opportunity to redefine our life and ourselves and hence are powerless. With James and Hemingway, in death, we simply lose consciousness. For Heidegger, as death moves toward non-being, we are introduced to nothingness- the ultimate loss, which Heidegger tries to describe to us as "being-towards-death", a state which fills us with anxiety and awe. With societal definitions of death found in deathbed practices, funeral services and burial practices, death marks the loss of our own power to define our death and an inevitable delegation of the many meanings of our life and death to surviving society and loved ones.

Once the anticipation of our death is over, biological functioning stops, consciousness extinguished, life completed, nothingness reigns, the funeral and burial practices begin, and the thoughts and emotions that are experienced at death are the emotions of on-lookers, not the dead. A central emotion experienced by others at the time of death is grief and mourning for the dead. Such emotions of grief and its mourning is expressed in eulogy, elegy and requiem. The words of the archetypal elegy, Milton's *Lycidas*, captures the sadness in its opening lines:

> Yet once more, O ye laurels and once more,
> Ye myrtles brown, with ivy never sear,
> I come to pluck your berries harsh and crude,
> And with forced fingers rude
> Shatter your leaves before the mellowing year.

It is "plucked berries" of Milton's elegy for his drowned friend, which enables him and us to begin detachment from the loss and sadness of death.

Detachment

The accounts of the facts of death rarely describe a state of detachment. But in the course of old age, detachment from the prospect of death and the process of dying may be achieved, if at all, by a social, imaginative, and intellectual effort. Social detachment involves the literal withdrawal from social relationships. I have already identified a variety of thinkers such as Petrarch and Montaigne, who sought such withdrawal in old age and, while doing so, have written movingly about the benefits of such solitude. Even if one's life is not one of solitude and one's old age is filled with busy social contacts, as death approaches, withdrawal in the final stages is not uncommon. The ancient philosopher, Plotinus, separated himself from his friends and followers as death approached. The modern psychologist, Erik Erikson began to withdraw in his last years. So, for that matter, did Winston Churchill. The effect of such withdrawal, whether intended or not, is to separate oneself from the day-to-day involvements of ordinary life, in effect, "mirroring death". Such withdrawal may permit the contemplation of one's death both as a completion of a life and as an event within the cycles of nature.

Such a withdrawal may provide the circumstance for imaginative detachment.

Imaginative detachment involves the imaginative rehearsing of one's approach to death, the death itself, and even its aftermath. A myriad of literary works helps in such a rehearsal. The preparation for death is portrayed in Plato's *Phaedo,* in which Socrates calmly discusses death and then drinks the hemlock. We have already mentioned Thomas Mann's *Death in Venice* which describes the old Aschenbach's final search for the last glimpse of beauty. An extensive treatment of after -death may be found in such works as Dante's *Divine Comedy,* where, with the help of his Catholic faith, he can imaginatively recreate the afterlife in hell, purgatory and heaven. All of these works create alternative pictures of dying, death, and after-death for us to entertain – possibilities which we may or may not be able to follow or reject as we contemplate our own deaths.

The method of intellectual detachment from the prospect of death and dying should be guided as outlined in the Chapter 12's account of reflective meditation. One begins reflection by identifying the prejudgments which one holds in relation to the topic. As suggested above, some of my prejudgments include the belief that death is important as the loss of life, suicide is a reasonable option at the end of life, and the portrayal of an after-life of heaven, hell, or purgatory is simply not a live option. Each individual must identify his or her own prejudgments. The next step is a canvassing of relevant classics. Death is a perennial topic of the canon classics including great works of fine art, such as Michelangelo's *Pieta,* Picasso's *Guernica* and Mozart's *Requiem.* The death of Socrates as recounted in the *Phaedo,* and the crucifixion of Jesus in the *New Testament* are simply two of a myriad of treatments of death which are repeated in works of sculpture, painting and literature throughout the ages, (although, to be sure, neither the death of Socrates nor Jesus took place in old age). The canon includes many works dealing with death in old age including many of the biographies in Plutarch's *Lives*, Montaigne's late *Essays*, Sophocles' *Oedipus at Colonus*, Shakespeare's *King Lear*, Cervantes *Don Quixote*, Eliot's *Middlemarch*, Dickens' *Curiosity Shop*, Tolstoy's *The Death of Ivan Ilyich*, Huizinga's *The Waning of the Middle Ages*, Frazier's *The Golden Bough*, Hardy's *Jude the Obscure*, Willa Cather's *Death Comes to the Archbishop*, Brecht's *Mother Courage and her Children*, Beckett's *Waiting for Godot*, Yeats' late poems, much of Emily Dickenson's poetry, and many other works. Similarly, philosophical works, many of them mentioned above, explore the nature of life and death.

These classic works supply a myriad of ideas for interpreting the reality of old age death. *Life* and *death* themselves are examples of such ideas. The process of death may be subsumed under more general notions of *change* in *substance*, (Aristotle). *Death* and *decay* which follows may be viewed as part of the *life cycles* in *nature* and *evolution*. (Darwin). As part of this process, the human *body* loses its *form*, and, some believe that its' *soul* departs. (Aquinas). At a metaphysical level, some assert that there is a change from *being* to *non-being*, (Heidegger). Some discuss death in the context of a discussion of fate (Cicero, Thornton Wilder). These ideas take different forms, descriptions and explanations within the myriad of classics in which they are found. And one of the difficult tasks of old age meditation is the sorting out and finding or creating a coherent account among these ideas.

We must also explore how our own individual deaths "participate" in these ideas. Many philosophers, both ancient (Plato, Plotinus) and modern, (Russell, Whitehead), argue that our particular deaths do "participate" in these universals, while, at the same time, the universals themselves are eternal, that is, they are timeless ideas which, in their abstraction, are not located in either time or space. Of course it is possible to maintain, (and I do), that even if we participate in these timeless ideas in this life, such participation takes place only during our own bodily lives and need not extend beyond our these lives, despite the paradoxical fact that the ideas themselves may remain timeless. *Thus, one possible definition of death, from this point of view, is our own cessation of participation in the timeless ideas.*

After identifying our own prejudgments, defining the topic, identifying classics and their ideas, we must bring "these ideas home." Thus, we can ask how we view our own approach to death as part of change in our substance, as part of the cycles and evolution of nature, resulting in loss of our bodily form, the departure of one's soul and our movement towards a possible non-being. In order to "bring these ideas home" we must not only relate them to our own experience, but also assess their truth. Thus, the final step in reflective meditation is the ascertaining of the truth of these ideas as they apply to our own lives. We have already begun to search for that truth when we seek a coherent account of the myriad of ideas which deal with death. But, as applied to our own lives, we must seek an account of death which is also coherent within our own lives and prospective deaths and which corresponds with the reality of death as we know it.

Coherence and incoherence of ideas about death may be illustrated by the deaths of Augustine and Aquinas. Both philosophers were committed in their lives to the role of reason and both philosophers, especially Aquinas who, in his *Summa Theologica,* sought coherence in philosophical views covering a myriad of subjects. Yet, it was Augustine who found a coherent death, in which, at the time of dying, he read until his death, thus confirming his belief in the prime importance of reading. By contrast, at the time of his death, Aquinas allegedly renounced all of his writings as "straw" which, to me, seems to be an incoherent act which is inconsistent with the remainder of his life.

Death, in addition to being coherent with life, must also correspond with reality. Ivan Ilyich, in Tolstoy's short story, and Thomas Aquinas, in the accounts of their dying, may have discovered new truths, new realities, which apparently made their previous lives a lie. Ilyich's found his self-centered life to be inadequate in light of his discovery of love when dying. Aquinas apparently discovered a deeper reality in his religious faith – a "last minute" discovery which led him to place no further value on his remarkable writings! In such a situation, the coherence of their deaths with their lives was challenged by newly discovered and inconsistent truths which correspond with a reality different from the reality they lived!

Consolation

Consolation for the dying, either self-administered or with the help of loved ones, takes place through a process of placing death in perspective, familiarizing the dying with death in advance, finding substitutes for the losses connected with death, transforming the dying in death, purging feelings of fear, anger, regret or grief at the advent of death, and assenting to the truths found within the experience of death.

Two of the consolatory classics, Boethius's *Consolation of Philosophy* and Thomas More's *Dialogue of Comfort Against Tribulation* seek to cope with the prospect of death by placing it within a broader perspective. In Boethius's case, the perspective is a philosophic framework in which all suffering including death is seen the result of God's bestowal of freedom on man in an otherwise determined universe. In More's perspective, God has given man suffering and death as punishment for his sins on earth. An ancient or modern scientific perspective of death places it in the cycles of life, the evolution of man, and the movement of atomic particles, dictating the necessity of the death of the individual, perhaps to advance the career of the species or competing species or simply as part of the accidental movements of particles in a unknowing or uncaring universe.

Consolation may arrive through the familiarization with death. That familiarization may take the form of simply contemplating the fact of one's mortality, a "momento mori" or planning one's death. ("ars moriendi"). Modern versions can be found in such works as Marylyn Webb's *The Good Death.* By means of such works, we may familiarize ourselves to face the end of our lives, if not the pains of dying itself. Familiarizing oneself with these pains is found in reading such works as Dostoevsky's *House of the Dead,* Sherwin Nuland's *How We Die,* Kubler Ross's *On Death and Dying* and Leonid Andreyev's *Seven Who Were Hanged.* Each of these works book seeks to remove the mystery of dying by describing in detail the physiological or psychological changes undergone during the final period of the lives question; such accounts may be needed to help the dying, their relatives and the caregivers to cope with their own death.

The purging of emotions resulting from death is best captured by attendance to the musical requiem and the elegy. The requiem is most identified with the Catholic mass for the dead or the music associated with that mass; it recognizes the glory of God, punishment for sins of the world in death and a plea for mercy for the dead. Obviously these works are directed at survivors, but there is room for elegies to be directed to those anticipating or experiencing death, Requiems imaginatively allow a person, while mourning another, to entertain the prospect of his own death, mourn for himself, detach from the experience of that loss and thus, in mourning find consolation, not only for the deceased, but also for the mourner.

In one sense, there may be no substitutes available to the dying for the loss encountered in death, since the loss is so profound. Perhaps legacies can offer weak substitutes for the final loss of death or holding onto the notion of being part of a cycle of life or history. Also, it may be possible to familiarize oneself with the dying process, whether experienced by oneself or by witnessing the death of one's loved ones. In those moments of dying, a transformation may take place in which the natural goods of life being lost in death are replaced by other goods - the love of others, a belief in god, or if rationality holds to the end, a sense of the presence of the eternal ideas themselves. The sudden growth of love is described in Tolstoy's *The Death of Ivan Ilyich*, the experience of a love of God at the time of death is described in Dante's ascent into heaven, and the love of eternal ideas for their own sake is portrayed in Socrates' facing of death in Plato's *Phaedo*. Such a transformation may be closely related to the ultimate consolation in dying and death, whether of oneself or another, the discovery of a unique truth – the meaning of one's own life in general and for oneself and others.

Conclusion

Death then is the end of life – the ultimate loss, bringing with it all the other losses which take place in the period of its anticipation, its advent in dying, and perhaps even the moment of cessation of the metabolic processes. But I have suggested that it is best conceived as an end -the end of a life. It is like a picture frame, which encircles and limits a picture of our life, taking whatever value it has from the life that precedes it. In old age, we become aware of impending death and such awareness may help us to define our entire life. Spurred to reflect upon our entire life, we are ennobled and consoled by this aspect of death. Beyond our own death is our own non-being - the non-existence of our individuality. For some, such non-existence takes with it the very existence of the world itself. But, at least before death, it is possible to imagine the world continues after death and our capacity to love enables us to desire the continuation of our loved ones, our culture, and nature itself.

CHAPTER XX

Conclusion: Old Age, Loss, and the Rest of Life

Human good turns out to be activity of the soul … in a complete life – Aristotle

Veritable truth …is self-accordance; …it is at once existence and self-affirmation – Plotinus

It is with a certain sadness that I write this conclusion sixteen years after I began my exploration of old age at age 72. During this time, I have savored my old age by reading and appreciating many of the classics of old age loss. Each morning, with a hot cup of coffee, I sit in my favorite living room chair, read and meditate, solemnly jotting notes which I then often misplace. Each morning my cat, Oliver, joins me on my lap, although I don't think he appreciates the seriousness of my meditations. Each morning I have found some consolation in my reading and meditations. But I am under no illusion. My current comfortable state is temporary - primarily the product of good genes and doctoring, a loving wife, family, friends, and relative prosperity. I have been lucky. I shall die soon.

Around the edges of my old age comfort is a vague fear – a sense of vulnerability – the threat of my own serious illness and death. In old age, our lives are a "holding on". We hold on to our respective largely trivial

routines. We hold on to largely meaningless conversations, conducted with a touch of love, mixed with denial of what comes next. I hold on as I read and write avidly about death without taking the basic practical steps in anticipation of its advent. (I really do have to order our cemetery stones).

My blanket of consolation which the classics provide does not extend to covering all the losses I face in old age. To be sure, it has eased the pains of retirement, helped me cope with the eclipse of the past and the foreshortening of the future – an easing of ambitions. I have adopted a comfortable old age conservatism in response to my loss of faith in progress. But the consolation of the classics does little to ease pain of biological decline and the onrushing reality of death evidenced by the recent deaths of my wife and best friend. The blanket of consolation has failed to provide sufficient warmth of compassion needed to fully console the end.

But I have discovered during these sixteen years that old age is more than simply a response to loss. I have discovered that old age is not only a time of loss; it is also the time of completion of an entire life. How does one properly complete one's life? Having given enough attention to loss and its consolation in this book, I will turn to seek understanding of my entire life – its stages and threads – and how these fit (or fail to fit) with the lives of others. I am certain this new inquiry will lead me to other classics in my effort to understand the life I am completing. But I need more time! Old age does not promise more time.

Introduction

In earlier chapters, I concluded that reflective meditation in old age – a meditation designed to provide detachment and consolation- should conclude with a test of the lessons yielded by such meditation. Such testing seeks to determine their truth. In this chapter, I report upon the truth of these meditations based upon my own experience over the past years of old age life. During this time, I have continually sought to assess the implications of those conclusions from my reading.

The classics offer three principal theories of truth, and all are relevant here. The first theory, the "correspondence theory", defines "truth" in terms of the extent to which statements or knowledge claimed correspond with reality. Thus, do the conclusions of my meditations fit with the "corresponding" reality of old age? Do they mirror my experience? The second theory is the "coherence theory" in which truth is measured in terms of its' conformity or consistency with other established assertions, beliefs and actions? Do my conclusions fit with other truths of my life - truths yielded by my other experiences and other classics? Do the conclusions of my meditation cohere with other truths in my life? The third theory is a "pragmatic theory" in which truth is measured by "what works". Have the conclusions reached by my reflective meditation helped me to cope successfully with old age?

When I "test" the conclusions set forth above, I begin with a correspondence theory in which I explore the extent to which my conclusions mirror my own experience of the reality of old age. In other words, I test whether the conclusions are true *for me,* (which acknowledges that other persons may have very different experiences from mine). I recognize that my experiences are limited to "early old age" i.e. ages 72-87, experiences of an overeducated retiree who has led an easy life. Hence such experiences may not prove valid for my later old age when I presumably will confront more serious losses or other life experiences nor for others who have led different lives. Yet, I believe that I have already experienced many universal losses consolations found in any period of old age.

Following my test measuring the extent to which my conclusions correspond to old age reality, I shall place the subject of old age response to loss within the broader framework of "an entire life", asking whether my conclusions about old age losses are consistent with my entire life. In other words, I ask the question: *even if my conclusions regarding old age losses mirror the reality of old age, how do these conclusions fit within the entire life that I have led? And conversely, how does my entire life fit with how I have responded to old age?* In seeking to answer these questions, I adopt the coherence theory of truth, since I shall explore whether the conclusions I have reached regarding old age losses are consistent with the conclusions drawn from my entire life. By "entire life", I refer both to my past life and that part of my current life which is not devoted to old age loss.

Finally, I discuss whether becoming aware of the conclusions reached in the earlier chapters has improved the quality of my old age. This reflection leads to a discussion of the core assumption of this book: *does a reading and appreciation of the classics in general successfully support detachment and provide consolation for old age losses while permitting the completion of a successful old age.* In this inquiry, I adopt a pragmatic theory of truth, since I am reviewing the conclusions I have reached and asking whether "they work" in old age.

The "Conclusions": Hypotheses About Old Age

In the previous chapters, I sought answers to the following questions: To what extent is the central meaning of old age to be found in its losses and our response to them? To what extent has elegy proved to be an adequate framework for understanding the losses of old age in general and, specifically, my old age? Are the classics relevant to old age loss? If so, how does one select the relevant classics pertaining to old age losses? To what extent do these classics enable one to understand and accept the losses of old age and their consequent emotions? Do the classics help one to detach from these losses? Can they supply appropriate consolations? I offered the following conclusions regarding these questions.

1. Elegaci Reflection on Old Age Losses

In this book, I have assumed that old age is a unique period in life, in which, if we are fortunate, we can look back to survey and celebrate that life in its entirety. Unfortunately, old age is also a time of losses—permanent, cumulative, and irreversible – and these losses can interfere with any old age celebration. In the words of the poet, Robert Lowell, these losses of old age are a series of "subtractions" -- losses of the challenges of work and wealth due to retirement; losses of past time - eclipsed by the very passage of time as well as the failings of memory; losses of capacity taken away by our biological decline, often accompanied by a growing dependency; a foreshortening of our future, leaving little room for ambition; loss of faith in the inevitability of our own individual improvement and society's inevitable progress; loss of a future taken by the approach of our dying and death. We cannot ignore or deny these losses, although many seek to do so as they ask modern science and medicine to extend their lives, or seek salvation in religion, or heedlessly pursue old-age pleasures, or bury themselves in the denial of one or another busy practical enterprise.

My experiment for coping with old age loss was stimulated by the advent of my own old age, but, unlike Thoreau's brief experiment in living at Walden, this experience has lasted sixteen years and promises to linger on until death. The immediate prospect of old age stimulated me to extend my thoughts beyond everyday old age concerns, leading me to wonder what old age life and death are all about. To pursue such "philosophical wondering", I have adopted a way of life which I label, (somewhat pretentiously, I admit), "classical leisure" - a life of reflective meditation on the losses of old age and the routes, if any, of detachment from and consolation for these losses. In my view, such reflective meditation is one of the activities which constitute classical leisure. Such leisure is composed of voluntary activities which are "auto-telic", that is, activities whose goals, (which make the activities valuable), are inherent in the very activities themselves. We engage in these activities "for their own sake". Such activities include love, the reading of poetry, literature, history and philosophy, certain political and moral activities, aesthetic performance and appreciation, prayer and reflective meditation. I focus my "experiment" on one of these activities - *reflective meditation*. The objects of my reflection are those losses listed above, which I regard to be central to the experience of old age.

I have framed my reflections on old age loss by regarding it as part of "an elegy of old age". *Elegy is a literary form which, when applied to old age and death, captures a central theme - one in which losses and the feelings they generate are experienced and accepted, along with the possibility of detachment from these losses and the finding of consolations for them.* To be sure, traditional elegies are viewed as poetic mourning for the death of a loved one, but modern scholars have extended the meaning of "elegy" to apply to prose as well as poetry applying to different kinds of significant losses. I have adopted this expanded meaning of elegy to apply to the losses which accumulate in old age, and which can threaten to eclipse the self. This expansion of the meaning of elegy may also extend it beyond an evocation of sadness to embrace the myriad of emotions resulting from old age losses; these feelings crowd upon us, creating not only distinct moods of sadness but also their fellow traveling emotions of regret, alienation, anomie, anger, and nostalgia.

2. Detachment Secured in Reading the Classics

Once we face old age losses and their emotions in elegiac terms, we can adopt an elegiac detachment, not unlike the elegiac poet; we separate ourselves from the losses, reflectively meditate about them and explore avenues of solace for them. To do so, I suggest that we need the help of the classic works, in Yeats' terms- the "un-aging monuments" found in his "Sailing to Byzantium". With the help of these works, we may anticipate the losses and the feelings such losses bring in their wake, before they overwhelm us; or, if we are experiencing these losses in the present moment, we can interpret and find their meaning; or, if we have already experienced these feelings, we can, in the words that Wordsworth applied to lyric poetry, "recollect them in tranquility." Exploring losses and their emotions in the light of selected classics enables detachment and supplies the avenues of solace needed for consolation. With elegiac understanding, helped by the classics, we understand and accept the losses and feelings of old age, detach ourselves from these losses, and find a variety of possible consolations. Elegy supplies a unity of a literary form to understand and cope with our old age loss.

The detachment enabled by the classics requires a way of life in which we socially, imaginatively. and intellectually withdraw from attachments to many activities we had once engaged in and the objects we once possessed in our earlier lives, but which, in old age, are receding from our grasp. I suggest what admittedly may be an unwelcome solution to coping with old age: detachment - a "letting go" of the vitality of youth and middle age, the excitement of productive work, and the ambitions we can no longer ably carry out. Instead, I shall recommend for my readers an old age solitude (social detachment), imaginative explorations in literature and fine arts, (imaginative detachment), and reflective meditation upon the classic works, especially science, history and philosophy, (intellectual detachment). (Obviously, such detachment is not suited to everyone facing old age).

All three kinds of detachment can receive help from the tradition of the classics. The savoring of solitude can be helped with reading of the array of many classics which describe the dimensions of solitude and appreciating the many works of art and music which portray or express such solitude. When we read and behold classic works, we enter a different world – the imaginative world of the literature, music, and fine arts. In facing his own solitude of suffering, the late ancient philosopher, Boethius regarded such works as "poultices" for the wounds of his captivity and torture. For Boethius, these pleasant remedies were to be followed by a deeper treatment of philosophy, which could explain how such events could take place in a world created by God. Similarly, I suggest that Intellectual detachment from the losses of old age is to be found in reading and appreciating the rational systems of thought found in the sciences, history and philosophy. All three kinds of detachment, (social, imaginative, intellectual) are part of a reflective meditation in old age. Such meditation is that part of classical leisure, which, in the Andrew Marvell's words, constitutes the "garlands of repose" in old age.

The tradition of the classics is that collection of interrelated intellectual and artistic works of our respective eastern and western civilizations, described in Matthew Arnold's felicitous phrase:" …the best which has been thought and said in the world", (and I would add, "or found in the fine arts"). I have devoted a chapter of this book to describing and defending the canon of classics. To gain initial access to this tradition, retain our attachment to it throughout our lives, and enable us to meditate upon these works in old age, a lifelong liberal education is required. Fortunately, the beginning of such an education has been available for many citizens in the United States and elsewhere; there are thousands of graduates, who, (to a lesser or greater degree) have benefitted or will soon benefit from such an education in academic high schools, liberal arts colleges, universities, and adult liberal studies programs

If a liberal education in college is to lead to a lifelong liberal education, it should begin in youth with an introduction to the liberal disciplines, the great works and the significant problems of our civilization. Hopefully, as two great expositors of liberal education, Cardinal Newman and Robert Hutchins, have recommended, such an education would help its students to integrate these liberal disciplines, one with another. As John Stuart Mill has pointed out, the second stage of liberal education is found in the experiences of our adult lives. These mid-life experiences can test the conclusions of a youthful liberal education. Such a continuing adult education creates a bridge to old age. I view old-age reflective meditation based upon the classics as "the curriculum" of the third stage of lifelong education. In this book, I have described these stages of education and set forth a method of old age reflective meditation which begins with seeking a general understanding of old age and its' place in the stages of life followed by an elegiac examination of the losses and emotions of old age, the detachments from them and consolation for them.

All of these early parts of the book – a brief description of old age, (Introduction), the generic description of the four elements of elegy,(Part I), the discussion of the "enemies of elegy", (Part II), a description and defense of the tradition of classics and the outline of the three stages of liberal education including a general account of reflective meditation (Part III) are preliminary to my specific reflective meditations upon the eight major losses in old age mentioned above: biological decline, retirement, old age poverty and inequality, eclipse of the past, foreshortening of the future, increased dependency abandonment of belief in progress and dying/death, (Part IV). This old age reflective meditation on specific losses in old age draws not only from my own experience of old age, but also from the significant works of the classical tradition. These classics have enhanced my "powers of distance", which are part of what the French philosopher, Pierre Hadot calls "spiritual exercises" – exercises which include reading, writing, and aesthetic appreciation, all of which help me to understand the specific losses and emotions of old age and help with intellectual detachment and consolation.

In reflective meditation, a cluster of ideas and principles, (which I refer to as "the house of ideas"), can be abstracted both from the old age experience of loss and the variety of classical works relevant to understanding this loss and its accompanying emotions. These ideas assist in securing detachment, since it is *through* these ideas that we grasp the reality of old age losses, understand their accompanying emotions, and experience consolations. These ideas act as the spectacles for old age reflective meditation. For example, as I have shown above, ideas contributing to understanding of the losses due to retirement include the ideas of *work* and *leisure*. Ideas pertaining to the feelings accompanying this loss include *anomie* and *alienation*. The ideas contributing to understanding consolation include (but are not limited to) *classical leisure* and *solitude*.

How do universal ideas and principles arise to support detachment from instances of old age loss? Ideas are found or postulated through a process of memory (Plato), grouped in their commonality (Mill), induced and abstracted from experience, (Aristotle and Aquinas), experimented with and imagined, (Bacon), and subjected as part of a textual analysis or interpretation of the classics themselves, (Augustine). Since ideas are universals, they apply to more than one instance of the loss, emotion, or consolation in question. Since such ideas may have a complex architecture of interrelated parts as well as relations to a larger context of ideas, arguments, narratives, and intellectual systems, and since they acquire changing meanings throughout history, (while retaining a common thread), these ideas require substantial analysis. In fact, many scholarly works have been written about one or another single idea.

3. Consolation

Once I explored ideas pertaining to each loss, I sought consolation. I have found avenues of solace to include *familiarization, substitution, catharsis, transformation, adoption of larger perspectives,* and *permanent truths.* Many of the classic works *familiarize* us in advance with the losses we will meet in our old age. Other works *suggest substitutes* for the goods of life we have lost in old age. A few unique works may also offer opportunities for some *catharsis* for the sadness or other emotions we experience. In some instances, such works may even help to *transform our selves* so that we may live well without many of the goods of our earlier years. Another significant contribution of the classics is to see old age, its losses and consolations against the backdrop of *a larger perspective* of universal ideas supplied by experience and the classics. Since the universal ideas through which we understand our losses and their consolations may be treated as objects in themselves, these ideas carry intimations of a permanency extending beyond the present moment or, for that matter beyond one's own life and death. If one listens to Plato and Whitehead, there is a touch of eternity in ideas themselves and, as we participate in these ideas through our knowledge of them, we achieve what might seem to be a contraction in terms - a momentary immortality. Or, as one author phrased it, "an eternal now".

"Testing" the Conclusions

Are these conclusions true? Do they correspond to reality, specifically, the reality of my old age? In the past years, I have been gradually "testing" the conclusions I have reached with my own life, and, in the process, pursued a faint imitation of the scientific method so well described by both Francis Bacon and John Dewey. Thus, when encountering one or another old age loss in my life, I ask whether the classics I have read or undertake to read, help me to understand and accept the loss and its accompanying emotions, help me to detach myself from it and help me to find some consolation. As shall be revealed below, I have concluded that the classics have very much helped me to cope with some old age losses, produced mixed results with other losses and have been largely unhelpful with two of the major losses of old age.

Successful Ventures in Detachment and Consolation

The classics have been successful in helping me cope with three of the principal losses of old age: retirement, "the eclipse" of my past, and the foreclosure of my future. Upon experiencing the emotional wrench of retirement years ago, I turned to a way of life which I have called "classical leisure" in which I have read and appreciated a variety of classics. After the first few years in which this reading was accompanied by a continuation of my work (i.e., tutorials of legal classics and editing a series of modern commentaries on Plato, Aristotle, Cicero, Augustine and Aquinas). After a few years, I turned away from work completely to solitary reflections on the classics and their ideas which had something to say about old age losses.

Let me give one example (discussed in Chapter XIV) from my coping with retirement. To better understand the losses encountered with retirement, I reread parts of Adam Smith's *Wealth of Nations,* Marx's *Economic and Political Manuscripts,* and Emile Durkheim's *The Division of Labor* which helped me to understand the nature of retirement and the frequent alienation which follows in its wake. Through such works, I realized that in my retirement I was being separated from society's productive enterprises, resulting in my own sense of uselessness, powerlessness, normlessness, and meaninglessness. Turning to other classics, I gradually found avenues for coping with the alienation of retirement in the many works, such as Aristotle's *Nicomachean Ethics,* Pieper's *Leisure,* de Grazia's *Time, Work and Leisure,* and O'Loughlin's *Garlands of Repose,* all of which set forth a view of classical leisure as a way of life in which certain activities, both practical and theoretical, are valued for their own sake, and not to advance economic "productivity". In short, I "substituted" the ideal of classical leisure for that of productive work and I have pursued happily one leisure activity - reflective meditation, for the past sixteen years.

One unexpected delight resulted from this pursuit of classical leisure. During most of my retirement, since I have lived in moderate solitude, (with in the early years the important exception of my now deceased wife, and in later years, occasional visits and daily telephone calls from my son and daughter and occasional meetings with my few friends), *I have been alone with my books.* This experience of solitude, not unknown to many elderly persons, has led me over the years to a reading of the classics of solitude especially those authored by Petrarch, (*The Solitary Life*), Montaigne, (*Essays*) and Rousseau, (*The Reveries of a Solitary Walker*). These works have helped me to reflect upon the nature of solitude, and savor and cherish a solitary life – a special kind of consolation for my retirement's loss of the opportunity to participate in economically productive work.

In a similar manner, I have coped well with the loss of the past, especially the loss of memory of my own past. Here I have supplemented my reading of the classics with historical accounts of the communities in which I have lived, (Lake Forest, Illinois; Chicago, Illinois; New Haven, Connecticut; London, England; Norwich, Vermont); the study of works dealing with the three major reform efforts in which I was engaged during my work life: urban development, (Rae, *City*), anti-poverty, (Sachs, *The End of Poverty*) and environmental protection, (Easterbrook, *A Moment on Earth*); and the history of some of the educational institutions at which I have attended or taught, the University of Colorado, (Allen et al.,*The University of Colorado 1876-1976*); University of Chicago, (Boyer, *The University of Chicago: A History*); Yale Law School, (Kronman, *History of the Yale Law School*); Dartmouth College, (Bradley, ed. *Dartmouth*).

Perhaps most enjoyable has been the reading of the many works written by my past teachers: Richard McKeon, Walter Watson, Alan Gewirth, Albert Levi, Thomas Bottomore, Ernest Gellner, Myres McDougal, Joseph Goldstein, Charles Schottland, Roland Warren; these works were written either before, during and after my student days. This reading has sparked many memories of the past, clarification on the subjects I once studied, and new learning. In some cases, such readings have forced me to reassess the significance of my past educational experience with a perspective gained from the later years of my life. This reading has helped me to recreate some parts of my past life which were lost in old age or, perhaps, were never part of my past life!

A third loss which I have accepted is the foreshortening of my future in old age. In Chapter XV"I, I suggested that abandoning ambitions, establishing a legacy in the lives of children, enjoying the love of a spouse, the receipt of some belated honors, and participation in community projects – are proper responses to the foreshortening of one's life, and are reasonable ways of extending one's future. However, in my retirement, I have focused primarily upon my participation in the eternal ideas which the classics supply in abundance, (despite the changes in the meanings of ideas over time and the transience of one's own participation in them. The participation in eternal and universal ideas and principles is attained through a reading of and writing about the history and exposition of many ideas as set forth, not only in the classics themselves, but also in the *Syntopicon,* the annual editions of the *Great Ideas,* the works of the Chicago Institute of Philosophical Research, the Dictionary of the History of Ideas, recent studies of ideas issued by Oxford press and the on-line Stanford Encyclopedia of Philosophy. These ideas and principles are also embodied in the variety of works of fine arts. As for principles, philosophical work, Walter Watson's *The Architectonics of Meaning,* and the many works of John Kekes has had a great influence on my understanding of the principles which animate the major works of western civilization.

- Ventures of Mixed Consolation

I have been less successful in my efforts at securing consolation for losses such as my growth in dependency in old age, my abandonment of belief in progress and individual improvement, and my recognition of old age poverty in others. While she lived, my wife and I were co-dependent as we slowly lost some of our adult capacities through loss of energy and vitality, and since her death, I have grown increasingly dependent upon others for the management of my life. Curiously, I find myself less willing to consult those classics which discuss love and compassion, (such as the *Bible,* St. Thomas Aquinas' *Summa Theologica,* or Garret Keizer's delightful *Help),* to help me cope with our dependencies. These and other classics urge one to develop the capacity for compassion, (whether that compassion is naturally or religiously inspired), for such losses, including dependency of others. Although I am (somewhat) happy to receive help, I am less able to provide it with the grace and love which should accompany such help.

In contemplating the poverty which many elderly encounter in old age, I recognize that I am quite well off; in fact, this relative prosperity undergirds the leisure I have had to conduct this very reflective meditation on old age. In any case, the old age loss of poverty does not apply to me now; nevertheless, since the poverty of the elderly – loss of income, whether due to retirement, health and related social problems – is an important loss for many elderly persons, I have contemplated devoting a chapter to the topic. Simone de Beauvoir's *Coming of Age* offers a wrenching portrait of that poverty. Although I have grown conservative in many ways, I strongly support the welfare state and its expansion of help to all elderly (as well as others in poverty). Despite believing that equalization of capital ownership would reduce poverty of all, including the elderly, and that adoption of a temperate life style adopted by all would help to prevent elderly poverty, I have not written about such topics since I have not undertaken any personal effort at promoting such capital ownership, nor have I sought to promote temperate and moderate non-consumption-oriented life styles ("the simple life") for myself or others.

Regarding another loss, namely, the abandonment of belief in the inevitability of progress and continued individual improvement, I have intellectually abandoned a belief in social progress and the capacity for individual self-improvement in old age. After extensive reading, I have adopted a conservative perspective as set forth in Aristotle's *Politics;* Burke's *Reflections on the Revolution in France,* Oakeshott's *Rationalism in Politics* and Kekes', *The Case for Conservatism,* all of which set forth a persuasive case for traditions, pessimism, skepticism and pluralism. Despite this newly acquired old age conservatism, I continue to experience liberal democratic emotions and ideals, undoubtedly the result of my past life when I believed in progress, and I realize that I have yet to reconcile them with my newfound conservatism.

- Losses without Acceptance or Consolation

I have had less success with accepting and finding consolation for old age biological decline and the prospect of death. Although I have continued to read and meditate about such losses in old age, and, because of this reading, I have been able to accept the relatively minor decline in my own physical capacity, (which comes with age), I have found in myself very little understanding and no acceptance of more serious old age ailments, nor have I found consolations when minor but painful old age diseases occur. As for the prospect of death, (my own or my loved ones), although I have read extensively on the topic, death remains an unknown and perhaps an unknowable country. I continue to dread the prospect of death of my loved ones.

The Scorecard

In reviewing this "score card" of my approach to old age, I can observe that those losses for which I reach understanding, detachment, and consolation, appear to be losses which I have been "prepared for" earlier in life. Thus, my earlier study of philosophy and my habits of solitude equip me well for retirement, my love of history helps me to recreate the loss of the past, and my love of universal ideas in which I might participate helps to extend a foreshortened future. A more mixed picture results in the case of abandoning faith in progress, coping with dependency and responding to the old age poverty of others. I have had less relevant preparation in my early life to enable me to emotionally embrace conservatism, to provide or accept personal help, or to pursue acts of private and public compassion to compensate for others' losses. Nevertheless, I believe I can learn to embrace conservative thought, compassion for others and myself, and cope with dependency. As for confronting sickness and death with equanimity, I have had little opportunity to develop the kind of courage or detachment required to confront these losses in old age. I have managed to avoid opportunities to exercise such courage by facing risks of death in the military, extreme sports or dangerous jobs; I have not encountered serious illness in my life, and, for the most part, have been sheltered from the immediate impacts of the sickness, dying and deaths of friends and family. (Of course, Montaigne, in his later essays, doubts whether one can prepare for death at all). Of course, it is biological decline and anticipation of death which are the central losses in old age. As I encounter these losses, as Montaigne did, the practical experience itself may offer its own consolation.

Old Age and Its Losses Within an Entire Life

I recognize that the focus of this book – fashioning a response to old age losses -is only part of the old age experience. *Loss is not all there is to old age; there are other activities and values which are also an important part of our old age.* For example,in earlier chapters I banished those who deny old age loss, calling them "enemies of elegy", (Part II). Despite my belief that such denial cannot cope with the losses of old age, I recognize that the pursuits of old age delight, the application of science to improve the quality of old age health, the recognition of important secular principles found within religious beliefs, and a necessary participation in the world's activities are important in old age.

I also recognize that old age is only one stage of life and if one is seeking in old age to make sense of one's entire life, (an important activity in old age), one must reflect upon that entire life. That entire life contains both a series of stages marking its narrative and a series of "threads" – ideas and principles - running through the length of life. Consequently, one must meditatively reflect upon the stages and threads of one's life- apart from and in addition to meditation on old age losses. Once one recognizes the three dimensions of old age – coping with loss, engaging in current ongoing pursuits, reflecting upon the stages and threads of one's entire life, it is necessary to briefly review these other dimensions of old age, although a detailed treatment of these latter themes awaits more reflection and, perhaps, another book.

1- Aspects of Old Age Outside of Loss

Old age is not merely a bundle of loss and sadness. In reflecting upon my own aged life, there are other dimensions of everyday life outside of loss – the life of family and friends; the residue of former interests and duties; the practical conduct of living; everyday pleasures, as well as community and political activities. How does my emphasis upon the consolation of old age loss fit within this broader fabric of old age? Focusing upon these dimensions of old age outside of old age loss may appear to divert attention from such loss and provide opportunities for denial and escape from attention to that loss.

On the other hand, this everyday aspect of old age may be affected by the losses themselves. As the losses increase, they interfere with ongoing relationships to family and friends, the effective performance of everyday activities and pleasures, and diminishing interest in community and political activities. The impact experienced from each loss upon these other dimensions of old age will differ with each person. In my own case, I can see the gradual impact of old age loss as the years go by. To give but one example, my loss of faith in progress has diminished my motivation to participate in community and political activities- activities which I loved in earlier years.

If old age losses influence the other activities we pursue in our old age lives, the responses to such losses may also affect the rest of our lives. For me, the time spent with the classics, detaching from the losses and their emotions, and accepting some forms of consolation does interfere with other activities of everyday life. For example, my frequent detachment in the face of old age loss has carried over to my interaction with friends and families! Obviously, each aged person must find her own point of balance between the coping with old age loss and pursuing the other ordinary activities which make up the remainder of old age life.

The Stages of an Entire Life

The response to old age loss requires placing one's old age into one's own lived biography – written or unwritten. That biography implies viewing one's old age as part of a narrative of an entire life. Such a narrative will have a plot with stages, steppingstones, decision-points, or key events which drive the plots of our lives. We may find these key moments by simple biographical reflection. (According to such reflection, I can readily organize my life into roughly chronological but overlapping stages of childhood and youth in Lake Forest; late adolescence and youth at the several universities; preparation in graduate and law school for my legal and administration career; marriage to Mollie and the birth of our children and parenthood; my active occupational engagements in legal services, urban development, anti-poverty and environmental law work; the study and teaching of planning and law; the founding and direction of an Environmental Law Center and the late life teaching environmental law and other law related subjects, a return to scholarship in the classics near retirement). Such a prosaic outline may parallel historical events taking place at the same time- birth in the depression; childhood during the Second World War; education during America's postwar prosperity, the Korean War and the civil rights movement; my "first career" during the "Great Society" and "Earth Day" periods of the urban redevelopment, anti-poverty and the environmental movements; the growing importance of public planning and my study and teaching of it, the 70's flowering of the environmental movement and my founding of an Environmental Law Center, a move towards retirement shortly after 9/11 and the advent of the "age of terrorism" .

Such an outline, however, does not provide meaning for such a life, since it does not reveal how the stages or events shaped my life and character or created and reflected the values I pursue. Just as I have turned to the classics to understand old age loss, I now turn to the classics to consider how an entire life may be understood. There are a variety of classic sources for such an understanding. There are philosophies, especially ancient philosophies, which suggest ways of life which may be embraced. For example, Plato outlines the steps in life of preparation of the guardians of *The Republic*. Another more recent attempt to provide a map of stages of life is Erik Erikson's *Identity and the Life Cycle, which* suggests eight stages of life, each starting with a basic crisis and ending with a resolution; in *The Life Cycle Completed,* he focuses upon old age and adds, with the help of his wife, a ninth stage. In addition to Erikson, helping one to view one's entire life are a myriad of novels describing life stories as well as biographies and autobiographies. Recent scholars, (Smith and Watson, in *Reading Autobiography)* have identified 52 autobiographical forms including bildungsroman, conversion stories, meditations on life, personal essays, self-help tracts, spiritual appeals, and many others. Each kind of autobiography suggests one or more patterns of life. Consultation among these sources help in the exploration of one's own life

In beginning to undertake such a task, I have been much influenced by David Norton's fine work, *Personal Destinies: A Philosophy of Ethical Individualism,* which embraces the philosophy of Aristotle, but incorporates the modern contributions of Erikson and others to set forth a philosophic understanding of the stages of life. For Norton, the stages of life embrace youth, adolescence, maturation and old age. Each stage has its own distinct and essential principles and hence each stage is discontinuous with the earlier or later stage. Childhood is a stage of essential dependence, adolescence is the stage of the quest for autonomy and a review of alternative principles for living one's future life, and maturation is the choice of those principles which yield an identity to the life of the individual. *Old age for Norton is a stage in which we discover that we no longer have a future.*

Like Norton, my reflections upon my entire life views it as largely a series of stages. Childhood and youth were one of dependency in the secure confines of family and my Lake Forest home. During an extended adolescence, I explored the options for life, including alternative religions, sexual preferences, and occupations. In maturation, I chose a life of conventional marriage and parenthood, as well as legal practice, public administration and teaching, all in the name of public reform. Unlike Norton, however, I view these stages as leaving "residues of character': habits, thoughts and feelings which make up the threads of my identity over time and into old age.

In important ways, Norton's account of old age as a stage of life lacking a future anticipates my own discussion of one old age loss as a "foreshortened future". Norton suggests that the appropriate response or principle of old age is "recovery of the past as a foundation of present and future living"; similarly, I found the need to recreate a lost past in old age. And, when I discuss the need to establish a legacy for a foreshortened future, I *find that legacy for the future in a participation in the tradition of the classics, while Norton finds the past "not in the past of a given present, but the eternal past ...the past of humankind, the past of the world, the past of historical being."* In Norton's quote of the philosopher, Santayana, piety towards the past, like my piety towards the classics is "man's reverent attachment to the sources of his being and the steadying of his life by that attachment".

The Threads of An Entire Life

Despite a recognition of the stages of life, there is also continuity. There are threads of life, i.e., those habits, traits of character, themes and ideas which run through our lives, helping to establish a continuity of identity. There are many such threads, only some of which pertain to old age loss, emotion, detachment and consolation. My own life, prior to old age, serves as the origin of multiple threads of my life and these threads are reflected in my approach to the losses of old age. For example, my adoption of a solitary life of detached reflection upon the classics is based, at least in part, upon the thread of prior acquaintance with the classics through exposure to a classical liberal education.

To offer another example, take the thread of solitude in my life. Solitude has been part of my life in most of its stages. My old age engagement in the solitary practice within a classical leisure as a consolation for the losses of retirement is the result of upon a prior acclimatization to such solitude in my earlier life. The retirement from a career which I enjoyed and believed to be important was a serious loss and made the search for a substitute way of life in old age essential. Upon retirement, I experienced a deep sense of alienation from my former activist and academic life and withdrew into a world of reading and writing. Such solitude, however, was not new; one thread in my life had been the experience of solitude. As part of that solitude, I had acquired a detached reflective stance to my own work, and I drew upon my past liberal education to support such a stance. In addition, while working, I held onto the love of the solitary study of the classics during my adult work life and sporadically continued the study of them, returning to university to take one or another course throughout my middle age. Thus, I had the classics "in my back pocket" to fall back upon in seeking a solitary consolation in my old age. I can easily imagine other old persons, drawing upon threads within their previous lives to cope with the losses in their old age.

The Integrity of Old Age

Old age is not solely loss. There is a life existing outside of the experience of old age loss. We have seen that there are earlier stages of a narrative of our life, and threads of our past lives, and, of course, the everyday aspects of our old age lives which are not covered by our responses to loss. Or consciousness of our entire biography. Given these elements, the final question becomes: *how do we achieve and maintain coherence among the different aspects of our old age life?* The question is a pragmatic one which seeks truth in the form of an answer to William James' question: what works in old age?

Such a question prompts attention to the ideal of integrity to be sought in old age. Integrity, as a concept has an extensive history which has offered different definitions. Its' dictionary definition includes both the notion of having moral principles and having a whole and undivided character. In its latter meaning, the coherent interlocking of mental functions, virtues or parts of the character is suggested. David Norton suggests that integrity requires the past and future to be contained in one's present and that one's analytically separate acts are related by mutual implication in accordance with a strong central principle. Thus, in an integrated old age, the stages and threads of one's life, the other residues of an earlier life, the practical duties of present living and the responses to the losses of old age are organized around or within a central principle.

In my old age, the stages of my life and its' many threads are guided by the principle which recognizes the practice and value of reflective meditation. In my old age, my family and friends, the practical duties of my present life, the traces of my former life, whether stages or threads, all of which appear external to my principle of reflective meditation, revolve around the central ideal of a way of life devoted to reflective meditation. Some elders will be attracted to such an ideal; others must find their own principles and shape their own response to this challenging period of our lives.

For those who find my ideal of reflective meditation attractive, I propose *a way of life* for myself and my readers which will result from taking this book seriously. In recent years, some philosophers, such as Pierre Hadot, John Cooper, and John Kekes have suggested that the purpose of philosophy is not simply to create elaborate systems of thought but also to urge the thoughtful adoption and pursuit of specific satisfactory ways of life. In *Philosophy as a Way of Life, Hadot* lays out the ways of life which the ancient Hellenistic philosophers envisaged. John Cooper in his *Pursuits of Wisdom* extends and modifies Hadot's work and demonstrates how a wider range of ancient thinkers have articulated systems of thought which might inform and guide the ways of life which might be adopted by the reader. John Kekes, in his many books, including *Moral Wisdom and Good Lives* has suggested how a variety of satisfactory lives may be pursued with or without philosophy, but with a certain kind of moral control. In a similar spirit, I suggest that in old age, one such way of life is based upon an effort to continue and revive one's previous liberal education, renew one's commitment to the reading and appreciation of the classics, reject "the enemies of elegy" (religion, scientism, pragmatism, and epicureanism), and embrace a solitude of leisure in which the losses of old age may be confronted and, if not conquered, at least consoled.

To achieve this way of life, I have urged a revival of this classical concept of leisure – the practices of humanity independent of societal goals of economic production. The importance of leisure in society requires a profound revolution in our understanding of the aims of a good society and may require a revolution in our present society. A good society should enable universal leisure in youth, at certain intervals during the adult years, i.e., "sabbaticals" for all, and in old age. Such leisure requires a recognition of "auto-telic" activities of leisure, that is, activities for their own sake, in which the purposes of the activities are found within the practices themselves and not in the external consequences of those practices. I am under no illusion that in the immediate future, there will be political and economic revolution in which leisure is understood to be the principal purpose of social and political life. Until our political society changes, such a classical leisure may be recognized and realized only by a liberally educated minority of the elderly. In some past societies, for a brief period, the societal practices of leisure were thought to embrace appropriate personal relations of family and friends, religious practices, political participation for the common good, moral action, and "pastoral leisure", (reading and writing, artistic creation, appreciation of the fine arts and nature). In this book, I have urged the adoption of a "pastoral leisure" - the reading and appreciation of the classics in old age retirement. I have followed my own advice.

APPENDIX A

Old Age in the Classics

The following is a selected list of western classics, i.e. "great books" which in some way or other treat the topic of old age. I say "selected" since it does not include all major works which treat old age in English. Other collections of "great works" dealing with old age include Wayne Booth's *The Art of Growing Older: Writers on Living and Aging* (1992), which includes a bibliography of books which contain lists of books on aging, and Cole, T., R. Kastenbaum, and R.E. Ray, *Handbook of Humanities and the Aging, (2000).* Each work listed here may focus upon old age exclusively, such as Cicero's *On Old Age,* or in passing, such as Erikson's account of old age as a stage of life in *The Cycle of Life Completed or* the character of Casaubon in Eliot's *Middlemarch.* I have not included other works discussed in the body of this book – works dealing with themes related t old age such as elegy, (and its phases of loss, sadness, detachment and consolation), nor the myriad books on death, the classical tradition and liberal education. I have not included references to the fine arts, nor to eastern classics. The list is chronological, according to the original (approximate) date of publication of the work in question. Some readers may wish to place their reading of any work in the larger context of western history, which has been done in Will and Ariel Durant, *The Story of Civilization (1975),* or in the history of the canon and classics, as in Harold Bloom's *The Western Canon (1994)* or Gilbert Highet's *The Classical Tradition, (1949)* or within the history of old age as in Pat Thane, Ed., *The History of Old Age (2005).* I have also listed the kind of book and the country of origin of the author, (or, in some cases, the place where the author settled). I have not listed specific page numbers of the descriptions or analyses of old age within the texts, since there are multiple editions of these works and often old age is described or discussed in many places within the text. Besides, the reader is advised not to simply "cherry pick" the mentions of old age, but read these mentions in the context of the entire book. Such a list is intended to familiarize the reader with the book cited and to help the reader wishing to pursue further reading in the classics in order to explore how such classic may help in the coping with old age losses.

1. The Ancient Greeks
    Homer, (Greek authors/tradition), *The Iliad, The Odyssey (Before 550 B.C.)*
    Aeschylus, (Greek playwright), *Agamemnon,* (458 B.C.)
    Aristophanes, (Greek playwright), *Clouds, Plutus, Archanians, Wasps, (425- 375 B.C.)*
    Sophocles, (Greek playwright), *Oedipus at Colonus, (406 B.C.)*
    Euripides, (Greek playwright) *The Suppliants, Heracles Mad, Alcestes, (438-417 B. C.)*
    Hippocrates, Alexandrian physician), *Writings,* (400 B.C.)
    Plato, (Greek philosopher) *Republic, The Laws)* (370, 348 B.C.)
    Aristotle, (Greek philosopher), *On Youth and Old Age. On Life and Death, Nicomachean Ethics,   Politics, Rhetoric, (336-322)*
    Epicurus, (Greek Philosopher), *Letter to Menoeceus, (270-300)*
2 The Bible
    The Old Testament (Hebraic) *Ecclesiasticus, Psalms, Proverbs, Numbers, Kings, Job,* (1000-250 B.C.)
3. The Roman and Hellenistic World
    Cicero, (Roman Statesman, Orator, Philosopher), *On Old Age, (45-44 B.C.)*
    Horace, *(Roman Poet, Epodes; Odes (c. 20 B.C.)*
    Seneca, *(Roman Statesman, essayist), Letters, Moral Essays, (c. 63-65)*

Lucretius, (Greek poet and philosopher), *The Nature of Things*, (c. 100)

Plutarch, (Greek biographer), *On Contentment, Lives, (c.100)*

Epictetus, (Roman slave), *The Discourses, (c. 60-138)*

Galen, (Alexandrian physician), *On the Natural Faculties, (c.130-200)*

Aurelius, Marcus, (Roman Emperor), *Meditations,* (171 B.C.)

4. The Medieval World

Thomas Aquinas, (Italian theologian), *Summa Theologica, (1267-1273)*

Dante, (Italian poet and philosopher), *Divine Comedy: Inferno, (1308-1321)*

Boccaccio, Giovanni, (Italian Poet), *Decameron, (1348-1353)*

Chaucer, (English poet), *Canterbury Tales: The Merchant's Tale (1385-1400)*

5. The Early Modern Period

Montaigne, Michel (city official, essayist), *Essays* (1580)

Bacon, Francis (English jurist, essayist) Essays: *Of Youth and Age* (1597)

Cervantes, Miguel de, (Spanish novelist), *Don Quixote, (1605)*

Shakespeare, William (English poet, playwright), *King Henry, the Sixth; Henry IV; The Life of King Henry the Fifth, As You Like It, Winter's Tale, Hamlet, King Lear, Macbeth, The Sonnets.* (1589-1611)

Browne, Sir Thomas (English essayist) *The Urn Burial (1658)*

Harvey, William, *On the Motion of the Heart and the Blood, (1658)*

Moliere (French playwright*) Le Misanthrope (1666)*

Dryden, John, (English poet), *Song from the Tyrannic Love,* (1670)

Swift, Jonathan (English essayist), *Resolutions When I come to be Old; Gulliver's Travels,* (1699, 1726)

6. The Enlightenment and Romantic Era

Montesquieu, Baron, (French author and political theorist), *Persian Letters, (1721)*

Voltaire, Francois, (French author, playwright, encyclopedist), *Mahomet, Candide,* (1736, 1759)

Hume, David, (English philosopher), *Enquiry Concerning Human Understanding,* (1748)

Johnson, Samuel (English lexicographer, poet, critic), *The Vanity of Human Wishes,* (1749)

Rousseau, Jean Jacques, (French philosopher), *Reveries of a Solitary Walker, (1776)*

Boswell, James, (English biographer), *The Life of Samuel Johnson, (1791)*

Coleridge, Samuel Taylor, (English poet), *The Rime of the Ancient Mariner, (1797)*

Goethe, Johann Wolfgang, (German scientist, poet, philosopher), *Faust,* (1770-1832)

7. The Nineteenth Century

Hegel, Georg, (German philosopher), *The Philosophy of History, (1821)*

Austin, Jane, (English novelist) *Pride and Prejudice, Emma, (1814-1816)*

Balzac, Honore de, (French novelist) *The Centenarian, Gobseck, Elixir of Life, The Colonel Chabert, Le Cure de Tour, Eugenie Grandet, Le Pere Goriot, (1799-1850)*

Wordsworth, William (English poet), Collected Poems, (1849-50)

Dickens, Charles, (English novelist) *Old Curiosity Shop, Christmas Carol, Tale of Two Cities; Bleak House; Great Expectations, (1840-1861)*

Browning, Robert, (English poet), *Rabbi Ben Ezra, (1864)*

Arnold, Matthew, (English essayist, Poet), *Growing Old, (1864-67)*

Eliot, George, (English novelist), *Middlemarch,* (1874)

Dostoevsky, Fyodor, (Russian novelist), *Brothers Karamazov, (1880)*

Tolstoy, Leo, (Russian novelist), *The Death of Ivan Ilyich,* (1886)

James, William, (American psychologist, Philosopher) *Principles of Psychology,* (1890)

James, Henry, (American novelist), *The Middle Years,* (1895)

8. The Twentieth Century

Mann, Thomas, (German novelist), *Buddenbrooks; The Magic Mountain, (1901, 1924)*

Cather, Willa, (American novelist), *Death Comes to the Archbishop* (1927)

Proust, Marcel, (French novelist) (*Remembrance of Times Past*, (1913-1927)

Whitehead, Alfred North, (American philosopher), *Religion in the Making, (1926)*

Yeats, William, (Irish poet), *The Poems of W.B.Yeats,* (1928)

Jung, C.G. (Swiss Psychoanalyst), *Modern Man in Search of a Soul, (1933)*

Faulkner, William, (American novelist), *As I Lay Dying, (1930)*

Hemingway, Ernest, (American Novelist), *Old Man and the Sea,* (1952)

Waddington, Conrad, (*English Biologist), Biology for the Modern World,* (1962)

Beckett, Samuel, (French Playwright), *Endgame, Waiting for Godot,* (1953, 1957)

Erikson, Eric, (German-born American Psychoanalyst), *The Life Cycle Completed,* (1987)

APPENDIX B

Selected Recent Works on Old Age

I have not included the myriad of books, old and new, bearing upon each of the specific losses in old age, the present debates over the classical tradition and of liberal education, the roles of religion, life extension, and pleasure seeking in old age – all of which are discussed in my book.

The Elegy of Old Age

John Bayley, *Elegy for Iris* (1999)

> *This book is the moving story of the decline of the well-known English philosopher, Iris Murdoch, into the loving care given by her husband, the author.*

Thomas Vickery, *The Modern Elegiac Temper* (2006)

> *This book extends the notion of elegy to modern works, expanding its notion of loss to embrace not only the tradition notion of mourning for a lost lover or friend, but also other kinds of losses as exemplified in modern poetry. Vickery has also written another book on elegy in modern prose works.*

These works pertain to the framework theme of my book on the elegy of old age. Bayley's book is limited to the admitted serious loss of mental capacity in old age, whereas, like Vickery, my focus in upon a range of losses. Vickery does not focus upon old age loss.

Old Age, Literature and Art

Arnold Weinstein, *Morning, Noon, and Night* (2011)

> *This book explores the meaning of the various stages of life in light of literature. As might be expected by a literature professor, the book offers extensive interpretations of selected literature treating the themes of youth, adulthood and old age.*

Wayne Booth, *The Art of Growing Older* (1992)

> *This book is a delightful compilation of poetry and short excerpts of written essays, grouped into the themes of losses and lamentations as well as celebrations and cures. Booth has also authored* The Company We Keep, *which lays out the essential ways in which fiction may influence the actions attitudes and characters of the readers.*

Nicholas Delbanco, *Lastingness: The Art of Old Age* (2011)

> *This fine little work explores some of the works of painters, poets and composers in their later years. In doing so, he finds "power in reserve", a commitment to continuity, and consistency in these works and he explores what makes these artists productive in their old age and their works lasting.*

William Ian Miller, *Losing It* (2011)

> *The delightful satirical autobiographical work romps through the classics and other good works in an effort to*

understand some of the losses of old age and how our and past societies regarded them.

Helen Vendler, *Last Looks, Last Books: Stevens, Plath, Lowell, Bishop, Merrill*

> *Vendler, a master critic of poetry, shows how the last works of these poets respond to their end of life and death.*

These fine works supply excerpts and interpretations of literature, but, unlike my work, do not extend their reach to other classics, such as history, biology, philosophy and so forth. Moreover, none of the books seek to develop a systematic philosophy of aging as I have tried to do. In the book by Delbanco, there is little attention to the very real losses in old age – a theme which I have sought to pursue. Miller touches on several of the losses I treat, but he treats them more lightly; humor is his principal method of detachment.

The Tradition of the Classics, Liberal Education, and the Meaning of Life

Harold Bloom, *The Western Canon* (1994)

> *Bloom's book, along with a volumes of the "best poems" in the English language are discussions of many of the works of the humanities which he places in a historical framework of an aristocratic, democratic and chaotic age. Despite his pessimism about the future of the literary canon, he defends it against the reductionism of much modern thought.*

William Casement, *The Great Canon Controversy* (1997)

> *This well-crafted book explores the nature of the ancient canon and its teaching, the anti-canon movement and arguments for and against. Casement argues for a revised canon which recognizes the need to "update" the canon without losing its essential values.*

Gilbert Highet, *The Classical Tradition* (1949,1959)

> *An effort to show how the ancient classics shaped the literature of modern Europe and America.*

Erich Auerbach, *Mimesis* (1942, 1956)

> *This book examines carefully a variety of texts to show the different ways in which Reality is portrayed in these works.*

Jaroslav Pelikan, *The Vindication of Tradition* (1984)

> *This book offers a spirited defense of tradition both as history and heritage.*

Eva Brann, *Paradoxes of Education in a Republic* (1979)

> *Brann views liberal education through the principles of utility, tradition and rationality.*

Mortimer J. Adler and Milton S. Mayer, *The Revolution in Education* (1958)

> *The authors place traditional liberal education in a carefully constructed set of debates over the nature of liberal education.*

Anthony Kronman, *Education's End* (2007)

> *This book argues for the capacity of the classics to provide a liberal education in secular humanism in the face of the current ideals of the research ideal and political correctness which dominate the curricula of our current colleges and universities.*

Hubert Dreyfus and Sean Kelly, *All Things Shining: Reading the Western Classics to Find Meaning in a Secular Age* (2011)

> *Dreyfus and Kelley argue that a careful reading of the classics will reveal the sources of our modern nihilism and will supply other sources by which we can rediscover the sacred in the practices of our modern life.*

These works, like my book, accept the importance of the western classics, the canon, and liberal education, but, unlike my book, do not explore how a reading and appreciation of these classics may facilitate detachment and a consolation of the losses of old age. With Bloom, I share a deep commitment to the reading of the classics but suggest that the kind of reading will differ depending upon the reader's stage of life. The works of Highet and Auerbach, in different ways offer implicit defenses of the importance of the classics. Like Casement, I accept the need to revise the canon and embrace the broader view of the canon he espouses to include scientific and political works; however, the selection of these works, during the period of adult and old age education will be dictated not by a list of canon works, but by the relevance of those works to the problems of adulthood and the losses of old age. Moreover, I do not reject completely the insights of the modern enlightenment, as eand Kelley appear to do, nor do I totally reject, with Dreyfus, Kelley and Kronman, the importance of monotheistic beliefs as reflected in many of the classics. As set forth in my discussion of religion in old age, I find some redeeming secular principles and truths in the western religious works.

Philosophy and Old Age

Joseph Esposito, *The Obsolete Self* (1987)

> *This book explicitly draws upon each of the disciplines dealing with the aged — biology, psychology, sociology, economics, law and political theory Esposito's contribution*

is to trace the philosophical implications of these disciplines for the phenomenon of aging and its apparent movement toward the creation of "an obsolete self". In doing so, Esposito is able to offer a critique of unwarranted conclusions from these disciplines and how it may be possible to move beyond the underlying assumptions of obsolescence in old age.

Helen Small, *The Long Life* (2007)

Helen Small explores certain assumptions about old age – what is life, what is a good life, what is a person and what is social justice. These assumptions are explored in relation to certain modern philosophies and their applicability by drawing upon selected works of literature.

Simone de Beauvoir, *Coming of Age* (1970, 1972)

This classic work on old age explores the existential subjectivity of old age on the one hand and the economic and social oppression of the aged on the other – both inquiries are products of the late French existentialism which sought to combine existentialism with Marxism.

John Cooper, *Pursuits of Wisdom* (2012)

Cooper, following in the footsteps of Pierre Hadot, identifies and describes in considerable detail different conceptions of wisdom set forth in ancient philosophies, including, Socrates, Plato, Aristotle, the Stoics, the Epicureans, Skeptics and Plotinus. Although not specifically focused upon old age, the easy identification of old age with some form of wisdom makes this book particularly relevant to the philosophical treatment of aging.

Jean Amery, *On Aging* (1968, 1994)

This remarkable and eloquent essay on aging discusses the importance of time, alienation, a feeling of invisibility, the inability to understand the world and the presence of dying are described in detail. Amery has also completed a book on Suicide, and then he killed himself.

Christine Overall, *Aging, Death, and Human Longevity* (2003)

In this work, Christine Overall discusses the philosophical problems which arise from the efforts to extend longevity.

David C. VanTassel, Ed. *Aging, Death, and the Completion of Being (1979)*

This is a collection of scholarly essays on old age and death

Patrick L. McKee, Philosophical *Foundations of Gerontology 1982)*

An excellent collection of essays dealing with philosophical, ethical, and epistemological aspects of aging as well as a selection of early gerontological writings.

All of these works, given their breadth, overlap in one way or another with my book. For example, I devote a chapter to the discussion of longevity, although my discussion is very different from Overall. Like Amery, I identify some of the losses experienced in old age. Throughout the book, like Cooper and the essays in McKee, I draw upon the conclusions of ancient philosophers. Like Small, I too am interested in defining old age in the context of a whole life. Like Esposito, I am interested in reviewing the documented facts of aging. All of these topics, however, are not the focus of my argument, structured upon the insight of the elegiac nature of old age. Equally important, with the exception of Amery's work, my book is not a systematic work of philosophy but rather a series of ordered reflections which I hope are readily available to the educated reader.

The Western History of Old Age and Death

Pat Thane, ed. *The History of Old Age* (2005)

> *In this beautiful book, filled with reproductions of paintings, sculpture and photographs through the ages, traces the changing history of the culture of the aging and the history of that culture. In doing so, Thane and her coauthors treat a broad cross section of the elderly in all stations of life.*

Philippe Aries, *The Hour of Our Death* (1981)

> *This book traces the history of the ways in which dying and after death is regarded in the customs and practices of western societies.*

Jacques Choron, *Death and Modern Man* (1964)

> *Based upon Charon's previous book, Death and Western Thought, Charon reviews the works of Malraux, Rilke and others, seeking to articulate how modern man with a scientific world view can encounter death. In this book, he offers his own view of death.*

Susan Jacoby, *Never Say Die* (2012)

> *A spirited attach upon the modern effort to create the image of a happy old age.*

In my book, I refer to classic works throughout the ages, however, without placing them in the context of a chronological history of old age and its losses. History, however, becomes an important topic when I address the eclipse of the past in old age and the decline in the faith of progress.

Aging and the Stages and Cycles of Life

Tom Kirkwood, *Time of Our Lives* (1999)

> *Based upon biological and genetic studies, this book explores the nature of aging, its biological causes, and the scientific approaches to the possible extension of life.*

Erik Erikson, *The Life Cycle Completed* (1998)

> *This book and the other Erikson books are the locus classicus of the treatment of the stages and cycles of life. Erikson offers a detail theory of the various stages based primarily upon an extension of Freudian thought.*

James Feibleman, *The Stages of Human Life* (1975)

> *Feibleman seeks to identify which philosophy is appropriate for understanding each stage of life. In the stage of old age, Feibleman believes the work of Heraclitus, the later Plato, and Bergson are most applicable.*

Bernice L. Neugarten, et al., *The Meanings of Age* (1996)

> *Many of the essays in this volume deal with the social and psychological characteristics of people at the middle or old age stages of life and explore the changing meaning of age in the stages of life.*

Edward Mendelson, *The Things that Matter* (2006)

> *Mendelson chooses to discuss one classic for each stage of life including the end of life.*

My book accepts the assumption of stages of life, hence addressing the stage of old age. However, I do not regard the stages as fully biologically or psychologically determined and, in one chapter, I argue that certain kinds of freedom may be obtained in old age, despite the aging process. Unlike Feibleman, I regard many of the classic works appropriate to each stage of life including the understanding of old age, depending upon what old age issue is being discussed or what old age loss is the subject of discussion.

Medical Reflections on Old Age

Sherwin Nuland, *The Art of Aging* (2007)

> *Sherwin Nuland, on the basis of two previous remarkable books, How We Live, and How We Die, has written a human book as to how to live well in old age. Drawing not only on his medical expertise, but also his own experience and that of his friends, Nuland suggests ways in which creativity and joy can be found in old age and how, in the future, old age might be extended.*

Andrew Weil, *Healthy Aging* (2007)

> *Weil, a successful health "guru", argues against the denial of aging and or the value of aging. He suggests a variety of specific physical and mental steps to be taken to "age gracefully".*

David Haycock, *Mortal Coil* (2008)

> *Haycock traces the history of efforts to extend life.*

Atul Gawande, *Being Mortal* (2014)

> *Gawande suggests that facing death in aging requires giving meaning to life and that meaning can embrace a wide variety of objects and capacities, e.g., the capacity to enjoy chocolate and football games. He documents this*

argument with numerous accounts of aging, some which he encountered himself as a doctor.

Although Nuland, Weil and Gawande are wise and humane doctors, they exude optimism about old age which I reject. To be sure, Nuland, in his previous work, *How We Die,* was brutally honest about the process of dying. In his later book, as well as in Weil's book, neither doctor is willing to face the inevitable losses to be confronted in old age. Haycock addresses the efforts to extend life – an effort which I and others have rejected. Gawande is willing to face and describe the difficulties that doctors have in facing the end of life of their patients.

Memoirs, Autobiographies and Last Books

William Zinsser, *Writing About Your Life* and *Inventing the Truth* (2005)

> *These two books, one authored, the other edited, about memoir writing offer good advice on the art and craft of memoir, a genre which is often written in old age and not infrequently about old age. Zinsser is regarded as the master of the memoir, and his second book includes articles by other masters, such as Frank McCourt, Annie Dillard, and others.*

William Randall, A. Elizabeth McKim, *Reading Our Lives, The Poetics of Growing Old* (2008)

> *This is a remarkable and detailed exploration of how to "story lives", that is, how to place one's life in a narrative, and employing literature as part of that narrative, to give one's life meaning and unfold the wisdom of old age. (This book contains a remarkable bibliography on the topic).*

Helen Vendler, *Last Looks, Last Books* (2010)

This books, authored by a "master" of the study of poetic style, looks at the poetry of Stevens, Plath, Lowell, Bishop, and Merrill as they confront the last years of their lives and their mortality.

Since part of my book, that is, the epigraphs of each chapter, is an autobiographical excerpt which illustrates, I hope, the more general issues discussed in the chapter, it seemed appropriate to list at least some of the major memoir-in-old-age writings. In fact, the Randall, McKim and Vendler books also touch upon the theme of elegy. These books, however, are focused upon writing and texts themselves. I am interested in reaching *through* the canon texts to discover the truths of the reality of old age.

In summary, after reviewing a selection of recent old age literature, I find it difficult to know which book a prospective book purchaser who is interested in old age, might select and whether he or she might prefer one of these fine books to my own. And the choice is even more complicated than I have indicated since I have not listed the many recent old age and death related novels of Philip Roth, the public policy books of Daniel Callahan, which deal with aging and death, the myriad medical writings on old age, and many memoirs. In fact, there is an incredible variety of books dealing with one or another aspect of old age. *Perhaps the best way to distinguish my book might be to regard it as a reflective meditation which seeks, with the help of the classics, to produce a mood of detached consolation about the losses in old age – a mood which grows over a life time from the time of one's reading of classics early in life as part of a liberal education, through the time of adult work life, and then later – into old age. None of the above listed books offers such a meditation.*

Printed in Great Britain
by Amazon

24412063R00260